W9-BVU-562

The Missouri Controversy
1819-1821

GLOVER MOORE

The
Missouri
Controversy
1819-1821

KENTUCKY PAPERBACKS

UNIVERSITY OF KENTUCKY PRESS

Lexington, 1966

*Publication of this book is possible partly
by reason of a grant from the
Margaret Voorhies Haggin Trust
Established in memory of her husband
James Ben Ali Haggin*

PREFACE

*T*HIS STUDY HAD its beginnings twenty years ago when Professor Frank L. Owsley of Vanderbilt University called my attention to the fact that the Missouri Controversy of 1819-1821 was a subject about which comparatively little had been written, with the exception of Floyd Shoemaker's excellent book on Missouri's part in the controversy. I should never have completed the present work without Professor Owsley's constant advice and encouragement and without the assistance of two of my colleagues in the History Department of Mississippi State College, John K. Bettersworth and Harold Snellgrove. Professor Bettersworth read portions of the manuscript and made valuable suggestions for its improvement. For reading the entire manuscript and assisting in its revision, I wish to thank Professor Owsley, Professor Snellgrove, Mrs. Henry T. Ware of Mississippi State College, and the director and editors of the University of Kentucky Press. Among those to whom I am indebted for assistance and encouragement are Professor William C. Binkley of Vanderbilt University, Professor Arthur Link of Northwestern University, Miss Dorothy C. Barck of the New-York Historical Society, Professors William J. Evans, Marion Loftin, Robert A. Brent, and James H. McLendon of Mississippi State College, Miss Nannie Rice of the Interlibrary Loan Service of Mississippi State College, Miss Ethel Halbert of Starkville, Mississippi, and Miss Sara Woodward of the Decatur, Mississippi, Junior College.

I am indebted to Mississippi State College for clerical assistance in the preparation of the manuscript and to my graduate students at Mississippi State College for the use of their seminar studies in supplementing my research. Finally, I wish to express gratitude to the library staffs of Mississippi State College; Vanderbilt, Harvard, Princeton, and Columbia universities; the Library of Congress; the National Archives; the public libraries of New York and Birmingham; the Ridgway Branch Library of Philadelphia; the Illinois State Historical Library of Springfield; the Alabama and Mississippi Departments of Archives and History; and the New York, Long Island, Pennsylvania, Massachusetts, Maine, Western Reserve, Chicago, and Missouri Historical Societies.

To all of these and many more the author is grateful, though of course he would not hold anyone except himself responsible for the shortcomings of his work.

State College, Mississippi   GLOVER MOORE
December, 1952

TABLE OF CONTENTS

Preface   v

  I. A Background of Sectionalism   1

 II. Tallmadge Lights the Fuse   33

III. Burlington County, New Jersey, Starts a Crusade   65

 IV. Congress Debates   84

  V. The Issue Is Rejoined and Finally Laid to Rest   129

 VI. Public Opinion in the Free States   170

VII. Public Opinion in the Slaveholding States   218

VIII. Special Parties to the Missouri Controversy:
        Missouri, Maine, and Illinois   258

 IX. Race Relations, Democracy, and State Rights   288

  X. An Economic Basis for Sectionalism   318

 XI. Significance of the Missouri Controversy   339

Bibliography   353

Index   377

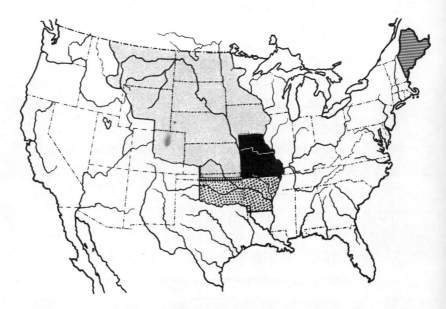

THE MISSOURI COMPROMISE

- Louisiana Purchase territory closed to slavery
- Compromise line of 36° 30′
- Louisiana Purchase territory left open to slavery
- New free state, Maine
- New slave state, Missouri

"We think sectionally and do not fully understand one another."—FREDERICK JACKSON TURNER[1]

CHAPTER I

A BACKGROUND OF SECTIONALISM

*M*EN AT THE TIME, and historians since, have commented on the suddenness with which the Missouri Controversy arose. Jefferson compared it to "a fire bell in the night" that had awakened and filled him with terror.[2] Sudden and terrifying though the controversy was, however, the forces which produced it had been accumulating for many years.

Prior to the Revolutionary period there was, of course, scant occasion for any clash between Northern and Southern interests. There was then no central legislative body in British America where representatives from all of the colonies could meet either to air their differences or to unite in a common effort. Even so, it was inevitable that certain adjoining colonies should feel a sense of sectional solidarity and develop characteristics which distinguished them from other areas. During the greater part of the colonial period, the seaboard colonies could logically be divided into three groups: Eastern (or New England), Middle, and Southern. An eighteenth-century writer suggested that three regional governments be established on such a basis.[3] This was never done, and eventually a more significant distinction began to arise—between the North and the South.

At an early date Northern visitors in the South began to make caustic comments on Southern manners and customs, comments which have continued to this day. During a year's stay in Virginia in 1773-1774, Philip Fithian of New Jersey found himself among a polite and hospitable people but was appalled by the cruelty of slaveholders and overseers. "Good God," he exclaimed, "are these Christians?" While traveling in South Carolina in the same period, Josiah Quincy, Jr., of Massachusetts was critical of almost everything, from the "repugnant" religion of the inhabitants to the listless ladies of Charleston, who lacked "the fire and vivacity of the North." Quincy's criticism of Carolina was no more severe than that of a distinguished Virginian regarding New England. As early as 1736 Colonel William Byrd had found "the saints of New England" not to his liking, and he denounced them as "foul Traders." "They have," he said, "a great dexterity at palliating a perjury so well as to leave no taste of it in the mouth, nor can any people like them slip through a penal statute."[4]

The mutual fear and distrust which has characterized the relations between New England and the South represents one of the oldest forms of American sectionalism. One reason which the Massachusetts General Court gave for rejecting the Albany Plan of Union was "the great sway which the Southern Colonies (the Inhabitants whereof are but little disposed to and less acquainted with the affairs of war) would have in all the determinations of the Grand Council, &c."[5] A few years later Jonathan Boucher, the Tory parson, warned the Southern colonists that for them independence would mean only a change of masters, with New England wielding the scepter formerly held by old England. In "what a case we are likely

[1] *The Significance of Sections in American History* (New York, 1932), 326.

[2] Paul L. Ford (ed.), *The Writings of Thomas Jefferson* (10 vols., New York, 1892-1899), X, 157.

[3] Turner, *Significance of Sections*, 290.

[4] Hunter D. Farish (ed.), *Journal & Letters of Philip Vickers Fithian, 1773-1774* (Williamsburg, 1943), 39, 51; "Journal of Josiah Quincy, Junior, 1773," in *Massachusetts Historical Society Proceedings*, XLIX (1916), 455-56; "Colonel William Byrd on Slavery and Indented Servants, 1736, 1739," in *American Historical Review*, I (1895), 88; David M. Potter and Thomas G. Manning, *Nationalism and Sectionalism in America 1775-1877* (New York, 1949), 18-24.

[5] Max Savelle, *Seeds of Liberty, The Genesis of the American Mind* (New York, 1948), 332.

tu be" then, said the parson, and he entreated Southerners "to remember that you are—*from the Southern Provinces.*"[6]

Throughout the entire history of the Continental Congress there was an undercurrent of friction between the New England and Southern delegates. Disagreements arose over the fisheries, the apportionment of taxes, the disposal of western lands, and the navigation of the Mississippi River.[7] These regional differences were overshadowed by contests between radicals and conservatives, large and small states, and the states which had western lands and those which were landless. Periodically, however, the Southern and New England delegations would line up solidly, or nearly so, on opposite sides of a question. On such occasions the Middle states held the balance of power. When they voted with New England, Congress presented the spectacle of a solid North arrayed against a solid South. This was notably the case in 1776 and again in 1786-1787.

In 1776 there was a controversy regarding the method to be used in apportioning taxes among the states. It was suggested at first that each state's contribution should be determined by the size of its population, including slaves. The South objected and insisted that only the white population should be taken into account. The alignment on this issue was almost entirely sectional—North against South—and resulted in a threat of disunion from South Carolina. In 1777, after a division had developed among the representatives from the Middle states, it was finally decided that the quotas of the states should be based on the value of their lands and improvements.[8]

In 1786-1787, under the Articles of Confederation, the Jay-Gardoqui Treaty negotiations produced a major collision between the North and South which seriously threatened to dis-

[6] Jonathan Bouchier (ed.), *Reminiscences of an American Loyalist 1738-1789 Being the Autobiography of the Revd. Jonathan Boucher* (Boston, 1925), 132-34.

[7] Edmund C. Burnett, *The Continental Congress* (New York, 1941), 249-50, 433-38, 622-25, 654-59, 679-80.

[8] Merrill Jensen, *The Articles of Confederation* (Madison, Wisc., 1948), 145-50.

member the Union. At that time the mouth of the Mississippi River lay in Spanish territory. John Jay, Secretary for Foreign Affairs, was empowered by Congress to negotiate a treaty with Spain, in which it was hoped that he might be able to secure commercial advantages for the United States as well as a recognition of America's claim that its citizens possessed the right to navigate the Mississippi freely. Finding that he must yield to the Spanish on some points in order to secure a treaty, Jay suggested to Congress that America surrender the right of free navigation on the lower Mississippi for twenty-five or thirty years in return for commercial concessions.

There were sound arguments in favor of Jay's proposal,[9] but it elicited a storm of protest from Southerners and Westerners, who rightly felt that their interests were about to be sacrificed for the benefit of Northern merchants. Congress had previously given Jay instructions to insist on "the right of the United States to . . . the free navigation of the Mississippi, from the source to the Ocean." It now voted to rescind these instructions and give Jay a free hand to cede away the navigation of the river for a limited period. The vote to rescind was strictly sectional, seven Northern states against five of the South, with Delaware not voting.[10] While Jay thus received the sanction of a congressional majority for his plans, he had actually sustained a defeat, since the approval of nine states was necessary for the ratification of a treaty. With little prospect that a treaty would be ratified and amid threats of secession from irate Southerners and Westerners, Jay and the Spanish envoy, Gardoqui, conducted the remainder of their negotiations in an atmosphere of futility. The unsolved Mississippi question was bequeathed to the new government established by the Constitution and was ultimately settled in accordance with Southern wishes.

The quarrels over the navigation of the Mississippi led many men to conclude that the Union was a mere "rope of sand," and the possibility of rival Northern, Southern, and Western

9 For Jay's own argument, see *Journals of the Continental Congress*, XXXI, 473-84.
10 *Ibid.*, 595-96.

confederacies was seriously discussed. In 1786 Theodore Sedgwick, a Massachusetts delegate to Congress, declared that the Eastern and Middle states would do well to separate from the South unless that section should grant them a greater participation in its commerce as an equivalent for the protection which it derived from them.[11] A few months later it was said that in North Carolina "a Dissolution of the Union was publickly and openly spoke as a thing that would and ought to happen because the Northern states were injurious to the southern."[12] For a time it was not certain whether the greatest danger of division lay between the North and South or the East and West. There was a strong separatist movement in the West in the 1780's and 1790's, and for this the Mississippi question was partly responsible, since Westerners felt that their welfare was of no concern to Secretary Jay or the national government. Jay was an able man and a patriot, but being a New Yorker and having never been south or west of Philadelphia, he did not understand the psychology and aspirations of the Western people.[13]

Although the solid vote of seven Northern states could not secure the ratification of a treaty, it did present to the Southern mind the nightmare of a Northern majority which was willing, and at some future time might be able, to inflict grave injury on the South. Jay's diplomacy was used as an argument to dissuade the Southern states from ratifying the Constitution.[14] Indeed, it was still a burning issue with many Americans thirty-three years later, and numerous references to it cropped out in the debates and correspondence dealing with the Missouri Controversy. When in 1819 the aged Jay bestowed his blessing on the movement to prohibit slavery in Missouri, President Monroe declared that a "monopoly of power in the Eastern portion of the Union, to be perverted to improper purposes, was then [1786] the motive. It is the same now. In this sentiment I

[11] Edmund C. Burnett (ed.), *Letters of Members of the Continental Congress* (8 vols., Washington, 1921-1936), VIII, 415-16.

[12] *Ibid.*, 533.

[13] Arthur P. Whitaker, *The Spanish-American Frontier: 1783-1795* (Boston, 1927), 77, 90-122; Frank Monaghan, *John Jay* (New York, 1935), 259.

[14] Burnett, *Letters of Members of the Continental Congress*, VIII, 722.

should have been confirmed, as soon as I saw the association of Mr. Jay with Mr. King, in this [Missouri] business, as was lately apparent, had I doubted before."[15] Charles Pinckney of South Carolina opposed Jay in 1786 and lived long enough to vote against the North in the Missouri dispute, which prompted him to remark that having "contributed, at that distant day, to save the parent [the West], he felt great pleasure on the late great occasion, in contributing his humble efforts to save her children [the Missourians]."[16]

Before the Articles of Confederation were replaced by the Constitution, the South had already attained a certain degree of solidarity in its thinking. Men like Richard Henry Lee, James Monroe, Timothy Bloodworth, William Blount, and Benjamin Hawkins were conscious of being "Southerners," and their correspondence while they were members of the Continental Congress was filled with such expressions as "Southern States," "Southern interest," "Southern scale," and "Southern States . . . rights."[17] In 1786 Monroe ardently desired "the admission of a few additional States into the Confederacy in the Southern scale," while Timothy Bloodworth of North Carolina regarded the Jay-Gardoqui negotiations as "Dangerous to the Liberty of the southern States."[18]

The North as yet had achieved no such unity. The word "Northern" was frequently used as a synonym for "New England," and in order to designate all of the states above the Mason and Dixon line, one had to use some such expression as "Eastern (or Northern) and Middle states."[19] Nor were the

15 Letter from Monroe to an unnamed person, Washington, 1820. This letter was found by Northern soldiers in Virginia during the Civil War and was published in the Columbus (Ohio) *Crisis*, December 14, 1864. The *Crisis* incorrectly dated the letter July 12, 1820. It was probably written in January or February of that year.

16 *Annals of Congress*, 16 Cong., 1 Sess., 1629. See also Richmond *Enquirer*, January 25, 1820.

17 Burnett, *Letters of Members of the Continental Congress*, VIII, 181, 461, 462, 474, 533, 619.

18 *Ibid.*, 462, 474.

19 *Ibid.*, 415, 518, 611; Merrill Jensen (ed.), *Regionalism in America* (Madison, Wisc., 1951), 41.

Middle states securely attached to the "Eastern Interest." Rufus King was afraid that Pennsylvania and New Jersey would fall under *"southern Influence."*[20] This fear was well warranted, and until the Civil War the Middle states were a political borderland, voting often with New England, as in 1786, but at times with the South.[21]

In the Constitutional Convention at Philadelphia in 1787 Northerners and Southerners co-operated on many matters, and sectional rancor was not the dominant feature of the Convention.[22] Nevertheless, it was present in the deliberations of the delegates, assuming such proportions at one time that Rufus King of Massachusetts was led to declare that "the question concerning a difference of interests did not lie where it had hitherto been discussed, between the great and small states; but between the southern and eastern."[23]

It has been said that the Constitution is a bundle of many compromises. At least two of them owe their origin to the necessity for reconciling the divergent views of the North and South: the commerce–slave-trade compromise and the three-fifths compromise. Both of these settlements were to be the source of sectional animosity in later years; the three-fifths ratio was to be a major issue in the Missouri Controversy.

The three-fifths compromise of the Constitution provided that in apportioning representation and direct taxes among the states, three fifths of the slaves should be counted as a part of the population. This arrangement caused a long and bitter debate in the Philadelphia Convention. At that time there were comparatively few slaves in the Northern states. Indeed, for climatic and other reasons slavery in the North was definitely on the road to extinction. In the South slaves were numerous and, because of economic and social considerations,

[20] Burnett, *Letters of Members of the Continental Congress,* VIII, 541.

[21] Turner, *Significance of Sections,* 291.

[22] On this point, see Max Farrand, "Compromises of the Constitution," in *American Historical Review,* IX (1904), 479-89.

[23] Charles R. King (ed.), *The Life and Correspondence of Rufus King* (6 vols., New York, 1894-1900), I, 241. See also Carl Van Doren, *The Great Rehearsal* (New York, 1948), 149-57.

were not likely to be freed in the near future. Since the size of each state's population would determine the number of representatives it should have in the lower house of Congress, the balance of power would be affected by counting the slaves as people. Northerners insisted that they were mere property and hence no more entitled to representation than cattle and horses.[24] But the South was determined to have additional representation on account of its slaves, and a union of the states would not have been possible without the three-fifths compromise or a similar one. "The North paid that price in order to obtain a government that would protect its commercial, financial, and industrial interests."[25]

In the period after 1787, the Eastern and Southern seaboard states were destined to become increasingly hostile to each other. The East was commercial and conservative. Partly for economic reasons, its leading statesmen allied themselves with the Federalist party of Washington and Hamilton. Because of the French Revolution, the people of New England became pro-British in their attitude toward foreign affairs. On the other hand, the agrarian South during the early years of the Republic opposed much of the Hamiltonian fiscal program and generally attached itself to the rising Jeffersonian Democratic party. In foreign policy, moreover, the leaders of Southern opinion were strongly Francophile.

As a result of such differences, rival sectional interests battled for control of the federal government as soon as the Constitution was adopted. In this struggle the Federalist East maintained the ascendancy over the South from 1789 to 1800. The South became a self-conscious minority in the national body

24 Max Farrand (ed.), *The Records of the Federal Convention of 1787* (3 vols., New Haven, 1911), I, 201.

25 Albert F. Simpson, "The Political Significance of Slave Representation, 1787-1821," in *Journal of Southern History*, VII (1941), 319. This article is a summary of a doctoral dissertation written by Mr. Simpson at Vanderbilt University in 1940. The dissertation contains a detailed study of the debates in the Federal Convention on slave representation (pages 6-37) and shows rather conclusively that the adoption of the three-fifths ratio was a major sectional compromise. For a contrary viewpoint, see Farrand, "Compromises of the Constitution," 481.

politic.[26] The Eastern Federalists wrote most of the national legislation, and many Southerners believed that the tariff and kindred measures were draining their section of its wealth and reducing it to servitude. The course of events seemed to justify the forebodings of Patrick Henry and the other prophets of doom who had warned the Southern states not to ratify the Constitution, lest it result in their exploitation by a Northern majority.[27] Below the Potomac, everything done by the new government "was thought to be wrong. The salaries bill, the residence bill, the revenue bill, the funding bill, were [regarded as] so many pieces of jobbery in the interest of the East."[28] Against this state of things believed to be unfavorable to the South, Southern leaders protested with great vehemence. Jefferson complained that "we are completely under the saddle of Massachusetts and Connecticut, and . . . they ride us very hard." Governor Henry Lee of Virginia, father of Robert E. Lee, even talked of dissolving the Union in preference to enduring "the rule of a fixed and insolent majority."[29]

But the South did not long remain a minority in the federal government. Rather, the Jeffersonian Democratic party—composed of Southern planters, Western frontiersmen, and Eastern farmers and mechanics—soon was threatening to wrest control from the Federalists. In a desperate effort to retain their slipping power the Federalist leaders in 1798 secured the passage of the famous Alien and Sedition Acts. In the equally famous Virginia and Kentucky Resolutions, the South replied to these measures with a thinly veiled threat of secession. Finally in 1800 Federalism was overthrown. In 1801 the Democratic Jefferson, a native of Virginia, became President.

[26] Jesse T. Carpenter, *The South as a Conscious Minority 1789-1861* (New York, 1930), 26-27, 29-30; Ulrich B. Phillips, *The Course of the South to Secession* (New York, 1939), 60-71.

[27] Jonathan Elliot (ed.), *The Debates, Resolutions, and Other Proceedings, in Convention, on the Adoption of the Federal Constitution* (4 vols., Washington, 1827-1830), II, 431-32.

[28] John B. McMaster, *A History of the People of the United States* (8 vols., New York, 1884-1913), I, 593.

[29] Ford, *Writings of Jefferson*, VII, 263; Carpenter, *The South as a Conscious Minority*, 26.

After Jefferson's election a great change occurred in the relations between the South and the national government. The Southern states from 1801 to 1819 were no longer a minority. All of the Presidents were Virginians, Southerners occupied key positions in Congress, and the South was too much a part of the central authority to view it any longer with suspicion. A few farsighted men like John Randolph and John Taylor could still foresee dangers ahead, but for the most part the South was a land of political contentment and intense patriotism in the first two decades of the nineteenth century.[30]

It was now the turn of New England and her Federalist leaders to be the self-conscious and bitter minority of the Union. For more than twenty years after Jefferson's election they were to occupy that position. They were to see themselves deserted by the Middle states and governed from Washington by a coalition of Southern planters and Western frontiersmen. They beheld the Democratic party gaining strength in their own back country; they saw their own emigrants moving to Ohio and there deserting Federalism for Democracy. In 1803, moreover, the size of the Union was suddenly doubled by Jefferson's acquisition of the Louisiana Purchase. The Federalists feared that an endless number of new Democratic and slaveholding states would be established in this vast region, thus ensuring the perpetual hegemony of the South and West in national politics. Meanwhile, Eastern commerce suffered from Jefferson's embargo and Non-Intercourse Act. When at length in 1812 the nation was plunged into war with England by the South and West, the Federalist cup of woe flowed over.

After 1800 New Englanders made a careful survey of the political situation to determine the cause of their fall from power. The real cause lay in the fact that the Federalist party

[30] Charles S. Sydnor, *The Development of Southern Sectionalism 1819-1848* (Baton Rouge, 1948), 1-2; Merle Curti, *The Roots of American Loyalty* (New York, 1946), 151-53; Ulrich B. Phillips, *Georgia and State Rights*, in *Annual Report of the American Historical Association for the Year 1901*, II (Washington, 1902), 38. Phillips says: "We have reached, then, a period coinciding roughly with the first two decades of the nineteenth century, where a distinct lull occurred in Georgia's contentions for the recognition of her sovereign rights."

was too aristocratic for the age and actually rested upon too small a group to give it real strength.[31] Its philosophy of government did not suit the average American as well as Jefferson's. But New England's leaders, ignoring this fact, attempted to make a scapegoat out of the three-fifths compromise of the Constitution. From 1789 to 1800 there had been isolated protests in the North against "slave representation." After Jefferson's election these protests were revived and elaborated.[32]

It was said, for instance, "that, at the 4th Presidential Election, when Mr. Jefferson was first chosen President, he had 73 electoral votes, and Mr. Adams 64; making a majority of 9; and that, at that very time, the black representation from the SLAVE COUNTRY amounted to 15: so that *the negroes turned the majority, and actually put in the President!*"[33] John Quincy Adams wrote in 1804 that the North need not expect an equal balance in the national councils, since the "slave representation, like the sword of Brennus, will forever be thrown into the Southern scale, and must forever make our's kick the beam."[34] It would be difficult to overestimate the bitterness which New Englanders harbored against the three-fifths ratio after 1800— a bitterness that led Fisher Ames to ridicule those of his compatriots who compared themselves to Romans. "If we resemble any thing Roman," he wrote, "it is such a domination as Spartacus and his gladiators and slaves would have established. . . .

[31] The aristocratic Federalist concept of government is admirably illustrated by the following editorial from the Hartford *Connecticut Courant*, April 13, 1819: "We congratulate our friends in East-Hartford on the issue of the late election. This has always been one of the most decidedly federal towns in the state, until the universal suffrage law was made last year; since that such has been the remissness of the federal party, and such the activity of the other, in qualifying their voters, that the town has been twice discredited by the election of tolerationists [anti-Federalists and Democrats]. On Monday last, the landholders, and the *real* proprietors of the wealth and resources of the town, came forward with the spirit of freemen, and by a decided majority elected men to represent them in the assembly, who command the confidence of their fellowcitizens, and feel interested in their welfare as well as in that of the state."

[32] Simpson, "Significance of Slave Representation," 320-21.

[33] "Boreas" [Sereno E. Dwight], *Slave Representation* (n.p., 1812), 21.

[34] Worthington C. Ford (ed.), *Writings of John Quincy Adams* (7 vols., New York, 1913-1917), III, 71.

The government of the *three fifths* of the ancient dominion [Virginia], and the offscourings of Europe, has no more exact ancient parallel."[35] After Madison's re-election in 1812, many New Englanders believed that under the operation of the three-fifths rule they were subjected to a "foreign" government.[36]

Many and devious were the methods by which the Federalists sought to recover their lost power. In 1803 they asserted that the Louisiana Purchase treaty was unconstitutional and opposed its ratification in the Senate. Later, objections were made when Louisiana sought admission to statehood. "If this bill [for her admission] passes," said Josiah Quincy of Massachusetts, "it is my deliberate opinion that it is virtually a dissolution of this Union; that it will free the States from their moral obligation, and, as it will be the right of all, so it will be the duty of some, definitely to prepare for a separation, amicably if they can, violently if they must."[37] There was also a movement to secure the adoption of a constitutional amendment to abrogate the three-fifths compromise.[38]

After 1800, when not decrying the acquisition of foreign territory or pressing for alterations in the Constitution, the Federalist East frequently was toying with the idea of secession as a means of throwing off the so-called Southern yoke. Disunion was seriously contemplated in 1804 and 1808 and again in 1814-1815 at the time of the Hartford Convention.[39] But these separatist movements all proved abortive and succeeded only in discrediting Federalism in the eyes of the remainder of the nation.

The disintegration of the Federalist party was hastened by the pro-British activity of its adherents, particularly in New England, during the War of 1812. The New Englanders were averse to fighting England in a war which was forced upon

[35] Seth Ames (ed.), *Works of Fisher Ames* (2 vols., Boston, 1854), II, 248-49.

[36] McMaster, *History of the United States*, IV, 202.

[37] *Annals of Congress*, 11 Cong., 3 Sess., 525.

[38] Simpson, "Significance of Slave Representation," 325-26.

[39] Henry Adams, *History of the United States of America* (9 vols., New York, 1891-1898), II, 160-91, IV, 402-407, VIII, 305-309.

them by Southern and frontier congressmen. They accordingly sought to hamper the war effort in various ways, and some extremists suggested that the Eastern states withdraw from the war and make a separate peace with the British. By the time the war was over, many Americans regarded the words "Federalist" and "traitor" as synonyms, and within a few years the Federalist party was virtually dead.

While the party of New England was thus being reduced to a cipher in the national government, the people of New England were acquiring an odious reputation in other parts of the country. This reputation, otherwise known as anti-Yankee sentiment, is a phenomenon in American history, and an understanding of it is essential in considering the background of the Missouri Controversy. The origin of the word "Yankee" is uncertain.[40] In 1819 it was used to designate a resident of New England and did not yet apply to people living in other parts of the North. The Indians of Massachusetts seem to have been the first to dislike Yankees, and their feelings on the subject soon were shared by the Dutch in the neighboring colony of New York. When New Englanders swarmed into New York in quest of land and trade, friction developed between Yankees and Yorkers.[41] "God damn all Yankees," says an upstate New Yorker in a well-known historical novel.[42]

As the years went by, Yankee peddlers made their way into the South and West, where they were regarded popularly as crafty traders who pawned off wooden nutmegs and inferior wares on honest farmers.[43] Much of the prejudice against the peddlers, and perhaps most of it, was undeserved,[44] but still it

[40] George E. Shankle, *American Nicknames, Their Origin and Significance* (New York, 1937), 595.

[41] Dixon R. Fox, *Yankees and Yorkers* (New York, 1940), especially 57-151.

[42] Walter D. Edmonds, *Drums Along the Mohawk* (Boston, 1936), 548.

[43] "The seeds of some of the ill-feeling between the North and the South unquestionably were first planted through the activities of these Yankee peddlers." Richardson Wright, *Hawkers & Walkers in Early America* (Philadelphia, 1927), 40. See also Washington *Gazette*, February 15, 1820; Lexington (Kentucky) *Gazette*, March 10, 1820.

[44] Lewis E. Atherton, "Itinerant Merchandising in the Ante-bellum South," in *Bulletin of the Business Historical Society*, XIX (1945), 59.

was a factor to be reckoned with. When, moreover, New Englanders were suspected of collaboration with the enemy in the War of 1812 and when Commodore Decatur accused them of placing blue lights on the coast to inform the British of American ship movements, Southerners and Westerners required no further proof that Yankees were a depraved and wicked race. Henceforth every New Englander was suspected of being a "Bluelight" Federalist as well as a crook in business.[45]

At the time of the Missouri Controversy, anti-Yankee feeling had reached amazing proportions. Daniel Boone, greatest of frontiersmen, asserted that Indians were more trustworthy than New Englanders and that he never wanted to live "within 100 miles of a d—d Yankee."[46] In the summer of 1819 a Southerner wrote a letter to a Darien, Georgia, newspaper to protest against the sectionalism of Darien and "the sneers and sarcasms continually lavished, by the unthinking and illiberal, upon that class of our citizens vulgarly denominated *Yankees*."[47] In Illinois, where it was a political liability in the early 1820's to be known as a native of New England, it was said that nearly all of the Yankee politicians sought to conceal their true origin by posing as New Yorkers.[48] Some frontiersmen were not able to make so fine a distinction. The English traveler Faux tells the story of a New Yorker who was whipped out of Indiana "as a warning and terror to all future coming Yankees."[49] New Yorkers knew the difference between Yankees and Yorkers, whether Indianians did or not, and a member of the New York

[45] Thomas D. Clark, *The Rampaging Frontier* (Indianapolis, 1939), 301-20; Elias P. Fordham, *Personal Narrative of Travels in Virginia, Maryland, Pennsylvania, Ohio, Indiana, Kentucky; and of a Residence in the Illinois Territory: 1817-1818*, ed. by F. A. Ogg (Cleveland, 1906), 223.

[46] John Bakeless, *Master of the Wilderness Daniel Boone* (New York, 1939), 357-58; *Niles' Weekly Register* (Baltimore), XXIV (1823), 166.

[47] Darien (Georgia) *Gazette*, quoted in Washington *Daily National Intelligencer*, April 1, 1819.

[48] Ninian W. Edwards, *History of Illinois, from 1778 to 1833; and Life and Times of Ninian Edwards* (Springfield, 1870), 191.

[49] William Faux, *Memorable Days in America: Being a Journal of a Tour to the United States* (London, 1823), 304-305.

legislature declined to participate in the movement to prohibit slavery in Missouri because he suspected that it was "of Yankee [New England Federalist] origin."[50]

By 1819, then, the prestige of New England and the Federalist party was at a low ebb. The Federalists in Congress were reduced to a corporal's guard. Even in New England they now controlled but one state, Massachusetts. Nevertheless, moribund though Federalism might be, it still included in its ranks a large percentage of the nation's wealth and aristocracy. It had influential newspapers and pamphleteers at its command and was still capable of making as much noise as all the rest of the country put together. The Northern Federalists—those of the Middle states as well as of New England—were probably the most frustrated group in all American history. Having known nothing but defeat and disappointment for twenty years, they were finally little more than onlookers at the national scene. The Federalists in the Middle states differed from their New England brethren chiefly in this respect, that, being usually in the minority in their states, they did not have governors and legislatures to serve as their mouthpieces; consequently their unhappiness had not attracted as much attention as that of the New Englanders. The Federalist frame of mind was indicated by an editorial which appeared in the New York *Daily Advertiser* in 1818. After speculating on whether the next President would come from the South or West, the *Advertiser* spoke of the customary role to be played by the East. "It will be curious," said the editorial, "for the inhabitants of those parts of the country who live *without the pale of dominion,* to watch the course of proceedings."[51]

Once the Missouri Controversy arose, and entirely regardless of the motives of those who precipitated it, it provided an outlet for twenty years of Federalist frustration. It also presented the prospect of a new alignment of parties in which Federalists

[50] New York *Columbian*, January 21, 1820; Albany *Argus*, January 21, 1820. For hostility to Yankees in Pennsylvania, see Everett Dick, *The Dixie Frontier* (New York, 1948), 338.

[51] New York *Daily Advertiser*, April 9, 1818.

might reintegrate themselves with the majority of the Northern people in a common front against the South. This was only one of many elements which went into the making of the Missouri Controversy, but it was a most important one.

The Clintonian faction of the Democratic party represented yet another frustrated group which was to figure prominently in the dispute over Missouri. In 1819 the Democratic party in the state of New York was divided into two rival groups, the Bucktails and the Clintonians. The personality of Governor De Witt Clinton was largely responsible for the cleavage in New York, the Bucktails being opposed to the governor while the Clintonians were his supporters. These local differences were projected into national politics. The Bucktails were often accused of being pro-Southern,[52] and the Clintonians were conspicuous for their opposition to "Virginia influence" and "Southern rule."

The anti-Southern bias of the Clintonian Democrats was of long standing. Gideon Granger, a New Yorker who was Postmaster General in Madison's cabinet, had attempted to raise the standard of revolt against the Virginia Dynasty in 1810, when he corresponded secretly with Clinton and urged him to be a candidate for the presidency. The next year, in a letter to the Speaker of the Pennsylvania House of Representatives, Granger inveighed against slave representation and deplored the subservience of Pennsylvania to the Old Dominion.[53] In 1812 Clinton actually ran for President, as a coalition candidate of Federalists and New York Democrats, against Madison, the regular Democratic nominee. Since he accepted Federalist aid, he was regarded henceforth as an apostate by Democratic stalwarts. Opposition to Southern dictation was a major issue in the 1812 campaign.[54] Four years later the Democratic mem-

---

[52] Everett S. Brown (ed.), *The Missouri Compromises and Presidential Politics 1820-1825 from the Letters of William Plumer, Junior* (St. Louis, 1926), 16, 33, 74.

[53] Gideon Granger to De Witt Clinton, March 27, 1810; Granger to John Tod, December 26, 1811, Gideon and Francis Granger Papers, Library of Congress.

[54] Edward Stanwood, *A History of the Presidency* (Boston, 1898), 100.

bers of the New York legislature unanimously passed resolutions warning that the ascendancy of the party would be jeopardized if another Virginian were nominated and appealing "to the forbearance" of Virginia herself.[55]

In 1819 Clinton was serving as governor, and he and his friends definitely had a chip on their shoulder. Resenting the Southern leadership of the national Democracy, they considered themselves the stepchildren of the Monroe administration. Judge Matthias Tallmadge was quite certain that the administration was "decidedly opposed to the Repbn. prosperity of N. Y." Congressman James Tallmadge, Jr., even complained to President Monroe that all the officials of the government except Monroe himself were hostile to New York. In 1820 Gideon Granger refused to attend a meeting of the state legislature to vote for Monroe electors. "I did not anticipate," he wrote, "that any important business, other than the choice of Electors would be acted on, and I was unwilling to poach through the mud 225 miles to perpetuate the slavery of the north."[56]

It was natural that the Clintonians, like the Federalists, should seek to make political capital out of the slavery question. The only cause for surprise was that a majority of the Northern Democrats united with them in the dispute over Missouri. Prior to 1819 the attacks on the three-fifths ratio and the political power of the slave states had come principally from Federalists and Clintonians. These attacks had been regarded by most Northern Democrats "as assaults upon their political brethren" of the South and were "resented accordingly."[57] For a number of reasons, however, a change occurred in the relations between Northern and Southern Democrats in 1819.

[55] "Resolutions of the Republican Members of the New York Legislature— Feby 14, 1816," John W. Taylor Papers, Miscellaneous, New-York Historical Society.

[56] Matthias B. Tallmadge to De Witt Clinton, January 7, 1819; James Tallmadge, Jr., to Clinton, February 11, 1818; Gideon Granger to Clinton, December 13, 1820, De Witt Clinton Papers, Columbia University.

[57] See letter of Martin Van Buren to Thomas Ritchie, January 13, 1827, in Charles H. Ambler, *Thomas Ritchie* (Richmond, 1913), 107-108.

In the first place, some Northern Democrats were not anti-Southern but, for humanitarian reasons, felt bound to vote against the admission of Missouri as a slave state. It might be well to add that the Federalists and Clintonians were likewise influenced, in part, by a humanitarian motive and that Clinton had been an antislavery legislator from his youth.[58] The Missouri question was complex, and many motives and issues were involved. Some among the Northern Democracy were alienated by the Southern monopoly of high government offices. From 1801 to 1819 the presidency appeared to be the exclusive property of Virginia, and most of the Speakers of the House of Representatives were Southerners. A Federalist newspaper spoke all too truly when it declared that fifty able men in Virginia, "supported by and supporting each other, have enabled her to exercise a controlling influence over this Union for the last twenty years."[59] It was inevitable that Northern Democrats should grow restless under such top-heavy Southern leadership. They were not apt to kick the traces as long as the fear of a Federalist victory hung over their heads, but by 1819 there seemed little likelihood of that event. In the House of Representatives there were only about twenty-five Federalists in a total membership of 186.[60] The Democratic party was losing cohesion from lack of opposition and was not able to bind its Northern and Southern members together as effectively as in the past.

The South might have received more aid from the Middle states in 1819-1821 if it had not been at daggers' points with that section on the subject of the tariff and internal improvements. Furthermore, the disagreement over the tariff was accentuated by the Panic of 1819, which began shortly before the Missouri Controversy. American manufacturers, finding themselves driven to the wall by the panic, sought salvation in clamoring for higher protective duties. Great was their dismay when they beheld the congressional delegation from the slave

[58] Dorothie Bobbé, *De Witt Clinton* (New York, 1933), 256.
[59] West Chester (Pennsylvania) *Village Record*, January 31, 1821.
[60] Washington *Daily National Intelligencer*, October 30, 1819.

states ranging itself in almost solid opposition to a higher tariff. This stand was not altogether in keeping with the previous history of the South. There had been dreams of industrialization and much protectionist fervor below the Potomac in the years immediately after the War of 1812, and many Southerners supported the tariff of 1816.[61]   In 1819 conditions had changed somewhat, and the South now was regarded as the chief stumbling block in the way of the protection so ardently desired by the Middle states. Ironically, about half of the New England congressmen, including a number of Federalists, tagged along with the South on this issue, but there were so few of them that they formed no more than the tail of the Southern kite. This was an unusual role for Federalists, but economic interests make strange bedfellows.

It was upon the South, representing the bulk of the opposition to the tariff, that the protectionists of the Middle states unlimbered their biggest guns, beginning in 1819 at the very time when rival forces were lining up for the Missouri contest. "It is undeniable," said a writer in a New Jersey newspaper, "that the slave holding states to the Southward originate and uphold this pernicious system [of dependence on foreign manufactures], which must ere long reduce us (unless corrected) to a state more wretched than colonial servitude."[62] "The rise of cotton," lamented the Pittsburgh *Gazette*, "is a host in itself against us."[63] "COLBERT," writing in the Washington *Gazette*, concluded that the North was "a prey to English cupidity and Southern *plantation* avarice."[64] A writer in the Philadelphia *Aurora* recommended the formation of an association for wearing only American manufactures, since it was useless to expect any tariff increase "from the prevailing influence of the slave states over the general government."[65]

[61] For maps showing the congressional vote on the tariff of 1816 by states and districts, see Charles O. Paullin, *Atlas of the Historical Geography of the United States* (Washington, 1932), plate 113 B; Kendric C. Babcock, *The Rise of American Nationality 1811-1819* (New York, 1906), 238.

[62] Trenton *True American,* April 12, 1819.

[63] November 16, 1819.   [64] May 18, 1819. See also for May 13, 1819.

[65] Philadelphia *Aurora,* July 9, 1819.

At the same time that the votes of Southern congressmen were denying tariff protection to the Middle states, the vetoes of Virginia Presidents were thwarting them also in the matter of internal improvements. In 1817 John C. Calhoun's Bonus Bill, which provided for the construction of roads and canals at federal expense, was vetoed by Madison on the ground of unconstitutionality. President Monroe, in his first message to Congress, followed the lead of his predecessor in pronouncing federal internal improvements to be unconstitutional, although he pointed out that this difficulty could be removed by a constitutional amendment.[66] The Bonus Bill received its greatest support from New York and Pennsylvania, which cast half of the votes given in its favor in the House of Representatives.[67] It was upon these states that Madison's veto and Monroe's subsequent support of Madisonian principles bore hardest.

While many Southerners ardently advocated federal internal improvements, there was a tendency in the Middle states to associate the constitutional views of Madison and Monroe with the political ascendancy of Virginia and the slave states. In a letter to Rufus King in 1817, De Witt Clinton expressed a belief that there would be no more federal assistance for roads and canals and that New York would have to complete the Erie Canal without outside aid. "After swallowing the national Bank and the Cumberland Road &c.," he wrote, "it was not to be supposed that Mr. Madison would strain at Canals—but so it is, and the gallantry of his successor in protecting him with his Telamonian Shield is more to be admired for its spirit than its prudence."[68] John Savage, a New York Democratic congressman who wrote to Clinton in 1818 to complain of the attempts made at Washington to belittle New York, went so far as to declare that all opposition to internal improvements

66 James D. Richardson (ed.), *A Compilation of the Messages and Papers of the Presidents 1789-1907* (11 vols., New York, 1908), I, 584-85, II, 18.

67 There is a map showing the vote by districts in Paullin, *Atlas of the Historical Geography of the United States*, plate 113 C. For an analysis of the vote by sections, see Charles M. Wiltse, *John C. Calhoun Nationalist, 1782-1828* (Indianapolis, 1944), 135-36, 403.

68 De Witt Clinton to Rufus King, December 13, 1817, Clinton Papers.

by the national government was resolvable into enmity to New York or Clinton. Another of Clinton's correspondents wrote of his fear that Monroe was seeking to subordinate the commercial interests of New York "to the domineering aristocracy of Virginia."[69] During the Missouri Controversy, Evert K. Vanderveer accused the South of being unfriendly to New York and of instigating the Tammany opposition to Clinton. He asserted that if "Mr. Clinton would write Mr. Pinckney, or General Stokes, or Mr. Barbour, pledging his word in black and white, not to finish your canal—not to oppose a Virginia President—not to encourage your manufactures—and not to promote such a *union among yourselves* as would be most dreadful to the Virginia dynasty, be assured that Tammany Hall, taking her cue from the south, would very soon admire Mr. Clinton."[70]

Savage and Vanderveer were correct in their supposition that some Southerners were fearful of the prosperity that the Erie Canal might bring to New York. Felix Grundy of Tennessee objected in 1812 when the legislature of his state requested its congressmen to support the canal. Writing to Andrew Jackson he explained that this "Newyork Mammoth Canal" was merely an expensive and impractical electioneering hobby of Clinton and that it could serve no purpose "except to increase the power of the northern Section of the Union."[71]

Disagreement over the tariff and internal improvements undoubtedly played an important part in weakening the bonds between the Democrats of the Southern and Middle states in 1819-1821. After the defeat of the tariff bill in 1820, Hezekiah Niles, editor of *Niles' Register* and a former Democrat, declared that "*tory* I cannot be, but an *administration man* is becoming almost as bad."[72] Morgan Neville, editor of the Pitts-

[69] John Savage to De Witt Clinton, March 8, 1818; Elijah Hayward to Clinton, July 4, 1818, *ibid.*

[70] New York *Columbian*, April 14, 1820.

[71] John S. Bassett (ed.), *Correspondence of Andrew Jackson* (7 vols., Washington, 1926-1935), I, 216.

[72] Hezekiah Niles to William Darlington, May 5, 1820, William Darlington Papers, Library of Congress.

burgh *Gazette*, told of a conversation with a friend who remarked that "we don't like the manner in which you treat the President's Message [in your editorials]; Mr. Monroe is certainly hostile to manufactures, and as you have stepped forth the champion of domestic fabrics and internal improvements, you must throw a little more salt and pepper into your style when you speak of that gentleman; otherwise we shall suspect you retain your old Virginia notions and prejudices in favour of the south."[73] In 1821 a Democratic newspaper, the Washington *Gazette*, summarized the grievances of the Northern Democracy against the South. After confessing that its earliest political views had been derived from the writings of such Southern statesmen as Jefferson and Henry, the *Gazette* added that further experience had moderated its prepossessions in favor of the South. "In political economy," it said, "we behold some distinguished characters of the south *a full century* in rear of the knowledge of the age. We see them warped by sectional calculations: we behold *too many* of them turned giddy by an ascendancy *so long* possessed in the councils of the Union; an ascendancy destructive of the vital principle of protection; and, finally, we behold them apparently more attached to the welfare of Birmingham and Manchester, and Liverpool, than to the prosperity of our common country."[74]

Another element which went into the making of the Missouri Controversy was the concept of a balance of power between the Northern and Southern states, especially in the United States Senate. The astute John Taylor of Caroline not only regarded this as the main cause of the controversy but prophesied that it would lead finally to a war between the states, since it was equivalent in its consequences to the balance of power in Europe.[75]

The idea of admitting Northern and Southern states to the Union in pairs, to balance each other, originated in the Continental Congress. When Vermont sought admission in 1782,

73 Pittsburgh *Gazette*, December 11, 1820.

74 Washington *Gazette*, February 19, 1821.

75 John Taylor, *Construction Construed, and Constitutions Vindicated* (Richmond, 1820), 291.

the Rhode Island delegates observed that certain states would oppose this "because it might affect the balance of power by throwing an additional weight into the eastern Scale." In 1787 William Grayson of Virginia asserted that Kentucky would be balanced against Vermont, and thus both might be admitted. Northerners in their turn objected in 1788 to the admission of Kentucky without Vermont, "least another Vote should be added to the Southern States."[76]

After the adoption of the Constitution, the attempt to maintain a sectional equilibrium continued. In 1789, before North Carolina had acceded to the new Union, Senator Pierce Butler of South Carolina wrote to a North Carolinian: "I confess I wish you [North Carolina] to come into the confederacy, as the only chance the Southern interest has to preserve a balance of power."[77] Between 1803 and 1815 the Federalists often complained that their Democratic opponents had upset the balance, first by the Louisiana Purchase and later by the formation of new Western states.[78] It is interesting to note, however, that the Democrats themselves wanted to preserve an equilibrium. At the commencement of the War of 1812 there seems to have been a tacit understanding between Northern and Southern Democrats that an even adjustment should be attempted in the conquest of foreign territory, with Canada being added to the North and Florida to the South. During the course of the war this bargain broke down because of Southern reluctance to strengthen the North by the acquisition of Canada and a similar unwillingness on the part of Northern Democrats to sanction the occupation of Florida. Even the Western War Hawks were susceptible to the influence of North-South sectionalism.[79]

[76] Burnett, *Letters of Members of the Continental Congress,* VI, 329, VIII, 582, 741, 750, 757; Burnett, *The Continental Congress,* 708.

[77] Griffith J. McRee, *Life and Correspondence of James Iredell* (2 vols., New York, 1857-1858), II, 264.

[78] Everett S. Brown, *The Constitutional History of the Louisiana Purchase 1803-1812* (Berkeley, 1920), 32-33, 44-45; Edmund Quincy, *Life of Josiah Quincy* (Boston, 1868), 89-91; *Niles' Weekly Register,* VII (1815), 310.

[79] Julius W. Pratt, *Expansionists of 1812* (New York, 1925), 12-13, 134-52, 228-29.

Maine and Mississippi provided additional illustrations of the balance of power concept. An argument used in favor of separating Maine from Massachusetts in 1816 was that the new state would give the North two more senators and reduce the anxieties of some people over Southern influence.[80] Three years later Rufus King listed two reasons why it would be desirable to separate Maine and Massachusetts, one being "that as respects the balance of power in the Senate, which shifts rapidly towards the West, it is a good policy to multiply the numbers of this body from the North."[81] In 1813 an anonymous Massachusetts writer published a pamphlet to protest against the proposed division of the Mississippi Territory into two states. His contention was that the South was already bloated with slave representation and ought not to be further swollen.[82] In spite of such objections, the territory eventually was divided into two states, Alabama and Mississippi. One of those responsible for this was Senator Charles Tait of Georgia, who later rejoiced in the wisdom of the division. "It has," he said, "given us more strength in the Senate."[83]

The balance of power was a leading issue in the Missouri Controversy, but in view of the jockeying which had been going on ever since 1782, no originality could be claimed by the Illinoisan who wrote in the summer of 1819: "There is now, when Alabama is admitted, an equal number of free and slave states. Make Missouri a slave state, as also Florida and Arkansas, and the free states, which are the strength of the nation, are thrown in the background. I ask, are we prepared for this?"[84] The Ohio River formed a logical boundary between slave and free territory east of the Mississippi. Further west

[80] Louis C. Hatch (ed.), Maine, a History (3 vols., New York, 1919), I, 127.
[81] King, Rufus King, VI, 211-12.
[82] "Massachusetts," The New States . . . with a View to Expose the Injustice of Erecting New States at the South (Boston, 1813), 3.
[83] Charles Tait to John W. Walker, January 5, 1820, John W. Walker Papers, Alabama Department of Archives and History; Charles H. Moffat, "The Life of Charles Tait" (Ph.D. dissertation, Vanderbilt University, 1946), 95-96. See also address by David L. Yulee in U. S. Senate, August 6, 1850, in Appendix to Congressional Globe, 31 Cong., 1 Sess., 1164-66.
[84] Kaskaskia (Illinois) Intelligencer, June 30, 1819.

there was no natural dividing point. Should Missouri be admitted as a free state, the Mason and Dixon line would be pushed to a low latitude and little room left for Southern expansion. On the other hand, if slavery were permitted in Missouri, it would extend far above the area where Northerners felt it should be confined. Thus Missouri became and long remained a bone of contention between the North and South.

As the Missouri Controversy was tied up with the moral issue of slavery, it is necessary to consider briefly the history of the "peculiar institution." Slavery, which took firm root in the English colonies in the seventeenth century, seems to have troubled men's consciences little until late colonial times. In the Revolutionary period, with its emphasis on equality and the rights of man, a strong antislavery movement developed.[85] So strong was the equalitarian philosophy engendered by the Revolution that between 1780 and 1804 every Northern state either abolished slavery or provided for gradual emancipation.

There was much antislavery sentiment in the upper South, especially among the liberal aristocrats of Virginia and the Quakers. Though no Southern state abolished slavery, so many masters in the Chesapeake country freed their slaves that in 1790 a majority of the nation's free Negroes lived south of the Mason and Dixon line, as was still the case in 1819.[86] Doubtless Maryland and Virginia would have passed emancipation laws when the North did if they had not been frightened by the size of their Negro population. Liberating all of the slaves would have involved problems of economic adjustment and social control which were not present in the North. Nevertheless, gradual emancipation at some future date continued to be the hope of enlightened Virginians. The antislavery views of Washington and Jefferson are well known, and at the Constitutional Convention of 1787 the Virginia delegation wished to prohibit

[85] John H. Franklin, *From Slavery to Freedom, a History of American Negroes* (New York, 1948), 125-29; Mary S. Locke, *Anti-Slavery in America* (Boston, 1901), 9-87.
[86] *The Seventh Census of the United States: 1850*, ix.

the African slave trade immediately. This could not be done because of the opposition of the deep South, where slave labor was regarded as indispensable.

In 1819 there were grounds for believing that the Southern states might eventually abolish slavery, and as late as 1827 there were more antislavery societies in the South than in the North.[87] Significant as that fact is, it must be kept in mind that the Southern societies were not evenly distributed. All of them were in the upper South, with a noticeable concentration in east Tennessee and the Quaker counties of North Carolina. East Tennessee had the additional distinction in 1819 of having America's most avowedly abolitionist newspaper, the Jonesboro *Manumission Intelligencer*.[88]

The American Colonization Society furnished an additional outlet for Southerners who wanted to end slavery. This society had been organized in 1816-1817 for the purpose of removing free Negroes (with their consent) to Africa. Of course, mere membership in the Colonization Society did not constitute evidence of antislavery convictions. Planters wished to expatriate the free Negroes because of the evil influence which they were alleged to exert on the slave population, while some colonizationists seem to have had no other motive than race prejudice and a desire to rid America of all Negroes.[89] At the same time, there can be no doubt that much abolitionist energy was funneled into the colonization project, and its advocates often expressed the hope that it would encourage emancipation and finally result in the total disappearance of slavery.[90] Although the society was accused of being "an organized conspiracy

---

[87] Stephen B. Weeks, "Anti-Slavery Sentiment in the South," in *Publications of the Southern History Association*, II (1898), 88-89; Alice D. Adams, *The Neglected Period of Anti-Slavery in America (1808-1831)* (Boston, 1908), 117.

[88] The name of the paper was changed to *Emancipator* in 1820. Clarence S. Brigham, *History and Bibliography of American Newspapers 1690-1820* (2 vols., Worcester, 1947), II, 1058; Asa E. Martin, "Pioneer Anti-Slavery Press," in *Mississippi Valley Historical Review*, II (1916), 514-15.

[89] Dwight L. Dumond, *Antislavery Origins of the Civil War in the United States* (Ann Arbor, Mich., 1939), 13-14.

[90] Albany *Argus*, August 25, 1820; Early L. Fox, *The American Colonization Society 1817-1840* (Baltimore, 1919), 48-50, 53.

against the property of the southern country,"[91] it was accorded a warm welcome in influential Southern circles. In 1819 it reported the receipt of large contributions from the citizens of various towns in Maryland, Virginia, and Georgia.[92] Bushrod Washington of Virginia was president of the organization, and most of the vice-presidents—who included William H. Crawford, Henry Clay, John Taylor, and Andrew Jackson—were Southerners.[93] These toasts, given at a dinner in honor of President Monroe at Athens, Georgia, throw some light on public opinion in 1819: "*The Colonization Society.*—Planned by the wisest heads and purest hearts. May it eventuate in the happiness of millions." "The Slave Trade.—The scourge of Africa; the disgrace of humanity. May it cease for ever, and may the voice of peace, of christianity, and of civilization, be heard on the savage shores."[94]

While the benevolent-minded in the South were groping for a solution of the slavery problem, Northerners continued to take an interest in the question. In the months immediately before the outbreak of the Missouri Controversy, when it was reported that cargoes of Africans were being smuggled into the country, Congress received a number of petitions from the free states, some bearing numerous signatures, requesting a more vigorous enforcement of the laws against the slave trade.[95] Further attention was focused on the activities of desperadoes who went about the land kidnaping free Negroes in order to sell them into servitude. In New Jersey this practice was so prevalent and aroused so much resentment that an association was formed in Middlesex County in 1818 to combat it.[96] New York City had a manumission society which was es-

[91] Milledgeville (Georgia) *Journal,* January 18, 1820.

[92] Charleston *Southern Patriot, And Commercial Advertiser,* May 25, 1819.

[93] Baltimore *American & Commercial Daily Advertiser,* January 20, 1820.

[94] New York *American,* June 19, 1819.

[95] These petitions are now preserved in the National Archives at Washington. Those in the Senate files, Legislative Division, are open to the public.

[96] New York *Daily Advertiser,* August 7, 1818. For stories of kidnaping, see *ibid.,* April 20, June 5, June 11, July 4, October 24, December 5, 1818, April 8, May 20, 1819; also Mount Holly (New Jersey) *Burlington Mirror,* December 16, 23, 1818.

pecially zealous in rescuing free Negroes from kidnapers. It also seems to have protected runaway slaves, and a New York judge declared that it was difficult for Southerners to recover fugitive slaves from New York because of the opposition of the Manumission Society and of Mayor Colden and other city officials.[97] On the eve of the dispute over Missouri, the Quakers were conducting a campaign to strengthen the laws against the African slave trade and to protect free Negroes from kidnaping.[98]

Meanwhile, books and pamphlets on the subject continued to appear. George Bourne wrote in 1816 that "every man who holds Slaves and who pretends to be a Christian or a Republican, is either an incurable Idiot who cannot distinguish good from evil, or an obdurate sinner who resolutely defies every social, moral, and divine requisition."[99] In 1818 Senator William Smith of South Carolina complained that the bookstores of the country were filled with catchpenny prints and pamphlets against slavery written by people who knew no more of the actual condition of the slaves than they did of the man in the moon.[100] Smith was incensed especially by the writings of Jesse Torrey and John Kenrick. Kenrick's pamphlet, *Horrors of Slavery*, seems to have had wide circulation. The author himself sent one hundred copies to Governor Plumer for distribution among the legislators and prominent men of New Hampshire.[101]

The humanitarian impulse of the Missouri Controversy was partly the result of the great benevolent and philanthropical movement which swept over the country after 1815 and

[97] B. Livingston to John Sergeant, January 18, 1822, John Sergeant Papers, Historical Society of Pennsylvania. See also "Manumission Society New York City—Minutes July 15, 1817–Jan. 11, 1842," New-York Historical Society.

[98] Mount Pleasant (Ohio) *Philanthropist*, February 20, 1819.

[99] George Bourne, *The Book and Slavery Irreconcilable* (Philadelphia, 1816), 3.

[100] *Annals of Congress*, 15 Cong., 1 Sess., 236.

[101] William Plumer to John Kenrick, October 27, 1817, William Plumer Papers, Library of Congress; John Kenrick, *Horrors of Slavery* (Cambridge, 1817); Jesse Torrey, Jr., *A Portraiture of Domestic Slavery, in the United States* (Philadelphia, 1817).

reached full bloom in the 1820's.[102] In the twenties there were countless men of good will and great influence who were eager to reform everything from the penitentiary and poorhouse to the Southern plantation. In cities like New York the desire to be benevolent and aid one's fellow men became almost an obsession. The files of the Mount Pleasant, Ohio, *Philanthropist* provide an easy access to the mind of the reformer in the years from 1818 to 1821. This journal was strongly antislavery and also abounded in articles on justice for conscientious objectors, temperance, war and peace, dueling, debtors' prisons, the abolition of capital punishment, the reformation of criminals, instruction for the deaf and dumb, and new educational methods. In 1820 the editor Elisha Bates announced that he intended to publish yet another paper, *The Moral Advocate,* which would be devoted exclusively to the subjects of war, dueling, and capital punishment.[103] Bates joined other philanthropists in a nationwide campaign to secure better treatment for the Indians, and he lamented that "the light of science has not dawned on the mind of the Indian & that the negro is not included in the social compact, but remains, in the midst of an enlightened people, excluded from the common benefits of impartial laws."[104]

The social reform movement of the 1820's exerted considerable influence in the South. Southern benevolence found expression in the Colonization Society, in plans for the improvement of education, and in various humane measures.[105] On the Missouri question, however, some Southern reformers and humanitarians parted company with those of the North. Because of constitutional or other scruples, they could not favor the prohibition of slavery in Missouri by act of Congress.

During the dispute over Missouri, the antislavery views of Washington, Jefferson, and Patrick Henry were quoted, and

---

[102] For an account of the movement, see Alice F. Tyler, *Freedom's Ferment, Phases of American Social History to 1860* (Minneapolis, 1944), 274, 283-85, 287, 302; McMaster, *History of the United States,* IV, 522-69.

[103] Mount Pleasant (Ohio) *Philanthropist,* August 12, 1820.

[104] *Ibid.,* December 11, 1818, January 8, 15, February 20, 1819.

[105] Sydnor, *Development of Southern Sectionalism,* 89-103.

Southerners were accused of having repudiated the liberal principles to which they formerly subscribed. Actually there was no repudiation, for at no time in its previous history would the South have voted to prohibit slavery in a new state which contained a large slave population. The position of most Southern leaders on this subject from 1784 to 1821 was fairly consistent and may be summarized as this: We admit that slavery is an evil of great magnitude, but the slaves might cut our throats if set at liberty. We dare not free them now, though we hope that eventually emancipation and colonization will be possible. In the meantime, slaves are property, and it would be unfair to the owners to exclude them from the West. If they remain concentrated in a few seaboard states, it will be necessary to keep them under tight police control to prevent a rebellion. Scattering them over the western country will ameliorate their condition and reduce the danger to the whites in the older states.[106]

There were other considerations which were not likely to be mentioned in public debate. Many a tidewater planter looked forward to the day when he could move with his slaves from the worn-out tobacco lands of Virginia and Carolina to the fertile western territories. Barring slaveholders from that region would ruin the planters economically and would give New England an advantage in the settlement of the West, thereby upsetting the balance of power and strengthening the Federalist party, which was regarded as hostile to Southern interests.

Prior to 1819 there had been numerous attempts to prohibit slavery in the West, and the South had reacted to nearly all such propositions just as it did at the time of the Missouri Controversy. In the Continental Congress in 1784 Southern opposition defeated the antislavery clause of Jefferson's ordinance for

---

[106] See especially the debates in Congress on the question of prohibiting slavery in the Mississippi Territory in 1798 and on the Breckinridge Bill in 1804. *Annals of Congress*, 5 Cong., 1306-12; Everett S. Brown (ed.), "The Senate Debate on the Breckinridge Bill for the Government of Louisiana, 1804," in *American Historical Review*, XXII (1917), 354. There were always some Southerners, especially in the deep South, who defended slavery as a positive good, but the general attitude before 1820 was apologetic. William S. Jenkins, *Pro-Slavery Thought in the Old South* (Chapel Hill, 1935), 48-58.

a temporary government of the western territory.[107] In the next
year Virginia, Georgia, and the Carolinas voted against a similar proposal by Rufus King.[108] Southerners did not oppose the
antislavery provision of the Ordinance of 1787, but William
Grayson of Virginia, who was a member of Congress at the
time, declared that there were "political reasons" for making
such a concession.[109] North Carolina and Georgia, in ceding
their western lands to the federal government in 1789 and
1802 respectively, stipulated that slavery should be permitted
there.[110] In 1798 the South objected vigorously when Northern
congressmen sought to abolish slavery in the Mississippi Territory.[111] In 1804 most of the Southern senators, while voting
to forbid the importation of slaves into Louisiana from foreign
countries, insisted that American slaveholders who wished to
immigrate there should be allowed to carry their own slaves
with them. A motion by Senator James Hillhouse of Connecticut which provided for the gradual emancipation of all slaves
taken to Louisiana from other parts of the Union was defeated
by a vote of 17 to 11.[112]

The United States acquired what is now Missouri (and along
with it a dispute over slavery that lasted intermittently for
sixty years) by the Louisiana Purchase treaty of 1803. Slavery
existed throughout the Purchase under the French and Spanish
regimes, and in the treaty the American government promised
to maintain and protect the inhabitants in the free enjoyment
of their liberty, property, and religion.[113] Presumably the term
property included slaves. The people of Missouri not only
owned slaves in 1803 but were extremely anxious to continue

[107] *Journals of the Continental Congress*, XXVI, 247.

[108] *Ibid.*, XXVIII, 164-65, 239.

[109] Frederick D. Stone, "The Ordinance of 1787," in *Pennsylvania Magazine
of History and Biography*, XIII (1889), 328; Jay A. Barrett, *Evolution of the
Ordinance of 1787* (New York, 1891), 79.

[110] Samuel A. Ashe, *History of North Carolina* (2 vols., Greensboro and
Raleigh, 1925), II, 120; Phillips, *Georgia and State Rights*, 34.

[111] *Annals of Congress*, 5 Cong., 1306-12.

[112] Brown, "Senate Debate on the Breckinridge Bill," 351, 354-55.

[113] Hunter Miller (ed.), *Treaties and Other International Acts of the United
States of America* (8 vols. to date, Washington, 1931-   ), II, 501.

doing so. Fear of an attack on slavery similar to the Ordinance of 1787 may have been partly responsible for the cold reception extended to the United States by Missourians when they learned of their change of nationality.[114] Likewise, they were dissatisfied with the first act passed by Congress for their territorial government because it was silent in regard to slavery. Silence, they feared, might "create the presumption of a disposition in Congress to abolish at a future day slavery altogether in the district."[115] The influx of new American settlers after 1803 did not change the sentiments of the region concerning slavery. Indeed, since slaves were excluded from the Northwest Territory by the Ordinance of 1787, Missouri became a promised land for slaveholding immigrants from Virginia, North Carolina, Kentucky, and Tennessee. In 1810 it had a slave population of 3,011, and in 1820 nearly one sixth of its 66,000 inhabitants were Negroes.[116]

In 1812, when Congress raised Missouri to the second grade of territories, Representative Abner Lacock of Pennsylvania made a motion to prohibit the admission of slaves into the territory. The motion was defeated, receiving only seventeen votes. The debate on this occasion is not recorded in the *Annals of Congress*. Jonathan Roberts afterward asserted that "We were not then told the proposition was unconstitutional, nor in violation of the treaty; but that we were on the eve of a war, with almost one-half the community infatuated with the spirit of opposition to the Government; that further dissension at that time might be fatal. The question was thus deferred until a more convenient season."[117] As far as Missouri and the South were concerned, "a more convenient season" never arrived.

114 Floyd C. Shoemaker, *Missouri's Struggle for Statehood 1804-1821* (Jefferson City, 1916), 14; Clarence E. Carter (ed.), *The Territorial Papers of the United States* (18 vols. to date, Washington, 1934-   ), XIII, 29-30.

115 *Annals of Congress*, 8 Cong., 2 Sess., *Appendix*, 1613; *American State Papers*, XX, *Miscellaneous*, I, 401.

116 *Seventh Census: 1850*, 665.

117 *Annals of Congress*, 12 Cong., 1 Sess., 1248; *ibid.*, 16 Cong., 1 Sess., 337.

"The Missouri Bill . . . *is* our child—& *with me
a Darling favourite—But I fear an ill fated
offspring."*—James Tallmadge, Jr., to John
W. Taylor[1]

CHAPTER II

TALLMADGE LIGHTS THE FUSE

*I*n 1816 Missouri was raised to the highest grade of territories; in the next year its people began to petition Congress
for admission to statehood;[2] and in 1818-1819 the question of
admission was considered in Congress. When a dispute over
slavery in the proposed new state suddenly arose in February,
1819, Northerners and Southerners alike professed to have been
taken completely by surprise. During the previous months,
however, there had been a number of warnings of the storm
to come.

On April 3, 1818, a committee of the House of Representatives reported an enabling act for the admission of Missouri.
This bill got no further than the Committee of the Whole, but
it is significant that on the day after it was reported, Congressman Arthur Livermore, a New Hampshire Democrat, proposed
in the House that a constitutional amendment be adopted to
prohibit slavery in any states that might thereafter be admitted
to the Union. According to the *Annals,* Livermore's resolution
"was read, and, on the question of proceeding to its consideration, it was decided in the negative."[3] This proposed amendment is important as being perhaps the first intimation of a
Northern attempt to restrict slavery in Missouri. Apparently,
none of the Missouri petitions asking for statehood had anything to say about slavery. Since the territory had considerable

property in slaves, it was a natural assumption that Missouri would become a slave state if its people were left to their own devices.

Soon after the Fifteenth Congress reconvened in second session in November, 1818, a resolution for the admission of Illinois was presented. It was opposed by Representative James Tallmadge, Jr., of New York on the ground that the constitution of Illinois, although it might not sanction slavery, did not "sufficiently" prohibit it. The House passed the resolution, but with thirty-three Northern votes and one from Maryland against it. Tallmadge used strong language, asserting that Congress was "bound by a tie not to be broken" and that "the interest, honor, and faith of the nation, required it scrupulously to guard against slavery's passing into a territory where they have power to prevent its entrance." These remarks received a moderate amount of publicity from the press.[4]

On December 18, 1818, Speaker Henry Clay presented to the House a memorial from the Legislative Council and House of Representatives of Missouri, dated November 21, 1818, asking that the people of the territory be permitted to adopt a constitution and form a state government.[5] Meanwhile a significant move had been made by the American Convention for Promoting the Abolition of Slavery, and Improving the Condition of the African Race, which held a special meeting at Philadelphia in December, 1818, with delegates in attendance from antislavery societies in New York, Pennsylvania, and Delaware. The Convention appointed a committee to prepare

1 December 4, 1820, Taylor Papers.

2 Shoemaker, *Missouri's Struggle for Statehood*, 37-40, 321-23; *Annals of Congress*, 15 Cong., 1 Sess., 591, 840, 1391-92; *Memorial of the Citizens of Missouri Territory* (St. Louis, n.d.). This is a printed memorial with signatures in longhand. The Manuscripts Division of the Library of Congress and the State Historical Society of Missouri have original copies.

3 *Annals of Congress*, 15 Cong., 1 Sess., 1672, 1675-76.

4 *Ibid.*, 15 Cong., 2 Sess., 305-11; New York *Daily Advertiser*, November 28, 1818; Mount Pleasant (Ohio) *Philanthropist*, December 11, 1818.

5 *Annals of Congress*, 15 Cong., 2 Sess., 418. For a copy of the memorial, see *ibid.*, 16 Cong., 1 Sess., 42-44; *American State Papers*, XXI, *Miscellaneous*, II, 557-58; *Memorial of the Legislature of Missouri, for a Division of the Territory, &c.* (Washington, 1818).

a memorial to Congress, to be signed by American citizens, requesting that slavery be prohibited in all territories established in the future as well as in any states erected from such territories.[6]

In January, 1819, the House of Representatives received another warning of the impending Missouri Controversy. John Sergeant of Pennsylvania introduced a resolution instructing the Judiciary Committee to consider the enactment of a general ordinance which would guarantee the fundamental principles of civil and religious liberty to the inhabitants of the territories outside the original limits of the United States and be the basis of all governments established there. William Lowndes of South Carolina observed that the meaning of Sergeant's resolution was rather obscure but that he thought he could perceive the object of it. Sergeant replied that he did indeed have a particular object in view. The resolution was ordered to lie on the table[7] and would soon be forgotten in the excitement over Missouri.

On February 13, 1819, the House resolved itself into a Committee of the Whole to consider bills to enable the people of Missouri and Alabama to form state governments. The bill relating to Missouri was taken up first, and during its consideration, James Tallmadge, Jr., moved to amend it in the following manner: "And provided also, *That the further introduction of slavery or involuntary servitude be prohibited, except for the punishment of crimes, whereof the party shall be duly convicted; and that all children of slaves, born within the said state, after the admission thereof into the Union, shall be free, but may be held to service until the age of twenty-five years.*"[8]

To this proposed amendment to the bill for Missouri's admission—and hence to its author, James Tallmadge, Jr.—be-

[6] *Minutes of the Proceedings of a Special Meeting of the Fifteenth American Convention for Promoting the Abolition of Slavery, and Improving the Condition of the African Race* (Philadelphia, 1818), 42-43.

[7] *Annals of Congress*, 15 Cong., 2 Sess., 547.

[8] According to the House *Journal*, this was the wording of the amendment after it had been modified. The *Annals of Congress* gives a slightly different wording. See *Journal of the House of Representatives*, 15 Cong., 2 Sess., 272; *Annals of Congress*, 15 Cong., 2 Sess., 1166, 1170.

longs the distinction of having precipitated the famous Missouri Controversy. As Tallmadge's motives in introducing the amendment have been a subject of speculation from that day to this, it is well to know what manner of man he was and to understand his political background. He was a native of Dutchess County, New York, and the son of a Revolutionary patriot. At the time of the Missouri Controversy, he was representing the Poughkeepsie district in Congress. He was a Democrat and had once been private secretary to Governor George Clinton. In the War of 1812, in which he commanded a company of home guards, he secured the title of general.[9]

Tallmadge was a man of great ability. Nearly all of his contemporaries agreed that he had considerable talent. "And perhaps," said one who knew him, "there is no man in America, save one, (Henry Clay,) who, with so much grace, could blend the courtesy of a gentleman with the authority and dignity of a presiding officer in a deliberative assembly as Mr. Tallmadge."[10] At the same time, there was an eccentric and unpredictable streak in his nature which prevented him from rising as high as he might otherwise have done.[11] His desire for advancement made him too prone to change sides in politics,[12] and he was not above writing overly solicitous letters to those who controlled the patronage.[13]

Tallmadge's brother was related to De Witt Clinton by marriage, and he himself was affiliated with the Clintonian faction of the Democratic party at the time that he launched the Mis-

[9] *Dictionary of American Biography*, XVIII, 285-86.

[10] Jabez D. Hammond, *The History of Political Parties in the State of New-York* (2 vols., Albany, 1842), II, 228.

[11] *Ibid.*, 184; George Dangerfield, *The Era of Good Feelings* (New York, 1952), 200.

[12] Hammond, *History of Political Parties in New-York*, II, 170, 231; Charles F. Adams (ed.), *Memoirs of John Quincy Adams* (12 vols., Philadelphia, 1874-1877), VI, 298, VII, 411. Thurlow Weed, who was closely associated with Tallmadge, described him as inordinately ambitious, easy to anger but capable of being appeased, hopeful, confiding, efficient, zealous, and popular. Harriet A. Weed and Thurlow W. Barnes, *Life of Thurlow Weed* (2 vols., Boston, 1883-1884), I, 183.

[13] See his letter to President Monroe, August 14, 1819, James Monroe Papers, New York Public Library.

souri Controversy. Though not a candidate to succeed himself in Congress in 1818,[14] he was nominated by the Clintonians for the office of state senator in 1819. In the campaign that followed, the Missouri question was an issue, one of the arguments advanced in Tallmadge's behalf being that he had "dared to oppose that aristocratical southern influence, which, like the inundation of Gothic and Vandal power, threatens to overrun the Union."[15]

In New York City, which lay within Tallmadge's senatorial district, an appeal was made to the Negro voters to support him because of his stand on Missouri. The *Columbian*, the Clintonian organ of New York, declared that the Negroes regarded Tallmadge "as the enlightened and humane advocate of their oppressed race, and we presume will support him at the polls."[16] The Negro vote was an important factor in New York in 1819. Massed in doubtful wards, where it constituted a balance of power, it had actually swung the state to the Federalists in 1813 in spite of anything the Democrats could do.[17] One of Tallmadge's friends predicted that he would receive most of the Negro vote and also the support of the Quakers and the Manumission Society.[18] This was not enough to elect him, however, and he was defeated by the Tammany candidates.[19]

[14] According to Edmund Platt, *The Eagle's History of Poughkeepsie* (Poughkeepsie, 1905), 97, Tallmadge was defeated for re-election to Congress in 1818 by Randall S. Street, a Federalist. The election returns show, however, that Tallmadge was not a candidate. See New York *National Advocate*, June 9, 1818.

[15] Poughkeepsie *Dutchess Observer*, April 21, 1819.

[16] New York *Columbian*, April 22, 1819. On April 26 the *Columbian* asserted that "it is no 'novelty' in this state for people of color to assemble to express their sentiments on the subject of candidates for office. In this city that class of people are *numerous and respectable*—they are *voters*, and many of them are *well educated*."

[17] Dixon R. Fox, "The Negro Vote in Old New York," in *Political Science Quarterly*, XXXII (1917), 252-75; Dixon R. Fox, *The Decline of Aristocracy in the Politics of New York* (New York, 1919), 269-70.

[18] Theodorus Bailey to Matthias B. Tallmadge, April 27, 1819, Tallmadge Family Papers (Theodorus Bailey Folder), New-York Historical Society. The Tallmadge Papers contain many letters from James, Jr., and his relatives, though unfortunately they throw almost no light on the Missouri question.

[19] For the election returns, see Albany *Register*, June 4, 8, 1819.

Shortly after the election, Tallmadge broke with De Witt Clinton and went over to the rival Bucktail or Tammany faction of the New York Democracy.[20] He believed that he had alienated Clinton by supporting the Monroe administration in the debate on the Seminole War.[21] In any event it is certain that Clinton alienated him by not rewarding him with an appointive office.[22] Tallmadge later carried his animosity against Clinton to the extent of voting to remove him from the position of canal commissioner which he had so long and ably filled. This act hurt Tallmadge more than it did Clinton and in fact cost him the governorship.[23] Tallmadge's subsequent career was one of moderate distinction. He served as lieutenant governor of New York and was one of the founders of New York University. He also achieved a measure of fame through his daughter Mary Rebecca, who was so extraordinarily beautiful that Queen Victoria is said to have remarked that she would be willing to exchange her dominion for Miss Tallmadge's beauty.[24]

Though more of a politician than a statesman, Tallmadge did have deep convictions and seems to have been motivated primarily by humanitarian and patriotic considerations in opposing the extension of slavery to new states. He retired from Congress soon after the long contest over Missouri began but continued to take a lively interest in it and wrote letters to his friend Congressman John W. Taylor, urging him to keep up the fight. In his correspondence with Taylor he spoke of the contestants as being "cupidity" on one side and "principle" and

[20] The Bucktails got their name from the emblem of Tammany Hall, a buck's tail.

[21] James Tallmadge, Jr., to James Monroe, August 14, 1819, Monroe Papers, New York Public Library; Tallmadge to John W. Taylor, April 4, July 7, 1819, March 2, 1820, Taylor Papers.

[22] De Alva S. Alexander, *A Political History of the State of New York* (3 vols., New York, 1906-1909), I, 274. "Mr. Tallmadge asked and received *much*, but he did not obtain all he asked, and therefore turned about, . . . and turned bucktail." New York *Columbian*, July 27, 1820.

[23] Glyndon G. Van Deusen, *Thurlow Weed, Wizard of the Lobby* (Boston, 1947), 27.

[24] Arthur W. Talmadge, *The Talmadge, Tallmadge, and Talmage Genealogy* (New York, 1909), 217.

"suffering human nature" on the other. While doubtful that his amendment to the Missouri bill would ever pass, he expressed a hope that it "may have produced moral effects which will eventually redeem our beloved country from Disgrace & Danger."[25] These sentiments were shared heartily by his family. His wife memorized portions of a speech on the subject, and his parents were proud of him—"Especily," as his religious mother wrote, because they thought he was "on the Side of truth and justice."[26]

Tallmadge had other motives, of course, in seeking to check the spread of slavery. With his Clintonian background he was doubtless willing to fling darts at the South, and, as will be shown in discussing the congressional debates, he was thoroughly imbued with the old Federalist-Clintonian opposition to the three-fifths ratio of slave representation. Finally he had a fame and glory complex. An eloquent speaker, he obviously enjoyed delivering flamboyant and well-written addresses on slavery and hoped to send them sounding down the ages.[27]

As Tallmadge still was regarded as a protégé of De Witt Clinton when he introduced his amendment, Southerners were quick to charge that the attempt to prohibit slavery in Missouri was a deep-laid plot cooked up by their old enemy, the New York governor.[28] John W. Taylor, however, who was in a position to know, told John Quincy Adams that the South had ascribed the origin of the Missouri dispute to Clinton "without a shadow of foundation; that, so far from it, Clinton had in the first instance entirely discouraged, and never gave any counte-

[25] James Tallmadge, Jr., to John W. Taylor, January 11, March 2, December 4, 1820, Taylor Papers.

[26] *Ibid.*, March 2, 1820; Ann Tallmadge to her children, March 29, 1819, Tallmadge Papers (Ann Tallmadge Folder).

[27] His letters to John W. Taylor, January 11, March 2, 1820, Taylor Papers, contained such expressions as "monument to your fame," "cause of pride—& glory," and "great & glorious cause."

[28] De Witt Clinton "sent Talmage back with this accursed proposition last year. . . . I remember that I was laughed at last year for suggesting that Clinton originated this question—Everyone *now* thinks the same." Congressman Thomas W. Cobb of Georgia to Charles Tait, January 30, 1820, Charles Tait Papers, Alabama Department of Archives and History.

nance to it until he discovered its great popularity in the State."[29] Certainly Tallmadge was a strong-willed character and fully capable of acting on his own initiative without any stimulation from Clinton. John Quincy Adams thought that those who introduced the Tallmadge amendment (evidently meaning Tallmadge and Taylor) did not foresee its importance.[30] It was said that even Rufus King, who afterward became the leader of the Northern forces in Congress, did not at first realize the significance of the Missouri issue. When H. G. Otis told him of the debate in the House of Representatives, he seemed to consider it unimportant.[31]

Tallmadge regarded himself and John W. Taylor as the parents of the antislavery amendment.[32] Before presenting it he perhaps conferred with Taylor, Representative Elijah Mills of Massachusetts, and others who were known to share his views. He introduced the amendment on the same day that he returned from a visit to New York occasioned by the death of his son. As he was ill, he at first took little part in the debate, and Taylor and Mills bore the brunt of the fight. Taylor, who does not seem to have had sufficient advance notice of the role he was to play, explained in his first recorded address on the Missouri question that he could not do justice to the subject, "owing in part to the unexpected manner in which it was taken up."[33]

That the South was caught off guard is indicated by Thomas H. Benton's statement that John Scott, Missouri's territorial delegate in Congress, only learned of what was brewing "at a late period, at second hand, through the medium of a foreigner,

[29] Adams, *Memoirs of J. Q. Adams*, V, 203. The New-York Historical Society has Clinton's unpublished diary, but the entries in it for this period are too brief to be of much value to historians. In the Clinton letterbooks and manuscript correspondence, now preserved at Columbia University, the Missouri Controversy is scarcely mentioned.

[30] Adams, *Memoirs of J. Q. Adams*, IV, 528-29.

[31] Samuel E. Morison, *The Life and Letters of Harrison Gray Otis* (2 vols., Boston, 1913), II, 225-26.

[32] James Tallmadge, Jr., to John W. Taylor, December 4, 1820, Taylor Papers.

[33] *Annals of Congress*, 15 Cong., 2 Sess., 1061 n., 1179, 1204.

the Portuguese ambassador."[34] The Washington *Intelligencer* declared that the result of Tallmadge's motion "appears to have been wholly unexpected."[35]

It will be recalled that Tallmadge presented the antislavery amendment to the Missouri bill in the House of Representatives, in Committee of the Whole, on February 13, 1819. The debate that followed was not recorded fully, nor were those which took place in the next two sessions of Congress. Gales and Seaton, who were in charge of reporting the congressional addresses at this time, were rather slipshod in their work. Sometimes the reporter was absent, sometimes he might arrive late, and again he would merely record the fact that a congressman spoke in an inaudible tone. Often those who delivered speeches presented copies of them to Gales and Seaton. In such cases there was usually much alteration and embellishment between delivery and publication.[36]

The debate on the Tallmadge amendment in February and March, 1819, was short but able. The speeches preserved in Gales and Seaton's *Annals of Congress* on this occasion are worthy of careful analysis since they covered almost every phase of the arguments which would be used by the North and South for many years to come. The first speech on the Missouri question recorded in the *Annals* was made by John W. Taylor of Saratoga County, New York. Taylor was a Democrat of long standing who was later to become Speaker of the House. He and Tallmadge generally were recognized as the leaders of the antislavery forces in the House during the first

[34] St. Louis *Enquirer*, May 19, 1819.

[35] Washington *Daily National Intelligencer*, February 16, 1819.

[36] Gales and Seaton were printers to both houses of Congress. This item from their newspaper, the Washington *Daily National Intelligencer* (March 15, 1820), is typical: "When the resolution for directing the publication of the Journal of the Old Congress was ordered to be read a third time, a few days ago, our Reporter had not reached the Hall. There was some Debate on the question, therefore, which was not reported. A friend, who was present, has favored us with an account of it, from which the following is compiled: etc." Rufus King wrote in May, 1820, that "the speeches hitherto published have been prepared by those who delivered them: there was no note taker present in the Senate and I have not put a pen to paper in order to preserve what I said." King, *Rufus King*, VI, 336-37.

phase of the Missouri Controversy. This was a position for which Taylor was in many respects better qualified than Tallmadge, since he had the latter's ability without his eccentricities and political instability.[37]

Taylor began his address[38] with the assertion that the question under discussion was not one which concerned only the few people who then inhabited the Missouri Territory. Many states would eventually be formed on the Pacific coast and in the fertile region through which the Missouri River meandered for two thousand miles. The people of the new state of Missouri were the ones who were "to set in motion the machine of free government beyond the Mississippi." If slavery were allowed in Missouri, it would eventually, "with all its baleful consequences," inherit the entire West.

Next, Taylor attempted to show that Congress possessed the power to require of Missouri a constitutional prohibition against the future introduction of slavery before admitting it into the Union. The power of admission came under the constitutional provision that new states could be admitted to the Union by Congress. Obviously this power was discretionary. Congress might admit new states or refuse to admit them. But, argued Taylor, if Congress had the right of altogether refusing to admit them, much more had it the power of prescribing the terms of admission. Up to now, the exercise of the power had never been questioned. Ohio had been admitted in 1803 with the understanding that nothing in its constitution should be repugnant to the Ordinance of 1787. The sixth article of that ordinance stipulated that "there shall be neither slavery nor involuntary servitude in the said Territory, otherwise than in the punishment of crimes whereof the party shall have been duly convicted." In like manner slavery had been prohibited in Indiana and Illinois. Moreover, Congress had not doubted its right to annex conditions to the admission of new states from the Louisiana Purchase in 1811, for in that year, in passing a

37 Hammond, *History of Political Parties in New-York*, I, 305, 551-52, II, 172-73.
38 For the full address, see *Annals of Congress*, 15 Cong., 2 Sess., 1170-79.

law to enable the people of Orleans Territory to form a constitution and state government, it required them to establish
trial by jury and even to make English their official language.

Having, as he thought, shown that the Tallmadge amendment was constitutional, Taylor argued that it was expedient.
He declared that Southerners had long considered slavery an
"original sin" for which they were not responsible, it having
been fastened upon them by their ancestors. If now slavery
were perpetuated in Missouri by Southern members of Congress, future generations of Missourians would "say of them,
as they have been constrained to speak of their fathers, 'we
wish their decision had been different; we regret the existence
of this unfortunate population among us; but we found them
here; we know not what to do with them.'" If slavery were
permitted west of the Mississippi, said Taylor, slaves would
surely be smuggled in from Africa to perform the labor there.
Under such circumstances, it would be in vain to enact strict
laws against the foreign slave trade. Avarice would stimulate
the violation of law as long as a Negro man could be purchased
in Africa for a bottle of whiskey or a few gewgaws and sold for
twelve or fifteen hundred dollars in New Orleans.[39]

Taylor next answered the charge that the Tallmadge amendment would decrease the value of Southern property in slaves,
asserting that it would only do so incidentally. Nor would it
discourage Southern immigration to Missouri any more than
the admission of slavery would discourage immigration from
the North and East; for what white laborer would go where
he must be ranked with Negro slaves? The South had degraded
the working man. Even a liberal Southerner like Clay just had
spoken with abhorrence "of the performance, by your wives and
daughters, of those domestic offices which he was pleased to
call servile! What comparison did he make between the 'black
slaves' of Kentucky and the 'white slaves' of the North; and

[39] There can be no doubt that many slaves were being smuggled into the
United States at the time of the Missouri Controversy. See W. E. B. Du Bois,
*The Suppression of the African Slave-Trade to the United States of America
1638-1870* (New York, 1896), 108-30.

how instantly did he strike a balance in favor of the condition of the former!" And who but slaveholders were allowed to fill all the political offices of the South? Labor was considered disgraceful in the slave states, and the election of a laboring man, even if he were well educated, would be regarded as an unusual event.

Taylor maintained that slavery would reduce the value of farm property in Missouri. This, he said, could be demonstrated by comparing agricultural conditions in the slave state of Maryland with those in the free states of New York and Pennsylvania. In New York farms sold at rates ten times as high as those of similar fertility and situation in Maryland. Who, said Taylor, had traveled along the line which divided Maryland from Pennsylvania "and has not observed that no monuments are necessary to mark the boundary; that it is easily traced by following the dividing lines between farms highly cultivated and plantations laying open to the common and overrun with weeds; between stone barns and stone bridges on one side, and stalk cribs and no bridges on the other; between a neat, blooming, animated, rosy-cheeked peasantry on the one side, and a squalid, slow-motioned, black population on the other? Our vote this day will determine which of these descriptions will hereafter best suit the inhabitants of the new world beyond the Mississippi."

Besides Taylor's remarks, the *Annals* contain the addresses made in the Committee of the Whole by two other Northern congressmen, Timothy Fuller of Massachusetts and Arthur Livermore of New Hampshire. Fuller and Livermore were Democrats. Both demanded the exclusion of slavery from new states, though admitting that Congress could not interfere with it in states where it already existed.

Fuller laid great stress on the constitutional provision that every state in the Union must be guaranteed a republican form of government.[40] Certainly slavery was a departure from republican principles, he said, and cited the Declaration of Independence to prove it. Here he was interrupted by several

40 For Fuller's address, see *Annals of Congress,* 15 Cong., 2 Sess., 1179-84.

congressmen who deemed it improper to challenge the republican character of the slaveholding states. Such statements, said Colston of Virginia, tended to deny the right of those states to hold slaves. Colston expressed a fear that there might be slaves in the gallery who were listening. Fuller explained that he did not question the right of the older Southern states to continue holding slaves. The Constitution had republicanism as its "predominant principle," but an exception had been recognized in the case of the original slave states. The exception from "pure" republicanism, however, could not apply to new states. Congress, under the Constitution, must require every new state to have a "pure" republican form of government, which meant it must be free.

Fuller also maintained that the section of the Constitution declaring that Congress should not prohibit before 1808 the migration or importation of such persons as any of the States then existing should wish to admit empowered the federal legislature to prevent the transportation of slaves from one state to another after 1808. Fuller based his interpretation of this clause on the meaning of the phrase "migration or importation." According to him, "importation" meant the bringing in of slaves from abroad. Now, "migration" was not synonymous with "importation," nor would it have been used if it was. Obviously migration did not mean exportation. It could not mean the voluntary movement of free Negroes to America from abroad, as none ever came. What alternative remained then except to apply the term "migration" to the transportation of slaves from one state to another?

Livermore, in his address,[41] spoke feelingly of the cruelty and immorality of slavery. He reminded Southerners that even they had an interest in limiting the extension of the institution; for, should a servile insurrection break out, it was to the free states that the slaveholders must resort for aid.

The chief speakers on the Southern side at this stage of the debate were Henry Clay and Philip P. Barbour. Clay was Speaker of the House and Barbour was later to hold the same

[41] For Livermore's address, see *ibid.,* 1191-93.

position. Clay's address has not been preserved, but he spoke at some length and even "pressed into his service the cause of humanity" by using the popular Southern "diffusion" argument, namely, that the slaves would be happier and better fed if they were spread over the West instead of being cooped up in a few Southern states.[42]

Philip Barbour of Virginia began his remarks[43] with the assertion that while Congress could prohibit slavery in a territory, it could not do so in the new state of Missouri, for the Constitution stated that "New States may be admitted by the Congress into this Union." Obviously it was meant that a new state should be admitted to a union of equals and should enjoy all the rights of sovereignty retained by the original states. Slavery existed in some of the older states, and those where it did not exist could authorize it at any time they chose by laws of their own enactment. Missouri would be less sovereign than the other states if she were denied control over slavery in her borders. Besides, the Constitution provided that "The citizens of each State shall be entitled to all privileges and immunities of citizens in the several States." It would be illegal to prohibit the citizens of Missouri from holding slaves for all time when citizens of the Southern states were now holding them and citizens of the Northern states could do likewise if their legislatures consented. If Congress had a right to make a new state less sovereign in a single respect than the original states, there was no limit to which it might not legally go in this regard. It could even require a new state to sanction instead of abolish slavery. Slavery, argued Barbour, was a question of municipal legislation. In the territories Congress possessed the entire power of municipal legislation. But a state had the exclusive right to regulate slavery within its own limits, since the whole matter of municipal legislation appertained to a state legislature.

Barbour contended that even if Congress had the power to restrict slavery in Missouri, humanity, justice, and sound policy forbade the exercise of it. On the subject of humanity, he said,

[42] *Ibid.*, 1174-75.   [43] For Barbour's address, see *ibid.*, 1184-91.

he had little to add to the remarks of Speaker Clay. The latter had already shown that the condition of the Negroes would be improved if they were spread over a larger area. Because of the fertility of the West, its slave population would have cheaper and more abundant food than that of the Atlantic states. Southerners were attached personally to the slaves, whom they treated as their "most valuable" and "most favored property." Because of this fact, and because much labor was needed to clear the West, the South would be virtually barred from Missouri if not allowed to carry its slaves there. This meant that the whole trans-Mississippi country—"an illimitable tract of the most fertile land"—would in effect be opened to the North and closed to the South. Scatter the slaves over a wider area, said Barbour, and they would form a smaller proportion of the population, would be less liable to revolt, and in case of insurrection could be more easily suppressed. This would mean much from the point of view of the South's military efficiency in time of war. Not that there was any immediate danger of a slave insurrection. Barbour himself "slept quietly in his bed, notwithstanding the apprehension which some gentlemen seemed to entertain." He was thinking only of the future.

Barbour asserted that the existence of slavery in Missouri would not keep out Northern settlers, since the latter were constantly moving into the older slaveholding communities to engage in the mercantile business. Nor was it true that the South had degraded its nonslaveholding white laborers, who, on the contrary, had "all that erectness of character which belongs to them as freemen, conscious of their political and civil rights."

At the conclusion of the discussion, the Committee of the Whole decided by a vote of 79 to 67 to incorporate the Tallmadge amendment in the Missouri bill.[44]

The next day, February 16, the Committee of the Whole reported the amended bill to the House. Here a lengthy address against the Tallmadge amendment was made by John

[44] *Annals of Congress*, 15 Cong., 2 Sess., 1193. Neither the *Annals* nor the House *Journal* gives the votes of individual congressmen in this instance.

Scott, Missouri's territorial delegate to Congress.[45] Much of Scott's speech was a reiteration of what had already been said in Committee of the Whole. He particularly stressed the argument, which was popular with Missourians, that the treaty with France in 1803 prevented Congress from prohibiting slavery in any state that might be carved out of the Louisiana Purchase. In 1819 Missourians regarded the third article of the treaty as their Magna Carta, and interestingly enough, it was the same article which had caused the principal debate over constitutional interpretation when the treaty was ratified.[46] The article provided that "The inhabitants of the ceded territory shall be incorporated in the Union of the United States and admitted as soon as possible according to the principles of the federal Constitution to the enjoyment of all the rights, advantages and immunities of citizens of the United States, and in the mean time they shall be maintained and protected in the free enjoyment of their liberty, property and the Religion which they profess."[47]

Scott discussed the treaty point by point, beginning with the stipulation that the inhabitants of the ceded territory should "be incorporated in the Union of the United States." Statehood, he said, was necessary to "incorporation," as a territory did not have the same rights and privileges as a state. Under the terms of the treaty, the people of the ceded area were to be admitted to the Union as quickly as possible. This meant that any part of the Louisiana Purchase was entitled to admission if it was of sufficient size to form a state and had the population requisite for a representative in the lower house of Congress. According to the treaty, moreover, the people of the Purchase were to be admitted in accordance with the principles of the federal Constitution and, when admitted, to enjoy "all the rights, advantages, and immunities of citizens of the United States." That included the right to hold slaves.[48]

45 For Scott's address, see Annals of Congress, 15 Cong., 2 Sess., 1195-1203.
46 Brown, Constitutional History of the Louisiana Purchase, 65.
47 Miller, Treaties of the United States, II, 501.
48 Subsequent decisions of the Supreme Court have not sustained Scott's treaty argument. The Court has ruled on more than one occasion that a treaty

Scott's address contained a veiled threat of disunion. He declared that the people of Missouri "knew their own rights" and that the "spirit of freedom burned in the bosoms of the freemen of Missouri, and if admitted into the national family, they would be equal, or not come in at all."

Scott accused John W. Taylor of having a political motive in seeking to exclude slavery from Missouri. Taylor had said that if he ever left his present home, he would move to Illinois or Missouri. At any rate, he wished to send his brothers and sons there. Scott said he did not want this unwelcome accession to Missouri's population. Taylor opposed slavery in Missouri because of its northern latitude. Scott retorted that it was no further north than a portion of Kentucky, Virginia, and Maryland. He would thank Taylor "if he would condescend to tell him what precise line of latitude suited his conscience, his humanity, or his political views."

These remarks of Scott and Taylor revealed one of the fundamental causes of the Missouri Controversy—the desire of each great section of the nation to spread its own type of civilization over the western country and appropriate the resources of the West for its own use. In 1820, when the political tide was running temporarily in favor of the North, Tallmadge wrote Taylor that "Those brothers & sons, whom Mr. Scott last year prayed God to deliver them from—have in your speech & your exertions great cause of pride—& glory—& in common with your friends must & will exult."[49]

The House debates at this juncture were marked by considerable sectional animosity. "It was a painful scene," wrote Representative Salma Hale of New Hampshire, "& I hope a similar discussion will never again take place in our walls."[50] Scott concluded his address with the assertion that the question of slavery restriction was "big with the fate of Caesar and

---

can be overridden by an act of Congress. See Andrew C. McLaughlin, *A Constitutional History of the United States* (New York, 1935), 377; Head Money Cases, 112 *U.S.* 580 (1884); Chae Chan Ping *v.* United States, 130 *U.S.* 581 (1889).

[49] James Tallmadge, Jr., to John W. Taylor, March 2, 1820, Taylor Papers.

[50] Salma Hale to William Plumer, February 21, 1819, Plumer Papers.

of Rome." Thomas W. Cobb of Georgia declared that the Union would be dissolved if the restrictionists persisted. Tallmadge, he said, had "kindled a fire which all the waters of the ocean cannot put out, which seas of blood can only extinguish." Edward Colston of Virginia accused Livermore of "speaking to the galleries, and, by his language, endeavoring to excite a servile war," and added, "he is no better than Arbuthnot and Ambrister; and deserves no better fate."[51]

These attacks on Northern congressmen provoked a vigorous rejoinder from Tallmadge,[52] who, because of sickness and the death of his son, had taken only a minor part in the debate after presenting his amendment. He now repeated the statement, which he had made earlier, that he did not wish to interfere with slavery in the older states nor even in a region like Alabama Territory. Since Alabama was surrounded by slave states, the emancipation of its blacks might result in a servile war. But beyond the Mississippi, in new territory acquired by the funds of the whole nation, slavery was justly subject to national legislation.

Talk of civil war had no effect on Tallmadge. "If," he exclaimed, "blood is necessary to extinguish any fire which I have assisted to kindle, I can assure gentlemen, while I regret the necessity, I shall not forbear to contribute my mite." Extend slavery over the West, he continued, "and you prepare its dissolution; you turn its accumulated strength into positive weakness; you cherish a canker in your breast; you put poison in your bosom; you place a vulture on your heart—nay, you whet the dagger and place it in the hands of a portion of your population, stimulated to use it, by every tie, human and divine."

Tallmadge declared that about fourteen thousand slaves had been smuggled into the United States during the last year and that this illicit trade would be encouraged by extending slavery further west. The House, he said, had just beheld an elucida-

---

51 *Annals of Congress*, 15 Cong., 2 Sess., 1203-1205. Arbuthnot and Ambrister, two British citizens who were accused of fomenting Indian attacks on the American frontier, were captured in Florida by Andrew Jackson, tried by court-martial, and executed.

52 For Tallmadge's address, see *ibid.*, 1203-14.

tion of the Southern "diffusion" argument. "A slave driver, a trafficker in human flesh, as if sent by Providence, has passed the door of your Capitol, on his way to the West, driving before him about fifteen of these wretched victims of his power. The males, who might raise the arm of vengeance, and retaliate for their wrongs, were handcuffed, and chained to each other, while the females and children were marched in their rear, under the guidance of the driver's whip! Yes, sir, such has been the scene witnessed from the windows of Congress Hall, and viewed by members who compose the legislative councils of Republican America!" Earlier in the debate the assertion had been made that the South was ahead of the North in making contributions for Bible and missionary societies. Tallmadge ridiculed the inconsistency of thus sending missionaries abroad to civilize the savages of every country and to carry the gospel to the Hindu and the Hottentot, while at home, in Georgia, it was forbidden to teach a slave to read.[53] Yes, he said, the "dark benighted beings of all creation profit by our liberality—save those on our own plantations."

Mightily as Tallmadge inveighed against the moral iniquity of slavery, he frankly admitted that he also opposed its extension for political reasons. Southern slave representation rankled in his breast. It would be unfair, he argued, to count three fifths of the slaves in apportioning congressmen among new states west of the Mississippi. That region had "no claim to such an unequal representation, unjust in its results upon the other States." He asked: "Are the numerous slaves in extensive countries, which we may acquire by purchase, and admit as States into the Union, at once to be represented on this floor, under a clause of the Constitution, granted as a compromise and a benefit to the Southern States which had borne part in the Revolution?"

[53] Georgia had a law which made it illegal to teach a slave "to write, or read writing." One reason for this seems to have been that slaves, when they were away from their masters, were given passes to show to the patrol. It was feared that they would forge their own passes if taught to write. The law was also designed to make conspiracies and insurrections more difficult. Milledgeville (Georgia) *Journal*, October 12, 1819.

Finally, the House voted separately on each clause of the Tallmadge amendment. The first clause provided *"That the further introduction of slavery or involuntary servitude be prohibited, except for the punishment of crimes, whereof the party shall be duly convicted."* It was passed by a vote of 87 to 76. The second clause read, *"and that all children of slaves, born within the said state, after the admission thereof into the Union, shall be free, but may be held to service until the age of twenty-five years."* It was adopted by a vote of 82 to 78. In the case of each clause the vote was sectional,[54] with Southerners being almost unanimously on the negative side. From all the slave-holding states, only one representative (Willard Hall of Delaware) voted for both clauses. A Marylander, Samuel Smith, joined him in supporting the second one.[55] Only ten congressmen from free states voted with the South against the first clause. They were: John F. Parrott of New Hampshire; John Holmes, Jonathan Mason, and Henry Shaw of Massachusetts; Daniel Cruger, David Ogden, and Henry Storrs of New York; Joseph Bloomfield of New Jersey; William H. Harrison of Ohio (who later became President of the United States); and John McLean of Illinois. Philemon Beecher and John W. Campbell of Ohio, John Linn of New Jersey, and James Mason of Rhode Island joined these ten in voting with the South against the second clause.

The vote on the Tallmadge amendment by the representatives from the Old Northwest is significant. That region had been partly settled by people who had migrated from the South, many of whom in 1819 were still attached to the land of their birth. Considered as a unit, the congressmen from Ohio, Indiana, and Illinois cast six votes for the first clause of the amendment and two against it. But on the second clause the vote of the Northwestern representatives was a tie—four on each side. The four who favored the second clause had been

54 For the votes of individual congressmen, see *Journal of the House of Representatives*, 15 Cong., 2 Sess., 272-74; *Annals of Congress*, 15 Cong., 2 Sess., 1214-15.

55 Hall was born in Massachusetts, Smith in Pennsylvania. Both were Democrats.

born in the North, while three of the four who opposed it were natives of the South.[56]

After the passage of the amendment, several Southerners declared that they would now vote against the Missouri bill. Missouri's territorial delegate John Scott, however, as much as he opposed slavery restriction, would rather take the bill as it was than reject it. By a vote of 97 to 56 the House then ordered the bill to be engrossed for a third reading. Only eight Southerners voted for engrossment, and only six Northerners opposed it. The next day the bill was passed.[57]

In the Senate the Tallmadge amendment was foredoomed to defeat. Here the South had almost as many members as the free states. It could also count on the support of several Northern senators, including Jesse B. Thomas and Ninian Edwards of Illinois. Thomas and Edwards were to be a tower of strength to the South throughout the Missouri Controversy, and it would be perhaps anachronistic to characterize either

[56] The following is the vote in the House by states on each clause of the Tallmadge amendment:

STATE	FIRST CLAUSE for	against	SECOND CLAUSE for	against
New Hampshire	4	1	4	1
Vermont	5		5	
Massachusetts	15	3	15	3
Rhode Island	1			1
Connecticut	7		7	
New York	23	3	21	3
New Jersey	5	1	4	2
Pennsylvania	20		20	
Ohio	5	1	3	3
Indiana	1		1	
Illinois		1		1
Delaware	1	1	1	
Maryland		8	1	7
Virginia		20		20
North Carolina		13		13
South Carolina		6		6
Georgia		4		4
Kentucky		8		8
Tennessee		4		4
Mississippi		1		1
Louisiana		1		1
TOTAL	87	76	82	78

[57] *Annals of Congress*, 15 Cong., 2 Sess., 1215-17.

them or the state they represented as Northern in 1819. The people of Illinois at that time were mostly immigrants from the South. Indeed, the membership of the convention that framed the first constitution of the state was so overwhelmingly of Southern origin that the differences of opinion which appeared among the delegates were between rival groups of Southerners rather than between Northerners and Southerners.[58] Thomas and Edwards were not only Southerners by birth, but both were slaveholders, if indentured servants be considered slaves, which they were for all intents and purposes. The census of 1820 listed Thomas as the owner of five servants or slaves.[59] Edwards, who held slaves in Illinois in spite of the Ordinance of 1787, defended his right to do so in language that would have done justice to a Georgian or South Carolinian.[60]

The amended House Missouri bill reached the Senate on February 17, 1819, and on February 27 the Senate voted on the question of striking the Tallmadge amendment from the bill. The second clause of the amendment was taken up first and was struck out by a vote of 31 to 7.[61] Constitutional scruples were partly responsible for the one-sidedness of the vote. Senator Waller Taylor of Indiana, who favored the first clause, could not vote for the second because he considered it unconstitutional to free the offspring of the slaves already in Missouri.[62] Perhaps too it was thought that if the North agreed to the perpetual bondage of the slaves already in Missouri and their offspring, some Southerners would consent that no more slaves should be introduced there. But such was not the case, for when the vote was taken on the first clause of the amendment, it was struck out 22 to 16. Five senators from free states

58 John D. Barnhart, "The Southern Influence in the Formation of Illinois," in *Journal of the Illinois State Historical Society*, XXXII (1939), 366, 378.

59 Margaret C. Norton (ed.), *Illinois Census Returns 1820* (Springfield, 1934), 153.

60 Ninian Edwards to an unnamed person, n.d., Ninian Edwards Papers (Autograph Letters, Vol. 51., pp. 287-92), Chicago Historical Society.

61 *Journal of the Senate*, 15 Cong., 2 Sess., 321-22; *Annals of Congress*, 15 Cong., 2 Sess., 273. In listing the senators who voted to strike out this clause, the *Annals* did not include Waller Taylor.

62 Vincennes *Western Sun & General Advertiser*, April 15, 1820.

voted with the South to reject the first clause. They were: William Palmer of Vermont, Harrison Gray Otis of Massachusetts (of Hartford Convention fame), Abner Lacock of Pennsylvania, and Thomas and Edwards of Illinois. No senator from a slave state voted against striking out either clause.[63] On March 2 the Senate passed the Missouri bill without the Tallmadge amendment.[64]

The first senatorial debate on Missouri's admission was not recorded in the *Annals of Congress*. The two addresses made by Senator Rufus King of New York have been preserved, however. By request, King furnished the substance of his remarks to a committee appointed by the New York public meeting held in 1819 to discuss the Missouri question.[65] This "sub-

[63] *Annals of Congress*, 15 Cong., 2 Sess., 273. The table records the vote in the Senate by states on the question of striking the Tallmadge amendment from the Missouri bill:

STATE	FIRST CLAUSE yes	no	SECOND CLAUSE yes	no
New Hampshire		2	1	1
Vermont	1	1	2	
Massachusetts	1	1	1	1
Rhode Island		1		1
Connecticut		2	2	
New York		2	2	
New Jersey		2		2
Pennsylvania	1	1	2	
Ohio		2	1	1
Indiana		2	1	1
Illinois	2		2	
Delaware	2		2	
Maryland	1		1	
Virginia	2		2	
North Carolina	2		2	
South Carolina	1		1	
Georgia	1		1	
Kentucky	2		2	
Tennessee	2		2	
Mississippi	2		2	
Louisiana	2		2	
TOTAL	22	16	31	7

[64] *Annals of Congress*, 15 Cong., 2 Sess., 279.

[65] In sending the substance of the addresses to the committee, King wrote, "As my notes are imperfect, I may have omitted some remarks made on that occasion, and added others which were not made; the communication however contains the substance of my observations, and my present opinions upon this important subject." King, *Rufus King*, VI, 233.

stance" of the addresses, which was intended for publication, was printed in pamphlet form as well as in *Niles' Register* and various Northern newspapers. The preservation of King's speeches was most fortunate, for he was undoubtedly the leading figure on the side of the North in the Missouri Controversy.

King, who was a native of Maine, had had a long and varied political career, serving successively as a member of the Continental Congress, a delegate from Massachusetts to the Constitutional Convention of 1787, American minister to Great Britain, and United States senator from New York. Always an ardent Federalist, he was that party's candidate for Vice-President in 1804 and 1808 and for President in 1816.[66] Along with enormous ability, unquestionable integrity, a logical mind, and an uncanny knack for predicting political trends, King had a great dislike of all things Southern, and his fear of the South constituted one of the greatest obsessions in American history. As early as 1785 he made an unsuccessful attempt to prohibit slavery in the Northwest.[67] Two years later he expressed a fear that New Jersey and Pennsylvania would fall under Southern influence. He concluded that if this should happen there was "no mischief to public Credit, in the settlement of accounts, and in the just claim of the states" which might not be feared.[68]

In the period of Federalist ascendancy after the adoption of the Constitution, King realized that it was probably but a matter of time until the South and West would wrest control of the national government from the East. His logical mind made him wonder if a dismemberment of the Union would be preferable to such a state of affairs. In 1794 John Taylor of Caroline prepared a secret memorandum for James Madison in which he explained King's views on disunion. According to Taylor, King told him confidentially that it was impossible for

[66] The most complete biography of King is Charles R. King's *Life and Correspondence of Rufus King*, which has already been cited. For shorter accounts of his life, see Edward H. Brush, *Rufus King and His Times* (New York, 1926) and *Dictionary of American Biography*, X, 398-400.

[67] *Journals of the Continental Congress*, XXVIII, 164-65, 239.

[68] Burnett, *Letters of Members of the Continental Congress*, VIII, 541.

the Union to continue, since the South and East never agreed, and that as soon as Ralph Izard and William L. Smith of South Carolina left Congress, "the southern interest would prevail." Therefore King, and also Oliver Ellsworth of Connecticut who joined in the conversation, maintained that the only sensible solution was a friendly arrangement for dividing the country by mutual consent into separate nations. King seemed indifferent to whether the line of division should be the Hudson or Potomac. In Madison's opinion, King was not so anxious to disrupt the Union as Taylor thought, though it is obvious that at least he was considering the matter seriously.[69] In later years his views underwent a change, and in the closing days of the War of 1812 he frowned on the Northern separatist movement and vigorously supported the Madison administration in the prosecution of the war.[70] In 1819 King was certainly not a disunionist but rather was interested in securing predominance for his section within the Union. He was a perfect example of a sectionalist, for as a Northerner, he disliked the South, and as an Easterner, he distrusted the West.[71]

Although forceful and convincing, King's addresses[72] on the Missouri question were largely a repetition of what had already been said in the House of Representatives. They began with an exposition of constitutional principles and, in the opinion of former President John Adams, demonstrated Congress' right to restrict slavery in Missouri "in a manner, unanswerable by all the Cavils of Sophistry."[73] King disclaimed any intention of interfering with slavery in the states where it already existed. He declared that he would not dwell on the horrors of slavery, for fear of wounding Southern feelings, though he did mention some of the evils connected with the institution and maintained

[69] Gaillard Hunt (ed.), *Disunion Sentiment in Congress in 1794—a Confidential Memorandum Hitherto Unpublished Written by John Taylor of Caroline Senator from Virginia for James Madison* (Washington, 1905), 11-14, 21-23.

[70] Fox, *Decline of Aristocracy in New York*, 184.

[71] King, *Rufus King*, VI, 207-208, 215, 501.

[72] For the complete substance of the addresses, as compiled by King, see *ibid.*, 690-703; *Niles' Weekly Register*, XVII (1819), 215-21.

[73] King, *Rufus King*, VI, 240.

that "Freedom and slavery are the parties which stand this day before the senate; and upon its decision the empire of the one or the other will be established in the new state which we are about to admit into the union."

To anyone familiar with King it was evident that the portion of the speeches which was closest to his heart was that which dealt with the inequality of the three-fifths ratio of slave representation. When at a later stage in the Missouri debate, a Southerner questioned him specifically about his views on slavery, he replied that "The subject of domestic slavery is one with which Mr. K. is very imperfectly acquainted and on which he has not bestowed much consideration, and which he professes to look at and reflect upon solely in its bearing and effects upon great political interests, and upon the just and equal rights of the freemen of the nation."[74] King presented the Northern objections to slave representation much more forcefully than Tallmadge had done in the House. After marshaling impressive statistics to show that five white people in the South exerted as much influence in choosing representatives to Congress and appointing presidential electors as seven people in the free states, King argued that the North in 1787 had not fully realized the inequality which would arise under the operation of the three-fifths ratio. It had been supposed then that direct taxation on slaves would be a compensation for unequal representation. Such had not been the case. Unfair as the three-fifths clause of the Constitution was, said King, faith and honor stood pledged not to disturb it. It was a compact among the thirteen original states, however, and did not apply to new ones. "The extension of this disproportionate power to the new states," insisted King, "would be unjust and odious. The states whose power would be abridged, and whose burdens would be increased by the measure, cannot be expected to consent to it; and we may hope that the other states are too magnanimous to insist on it."

King's addresses made a deep impression on his contemporaries. In the words of Frederick Jackson Turner, they "un-

[74] *Ibid.*, 324-25.

blushingly raised [in the Southern mind] the prospect of the rule of a free majority over a slave-holding minority, the downfall of the ascendancy so long held by the south, and the creation of a new Union, in which the western states should be admitted on terms of subordination to the will of the majority, whose power would thus become perpetual."[75]

Meanwhile the Missouri bill, as modified by the Senate, was again considered in the House on March 2. By a vote of 78 to 76 the House refused to concur with the upper house in striking the antislavery amendment from the bill, which was returned to the Senate.[76] The Senate sent word that it still adhered to its position. This caused a renewal of debate in the House. Cobb of Georgia declared that the region beyond the Mississippi, having been purchased by the United States, belonged equally to both sections of the country. "The people of the slaveholding states, as they are called," he said, "know their rights, and will insist upon the enjoyment of them." Once more he asserted that the restrictionists "were kindling a fire which all the waters of the ocean could not extinguish. It could be extinguished only in blood!" But the House, by a vote of 78 to 66, again refused to concur with the Senate.[77] The next day, March 3, 1819, the Fifteenth Congress adjourned, leaving the fate of Missouri still in doubt.

The debate over slavery restriction in the second session of the Fifteenth Congress was not confined to the Missouri question. It was at this time that Congress created the Territory of Arkansas, which turned out to be another bone of contention between Northerners and Southerners. Up to now, the Arkansas country, consisting of the present states of Arkansas and Oklahoma, had been part of Missouri Territory. In 1820 it had a population of more than 14,000, including 12,579 white inhabitants, 59 free Negroes, and 1,617 slaves.[78]

[75] Frederick J. Turner, *Rise of the New West 1819-1829* (New York, 1906), 160.
[76] *Annals of Congress*, 15 Cong., 2 Sess., 1433-35.
[77] *Ibid.*, 1436-38.
[78] *Seventh Census: 1850*, 548.

When in February, 1819, the House was considering a bill to establish a territorial government in Arkansas, John W. Taylor attempted to insert in the bill an antislavery clause similar to that which Tallmadge was seeking to apply to Missouri.[79] The Arkansas debate was as animated as that over Missouri and revealed some interesting facts. From a constitutional standpoint, there was a much stronger case for restricting slavery in Arkansas than in Missouri, since many Southerners conceded that Congress could legally prohibit slavery in a territory but denied that it could do so in a new state. Logically, therefore, the restrictionists might have been expected to surrender Missouri to their adversaries in order to concentrate their efforts on Arkansas and the unorganized territories. The main issue in the Missouri Controversy was not constitutional, however, and either side would have reversed its interpretation of the Constitution on short notice if that had been to its interest.

The Arkansas debate showed clearly that lines of latitude were the determining factor with many congressmen. Basically, the chief objection to Missouri's admission as a slave state was that it lay in the same latitude with Ohio, Indiana, and Illinois—in a "sphere" of the West which the North had come to regard as rightly its own. Likewise, in the opinion of the South, the southerly location of Arkansas raised insurmountable objections to the prohibition of slavery there. As a Washington correspondent of the Philadelphia *Franklin Gazette* remarked during the discussion of the Arkansas bill, "It would almost seem as if an understanding prevailed, that a line of demarcation should take place in the west, so that a certain portion of the new states should be assigned for the non-slave-holding states of the Atlantic—while the more southern new states and territories, were to be left for the accommodation of emigrants from the old slave-holding states."[80]

The dispute over Arkansas was settled quickly in favor of the South, although the vote in the House was close. On several

79 *Annals of Congress*, 15 Cong., 2 Sess., 1222.
80 New York *Daily Advertiser*, February 24, 1819.

roll calls the division was about even. On one occasion it stood 88 to 88, and the Speaker had to break the tie.[81] On some ballotings the outcome was determined by a switch of one or two votes or by absentees. Four representatives from the Old Northwest who came to the South's aid provided the margin of victory in the significant vote of 89 to 87 on February 19.[82]

When the House bill, without any prohibition of slavery, reached the Senate, James Burrill of Rhode Island sought to amend it to prevent the further introduction of slaves into Arkansas. His motion was rejected by a vote of 19 to 14, and the bill was passed.[83] The defeat of the Burrill motion illustrates forcefully the strength of the Southern influence in the Old Northwest. Not a single senator from the slave states voted for the motion, and not one from the New England and Middle

[81] *Annals of Congress,* 15 Cong., 2 Sess., 1272-73.

[82] McLean of Illinois and Campbell, and Harrison of Ohio. The table records the vote by states on the question of striking the antislavery clause from the Arkansas bill on February 19 (*ibid.,* 1273-74):

STATE	Yes	No
New Hampshire	1	4
Vermont		5
Massachusetts	4	14
Rhode Island		2
Connecticut		7
New York	3	24
New Jersey	2	4
Pennsylvania	1	22
Ohio	3	3
Indiana		1
Illinois	1	
Delaware	1	1
Maryland	8	
Virginia	23	
North Carolina	13	
South Carolina	7	
Georgia	6	
Kentucky	9	
Tennessee	5	
Mississippi	1	
Louisiana	1	
TOTAL	89	87

[83] *Annals of Congress,* 15 Cong., 2 Sess., 274. The table shows the vote by states on the Burrill motion:

STATE	for	against
New Hampshire	1	
Vermont	1	
Massachusetts	1	
Rhode Island	1	
Connecticut	2	
New York	2	
New Jersey	2	
Pennsylvania	2	
Ohio	1	1
Indiana	1	1
Illinois		2
Delaware		
Maryland		1
Virginia		2
North Carolina		1
South Carolina		1
Georgia		1
Kentucky		2
Tennessee		2
Mississippi		2
Louisiana		2
TOTAL	14	19

states opposed it. Its defeat was due solely to the fact that four Northwestern senators joined the South in voting against it. They were: Edwards and Thomas of Illinois, both of whom were natives of Maryland; Waller Taylor of Indiana, who was born in Virginia; and Jeremiah Morrow of Ohio. Morrow had been born in Pennsylvania, but many of his Ohio constituents came originally from the South.[84]

So even was the alignment between restrictionists and anti-restrictionists in the Fifteenth Congress that Ezekiel Whitman, a Federalist representative from Massachusetts, was able to turn himself into a one man balance of power. This he did, voting with the North on the Missouri question, siding with the South in the case of Arkansas, and leaving no doubt about the reasons for his course. He pointed out that before that time Congress had attempted to divide the West equitably between the slaveholding and free states and could not well stop the process now. Because of the Northern majority in the House of Representatives, he assumed that Missouri would be made a free state and believed that Arkansas should be given to the South in compensation, especially since it was south of the southern boundary of Kentucky.

Whitman declared that the North need have no fear of a future Southern predominance in the government. The substantial majority which Northerners already had in the House of Representatives would increase with the taking of every census. Between 1800 and 1810, said Whitman, the population of the North had outstripped that of the South by 25 to 30 per cent, and two fifths of the slave portion of the Southern increase was not represented in the House.[85] As accurate as Whitman's prediction of population trends was, it was not accepted universally by his contemporaries. Louis McLane of Delaware considered the future predominance of the slaveholding interest far from improbable. He used this as an argument against slavery restriction. For, he said, if Congress set a prece-

[84] John D. Barnhart, "The Southern Influence in the Formation of Ohio," in *Journal of Southern History*, III (1937), 28-42.
[85] *Annals of Congress*, 15 Cong., 2 Sess., 1277-79.

dent in imposing conditions on new states, a Southern majority might someday force a new state to sanction slavery.[86]

The arguments over the Arkansas bill resembled those in the Missouri Controversy except that the issue was the imposition of a restriction on a territorial rather than a state government. While not attempting to defend slavery, Southern congressmen stressed the fact that it was "a delicate subject" with which Northerners ought not to meddle. Henry Clay accused the North of being under the influence of "negrophobia" and wanted to know what the people of the South had done, that they were to be proscribed.[87] Once more the relatives of John W. Taylor were injected into a public debate. Anticipating that his children and those of his constituents might immigrate to Arkansas, Taylor expressed a hope that they would not have to compete with slave labor. He also resented the monopoly which the slaveholding states held in the production of cotton and tobacco and urged that one section of the country, capable of growing these staples, be left open to immigration from the North and East.[88] Felix Walker of North Carolina countered with the assertion that Arkansas was too far south to support a laboring white population and could not be cultivated except by Negroes.[89]

Judging by the vote in the Senate and House on the Missouri Compromise of 1820, it would appear that a majority of Southern congressmen were then willing to concede that Congress possessed the power to prohibit slavery in a territory. A considerable minority, however, refused to make even that concession. Louis McLane denied that Congress could prevent the further introduction of slaves either into a new state or a territory which might become a state.[90] Felix Walker maintained that in organizing a territorial government, the local people "alone, have the right, and are the proper judges of that policy best adapted to their genius and interest, and it ought to

[86] *Ibid.*, 1231.   [87] *Ibid.*, 1223-24.   [88] *Ibid.*, 1222-24.
[89] *Ibid.*, 1226. The same argument had been used in 1804 in regard to Louisiana. Brown, "Senate Debate on the Breckinridge Bill," 349.
[90] *Annals of Congress*, 15 Cong., 2 Sess., 1230.

be exclusively left to them."[91] Stephen Douglas could hardly have summarized the doctrine of popular sovereignty better than this.

The most important thing about the Arkansas debate was the fact that it foreshadowed the Missouri Compromise of March, 1820. The first mention of a compromise in the *Annals of Congress* came from Louis McLane of Delaware on February 17, 1819. Noting that certain Southern and Western members of the House had expressed a willingness to agree to a line dividing the slave from the free states, McLane declared that the establishment of a line west of the Mississippi, north of which slavery should not be tolerated, had always been a favorite policy with him. He hoped it could be effected "upon principles of fair compromise" by a "compact" that would be binding on all parties and all subsequent legislatures.[92]

The next suggestion of a compromise came from John W. Taylor, the antislavery leader. After the House had voted against the prohibition of slavery in Arkansas, Taylor moved to amend the Arkansas bill to prevent the future introduction of slaves into any territories lying north of 36° 30', which was to be the southern boundary of the new state of Missouri. Arthur Livermore hailed Taylor's proposal as one "made in the true spirit of compromise," but he suggested another line, while William Henry Harrison proposed yet a third one. After much discussion, Taylor withdrew his motion, since he thought it unlikely that the House could agree on any line or compromise of opinion.[93] Actually, the enactment of a compromise law was still more than a year distant.

[91] *Ibid.*, 1227.   [92] *Ibid.*, 1228, 1235.   [93] *Ibid.*, 1280-82.

"[Dr. Boudinot's] last letter to me, on the Missouri question I shall preserve as an evidence of the strength & soundness of his mental faculties & judgment."—JOHN PINTARD[1]

CHAPTER III

BURLINGTON COUNTY, NEW JERSEY, STARTS A CRUSADE

*I*F THERE WAS anything more surprising than the sound and fury of the opening debate in Congress on the Missouri question, it was the complete indifference with which these verbal fireworks were received by the nation at large. Historians like McMaster have assumed that the North became violently excited as soon as Tallmadge presented his amendment and that from the moment the Fifteenth Congress expired on the fourth of March, leaving the issue, "raised by it, of freedom or slavery in the Territories undecided, the whole North, without distinction of party, was roused for action."[2] This was far from being the case. It would be more accurate to say that when the Fifteenth Congress adjourned, the Missouri Controversy adjourned with it (except in Missouri and Illinois) and created scarcely a ripple of interest for the next eight months. From the time it began until the fall of 1819, it was rarely mentioned either in newspaper editorials or private correspondence.

While antislavery toasts were drunk at a number of Fourth-of-July celebrations in 1819,[3] there is nothing to indicate that the mass of the people were really excited. In May the Boston *Yankee* had complained of the public indifference toward slavery. "We cannot conceive," said the *Yankee*, "of a question connected either with our political institutions, or the actual condition of a large portion of the human race, which is of so great moment to the American people. And yet it does not excite half the attention of a Royal birth-day, or the regimen of a Bonaparte."[4] In August there was so little concern over Missouri or any other question except the depression, which was bearing down with increasing severity, that a Virginia editor apologized for venturing to publish a new newspaper. The calm that existed in the political affairs of the country, he declared, was not calculated to render newspapers interesting to the general public.[5] As late as November, the New York *Evening Post* spoke of the Missouri issue as one which would "eventually" arouse the North.[6] At about the same time, the general apathy on this subject was a topic of conversation at a private dinner in Boston attended by Rufus King, Daniel Webster, Judge Story, and other notables.[7] Meanwhile, there were rumors that a special session of Congress would be called, but it was a raise in the tariff—to combat the depression—and not a blow at slavery that stirred the rumormongers.[8]

The public, then, was at first unconcerned over the Missouri dispute, and there is every reason to believe that it would have remained so if it had not been subjected to a carefully organized barrage of propaganda and a series of mass meetings by means of which those who favored slavery restriction managed to invest their cause with the aura of a moral crusade. It was later charged, by some Northern Democrats as well as Southerners, that Federalists took the lead in organizing meetings to

[1] Dorothy C. Barck (ed.), *Letters from John Pintard to His Daughter* (4 vols., New York, 1940-1941), I, 267.

[2] McMaster, *History of the United States*, IV, 576-77.

[3] See Trenton *True American*, September 6, 1819; *Supplement to the True American*, August 2, 1819; New York *Columbian*, July 15, 27, 1819; Philadelphia *Aurora*, July 15, 20, 21, 23, 24, 29, 1819; Kaskaskia (Illinois) *Intelligencer*, July 14, 1819; Steubenville (Ohio) *Western Herald*, July 24, 1819.

[4] Boston *Yankee*, May 20, 1819.

[5] Clarksburg *Independent Virginian*, August 4, 1819.

[6] New York *Evening Post*, November 25, 1819.

[7] William Tudor to Joseph Hopkinson, November 8, 1819, Joseph Hopkinson Papers, Historical Society of Pennsylvania.

[8] *Niles' Weekly Register*, XVI (1819), 220.

pass resolutions on the Missouri question and that their object was to destroy the Democratic party by discrediting its Southern leadership.[9] This accusation contained a half-truth. The initial impulse for the meetings did come from the Federalist stronghold of Burlington County, New Jersey, and was largely sponsored by Federalists. In the opening debate in Congress, Tallmadge and other Northern Democrats had sounded the Missouri antislavery tocsin, but in the fall of 1819, the Democrats yielded their leadership in this matter to the Federalists and never regained it. From then on, as the zeal of the Federalists mounted, many a Northern Democrat became increasingly suspicious of their motives and would have liked to withdraw from the contest altogether.

While Federalists took the lead in summoning meetings to discuss the Missouri question, they by no means had the field to themselves. Associated with them were Democrats, Clintonians, Quakers, humanitarians and reformers of every description, politicians who were eager to fish in troubled waters, and people in the Middle states who believed that their economic interests were being injured by the great political power of the South. The Federalists still were nursing their ancient grievance against the South and the Democratic party, whose success at their expense they attributed to the three-fifths ratio of slave representation; yet there is another point which must not be overlooked. Most of the great American philanthropists in 1819 were Federalists, and these had opposed slavery all their lives, regardless of whether or not they had a political ax to grind.

On August 30, 1819, a meeting was held in the town of Burlington, New Jersey, by a group wanting to prohibit slavery in Missouri. This was apparently the first gathering of its kind in the Northern states. In any event it marked the beginning of what might well be termed the "Anti-Missourian Crusade."[10]

[9] New York *National Advocate*, August 24, 1820; Trenton *True American*, September 9, 1820.

[10] The expression "Anti-Missourian" was used commonly by Jefferson and others to describe those who wished to restrict slavery in Missouri.

The venerable Elias Boudinot was chairman of the Burlington meeting, and William Newbold served as secretary.[11]

Elias Boudinot, who was to figure so prominently in the Missouri Controversy, was one of the greatest philanthropists in American history and combined philanthropy with an interest in politics. During the Revolution he had been commissary general of prisoners, a position he accepted to be of some service to the prisoners as well as to watch the military and safeguard the civil rights of his fellow citizens. Later he was president of the Continental Congress and active in the councils of the Federalist party. After retiring from public life, he devoted much of his time to the study of the Bible, being one of the founders of the American Bible Society. Like most of the benevolent-minded of his day, he was a lifelong antislavery man and a champion of the Indians. His interest in the aborigines led him to publish a book *(A Star in the West; or, A Humble Attempt to Discover the Long Lost Ten Tribes of Israel, Preparatory to Their Return to Their Beloved City, Jerusalem)* in which he attempted to identify the Indians with the lost tribes of Israel. Boudinot assisted the foreign mission school at Cornwall, Connecticut, and his name was assumed by a bright Cherokee lad at the school, who became almost as famous as his benefactor.[12]

While Boudinot, as chairman of the antislavery gathering at Burlington, appeared before the public as the chief sponsor of the meeting, the initiative in summoning it actually came from William Newbold of Springfield, Burlington County.[13] Newbold was a man of piety and good will, of whom it was said that "His benevolent mind deeply sympathized with the wrongs

[11] Trenton *True American,* September 6, 1819.

[12] George A. Boyd, *Elias Boudinot Patriot and Statesman* (Princeton, 1952); *Dictionary of American Biography,* II, 477-78. For Boudinot's conservative and Federalist political leanings, see Boyd, *Elias Boudinot,* 211, 250, 285; Walter R. Fee, *The Transition from Aristocracy to Democracy in New Jersey 1789-1829* (Somerville, N. J., 1933), 47, 105, 112, 121-22; Richard P. McCormick, *Experiment in Independence New Jersey in the Critical Period 1781-1789* (New Brunswick, 1950), 289, 290.

[13] Philadelphia *Friend,* I (1828), 360, IX (1836), 204. See also Thomas E. Drake, *Quakers and Slavery in America* (New Haven, 1950), 129.

and afflictions of the much injured African race, . . . while at the same time commiseration for the difficulties which pressed their masters on every side, induced him to avoid whatever was calculated unnecessarily to irritate and wound their feelings."[14] It was significant that Newbold should be an elder in the Society of Friends or Quakers. The town of Burlington was founded by Quakers,[15] and the nearby county seat of Mount Holly had been the home of John Woolman, a pioneer antislavery leader among the Friends. Another Quaker, Samuel Emlen of Burlington, was as indefatigable as Newbold and the Presbyterian Boudinot in his efforts to arouse public opinion against slavery in 1819.

Boudinot, Newbold, and Emlen found an able ally in Joseph Hopkinson, a Federalist attorney and former congressman of Philadelphia who was temporarily residing at Bordentown, New Jersey. Hopkinson may have done the cause more harm than good, however, since Northern Democrats were inclined to shy away from any movement which was supported by this high-powered Federalist lawyer.[16] The New York *National Advocate*, a Tammany organ, later charged that Hopkinson "got up" the first meeting on the subject of Missouri at the instigation of his law partner Daniel Webster as part of a plot for "the *erection of a northern party, the triumph of federalism,* or the *separation of the union.*"[17] An anonymous letter in a Philadelphia newspaper denied the *Advocate's* accusation and declared that a member of the Society of Friends in Burlington County invited Hopkinson to take part in the meeting and also sent notices to various other persons to attend. "If, therefore, any body can be said to have got up this meeting," concluded the letter, "it was this *Friend* [evidently meaning Newbold]."[18]

14 Philadelphia *Friend*, I (1828), 360.

15 William E. Schermerhorn, *The History of Burlington, New Jersey* (Burlington, 1927), vi; Amelia M. Gummere, *Friends in Burlington* (Philadelphia, 1884).

16 Jonathan Roberts to Nicholas Biddle, February 27, 1820, Nicholas Biddle Papers, Library of Congress.

17 New York *National Advocate*, August 24, 1820.

18 Philadelphia *National Gazette and Literary Register*, September 2, 1820.

It was not always easy, during the course of the Missouri Controversy, to know just where philanthropy ended and politics (in the form of Federalist opposition to the three-fifths ratio of slave representation) began. Though Burlington County abounded in men of good will and previously had played an active role in the campaign to rid New Jersey of slavery, it was also the Gibraltar of Federalism in the state.[19] Newbold was a member of a prominent Federalist family, while Boudinot, as a Federalist congressman in 1791, had been one of the first to protest against slave representation.[20] The three-fifths rule was also a major issue with Samuel Emlen, who even suggested that the Pennsylvania legislature use it as the sole grounds for objecting, in formal resolutions, to Missouri's admission as a slave state.[21]

The antislavery gathering at Burlington, sponsored by Newbold and Boudinot, issued a call for a state-wide meeting,[22] which convened at Trenton on October 29. The Trenton convention turned out to be a rather impressive affair. The governor of New Jersey and most of the legislature were present. Presiding over the assemblage was Jesse Upson, a Democrat who was vice-president of the state and also one of the managers of the New-Jersey Society for the Suppression of Vice and Immorality, and for the Encouragement of Virtue and Good Morals.[23] The secretary of the meeting was William Griffith, a Burlington Federalist leader who had been one of John Adams' "midnight judges" in 1801.[24] Boudinot was absent from

19 Henry S. Cooley, *A Study of Slavery in New Jersey* (Baltimore, 1896), 22-23; Fee, *Transition from Aristocracy to Democracy in New Jersey*, 245. Most of the Burlington Quakers were Federalists. See *ibid.*, 113-14, 239.

20 McCormick, *Experiment in Independence*, 294; Simpson, "Significance of Slave Representation," 320.

21 Samuel Emlen to Roberts Vaux, December 14, 1819, Roberts Vaux Papers, Historical Society of Pennsylvania.

22 Trenton *True American*, September 6, 1819.

23 *Constitution of the New-Jersey Society for the Suppression of Vice and Immorality, and for the Encouragement of Virtue and Good Morals* (New Brunswick, 1818), 2.

24 E. M. Woodward and John F. Hageman, *History of Burlington and Mercer Counties, New Jersey* (Philadelphia, 1883), 65; Fee, *Transition from Aristocracy to Democracy in New Jersey*, 228-29, 245.

Trenton because of age and indisposition,[25] but Hopkinson was there to make the principal address. His eloquence was said to have "rivetted the attention of every auditor," and he presented resolutions, which were unanimously adopted, stating that the meeting "would view, with unspeakable pain and mortification, any measure adopted by the *federal legislature,* tending to extend and perpetuate *slavery* among us; and holding out encouragement and temptation to the dealers in human flesh to continue their infamous trade, in defiance of the laws of the land, and the more sacred will of Heaven."[26]

The most important thing accomplished at Trenton was the appointment of a correspondence committee to seek aid from other sections of the country. A majority of the members of the committee, including Boudinot (who served as chairman), Emlen, Newbold, and Hopkinson,[27] were from Burlington County. The Federalist influence in the composition of the committee was obvious. The Federalist party of New Jersey has been described fittingly as "the party of Boudinot, Stockton, Dayton, Ogden, Parker and Griffith."[28] Of this list, Boudinot and James Parker were members of the correspondence committee appointed at Trenton, while Griffith was secretary of the Trenton meeting. The correspondence committee speedily prepared a printed circular, which it distributed far and wide to arouse the countryside. It announced its intention of calling "to our aid, the zealous co-operation of . . . our fellow Citizens in the different parts of these United States," and the recipients of the circular were urged, "in concert with such Gentlemen as you may associate with you in the design, to organize a plan of co-operation."[29]

[25] Perhaps his indisposition was an attack of the gout, a malady from which he suffered. See Elias Boudinot to Elias E. Boudinot, November 27, 1819, Elias Boudinot Papers, Princeton University.

[26] For an account of the Trenton meeting, see Trenton *True American,* November 1, 1819, and *Niles' Weekly Register,* XVII (1819), 189.

[27] The other members were James Parker and the Rev. Simon Wilmer.

[28] Fee, *Transition from Aristocracy to Democracy in New Jersey,* 270.

[29] For copies of the circular, see Elias Boudinot to William Tudor, November 5, 1819, William Tudor Papers, Massachusetts Historical Society; Elias Boudinot to Timothy Pickering, November 5, 1819, Timothy Pickering Papers, Massachusetts Historical Society.

By the middle of November, Boudinot had forwarded a considerable number of circulars to "persons of respectability & importance" in all of the Eastern states, New York, and Pennsylvania. Emlen sent fifty copies to Hopkinson for his disposal and, fearful that Vermont might be neglected, asked him to contact prominent people there.[30] Boudinot sent a circular to his nephew, accompanied by an exhortation. "Do exert yourself in this Business," he wrote, "—It is the most important question ever before Congress.—I consider that our Union depends upon it—If it is carried in favour of Slavery, in a few years, they will increase upon us in such a Manner, that we shall become a second Hayti—If it is difficult to get rid of Negroe Slavery now, when there are but a little above one million, what will it be when they are 10 millions." In another letter to his nephew concerning Missouri, Boudinot used the language that would be expected from the president of the American Bible Society: "For my own part, I devoutly trust that He, who has carried us thro Six & Seven troubles, will yet carry us thro' to the glory of his holy Name." Along with worries over Southern slavery, Boudinot had other troubles nearer home, judging by this excerpt from one of his letters: "As to Peter, I wish you do any thing you think best to secure him either in New York or New Ark Gaol, as I think in such case he may get some body to buy his time which I will fix at 10 years."[31] Whatever Peter may have been—slave, indentured servant, or apprentice—one wonders why the benevolent Boudinot did not set him free instead of fixing his time at ten years. Perhaps Boudinot's charity did not always begin at home.

One of those who received a circular from the Trenton committee was John Jay. In his reply to Boudinot, Jay bestowed his blessing on the committee's work, though he declared that his health would prevent him from taking an active part in organizing "a plan of co-operation."[32] Boudinot released Jay's

[30] Samuel Emlen to Joseph Hopkinson, November 13, 1819, Hopkinson Papers.

[31] Elias Boudinot to Elias E. Boudinot, November 27, December 15, 1819, Boudinot Papers.

[32] Trenton *True American*, December 13, 1819; Henry P. Johnston (ed.),

letter to the press for publication, and it gained wide publicity. Read in the North with a feeling akin to veneration, it horrified the South, where it conjured up memories of the Jay-Gardoqui Treaty fiasco of 1786.

While the North was being prodded by Boudinot and his friends, it received an additional powerful stimulus to action from the city of New York. Indeed, if Burlington had not started the crusade, New York undoubtedly would have, for here more than anywhere else could be found all of those groups which could be counted on to be most interested in a project of this nature: Federalists, Clintonians, reformers, and last but by no means least, the Federalist philanthropists, a strange but worthy breed of men of whom we shall hear more presently. Moreover, within a stone's throw of New York, at Jamaica, Long Island, lived the high priest of Anti-Missouri-anism, Rufus King.

After Tallmadge's retirement from Congress, King was re-garded popularly as the leader of the North in the Missouri Controversy. During the spring and summer of 1819 he strove to impress his friends and acquaintances with the importance of the issue at stake. A member of the Manumission Society wrote from New York in March that "Mr. Rufus King thinks the decision to be made at the next session of Congress on the Missouri & Arkansaw bills, the most important of any that Congress has ever been called upon to decide."[33] Writing to his brother William, who lived in Massachusetts, King listed the Northern senators who in the last Congress had voted with the South against slavery restriction, one of the offenders being "your Mr. Otis." "I think it wd. be well," he continued, "to instruct yr Senators, to vote agt. the admission of slavery in any New State west of the Mississippi, admitted into the Union—! I will write you further on this subject."[34] Later, on a visit to

---

The Correspondence and Public Papers of John Jay (4 vols., New York, 1890-1893), IV, 430-31.

[33] Isaac M. Ely to Roberts Vaux, March 26, 1819, Vaux Papers.

[34] Rufus King to William King, March 23, 1819, William King Papers (L. B. Chapman Collection, Rufus and James G. King Folder), Maine Historical Society.

Massachusetts, King informed Daniel Webster, William Tudor, Jeremiah Mason, and Judge Story that "the question was the most important one that had been brought forward since the adoption of the Constitution—it was in fact to decide whether the slave holding States should hereafter decidedly preponderate, and all the evils of the accursed slave trade be enhanced a hundred fold."[35]

Another New Yorker who exerted only slightly less influence than King on the course of the Missouri Controversy was the editor of the New York *Daily Advertiser,* Theodore Dwight, whose obsession against all things Southern was comparable to that of King. Dwight was a native of New England, a grandson of Jonathan Edwards, and a brother of Yale's renowned Timothy Dwight. He was an ultra-Federalist, having been secretary of the Hartford Convention. He was also "one of the most uncompromising of abolitionists, a forerunner of Garrison and Phillips," and was said to be willing to "take a lead in all questions which relate to the *purifying* our country, in this particular."[36]

Dwight was a humanitarian and, despite his political conservatism, had many reforming irons in the fire. His newspaper abounded in editorials condemning the flogging of soldiers and cruelty toward Negroes, Indians, Eskimos, mental patients, and even lobsters.[37] Just prior to the Missouri Controversy he had been conducting a campaign against the illicit African slave trade, and not long after that, he was urging Congress to abolish slavery in the District of Columbia.[38]

Dwight's paper, the *Daily Advertiser,* was one of the first to endorse the Tallmadge amendment to the Missouri bill.[39] In March and April, 1819, when most of the press was silent on the subject except for the reprinting of congressional speeches,

[35] William Tudor to Joseph Hopkinson, November 8, 1819, Hopkinson Papers.
[36] Locke, *Anti-Slavery in America,* 93; Isaac M. Ely to Roberts Vaux, March 26, 1819, Vaux Papers.
[37] For interesting editorial remarks on cruelty to lobsters, see New York *Daily Advertiser,* June 7, 1820.
[38] *Ibid.,* December 10, 11, 1818, June 1, 1819.
[39] *Ibid.,* February 19, 1819.

the *Advertiser* published a number of editorials and articles in favor of the amendment. Some of the articles were prepared by Isaac M. Ely of the New York Manumission Society.[40] On March 29 the *Advertiser* reminded its readers that if "the SIN OF SLAVERY be fastened, by the assent of the nation, upon that boundless region which the United States possess beyond the Mississippi, THE DEATH-WARRANT OF THE POLITICAL STANDING AND INFLUENCE OF THE FREE STATES WILL BE IRREVOCABLY SEALED." After pointing out that the North had a majority in both branches of Congress, the *Advertiser* concluded that if "this great question should be lost, in this situation of the great moral division of the nation, the event would be set down by all reflecting and virtuous people, as evidence of political insanity on the part of the majority."

By November the *Advertiser* was carrying editorial after editorial on the Missouri question. It spoke feelingly of the horrors of slavery: "The judgments of Heaven brood over a land cultivated by slaves—wealth acquired by injustice and cruelty. . . . The products of the soil that is watered with tears, and enriched by blood, etc."[41] While there could be no doubt of Dwight's humanitarianism, the moral aspect of slavery probably did not distress him as much as its political implications, for after all he had been the secretary of the Hartford Convention. On November 13, 1819, the *Advertiser* said: "We repeat an idea, which cannot be too often brought home to the consideration of the public, especially in this part of the United States THAT THIS QUESTION INVOLVES NOT ONLY THE FUTURE CHARACTER OF OUR NATION, BUT THE FUTURE WEIGHT AND INFLUENCE OF THE FREE STATES. IF NOW LOST—IT IS LOST FOREVER."

Dwight commanded enormous respect from the other Federalist editors, who regarded him as their oracle. They were quick to republish his cogent editorials on slavery restriction, and his articles deserved much of the credit for awakening the

[40] Isaac M. Ely to Roberts Vaux, March 26, 1819, Vaux Papers.
[41] New York *Daily Advertiser*, December 4, 1819.

North from its lethargy. Dwight's effectiveness was strictly limited, however, since Northern Democrats could never forgive him for participating in the Hartford Convention. In order to understand the warmth with which certain groups in New York embraced the Anti-Missourian Crusade, it must be kept in mind that the pre–Civil War humanitarian movement had permeated every phase of the city's intellectual life by 1819. New York of the year 1830 has been characterized as "the capital of the benevolent empire."[42] It might well have been called that in 1819, for it was already swarming with men of good will and benevolent and reformatory societies.[43] It was the favorite headquarters of national charitable and religious groups. There once a year, health permitting, journeyed the aged Dr. Boudinot, to preside over the annual meeting of the American Bible Society.

New York could boast of an impressive array of philanthropists in 1819. So many of these were Federalists that one almost is tempted to ask: Were they all Federalists? Were

[42] Sydnor, *Development of Southern Sectionalism*, 230.

[43] These societies were generally modeled after similar ones in England. Gilbert H. Barnes, *The Antislavery Impulse 1830-1844* (New York, 1933), 18. Below is a partial list of the New York humanitarian and benevolent societies in 1818-1821 (compiled from the files of the New York *Daily Advertiser*): Society for the Prevention of Pauperism, Humane Society of the City of New-York, New York Society for Promoting the Manumission of Slaves (usually referred to simply as the Manumission Society), New-York Bible Society, New-York Auxiliary Bible Society, United Foreign Missionary Society, New-York Marine Missionary Society, a society for erecting a mariners' church, The Port of New-York Society for the promotion of the Gospel among Seamen, Marine Bible Society of New-York, Pilot's Charitable Society, The Female Missionary Society for the poor of the city of New-York and vicinity, Female Association for the Education of poor Children, Free-School Society of New-York, Society for the Relief of Poor Widows with Small Children, Widows and Orphan Asylum Societies, The Wilberforce (African) Society, and the New-York County Society for the promotion of Agriculture and Domestic Manufactures. The city also had an African Free School for Negro children, established under the patronage of the Manumission Society, a Sunday School for the instruction of white male adults, a Sunday School Union, an Institution for the Instruction of the Deaf and Dumb, an Apprentices Library, and a Forum which debated such questions as: "Should Woman ever be placed in civil authority, or should she be restricted to the domestic circle?" New York *Daily Advertiser*, April 19, 1819.

there no Democratic philanthropists? A Federalist philanthropist might be patronizing and paternalistic in his benevolence, but still he was benevolent, even though he did not trust his white proletarian brothers when it came to voting. It would scarcely be amiss to say that in 1819 the Democrats in New York were those who favored universal white suffrage, while the Federalists advocated a restricted franchise but liked to indulge in acts of private philanthropy and usually had a kind spot in their hearts for minority groups such as Indians and Negroes.

A typical Federalist philanthropist was Peter A. Jay, "an able father's able son."[44] The father was that prince of Federalists and bogeyman of the South and West, John Jay. John Jay, for all his aristocracy and Federalism, had a heart as big as the Empire State Building as far as Negroes were concerned and had a habit of purchasing intelligent slaves that he might, after proper instruction, liberate them.[45] Peter Jay followed faithfully in his father's footsteps. While holding the office of city recorder, he used his influence to prevent Southern masters from recovering runaway slaves who took refuge in New York.[46] Early in 1819 he addressed a meeting which was called for the purpose of uplifting and civilizing the Indians. He spoke "with feeling and force," describing the miserable condition of the aborigines and showing by conclusive arguments "that the country was loudly called upon by a regard to its honour, its interest, and its duty, to make a serious, united, and energetic effort, to accomplish the great object in view."[47] Ten months later Jay took part in a meeting on the Missouri question. A year after that he was serving on a committee to prepare a report "on the results and tendency of the Penitentiary System" and was circulating a printed circular letter throughout the country to secure data for the project.[48] Finally in 1821, as the

[44] Fox, Decline of Aristocracy in New York, 243.
[45] Fox, "Negro Vote in Old New York," 253 n.
[46] B. Livingston to John Sergeant, January 18, 1822, Sergeant Papers.
[47] New York Daily Advertiser, January 12, 1819.
[48] Cadwallader D. Colden, Peter A. Jay, etc. to William Plumer, September, 1820, Plumer Papers.

Missouri Controversy was receding into the background, the indefatigable Mr. Jay, Theodore Dwight, and nine others, having organized a committee to "protect" an Eskimo couple in New York, were happily raising funds for this purpose.[49] Unfortunately the Eskimos did not want to be protected and succeeded in escaping from their benevolent custodians, to the great dismay of the latter. Of course Jay's Federalist benevolence stopped at the suffrage line. As a delegate to the state constitutional convention in 1821, he vigorously opposed universal suffrage. "When those who possess no property shall be more numerous than those who have it," he wrote his father, "the consequence of this alteration will, I fear, be severely felt."[50]

The New York meeting on the Missouri question followed closely on the heels of the one at Trenton. A preliminary meeting on November 6 made arrangements for a larger one to be held November 16 and inserted a notice in the newspapers, signed by John B. Coles and John T. Irving, to that effect.[51] Coles was a wealthy Federalist flour merchant and philanthropist.[52] Irving, a Bucktail Democratic member of the state legislature, had the distinction of being Washington Irving's brother.[53] On the evening of November 16, two thousand people gathered in the City Hotel. Present in all their glory were the Federalist philanthropists: Coles; Theodore Dwight; Peter Jay; General Matthew Clarkson, who was thrice a president—of the Humane Society, the Society for the Prevention of Pauperism, and the New York Bible Society;[54] Richard Varick,

49 New York *Daily Advertiser*, March 1, 1821. For Jay's philanthropy, see also John Jay, *Memorials of Peter A. Jay Compiled for his Descendants* (privately printed, 1929), 64-65, 123, 161.

50 Johnston, *Correspondence of John Jay*, IV, 455.

51 New York *Daily Advertiser*, November 13, 1819.

52 Walter Barrett (pseud. for Joseph A. Scoville), *The Old Merchants of New York City* (5 vols., New York, 1889), II, 41-45, 69-71; Fox, *Decline of Aristocracy in New York*, 18, 181, 182.

53 Barrett, *Old Merchants of New York*, II, 76-77, 80; Charles P. Daly, *Historical Sketch of the Judicial Tribunals of New York, from 1623 to 1846* (New York, 1855), 65.

54 New York *Daily Advertiser*, March 19, 1818, January 21, 1819; New York *Commercial Advertiser*, November 20, 1821.

treasurer of the American Bible Society; Isaac M. Ely of the Manumission Society; and Thomas Eddy, a Quaker merchant who has been called "the John Howard of America" because of his efforts in behalf of prison reform.[55] Matthew Clarkson presided over the gathering, and addresses were made by Peter Jay and John T. Irving. Jay spoke eloquently against slavery— of "its injustice and inhumanity, its immoral and irreligious character and tendency." Irving, "in an animated and feeling manner, depicted in glowing colors, the nature and consequences of Slavery, especially its abhorrent character in a Republic like ours."

In an address to the American people, the meeting declared that this "is no less a question, than whether, in this enlightened and philanthropic age, a mighty empire of slaves shall be permitted to be formed on the soil and under the sanction of Republican America, and admitted into her Union; or, whether that new empire is to be composed of men who shall have a *constitutional*, as well as natural, right, '*to life, liberty, and the pursuit of happiness.*'" As for the political motive, the address asserted that it would not "dwell upon the injustice of further extending *that* principle of representation, *that* was granted in a spirit of concession by which freemen are legislated for through votes derived from the possession of slaves."[56]

The New Yorkers appointed a large correspondence committee to secure an expression of opinion from other parts of the country. John B. Coles and John T. Irving were the leading spirits on the committee. These two gentlemen took their duties quite as seriously as the Trenton-Burlington committee and lost no time in issuing a printed circular, which was distributed in large quantities from Maine to Cincinnati.[57]

[55] "One of the most distinguished disciples of this university of charity, was Thomas Eddy, a merchant of the city of New York." Samuel L. Knapp, *The Life of Thomas Eddy* (New York, 1834), 41. See also Arthur A. Ekirch, Jr., "Thomas Eddy and the Beginnings of Prison Reform in New York," in *New York History*, XXIV (1943), 376-91.

[56] For accounts of the New York meeting, see New York *Daily Advertiser*, November 17, 1819; New York *Evening Post*, November 17, 1819; *Niles' Weekly Register*, XVII (1819), 199-200.

[57] For copies of the circular, see John B. Coles and John T. Irving to William

On November 23 Philadelphia had its say regarding Missouri.
A "very numerous and respectable" crowd assembled in the
chamber in which the Declaration of Independence had been
signed, listened to eloquent oratory, passed resolutions against
the further spread of slavery, and appointed the customary correspondence committee. A list of the committee members
might well have been entitled, *Who's Who in Philadelphia in
1819*, for it included such well-known names as Jared Ingersoll,
who had been De Witt Clinton's vice-presidential running mate
in the election of 1812, William Rawle, Horace Binney, Robert
Ralston, Robert Walsh, Jr., Peter S. Du Ponceau, Samuel Breck,
and Roberts Vaux.[58]

Meanwhile the circulars from Trenton and New York had
the desired effect of producing a multitude of meetings
throughout the land. Lancaster spoke out on November 23
(with James Buchanan helping to write the resolutions);[59]
West Chester, Pennsylvania, on November 27; Hartford and
Boston on December 3; Salem, Massachusetts (where Judge
Joseph Story used "passionate" language) on December 7;[60]
Albany, Providence, Newport, New Haven, and Cincinnati—
but why go on? The meetings operated like an endless chain,
with each meeting and correspondence committee begetting
other meetings and committees. Boston was moved by circulars
from Trenton and New York.[61] Hartford, Springfield, and
Canandaigua were inspired by New York;[62] New Brunswick
and Mount Holly, by Trenton.[63] The Cincinnati meeting af-

Plumer, November 17, 1819, Plumer Papers; John B. Coles and John T. Irving
to William King, November 17, 1819, William King Papers.

[58] Philadelphia *Aurora*, November 25, 1819; *Poulson's American Daily Advertiser* (Philadelphia), November 25, 1819; Philadelphia *Democratic Press*,
November 25, 1819; *Niles' Weekly Register*, XVII (1819), 241.

[59] *Poulson's American Daily Advertiser* (Philadelphia), November 29, 1819.

[60] James T. Adams, *New England in the Republic 1776-1850* (Boston, 1926),
326; Salem *Gazette*, December 10, 1819; Salem *Essex Register*, December 8,
1819.

[61] Boston *Daily Advertiser*, March 1, 1820.

[62] *Ibid.*, December 6, 1819; Hartford *Courant*, December 7, 1819; Canandaigua *Ontario Messenger*, December 7, 1819.

[63] Trenton *True American*, December 27, 1819; New Brunswick (New
Jersey) *Fredonian*, December 16, 1819.

fords a good illustration of the mechanics of the movement. Called at the instigation of the New York correspondence committee, it proceeded to appoint a similar committee of its own; and, said a Cincinnatian, "measures are about to be taken to procure a general expression of sentiment from the various parts of this state, and of Indiana; as also from the Legislatures of those States which are now in Session."[64] West Chester, Pennsylvania, was not a metropolis, yet when it held its meeting on the Missouri question it felt called upon to appoint a correspondence committee for circularizing the Pennsylvania congressional delegation and the other counties in the state.[65] Small wonder that by February, 1820, the St. Louis *Enquirer* was complaining that meetings were being held in "every dog-hole town and blacksmith's village in the northern states."[66]

It was noticeable that Boston, by comparison with Trenton, New York, and Philadelphia, was slow to speak its mind in 1819. The leaders of Massachusetts Federalism had now become what Disraeli once called the Gladstone Ministry, a "range of exhausted volcanoes." Having worn themselves out in combat with the South and West for twenty years, some of them at length adopted a platform of appeasement toward the victors. It was hoped that this change of policy would bring patronage favors from the Monroe administration as well as a remuneration from the national government for the expenses incurred by the Massachusetts militia in the War of 1812.[67] There was another reason why the Federalists of the Middle states should be more aggressive than those of Boston during the Missouri Controversy. Before 1819 New England had always led the opposition to slave representation and Southern political influence but had lagged behind the Middle states in moral and humanitarian concern over the institution of Southern slavery. Perhaps because it had fewer slaves of its own and was further removed from the South, it had no antislavery

<hr/>

[64] Boston *Daily Advertiser*, January 8, 1820; Cincinnati *Western Spy*, December 18, 1819; Cincinnati *Liberty Hall*, December 17, 21, 1819.
[65] West Chester *Village Record*, December 8, 1819.
[66] St. Louis *Enquirer*, February 5, 1820.
[67] Morison, *Harrison Gray Otis*, II, 224; King, *Rufus King*, VI, 274.

society that could compare in vigor with the New York Manumission Society, which had been organized in 1785 with John Jay as president, or the Pennsylvania Society for Promoting the Abolition of Slavery, which once had been headed by Benjamin Franklin.[68]

It was largely the influence of Rufus King and the Trenton and New York circulars which brought about the Boston meeting of December 3. King's friend William Tudor, editor of the *North American Review*, took the lead in getting up a meeting, and it was only with some difficulty that he arranged for one.[69] But whatever qualms any Bostonians may have had, they appeared to be enthusiastic enough when they convened in public assemblage in December. Most of the city's aristocracy and a large number of the "Reverend Clergy" were present, and the galleries were "adorned with circles of Ladies, who appeared to take a lively interest in a subject in which the Rights of Humanity are so deeply involved." The meeting was strictly nonpartisan. It had to be, of course, if the charge of "Bluelightism" and "Hartford Conventionism" was to be avoided. The arch-Federalists Webster and Josiah Quincy served on a committee with Democrats George Blake and James T. Austin to draw up a memorial to Congress. The only discordant note came from Alden Bradford, Secretary of the Commonwealth, who expressed doubts about the constitutionality of slavery restriction.[70]

When Congress reconvened in December, 1819, mass meetings throughout the country were in full swing, the state legis-

[68] Adams, *Neglected Period of Anti-Slavery*, 140-43; Adams, *New England in the Republic*, 326; Locke, *Anti-Slavery in America*, 98-99.

[69] William Tudor to Joseph Hopkinson, November 8, 1819, Hopkinson Papers; King, *Rufus King*, VI, 272.

[70] Boston *Commercial Gazette*, December 6, 1819, January 24, 1820; Boston *Daily Advertiser*, December 4, 1819; Boston *Columbian Centinel*, December 4, 1819; *Niles' Weekly Register*, XVII (1819), 241-42; Claude M. Fuess, *Daniel Webster* (2 vols., Boston, 1930), I, 271. For the memorial, see *A Memorial to the Congress of the United States, on the Subject of Restraining the Increase of Slavery in New States to be Admitted into the Union* (Boston, 1819). It is difficult to determine whether the memorial was actually written by Webster or by John Gallison, another member of the committee.

latures would soon be heard from, and pamphleteers had entered the lists. The New York correspondence committee published Rufus King's congressional addresses in pamphlet form, the New York Manumission Society did the same for Tallmadge, and Robert Walsh, a Philadelphia Federalist, made a profound impression by his brochure, *Free Remarks on the Spirit of the Federal Constitution.* Thus a considerable amount of antislavery enthusiasm temporarily had been drummed up.

There remains the question of how much the rank and file of the populace was concerned over the situation. In describing the public meetings, newspapers often stressed the fact that the audiences were highly respectable. No doubt they were respectable—top-heavy with Federalists, Clintonians, and other privileged groups; not drawn from the masses but full of benevolent folk who wished to uplift the masses. Arthur Schlesinger, Jr., maintains that conservatives have a penchant for sponsoring safe, sideshow reforms which do not interfere with their own prerogatives. This gratifies their humanitarianism and salves their consciences for the failure to grapple with other perplexing problems such as (in 1819) the extension of the suffrage.[71] The Schlesinger thesis may account for some of the zeal shown by Eastern Federalists in behalf of the Negro and Indian population of the South and West. The philanthropy of individual Federalists was something of which their party might well be proud. Nevertheless, in 1819-1821 Federalist philanthropy certainly contained a measure of escapism and political ax-grinding.

[71] Arthur M. Schlesinger, Jr., *The Age of Jackson* (Boston, 1945), 295-96, 364-68.

*"History tells us, I know not how truly, that
the Union reeled under the vehemence of that
great debate."—WILLIAM H. SEWARD[1]*

CHAPTER IV

CONGRESS DEBATES

*W*HEN THE SIXTEENTH Congress convened at Washington
on December 6, 1819, it was confronted with a multitude of
problems. A severe depression was in progress; manufacturers
were clamoring for higher tariff duties—a measure strongly opposed by Southern planters and New England shipping interests; the merchants were eager for the passage of a uniform
national bankruptcy law; and the West as usual was deeply
concerned with the perplexities of banking and credit.

To make matters worse, the Missouri Controversy, left unsolved by the Fifteenth Congress, had been passed on to the
Sixteenth. The Burlington–New York sponsored mass meetings
were urging the new Congress to prohibit slavery in Missouri,
while the Missourians themselves were calling on all to witness
that such a step would be unconstitutional and that they would
never tolerate "foreign" intermeddling in their domestic concerns. The grand jurors of Montgomery County, Missouri, had
already proclaimed to the world that they hoped congressional
restriction would never again be attempted but that if it should,
they expected "by the assistance of the genius of '76; and the
interposition of Divine Providence, to find means to protect
their rights."[2] It was obvious that it would be difficult to impose slavery restriction on such people, especially when the
rest of the South was rallying to their aid and the Senate was
still likely to be in disagreement with the House over the Tallmadge amendment.

Between the adjournment of the Fifteenth Congress and the convening of the Sixteenth, the voters of one state, Illinois, had the opportunity of expressing their sentiments on the Missouri question. This they did by defeating John McLean, who had opposed the Tallmadge amendment during the first Missouri debate, and giving his seat in Congress to Daniel Pope Cook, a militant restrictionist.[3] Cook's election gave the North one more vote in the House of Representatives, though it seemingly had little effect on the Southern-born senators from Illinois, Jesse B. Thomas and Ninian Edwards, who continued to vote on the Southern side with unswerving regularity.

With the antislavery pronouncements of mass meetings, state legislatures, and pamphleteers dinning their ears, it was natural that some Northern members of Congress should reverse the position they had held in the first Missouri debate. Interesting in this connection is the case of Senator Harrison Gray Otis of Massachusetts. Otis, an outstanding Federalist, had been one of the moving spirits of the Hartford Convention. In the Fifteenth Congress he voted against both clauses of the Tallmadge amendment. He later acknowledged that he had voted blindly, without perceiving the real importance of the subject. "It was not long before he realized his mistake, and saw that on this issue depended the question whether 'Virginian' rule should be perpetuated, or the balance of power be righted in favor of the free states." A speech of Rufus King in the Senate seems to have converted Otis to the restrictionist viewpoint. Once converted, he quickly made up for lost time and by 1820 was writing to a friend that "If the house gives way and the bill passes without restriction, their [Virginia's] feet will be upon our necks forever."[4]

Soon after the Sixteenth Congress convened, there was another attempt to settle the Missouri dispute by a compromise.

[1] *Congressional Globe*, 36 Cong., 1 Sess., 911.
[2] *Niles' Weekly Register*, XVII (1819), 71.
[3] Clarence W. Alvord (ed.), *Governor Edward Coles* (Springfield, 1920), 341; Kaskaskia *Intelligencer*, March 31, June 30, July 7, 14, 21, 28, 1819; Edwardsville *Spectator*, July 31, 1819.
[4] Morison, *Harrison Gray Otis*, II, 224-27.

At the suggestion of Tallmadge's friend John W. Taylor, a committee of seven was appointed in the House to see if a solution satisfactory to both sides could be worked out.[5] Though regarded by some as a fanatic, Taylor was really moderate in his views, and indeed some of his friends were afraid that he would go too far in the direction of compromise. His former colleague, Salma Hale of New Hampshire, wrote him that "I am not, I allow, where I can take a view of the whole ground, but here I see no necessity for a compromise. If we are firm for two years, changes of sentiment, & a new apportionment of representatives, will, I feel confident give us the victory."[6]

It was soon evident that Taylor's committee could never agree on a compromise. It was reported that Taylor himself proposed that the slaves already in Missouri, as well as their posterity, should be guaranteed to their owners forever and that the further introduction of slavery into Missouri and all the territory west of the Mississippi should be prohibited. He then suggested that the Missouri River or the line of the Missouri and Kansas rivers should be made the boundary between free and slave territory in the West, thus splitting the state of Missouri in two. William Lowndes favored yet another boundary. As the committee could not agree on any of these proposals, it was, at its own request, discharged from the further consideration of the subject on December 28.[7]

The Missouri question now had been complicated further by the application of Maine for admission as a state. By an act of June 19, 1819, Massachusetts had consented to its own division by permitting the people of that part of the Commonwealth known as Maine to set up an independent state. Maine was to revert to its old status as part of Massachusetts unless Congress consented to its admission to the Union before March 4, 1820.

Maine's application for statehood presented a golden opportunity to the opponents of slavery restriction in Congress. In

---

5 *Annals of Congress*, 16 Cong., 1 Sess., 732, 734-35.

6 Salma Hale to John W. Taylor, December 28, 1819, Taylor Papers.

7 Richmond *Enquirer*, December 21, 1819, January 11, 1820; *Annals of Congress*, 16 Cong., 1 Sess., 801-802.

1819 a large majority of the members of the House of Representatives came from free states, but after the admission of Alabama on December 14, the Senate's membership was evenly divided between the North and South. Moreover, in the Missouri Controversy, Southerners could always count on the support of the two slaveholding Illinois senators, Thomas and Edwards, and frequently they found yet other allies: Parrott of New Hampshire, Lanman of Connecticut, Waller Taylor of Indiana. Taylor, who was a native of Virginia, was reputed to be proslavery.[8] Thus those who opposed the restriction of slavery in Missouri had a clear-cut majority in the Senate. They speedily announced their intention of blocking Maine's admission in the Senate until the House should consent to Missouri's admission with slavery. On December 30 Speaker Henry Clay informed Northerners that "if you refuse to admit Missouri also free of condition, we see no reason why you shall take to yourselves privileges which you deny to her—and, until you grant them also to her, we will not admit you [Maine]." Clay declared that this "notion of an equivalent, . . . was not a new one; it was one upon which Commonwealths and States had acted from time immemorial."[9]

On December 8 Holmes of Massachusetts presented a petition from Maine asking for admission, and on January 3 the House passed a bill for this purpose.[10] The Senate, which had been considering a Maine bill of its own for some time, took up the House bill on January 13, together with an amendment suggested by the Senate Judiciary Committee. The amendment incorporated in the House Maine bill a provision enabling Missouri to form a constitution and state government without slavery restriction. As Clay had predicted, Maine and Missouri were to be connected and the admission of one made dependent on the unconditional admission of the other.

At this point Senator Roberts of Pennsylvania moved that the bill be recommitted to the Judiciary Committee with instructions to strike out the amendment relating to Missouri.

[8] Vincennes *Centinel*, February 26, 1820.
[9] *Annals of Congress*, 16 Cong., 1 Sess., 841.
[10] *Ibid.*, 704, 849.

Roberts' motion was debated at some length and was finally rejected by a vote of 25 to 18.[11] Later Roberts attempted to attach an antislavery proviso to the amendment admitting Missouri. After discussing the proviso for many days, the Senate rejected it by a vote of 27 to 16.[12] On February 3 Jesse B. Thomas of Illinois suggested amending the Missouri branch of the proposed Maine-Missouri bill by prohibiting slavery in the unorganized Louisiana Purchase north of 36° 30'. This proposal would eventually become the basis for the famous Missouri Compromise of 1820.[13]

On February 16 the Senate finally concurred in the report of its Judiciary Committee, uniting the Maine and Missouri bills in one. The vote was: for uniting the bills, 23; against it, 21.[14] Van Dyke and Horsey of Delaware were the only senators from a slaveholding state who voted in the negative. Three senators from free states voted with the South in the affirmative: Edwards and Thomas of Illinois and Taylor of Indiana.

As soon as the Maine and Missouri bills were combined, Thomas again offered an amendment, intended as a compromise, to prohibit slavery in the unorganized Louisiana Purchase north of 36° 30'. The amendment read:

And be it further enacted, That, in all that territory ceded by France to the United States, under the name of Louisiana, which lies north of thirty-six degrees and thirty minutes north latitude, excepting only such part thereof as is included within the limits of the State contemplated by this act, slavery and involuntary servitude, otherwise than in the punishment of crimes whereof the party shall have been duly convicted, shall be and is hereby forever prohibited: Provided, always, That any person escaping into the same, from whom labor or service is lawfully claimed in any State or Ter-

11 Ibid., 85, 118. The only senators from a slave state who voted for the motion were Van Dyke and Horsey of Delaware. Five Northern senators voted against it: Edwards and Thomas of Illinois, Taylor of Indiana, Palmer of Vermont, and Parrott of New Hampshire.

12 Ibid., 359. No senator from a slave state voted for the proviso. Six Northern senators voted against it: Palmer of Vermont, Parrott of New Hampshire, Hunter of Rhode Island, Lanman of Connecticut, and Edwards and Thomas of Illinois.

13 Ibid., 363, 367.   14 Ibid., 424.

ritory of the United States, such fugitive may be lawfully reclaimed and conveyed to the person claiming his or her labor or service as aforesaid.[15]

Thomas was proposing in substance to make Maine a free state, admit Missouri with slavery, leave Arkansas and Oklahoma open to future settlement by slaveholders, and prohibit slavery forever in the remainder of the Louisiana Purchase north of 36° 30′, the southern boundary of the contemplated state of Missouri. Such an arrangement, as an analysis of the vote by states shows, was acceptable to a majority of the Southern senators but was unsatisfactory to most of those from the North. It was regarded generally as a Southern measure. "The south have made offers of a compromise which the north & even Maine reject," wrote a Massachusetts congressman.[16] The Senate adopted Thomas' amendment by a vote of 34 to 10. Then, by a vote of 24 to 20, the joint Maine-Missouri bill, including the Thomas amendment, was ordered to be engrossed and read a third time. On February 18 it was passed.[17] By prohibiting slavery in the territories, the Senate majority hoped to reconcile the House of Representatives to Missouri's admission as a slave state. It was also supposed that the union of the Maine and Missouri bills would compel those Massachusetts congressmen who resided in Maine to vote for the unrestricted admission of Missouri rather than forfeit statehood for Maine.[18]

In the meantime the Senate's Maine-Missouri bill returned to the House, which had been considering a Missouri bill of its own and an antislavery amendment introduced by John W. Taylor. On February 23 the House rejected all of the Senate amendments. The one annexing the Missouri bill to the Maine bill was defeated by a vote of 93 to 72, while the Thomas compromise was rejected by the overwhelming majority of 141. The House then resumed consideration of its own Missouri bill

[15] *Ibid.*, 424, 427.

[16] John Holmes to William King, February 29, 1820, William King Papers.

[17] *Annals of Congress*, 16 Cong., 1 Sess., 428-30.

[18] John W. Walker to Charles Tait, February 11, 1820, Tait Papers.

and Taylor's restrictive amendment. After a lengthy debate, the amendment was at last approved "by from 12 to 18 votes."[19]

When the Senate informed the House on February 28 that it insisted on its amendments to the Maine bill, the House again disagreed to all of them.[20] The two houses were now so completely deadlocked that Representative Mark Hill of Maine wrote despairingly that it might take "a year or two for Congress to let us in."[21] The Senate next voted, on motion of Jesse B. Thomas, to request a conference with the House. As its conferees it selected Thomas, James Barbour of Virginia, and William Pinkney of Maryland. The House granted the request for a conference and appointed William Lowndes of South Carolina, John W. Taylor of New York, John Holmes and James Parker of Massachusetts, and Charles Kinsey of New Jersey as its conferees.[22]

Before considering the work of the conference committee and the events that followed, it is well to pause and take note of the atmosphere in which Congress was holding its deliberations: the frayed nerves of the members, the spectators in the galleries, the threats of violence and disunion emanating from Northerners and Southerners alike. Though the average American was undoubtedly more interested in the depression than in Missouri slavery,[23] Washington political circles had allowed the latter to push everything else from their minds. "The Missouri subject," wrote Henry Clay, "monopolizes all our conversation, all our thoughts and for three weeks at least to come will all our time. No body seems to think or care about any thing else."[24] At times during the discussion the halls of Congress were pervaded by a feeling of tenseness and awe. Nathaniel Macon stated on January 13, 1820, that "The appear-

19 *Annals of Congress,* 16 Cong., 1 Sess., 1455-57, 1540.

20 For the vote in the Senate against receding from the amendments, see *ibid.,* 457; for the House vote, *ibid.,* 1553-55.

21 Mark L. Hill to William King, February 28, 1820, William King Papers.

22 *Annals of Congress,* 16 Cong., 1 Sess., 459, 1558.

23 See Chapter VI.

24 Henry Clay to John J. Crittenden, January 29, 1820, John J. Crittenden Papers, Library of Congress.

ance of the Senate to-day is different from anything I have seen since I have been a member of it. It is the greatness of the question which has produced it."[25]

Crowded galleries in the Capitol heard orator after orator discuss the subject of slavery restriction from every conceivable angle. Never before had the deliberations of Congress aroused a deeper interest, said the Washington *Intelligencer*.[26] European diplomats were in constant attendance,[27] and of course, in an age of gentility and refined oratory, the fair sex was attracted irresistibly by such forensic exhibitions. It was at this time that Vice-President Tompkins gallantly invited a group of ladies to have seats on the floor of the Senate. Seeing the ladies so comfortably seated on sofas and footstools, the entire crowd in the gallery, young and old, descended to the Senate floor. That was too much. The Vice-President was dismayed, and senators were heard to mutter indignantly that there were too many women around for business to be transacted properly. When ladies flocked into the House of Representatives, John Randolph tartly suggested that they go home and attend to their knitting. Miffed by such advice, they remained away from the House for several days.[28]

The Negro population of Washington also flocked to hear the congressional debates. In February, 1820, Mrs. Seaton, wife of one of the publishers of the *Intelligencer*, declared that the galleries were crowded with Negroes almost to the exclusion of the whites. "They hear all," she wrote, "but understand much less than half. They know it to be a question of servitude or freedom, and imagine that the result will immediately affect their condition; so, as one side or other of the question preponderates, they rejoice or are depressed."[29]

[25] *Annals of Congress*, 16 Cong., 1 Sess., 97.
[26] Washington *Daily National Intelligencer*, January 22, 1820.
[27] Adams, *Memoirs of J. Q. Adams*, V, 40.
[28] Josephine Seaton, *William Winston Seaton of the "National Intelligencer"* (Boston, 1871), 146-47, 150-51; Margaret B. Smith, *The First Forty Years of Washington Society*, ed. by Gaillard Hunt (New York, 1906), 148-49.
[29] Seaton, *William Seaton*, 145.

As the debate over Missouri continued indefinitely, many of the speeches inevitably became repetitious and boring. Since congressmen believed that they must be heard in order to impress their constituents, the mails groaned with addresses in pamphlet form which were being dispatched, under the franking privilege, to every part of the country.[30] Finally, when Representative Felix Walker of North Carolina rose to speak on February 25, the House refused to listen to him.[31] Walker represented the Buncombe County district. According to tradition, he stated that his constituents expected him to say something about Missouri and that he was bound to "make a speech for Buncombe." In this manner, it is said, the word "bunkum" or "bunk" entered the American vocabulary.[32]

Threats of disunion became commonplace in the winter of 1819-1820. Henry Clay wrote from Washington in January that the words "civil war" and "disunion" were uttered almost without emotion.[33] John Scott, Missouri's territorial delegate, declared that if necessary Missourians would organize a state government without waiting for congressional sanction.[34] Should Missouri forcibly resist slavery restriction, John Tyler wanted to know if the North would try to reduce it by force and expect Southern aid in such an undertaking. He asked: "Do you believe that Southern bayonets will ever be plunged in Southern hearts?"[35] Representative John Holmes of Maine stated that a Southern senator told him that he would suffer "at the stake before he would submit to this outrage of the north upon *their rights*—That it was an attack upon their dearest interests a stab at their vitals." "By this," wrote Holmes, "you will judge of their feeling—& how can you expect to persuade such men?"[36]

30 Portsmouth (New Hampshire) *Oracle*, March 25, 1820.

31 *Annals of Congress*, 16 Cong., 1 Sess., 1539.

32 George W. Stimpson, *Nuggets of Knowledge* (New York, 1928), 88-89.

33 Calvin Colton (ed.), *The Private Correspondence of Henry Clay* (New York, 1855), 61. See also Richard Peters to Timothy Pickering, February 21, 1820, Pickering Papers.

34 *Annals of Congress*, 16 Cong., 1 Sess., 735.   35 *Ibid.*, 1394.

36 John Holmes to William King, February 27, 1820, William King Papers.

It was said that in the "hottest paroxysm" of the debate, Senator James Barbour of Virginia canvassed all the free state members of the upper house on the advisability of calling a convention to dissolve the Union and agree on the terms of separation.[37] Clay, William Lowndes, and Philip Barbour asserted that if the North had its way they would leave Congress and consult their constituents about whether or not they should ever come back, and Clay prophesied that within five years the country would be divided into three separate confederacies.[38] John Randolph of Roanoke was the most conspicuous of the disunionists. This picturesque and querulous descendant of Pocahontas opposed any compromise or concession to the North, declaring that "God has given us the Missouri and the devil shall not take it from us."[39] As if anticipating the events of 1861, he formulated a plan by which all the Southern delegation should abandon Congress in a body, but it is not certain whether he made this rash proposal in 1820 or 1821.[40]

It is surprising with what accuracy the contestants of 1820 predicted the war of 1861-1865. Senator Freeman Walker of Georgia could see in his mind's eye "intestine feuds, civil wars, . . . the father armed against the son, and the son against the father . . . a brother's sword crimsoned with a brother's blood . . . our houses wrapt in flames, and our wives and infant children driven from their homes." "Sir," said Robert Reid of Georgia, "the firebrand, which is even now cast into your society, will require blood—ay, and the blood of freemen—for its quenching." John Scott of Missouri warned his fellow congressmen that "the people they represented might one day bleed in contending for and against this restriction," and Francis Jones of Tennessee assured the people of the North that

---

[37] Adams, *Memoirs of J. Q. Adams,* V, 13.

[38] *Ibid.,* IV, 525-26; Brown, *Missouri Compromises,* 14.

[39] Boston *Daily Advertiser,* February 5, 1820.

[40] Epes Sargent and Horace Greeley, *The Life and Public Services of Henry Clay* (Philadelphia, 1852), 94; Glyndon G. Van Deusen, *The Life of Henry Clay* (Boston, 1937), 145; *Congressional Globe,* 25 Cong., 2 Sess., *Appendix,* 71.

"if ever Missouri subscribes to this humiliating condition, her name will be written in characters of blood."[41]

Northern congressmen made a number of bloodcurdling threats and prophecies, though on the whole the South easily carried off the honors in this field. Senator Walter Lowrie of Pennsylvania observed that between such a choice of evils as the dissolution of the Union or the extension of slavery over the entire West, he would choose the former.[42] Rufus King was said to have expressed a wish that Missouri should belong to the moon or be turned over to wild beasts,[43] while Harrison Gray Otis thought that if the treaty of 1803 made it impossible to abolish slavery in the Louisiana Purchase, "it would have been happier for us if the Mississippi had been an eternal torrent of burning lava, impassable as the lake which separates the evil from the good, and the regions beyond it destined to be covered forever with brakes and jungles, and the impenetrable haunts of the wolf and the panther."[44] Daniel Pope Cook of Illinois served notice that Missouri might return to the wilderness or unite with Mexico but should never, by vote of his, become a slave state.[45] Former Senator Lacock of Pennsylvania wrote President Monroe that "Some prudent & discreet men (in other aspects) in Congress have brought themselves to this awful alternative, 'to dissolve the union, rather than submit to the establishment of slave States over the Mississippi' This is met in a temper eqally fixt & determined on the other hand, these men Mutually 'throw firebrands arrows & death.' "[46]

The individual who exerted the greatest influence in the first session of the Sixteenth Congress was the Speaker Henry Clay. Clay was theoretically antislavery, and it was rumored widely that he advised the Missourians to abolish slavery gradually

[41] *Annals of Congress*, 16 Cong., 1 Sess., 175, 1033, 1462, 1523.
[42] *Ibid.*, 209.
[43] Richmond *Enquirer*, February 17, 1820.
[44] *Annals of Congress*, 16 Cong., 1 Sess., 239.
[45] *Ibid.*, 1113.
[46] Abner Lacock to James Monroe, January 30, 1820, James Monroe Papers, Library of Congress.

by state action.[47] Nevertheless, he vigorously supported the Southern position that slavery within a state was a subject for local and not congressional regulation. Discarding his usual role of politician for that of statesman, he used his utmost energies to effect a compromise which would be acceptable to Northerners and Southerners alike. Sometimes he blustered and threatened to go to Kentucky and raise troops to defend Missouri's rights, but this was obviously for the purpose of frightening the weak-kneed in the hope that they would vote for the compromise.[48]

It was a source of great grief to Southerners that their old ally Democratic Pennsylvania now was making common cause with New England and the Federalists. Clay made a powerful appeal to the Pennsylvanians for aid in solving the Missouri question. Addressing himself especially to the Pennsylvania Quakers through the medium of the aged Congressman Thomas Forrest, he "wielded the powers of pathos in a manner so sublime and touching, that the old man himself became restless, and half the House were in tears."[49]

By concentrating all of his charm and persuasiveness on Northern representatives who appeared to be wavering in their attitude toward the compromise, by utilizing to the fullest his power of making committee appointments, and by resorting to nearly every parliamentary trick and subterfuge in the bag, Clay succeeded in piloting three compromises through the House in 1820-1821. If his methods on this occasion were somewhat unscrupulous, it must be remembered that he was doing what he honestly believed that the welfare of the country demanded. He was also doing the things that a strong President would be expected to do today but from which President Monroe held aloof because of his temperament and his conception of the duties of his office.[50]

[47] Washington *Gazette*, February 27, 1821. For Clay's attitude toward slavery, see Bernard Mayo, *Henry Clay Spokesman of the New West* (Boston, 1937), 77, 80; Van Deusen, *Henry Clay*, 136-38.
[48] Brown, *Missouri Compromises*, 11-12.
[49] New York *Daily Advertiser*, April 18, 1820.
[50] William P. Cresson, *James Monroe* (Chapel Hill, 1946), 347.

In general, the South was represented more ably in the Sixteenth Congress than the North, Northerners themselves conceding that such was the case. Representative Plumer of New Hampshire wrote that "the great speakers are almost all in the other side."[51] "The Southern people have a great preponderancy of talent against us," admitted Congressman Dowse of Massachusetts.[52] John Quincy Adams asked by what fatality it happened that the most eloquent orators of Congress were on the "slavish side" of the Missouri dispute. "There is," said Adams, "a great mass of cool judgment and plain sense on the side of freedom and humanity, but the ardent spirits and passions are on the side of oppression."[53]

John Randolph was the most colorful figure on the Southern side in the Missouri debates. His brilliant wit and sarcasm always delighted the galleries, although the biased John Quincy Adams concluded, after listening to him for several hours, that "Egotism, Virginian aristocracy, slave-scourging liberty, religion, literature, science, wit, fancy, generous feelings, and malignant passions constitute a chaos in his mind, from which nothing orderly can ever flow."[54] John Sergeant of Pennsylvania was popularly regarded as the greatest Northern orator in the House in 1820. His address of February 10 in favor of slavery restriction was so forceful that it enraptured even Randolph, who said to him afterwards: *"Never speak again! Never speak again, sir!"* This was supposed to be a rare compliment, meaning that the speech could probably never again be equaled and certainly not excelled.[55]

At the opening of the Sixteenth Congress the antislavery forces appeared to be in danger of losing their leading orator in the Senate. Rufus King's term of office expired in 1819, and as he was a Federalist, the Democratic legislature of New York at first showed little inclination to re-elect him. He was re-elected almost unanimously in 1820, however, largely because

---

[51] Brown, *Missouri Compromises*, 5.   [52] Quincy, *Josiah Quincy*, 387.
[53] Adams, *Memoirs of J. Q. Adams*, IV, 506, 524.   [54] *Ibid.*, 532.
[55] For slightly differing versions of this episode, see Philadelphia *Franklin Gazette*, February 14, 1820; Philadelphia *Union*, February 16, 1820; Steubenville (Ohio) *Western Herald*, August 12, 1820.

the two factions of the New York Democracy, the Clintonians
and Bucktails, hated each other worse than they did Federalism
and partly, perhaps, because it was thought that the North
needed his services in the Senate.[56]

On returning to Washington, King made himself extremely
distasteful to the South. The slaveholders considered his
speeches seditious and inflammatory and could not "hear of
them without being seized with cramps."[57] King especially
antagonized Southerners by a two hour address on February 11.
This was the occasion on which he invoked the doctrine of
natural law to prove that one man could not legally enslave
another. The great slaveholders in the audience "gnawed their
lips and clenched their fists" during the course of his remarks.[58]
King's oratorical delivery was not of the spread-eagle type.
John Quincy Adams pronounced it "dignified, grave, earnest,
but not rapid or vehement." John A. Dix called it "calm, dignified, argumentative, forcible, and at times fervid." Dix considered King the perfect embodiment of the old Roman senators.[59]

The South's case was best presented to the Senate by William Pinkney of Maryland. Pinkney was a superb orator and a
leading member of the American bar. He was also noted for
his vanity, foppish dress, and love of applause—qualities which
led him to use cosmetics and corsets to improve his appearance.[60] On January 21 and 24 he delivered a long address in
the Senate against slavery restriction which was not recorded

[56] Fox, *Decline of Aristocracy in New York*, 207-208, 220-21; New York *Daily
Advertiser*, January 12, 1820; [Lemuel Shaw], "Slavery and the Missouri Question," in *North American Review*, X (1820), 167-68.

[57] Adams, *Memoirs of J. Q. Adams*, IV, 524.

[58] *Ibid.*, 522; *Annals of Congress*, 16 Cong., 1 Sess., 372-73, 380-81. For a
discussion of natural law as an issue in the Missouri debates, see Chapter IX.

[59] Adams, *Memoirs of J. Q. Adams*, IV, 522; Morgan Dix (ed.), *Memoirs of
John Adams Dix* (2 vols., New York, 1883), I, 60.

[60] "Do you know, that a corsetted Dandy of 60, or near it, having a wife &
12 or 14 children is my aversion;—God preserve me even from the sight of
such an animal." James M. Garnett to John Randolph, January 24, 1820, John
Randolph—James M. Garnett Correspondence, manuscript transcript, Library of
Congress. See also, *Dictionary of American Biography*, XIV, 628.

in the *Annals of Congress* but attracted considerable attention. Shortly after Pinkney closed his discourse on January 21, a venerable senator declared: "*I would rather have spoken that speech than be Emperor of all the Russias.*" Another admirer said of the speech: "I thought of Pitt, Burke, Fox, and Sheridan, of a Mirabeau and Maury, of a Patrick Henry, Ames, King, Randolph, Madison, Dexter, and Wirt, and I thought likewise of Demosthenes, of Cicero, and of the proudest days of Rome; but I felt convinced that the eloquence which once electrified Roman senates, never had surpassed that which sounded in the lofty dome of the American Capitol."[61]

Of course, Pinkney's address was not without its detractors. Rufus King called it "gaudy and captivating," and Mrs. John Quincy Adams and her sons were "somewhat disappointed" by it.[62] A member of Congress wrote to a citizen of Boston that Pinkney had "a disgusting visage and a disagreeable voice" and that he paraded the most commonplace arguments "with an air of ranting defiance, as if the orator thought them quite *new, beautiful,* and *unanswerable.*"[63]

Perhaps the fairest estimate of Pinkney's oration of January 21 and 24 is that given by Thomas H. Benton. "It was," says Benton, "the most gorgeous speech ever delivered in the Senate, and the most applauded; but it was only a magnificient exhibition, as Mr. Pinkney knew, and could not sustain in the reading the plaudits it received in delivery; and therefore he avoided its publication."[64]

On February 15 Pinkney spoke again for three hours in reply to King, and according to the Richmond *Enquirer,* "The Senator from New York was observed to wince and cower beneath the thunders of his eloquence." The speech of February 15, which contained a forceful discussion of state sovereignty, is preserved

[61] Charleston *Southern Patriot, And Commercial Advertiser,* January 31, 1820; *Niles' Weekly Register,* XVII (1820), 417.

[62] King, *Rufus King,* VI, 263; Adams, *Memoirs of J. Q. Adams,* IV, 510.

[63] Boston *Columbian Centinel,* February 2, 1820.

[64] Thomas H. Benton, *Thirty Years' View* (2 vols., New York, 1854-1856), I, 20.

in the *Annals*.[65] The Senate addresses of Pinkney and King assumed the character of a debate between these two eminent statesmen. In manner of oratory the two were quite dissimilar. King was calm and dignified, while Pinkney was emotional and flowery, though none the less cogent.[66]

Pinkney was handicapped in 1820 by equalitarian remarks which he had made in the Maryland legislature thirty years before. In discussing the slavery question in 1789 he had exclaimed: "Gracious God! can it be supposed that thy almighty providence intended to proscribe these victims of fraud and power, from the pale of society, because thou hast denied them the delicacy of an European complexion!" He had maintained then that Negroes "are in all respects our equal by nature" and had asked significantly: "Is their color, Mr Speaker, the mark of divine vengeance, or is it only the flimsy pretext upon which we attempt to justify our treatment of them?" These remarks were published and distributed by the Quakers at the time of the Missouri Controversy to show Pinkney's inconsistency.[67]

It may be well to recapitulate the course of events in the Sixteenth Congress up to this point. The House of Representatives on January 3, 1820, passed a bill for the admission of Maine and later took under consideration a bill to admit Missouri. The House Maine bill was passed by the Senate in February after being amended in two important respects. First, the Senate added to the bill a provision enabling Missouri to form a constitution and state government without slavery restriction. Next, by the Thomas amendment, the Senate prohibited slavery in the territory north and west of the proposed state of Missouri. Twice the House rejected the Senate amendments, and then at the Senate's suggestion, the two houses ap-

[65] Richmond *Enquirer*, February 19, 1820; *Annals of Congress*, 16 Cong., 1 Sess., 389-417.

[66] King, *Rufus King*, VI, 270 n., 277-78; Dix, *Memoirs of John Adams Dix*, I, 60-61.

[67] William Pinkney, *Speech of William Pinkney, Esq. in the House of Delegates of Maryland, At their Session in November, 1789* (Philadelphia, 1790), 15-17; *Dictionary of American Biography*, XIV, 627.

pointed a joint conference committee to see if a common agreement regarding Maine and Missouri could be reached.

Events now moved rapidly. On March 1, by a vote of 91 to 82, the House passed its own Missouri bill with restriction and sent it to the Senate for concurrence.[68] The Senate returned it the next day after striking out the section prohibiting slavery in Missouri and annexing the Thomas compromise to it.[69] On March 2 John Holmes presented the report of the joint conference committee to the House. The report recommended: (1) that the Senate withdraw its amendments to the Maine bill, (2) that both houses strike the slavery restriction clause from the House Missouri bill, and (3) that they add to the latter bill a provision forever excluding slavery from that part of the Louisiana Purchase lying north of 36° 30′ which was not included within the limits of the new state of Missouri.[70]

The well-known Missouri Compromise of 1820 consisted of these three recommendations and was made possible by Senator Thomas' territorial restriction proviso, of which Horace Greeley aptly said: "It was, in effect, an offer from the milder opponents of Slavery Restriction to the more moderate and flexible advocates of that Restriction—'Let us have Slavery in Missouri, and we will unite with you in excluding it from all the uninhabited territories North and West of that State.' "[71]

The dying request of Representative David Walker of Kentucky is evidence of the emotional state of Congress at this stage of the proceedings. He died on March 1 after directing his friends to carry him to the Capitol if he was still alive when the vote was taken in order that his last breath might be given in behalf of Missouri.[72]

After the recommendations of the conference committee had been presented to the House, Representative Charles Kinsey

[68] *Annals of Congress*, 16 Cong., 1 Sess., 1572-73. No Southerner voted for restriction. Nine Northerners voted against it: Holmes, Mason, and Shaw of Massachusetts; Foot of Connecticut; Meigs and Storrs of New York; Bloomfield of New Jersey; and Baldwin and Fullerton of Pennsylvania.

[69] *Ibid.*, 467-69.   [70] *Ibid.*, 1576-77.

[71] Horace Greeley and John F. Cleveland (comps.), *A Political Text-Book for 1860* (New York, 1860), 63.

[72] St. Louis *Enquirer*, March 29, 1820.

of New Jersey made a moving plea for their adoption. Kinsey, who up to then had voted with the restrictionist majority, seems to have been frightened by the threats of civil war and violence. Stressing the danger of disunion and the equitable division of territory, from a Northern standpoint, under the compromise, he concluded that should Northerners now "numerically, carry the question, it will be a victory snatched from our brothers . . . an inglorious triumph, gained at the hazard of the Union."[73]

After Kinsey and others had spoken, Charles F. Mercer of Virginia attempted to make an address but fainted before he had proceeded far. Then, while four Northern representatives were absent, the House voted on the second recommendation of the conference committee—that the antislavery proviso be eliminated from the House Missouri bill. The vote was: for eliminating the proviso, 90; for retaining it, 87. No representative from a slaveholding state voted for retention, though two— William L. Ball of Virginia and Willard Hall of Delaware— were absent. The four Northerners who were absent were: Caleb Tompkins of New York, brother of Vice-President Daniel D. Tompkins; Walter Case and Harmanus Peek of New York; and Henry W. Edwards of Connecticut. Fourteen Northern congressmen voted openly with the South to strike out the antislavery proviso: Mark L. Hill, John Holmes, Jonathan Mason, and Henry Shaw of Massachusetts; Samuel Eddy of Rhode Island; James Stevens of Connecticut; Samuel A. Foot of Connecticut (who is now remembered as the instigator of the Webster-Hayne Debate); Henry Meigs and Henry R. Storrs of New York; Joseph Bloomfield, Charles Kinsey, and Bernard Smith of New Jersey; and Henry Baldwin and David Fullerton of Pennsylvania.[74]

After striking the antislavery clause from the Missouri bill, the House turned its attention to the Thomas proviso excluding

[73] *Annals of Congress*, 16 Cong., 1 Sess., 1578-83.
[74] *Ibid.*, 1586-87. For a map showing the vote by congressional districts, see Paullin, *Atlas of the Historical Geography of the United States*, plate 113 D. One district in North Carolina and one in Kentucky did not have representatives in Congress at this time. The Speaker, of course, did not ordinarily vote except in case of a tie.

slavery from the remainder of the Louisiana Purchase north of 36° 30'. The proviso was approved by a vote of 134 to 42. Thirty-nine Southerners voted for it, while thirty-seven opposed it. Of its thirty-seven Southern opponents, eighteen were Virginians.[75]

One of the most noticeable things about the passage of the Missouri Compromise was that the House never voted "yea" or "nay" on the compromise as a whole. Such a vote could have produced only a negative decision, since all but eighteen of the Northerners, as well as a substantial minority of the Southerners (the diehards who opposed the Thomas proviso), probably would have voted "nay." Only by splitting the compromise into sections and voting separately on each one was it possible to push the measure through the House. Such procedure prompted two significant questions from writers in the Richmond *Enquirer:* (1) "Whether this question was not carried at last by a sort of parliamentary *coup de main?* That is, by voting on detached amendments from the Senate? Had the whole bill (or compromising system) come *at once* before the H. of R. would it have had a majority of votes?"; (2) whether "this bill has been in fact palmed upon the nation, without having fairly the consent of its representatives?"[76]

The compromise had the support of a safe majority in the Senate and an adroit Speaker in the House, but not of a majority of the House. As it sped toward enactment, the hand of Henry Clay was visibly pushing it along. Clay had been careful to appoint conciliatory men to represent the House in the conference committee, knowing in advance that a majority of them would be favorable to any reasonable settlement.[77] On March 3, the day after the decisive vote of 90 to 87, John Randolph made a final attempt to kill the compromise but was thwarted by Clay. On the night that the House voted to strike the antislavery clause from the Missouri bill, Randolph decided to ask for a reconsideration of the vote. As everyone seemed to

[75] *Annals of Congress,* 16 Cong., 1 Sess., 1587-88.
[76] Richmond *Enquirer,* March 7, 10, 1820.
[77] See letter from Representative Daniel Pope Cook in Shawneetown (Illinois) *Gazette,* March 30, 1820.

be exhausted and Representative Archer was ill, he postponed his motion until the next day, after Clay had told him that it would be in order then. The next morning Clay refused to receive the motion until he was sure that the Clerk had taken the bill to the Senate, removing it from the jurisdiction of the House. Not to be outdone, Randolph moved that the Clerk be censured for violating the rules of the House. By a vote of 71 to 61 the House refused to consider this motion; it would seem that some congressmen who disapproved of the compromise in theory and would not vote for it were yet glad to be rescued by Clay's strategy from the blind alley of their own intransigence.[78]

On March 3 the Senate withdrew its amendments to the Maine bill, and the second Missouri debate came to a close. Maine was admitted to the Union by act of March 3, 1820. By act of March 6 the people of Missouri were authorized to form a constitution and state government without slavery restriction, and in the unorganized territory to the north and west of the new state, slavery was prohibited forever.[79]

Much of the responsibility for the passage of the compromise of 1820 rested upon the eighteen Northern congressmen who either voted to strike the antislavery clause from the Missouri bill or were absent when the vote was taken. Once restriction in Missouri was defeated, a majority for the Thomas proviso could easily be secured. As for the Senate, the advocates of conciliation were so firmly in control there that they took the offensive, and senators appeared on the House floor to lobby for the compromise among the representatives.[80]

Because of a misinterpretation of a remark made by John Randolph, the eighteen Northerners who made it possible to admit Missouri without restriction became known as "dough faces." It is not certain exactly whom Randolph meant to designate by the term "dough faces." Apparently he was not

[78] *Annals of Congress,* 16 Cong., 1 Sess., 1588-90; Hugh A. Garland, *The Life of John Randolph of Roanoke* (2 vols., New York, 1850), II, 128-30.
[79] *Annals of Congress,* 16 Cong., 1 Sess., *Appendix,* 2554-59; 3 *U. S. Stat.* 544-48.
[80] Keene (New Hampshire) *Sentinel,* April 1, 1820.

referring to all Northern supporters of the compromise but only to those who assisted in its passage by being absent when the final vote was taken (March 2) on slavery restriction. He may also have had in mind those who had been voting for restriction and then switched to the other side on March 2. Perhaps he regarded absentees and last minute converts as half-baked or easily molded, or they may have reminded him of children who daubed their faces with dough and became frightened by a glance at the mirror. It is also possible that the epithet should be spelled "doe faces" and was an allusion to the timidity of the female deer.[81] Randolph declared that he had known all along that *these would give way.—*They were scared at their own dough faces—yes, *they were scared at their own dough faces!—*We had *them,* and if we had wanted *three* more, we could have had them: yes, and if *these* had failed, we could have three more of these men, *whose conscience, and morality, and religion, extend to 'thirty-six degrees and thirty minutes north latitude.' "*[82]

In the North, Randolph's expression "dough faces" was applied indiscriminately to all of the eighteen Northern congressmen who were responsible for eliminating the antislavery clause from the Missouri bill, and by that title they have ever since been known. They were denounced as traitors who had sold out to the South in return for patronage favors from the Monroe administration.[83] There was no proof of this accusation, however, nor was Monroe accustomed to using the patronage for such purposes.[84]

The most plausible explanation for being absent was that given by Henry W. Edwards of Connecticut in a public apology

81 For the meaning of "dough faces," see letter from "FAIR PLAY" in Newark *Centinel of Freedom,* May 23, 1820; Boston *Daily Advertiser,* June 22, 1820; King, *Rufus King,* VI, 291-92; Frank H. Hodder, "Dough-faces," in *The Nation,* C (1915), 245.

82 Pittsburgh *Statesman,* April 26, 1820.

83 New York *Columbian,* December 18, 22, 1820; Portsmouth (New Hampshire) *Oracle,* April 15, 1820; Mount Pleasant (Ohio) *Genius of Universal Emancipation,* August, 1821.

84 Cresson, *James Monroe,* 347.

to his constituents. He declared that on the evening of March 2, having had no food since morning, he had slipped home to get a bite to eat while Representative Mercer of Virginia was speaking. Before he could return, Mercer fainted, and the voting took place. This explanation did not satisfy everybody. The Hartford *Courant* believed that even if it was true it reflected on Edwards' stamina: "Mark here, Reader: The *fainting* Mercer, like a true son of Virginia, remained at his post, and voted for southern slavery and supremacy; while . . . our representative could not forego one *single meal* to prevent the extension of slavery."[85]

The fourteen Northern congressmen who voted openly with the South on March 2 explained their motives for doing so in public letters and private correspondence. For the most part they seem to have been conscientious in the stand which they took. Some of them regarded the proposed restriction on Missouri as unconstitutional,[86] and all were frightened by the threats of civil war and disunion. Henry Meigs of New York was unwilling to see the North and South ranged against each other in "eternal factions of *Up Town* and *Down Town Boys*."[87] Bernard Smith of New Jersey thought that a compromise was "*necessary* to prevent a dissolution of the Union."[88] In like vein, Mark Hill of Maine wrote that he was "for going as far as any body to restrict Slavery," but only if it could be done "without setting the United States on fire."[89] Henry Baldwin of Pittsburgh was willing to make concessions on the slavery issue in order to secure Southern votes for the tariff and bankruptcy

[85] Hartford *Courant*, March 28, 1820. Strangely enough, although Mercer championed Missouri's right to an unrestricted admission to the Union, he was a lifelong opponent of slavery. For his antislavery views, see Clement Eaton, *Freedom of Thought in the Old South* (Durham, 1940), 261-62.

[86] See Jonathan Mason's letter in Boston *Columbian Centinel*, March 25, 1820; letter from Henry Shaw quoted in Richmond *Enquirer*, May 21, 1819; Samuel A. Foot's letter in New Haven *Columbian Register*, June 10, 1820; and Pittsburgh *Gazette*'s defense of Henry Baldwin, March 16, 1820.

[87] *Annals of Congress*, 16 Cong., 1 Sess., 943.

[88] New Brunswick *Fredonian*, April 20, 1820; Newark *Centinel of Freedom*, May 2, 1820.

[89] Mark L. Hill to William King, January 28, 1820, William King Papers.

bills,[90] while Jonathan Mason of Boston hoped that a conciliatory policy would reconcile the South and West to the payment
of the Massachusetts militia claims. As for Missouri slavery,
Mason pronounced it to be "a question, there is not a Man in
New England cares one farthing about."[91]

All of the "dough faces" were Democrats except Henry
Storrs, who was a Federalist, and Baldwin and Mason, who
were rated as neutral in 1820.[92] One of the chief factors which
won Northern support for the Missouri Compromise in Congress was the fear that the Federalists and New York Clintonians were seeking to make political capital out of slavery
and use it as a lever to create a new alignment of parties based
on geographical distinctions. This was precisely what Rufus
King did have in mind; so the fears of the compromisers were
not groundless.[93] Jonathan Mason recorded his conviction that
the Missouri dispute was "got up entirely, for a political purpose, by De Witt Clinton & the Federalists, to enlist Pennsylvania with New York, in his & their future views of the Government of the Union."[94] Mark Hill of Maine considered it
imperative to settle the question at once, since "Clintonianism,
howsoever remarkable, seems to be the order of the day with
very many." Hill's colleague John Holmes noted that the
people of Maine had shown no interest in Missouri until the
arrival of the circular letters from the New York meeting. He
declared that most of the Maine delegation in Congress had
"been pushed on by Judge Storey & Mr King & by all the in-
trigues of Mr Webster & Mr Hopkinson—The object is to keep
up the excitement." As for himself, Holmes said: "I am not
fully satisfied with the motives of certain leaders who are getting up an excitement *at this time* on this subject."[95]

90 Claude H. Van Tyne (ed.), *The Letters of Daniel Webster* (New York,
1902), 83.

91 Jonathan Mason to William Eustis, January 29, 1820, William Eustis
Papers, Library of Congress; King, *Rufus King*, VI, 274.

92 For the political affiliations of all members of the Sixteenth Congress, see
Washington *Gazette*, December 4, 1819.

93 King, *Rufus King*, VI, 501.

94 Jonathan Mason to William Eustis, January 29, 1820, Eustis Papers.

95 Mark L. Hill to William King, February 9, 1820, John Holmes to King,

Some Northern Democrats were not frightened by the buga-
boo of Federalism and agreed with Representative Edward
Dowse of Massachusetts, a stanch Jeffersonian, that religion,
humanity, and sound policy were the motives back of the attempted restriction on Missouri.[96] There were other Democrats who, although not yet willing to admit Missouri as a slave
state, were becoming increasingly alarmed over rumors of Federalist plots and conspiracies. Senator Jonathan Roberts of
Pennsylvania was typical of that group. In January, 1820,
Roberts was willing to hazard any consequences rather than
consent to the extension of slavery, but at the end of February
he wrote to a friend in Missouri that the ultra-Federalists did
not want to see the controversy settled, and to his friend
Nicholas Biddle he confided that "I cannot hear such men as
Mr King and Mr Hopkinson and Mr Webster talk of keeping
the question open without horror."[97] Joseph Hopkinson and
Daniel Webster, who visited Washington in the winter of 1819-
1820 in connection with their legal practice, aroused suspicions
in Democratic circles by the zeal with which they advocated
slavery restriction. Senator Roberts and his Pennsylvania colleague Walter Lowrie did not vote for the compromise of 1820.
Nevertheless, before the issue was finally laid to rest in 1821,
both of them would be driven into the arms of the compromisers by the fear of a Federalist revival.

An analysis of the vote in Congress reveals the fact that the
compromise of 1820 was supported by a large majority of
Southern senators and a small majority of Southern representatives but was not acceptable to the Northern majority in either
branch of Congress. In this analysis it is not necessary to make
any distinction between the South and Southwest. Though in
many respects the people of the Southwest were more Western

December 25, 1819, February 22, 1820, William King Papers; John Holmes,
Mr. Holmes' Letter to the People of Maine (Washington, 1820), 1.

[96] Quincy, *Josiah Quincy,* 388. See also letter from anonymous Pennsylvania
Democratic congressman in Washington *Gazette,* March 22, 1820.

[97] Jonathan Roberts to John B. C. Lucas, February 27, 1820, John B. C.
Lucas Papers, Missouri Historical Society; Jonathan Roberts to Nicholas Biddle,
January 9, February 27, 1820, Biddle Papers.

than Southern in 1820, their attitude toward slavery was definitely in agreement with the Southern point of view.

In the Senate on February 17 the question of accepting or rejecting the compromise was presented squarely. On that day the vote was taken on ordering the Maine-Missouri bill to be engrossed and read a third time. As the bill embraced all of the compromise measures, a vote for engrossment was a vote for the compromise. The vote by states was recorded thus:[98]

STATE	for	against
New Hampshire	1	1
Vermont		2
Massachusetts		2
Rhode Island	1	1
Connecticut		2
New York		2
New Jersey		2
Pennsylvania		2
Ohio		2
Indiana		2
Illinois	2	
Delaware	2	
Maryland	2	
Virginia	2	
North Carolina	1	1
South Carolina	1	1
Georgia	2	
Kentucky	2	
Tennessee	2	
Alabama	2	
Mississippi	2	
Louisiana	2	
TOTAL	24	20

The vote leaves no doubt about which section of the country favored and which did not favor the compromise of 1820. Only four senators from the free states were willing to vote for the compromise measures as a whole: Edwards and Thomas of

[98] *Annals of Congress,* 16 Cong., 1 Sess., 428.

Illinois, William Hunter of Rhode Island, and John F. Parrott of New Hampshire. It was ironical that Hunter should be a Federalist, while Parrott's vote was dictated by the fear that restriction was a Federalist measure designed to injure the Democrats.[99] The two Southern senators who voted against engrossment were William Smith of South Carolina and Nathaniel Macon of North Carolina. Macon explained in a letter to a friend that nearly all of the leading men of the South were said to favor the compromise but that "to compromise is to acknowledge the right of Congress to interfere and to legislate on the subject, this would be acknowledging too much."[100]

In the Senate the South also indicated its approval of the compromise by voting to incorporate the Thomas proviso in the Maine-Missouri bill (February 17). The proviso, it will be recalled, prohibited slavery forever in the unorganized Louisiana Purchase north of 36° 30'. The vote of the Southern senators on the proviso was:[101]

STATE	for	against
Delaware	2	
Maryland	2	
Virginia		2
North Carolina	1	1
South Carolina		2
Georgia		2
Kentucky	2	
Tennessee	2	
Alabama	2	
Mississippi	1	1
Louisiana	2	
TOTAL	14	8

Again in the Senate on February 28 the South voted against receding from the Thomas proviso:[102]

[99] Brown, *Missouri Compromises*, 12-13.
[100] Nathaniel Macon to Bolling Hall, February 13, 1820, Bolling Hall Papers, Alabama Department of Archives and History.
[101] *Annals of Congress*, 16 Cong., 1 Sess., 428.
[102] *Ibid.*, 457.

STATE	for receding	against receding
Delaware		2
Maryland		2
Virginia	2	
North Carolina	1	1
South Carolina	2	
Georgia	2	
Kentucky		2
Tennessee		2
Alabama		2
Mississippi	1	1
Louisiana		2
TOTAL	8	14

Since the House of Representatives never voted on the compromise as a whole, the willingness of Northern representatives to compromise must be gauged by their vote against the second recommendation of the conference committee, that the antislavery clause be eliminated from the Missouri bill. The vote was:[103]

STATE	for striking out the antislavery clause	for retaining the clause
New Hampshire		6
Vermont		6
Massachusetts	4	16
Rhode Island	1	1
Connecticut	2	4
New York	2	22
New Jersey	3	3
Pennsylvania	2	21
Ohio		6
Indiana		1
Illinois		1
TOTAL	14	87

[103] Ibid., 1586-87.

Thus, by an overwhelming majority, Northern representatives rejected the only concession which the compromise of 1820 required of them.

The willingness of Southern representatives to compromise can only be judged by the vote on the Thomas proviso, the concession which the compromise required of the South:[104]

STATE	for	against
Delaware	1	
Maryland	8	1
Virginia	4	18
North Carolina	6	6
South Carolina	5	4
Georgia	2	4
Kentucky	7	1
Tennessee	4	2
Alabama	1	
Mississippi	1	
Louisiana		1
TOTAL	39	37

By voting 39 to 37 in favor of the Thomas proviso, Southern representatives approved the compromise of 1820. The majority they gave it was a slender one, but even that was in marked contrast with the uncompromising vote of the Northern congressmen.

It has often been said that the compromise of 1820 was a solemn compact between the North and South. From this analysis, however, it is evident that it was merely an agreement between a small majority of the Southern members of Congress and a small minority of the Northern ones.[105] It is true that the compromise was regarded by some, at the time of its adoption, as a compact between the sections. Certainly it was so regarded by John Taylor of Caroline and by *Niles' Reg-*

[104] *Ibid.,* 1587-88.

[105] On this point, see address by Stephen A. Douglas in United States Senate, March 3, 1854. *Appendix to Congressional Globe,* 33 Cong., 1 Sess., 328-31; George F. Milton, *The Eve of Conflict* (Boston, 1934), 136-38.

ister.[106] On the other hand, Representative Joseph Hemphill of Pennsylvania and Rufus King considered it simply an ordinary act of legislation, repealable at the will of Congress.[107]

To Senator Jesse Burgess Thomas of Illinois belonged the distinction of being the author of the compromise of 1820. The idea of settling the Missouri dispute by a compromise can be traced back to the debate over the Arkansas Territory in the Fifteenth Congress. In the Sixteenth Congress proposals looking toward a compromise were made, first and last, by Thomas and Ninian Edwards in the Senate and by John W. Taylor, Henry Storrs, and Samuel A. Foot in the House.[108] Though it would be impossible to determine in whose mind the compromise originated, Thomas introduced it in the Senate in the form in which it was finally adopted.

Thomas was a native of Maryland and a descendant of the Calvert family. In Illinois he was listed as a slaveholder by the census of 1820, and one of his biographers describes him as having "predilections . . . for the south and its people" and as being "invariably in unison with southern statesmen."[109] During the Missouri debates Congressman Whitman of Maine had the mistaken idea that Thomas was not strong in his convictions and might be persuaded to vote for the admission of Maine without Missouri, but a conversation with the Illinois senator

106 Taylor, *Construction Construed*, 295-96; *Niles' Weekly Register*, XVIII (1820), 26; Richmond *Enquirer*, March 7, 1820.

107 *Annals of Congress*, 16 Cong., 1 Sess., 1134; King, *Rufus King*, VI, 288-90.

108 *Annals of Congress*, 16 Cong., 1 Sess., 119, 157-59, 232-33, 732, 940, 947, 1171-72. For an indication that Edwards played an important part in framing the final compromise, see Edwards, *History of Illinois*, 124.

109 J. F. Snyder, "Forgotten Statesmen of Illinois. Hon. Jesse Burgess Thomas," in *Transactions of the Illinois State Historical Society for the Year 1904* (Springfield, 1904), 518. Snyder states that Thomas was not a slaveholder. For evidence to the contrary, see Norton, *Illinois Census Returns 1820*, 153; also, receipts for an indentured servant and a slave purchased by Thomas, August 7, 1813, June 21, 1814, Jesse B. Thomas Papers, Illinois State Historical Library. Some authorities give Shepherdstown, Virginia (now West Virginia) as Thomas' birthplace. Miss Elise S. Billmyer of Shepherdstown, who is descended from Thomas' stepson, thinks that he was born at Hagerstown, Maryland. Miss Billmyer to the author, October 24, 1938.

speedily dispelled any such notion. "I . . . find him," wrote Whitman, "very decidedly against us in this particular."[110]

In the division of the western territory, the Missouri Compromise gave to the North an area many times the size of that allotted to the South. It therefore seems strange that a majority of the Southern members of Congress supported the compromise while the North voted overwhelmingly against it. The general attitude of the Northerners, however, was that they represented the majority section of the nation and did not need to make concessions. Senator Harrison Gray Otis of Massachusetts predicted the passage of the compromise but added that "we ought to have stopped it [slavery extension], in toto—and the sceptre would then have passed from the ancient dominion forever."[111] Congressman William Plumer, Jr., a New Hampshire Democrat, summarized the prevailing attitude of the North in writing his father in February, 1820:

A compromise is much talked of in the Senate & by many in our House—The opponents of restriction see that they are likely not to succeed, & many of them are willing to give up the rest of the territories, if we will allow of Slavery in Missouri & Arcansaw—But in my opinion our true policy is to fight the first battle at the water's edge, & if repulsed there, to make our next stand as near as possible to the former—In other words, I would not yield Missouri, if it can be preserved—& if this is lost, I would still hold Arcansaw & all the rest—[112]

The Southern support of the compromise was based on the assumption that it represented the lesser of two evils. Senator James Barbour of Virginia called it a "proposition . . . which, I believe, unpleasant as it is, will be acceded to, as a lesser evil than either dividing the Union, or throwing it into confusion."[113] The best statement of the South's attitude was given

[110] Ezekiel Whitman to William King, February 24, 1820, William King Papers.
[111] Morison, Harrison Gray Otis, II, 226.
[112] Brown, Missouri Compromises, 6.
[113] Mrs. Chapman Coleman (ed.), The Life of John J. Crittenden (2 vols., Philadelphia, 1871), I, 41.

in a letter that was written by Senator Montfort Stokes of North Carolina to Governor Branch of the same state:

Those who are opposed to this unconstitutional restriction upon the people of Missouri, cannot and do not expect that Missouri will be admitted into the Union without the restriction, unless some concession or agreement shall take place excluding slavery from a portion of the west territory beyond the Mississippi. This is not mere opinion: it has been ascertained by several votes in the House of Representatives that a considerable majority of that body are in favor of restriction as to all the country purchased from France under the name of Louisiana. It is useless to examine at this time whether this is a correct principle or not. . . . All that we from the slave holding states can do at present is to rescue from the rapacious grasp of these consciencious fanatics a considerable portion of Louisiana, including all the settled parts of that extensive country. I can see no means either now or hereafter, of accomplishing this object but by consenting that slavery may be prohibited in the northern portion of the Louisiana purchase.[114]

One reason for the Northern opposition to the compromise was the fact that it gave a large western state to the South, while the territory given to the North, vast though it might be, was still unsettled and would probably be inhabited mainly by Indians for decades to come. Four Maine congressmen complained in an address to their constituents that the land north of 36° 30′ had not yet been purchased from the Indians and that perhaps it was the South's intention that it never should be.[115]

Representative Charles Pinckney of South Carolina added to the North's vexation by writing a letter to a Charleston newspaper in which he hailed the compromise as "a great triumph" for the South, since Missouri, Arkansas, and the Floridas would "give the Southern interest in a short time an addition of six, and perhaps eight, Members in the Senate of the United

[114] Brown, *Missouri Compromises*, 15; Raleigh *Register, and North-Carolina Gazette*, March 17, 1820.

[115] Martin Kinsley, Joshua Cushman, Ezekiel Whitman, and Enoch Lincoln, *An Address to the People of Maine* (Washington, 1820), 13.

States." As for the territory north of 36° 30′, Pinckney asserted that "it is at present of no moment; it is a vast Tract, inhabited only by savages and wild beasts, in which not a foot of the Indian claim to soil is extinguished; and in which, according to the ideas prevalent here at present, no Land Office will be open for a great length of time." After reading Pinckney's letter, the Boston *Centinel* published an editorial entitled *"The Cloven foot uncovered."* This incautious letter, said the *Centinel*, outweighed "a hundred speeches as a fair disclosure of the deep laid plan and anxious desire to establish forever the *ascendency of the slaveholding States*, and to control by means of the Senate the voice of the nation."[116] As a matter of fact, Pinckney was a proslavery extremist who had himself voted against the Thomas proviso, and his letter did not represent the views of a majority of the Southern members of Congress. To understand the attitude of most of the Southerners one should turn rather to the letter of Montfort Stokes, already quoted, or to the sagacious observation of Senator John W. Walker of Alabama, who wrote: "I hope the *Compromise* on the Missouri question gives satisfaction. It was a wise and *necessary* measure—and has saved the Republic."[117]

At this point there is a question which inevitably presents itself. The Missouri Compromise was essentially a bargain: the South got Missouri and Arkansas, and the North received the remainder of the Louisiana Purchase north of 36° 30′. It is generally known that from about 1820 to 1850 most of the region north of 36° 30′ was regarded as an immense waste unfit for human habitation—the "Great American Desert." Did the South favor and the North oppose the compromise because it was thought that the North's share of the compromise was a worthless desert?

The answer to the question is no. Northern opposition to the compromise cannot be accounted for on that basis. It was the western exploration of Stephen H. Long which did more

[116] Charleston *City Gazette And Commercial Daily Advertiser*, March 10, 1820; Boston *Columbian Centinel*, April 1, 1820.
[117] John W. Walker to Charles Tait, April 17, 1820, Tait Papers.

than anything else to create the Great American Desert myth, and Long did not conclude his journey until shortly after the compromise had been adopted.[118] Morever, in all the Missouri debates in Congress, as recorded in the *Annals*, not a single speaker referred to the northern part of the Louisiana Purchase as a desert. On the contrary, speaker after speaker described the whole western country as a fertile area from which numerous states would eventually be formed.[119]

It is true that some people subscribed to the Great American Desert myth even prior to the Missouri Compromise. In petitioning Congress for statehood in 1817, certain citizens of Missouri spoke of the interior of the trans-Mississippi country as being "composed of vast regions of naked and sterile plains, stretching to the Shining [Rocky] Mountains."[120] H. M. Brackenridge, the noted traveler, who contended in a public letter regarding the Missouri question that the country west of Missouri could only support a poor and scattered population, predicted that there would not be more than one tier of states west of the Mississippi for fifty years to come.[121] Similar views were expressed by Amos Kendall's *Argus of Western America*, which relied on the accounts of Lewis and Clark,[122] and by Rufus King. King did not raise this issue in the congressional debate but wrote privately that "One State more may be

[118] Ray A. Billington, *Westward Expansion* (New York, 1949), 452-53; Ralph H. Brown, *Historical Geography of the United States* (New York, 1948), 370-72; Frederic L. Paxson, *History of the American Frontier 1763-1893* (Boston, 1924), 215-16.

[119] Senator Morril of New Hampshire and William Pinkney referred to the existence of deserts somewhere in the West but did not locate them. The word "desert" as used in 1820 did not necessarily mean an uninhabitable region. Representative Hendricks of Indiana spoke with pride of the "deserts" of his section, upon which, he said, industry and agriculture smiled. *Annals of Congress*, 16 Cong., 1 Sess., 136, 402, 1354.

[120] Shoemaker, *Missouri's Struggle for Statehood*, 323.

[121] Philadelphia *Franklin Gazette*, February 4, 1820. Brackenridge had visited the country in question. See his *Views of Louisiana; Together With a Journal of a Voyage up the Missouri River, in 1811* (Pittsburgh, 1814). Zebulon M. Pike, who explored the western plains in 1806, also brought back an unfavorable account of them.

[122] Frankfort (Kentucky) *Argus of Western America*, March 9, 1820.

formed in the course of half a century on the Mississippi & north of the line 36° 30' N. Lat., . . . the country further west is a prairie, resembling the Steppes of Tartary, without wood or water exception the great River and its few branches."[123]

At the same time that the Missouri debates were raging, the Washington *Intelligencer* and St. Louis *Enquirer* were engaged in an interesting discussion on the subject of western deserts. In November, 1819, the *Intelligencer* proposed that new states west of the Mississippi be given narrow fronts on that river and extended inland to the Spanish frontier or to "the interior desart." The *Intelligencer* asserted that states located at any great distance west of the Mississippi and not bordering on the river would be remote and feeble, and it seemed to doubt that the western interior would ever be formed into states. In commenting on these remarks, the St. Louis *Enquirer* asked if the *Intelligencer* knew where the "desart" began. The *Enquirer*, which knew almost everything, did know, of course. It declared that six miles west of Mine a Burton, Missouri, "the inhabitable land gives out, and the naked and arid plains set in," while to the northwest of Missouri, "The *Grand Prairie*, a plain without wood or water, . . . extends . . . further than hunters or travellers have ever yet gone." Even so, the *Enquirer* maintained that many people could live in the valleys of the great rivers which flowed from the Rocky Mountains to the Mississippi and that there was room for twenty-six states west of the Mississippi and east of the Rockies, along the Arkansas, Missouri, Yellow-stone, Platte, Kansas, Red, and St. Pierre [Minnesota] rivers. The *Enquirer*'s reference to naked and arid plains displeased some Missourians. The St. Louis *Gazette* published a letter of refutation which was loud in its praise of the western prairies. The same issue of the *Gazette*, however, contained a refutation of the refutation—a letter from a member of the Yellowstone

[123] King, *Rufus King*, VI, 289. For further unfavorable comments on the trans-Mississippi country, made prior to the passage of the Missouri Compromise, see Boston *New-England Palladium & Commercial Advertiser*, February 4, 1820; Washington *Gazette*, January 22, 1820; Samuel R. Brown, *The Western Gazetteer; or Emigrant's Directory* (Auburn, N. Y., 1817), 189.

Expedition dated November 16, 1819. The writer of the letter stated that he had traveled for twenty or thirty miles on the prairie without finding a drop of water or a bush of wood.[124]

In short, though the myth of the Great American Desert was taking shape at the very moment that Congress was voting on the compromise of 1820, a majority of the congressmen and their constituents were not yet aware of it. There was no reference to it in the thousand pages of Missouri debates recorded in the *Annals of Congress,* nor was it often mentioned in connection with the abuse which was heaped upon the "dough faces" who voted for the compromise. In March, 1820, two of America's best informed newspapers, Theodore Dwight's New York *Advertiser* and Thomas Ritchie's Richmond *Enquirer,* were still anticipating the formation of state after state north of 36° 30'.[125] John C. Spencer, a New York Clintonian leader, characterized the whole area between the Mississippi and the Pacific as one "varying in climates, adapted to the constitutions and habits of the inhabitants of every part of the union, according to the accounts of travellers, rich in a fertile soil, inviting the migration of our posterity, if not of the present generation. This region . . . that fairest portion of the universe."[126] In the press and private correspondence of 1819-1821, such descriptions far outnumbered the references to western deserts.

It is impossible to do justice to all of the arguments advanced for and against slavery restriction during the second congressional debate over Missouri. Much of the argument, being a reiteration of the first debate, will not be discussed here at all, but these points require special attention: (1) the constitu-

124 For the newspaper discussion of deserts, see Washington *Daily National Intelligencer,* November 5, 1819; St. Louis *Enquirer,* December 1, 1819; St. Louis *Gazette & Public Advertiser,* January 19, 1820.

125 New York *Daily Advertiser,* March 7, 1820; Richmond *Enquirer,* February 10, March 7, 1820.

126 New York *Columbian,* January 20, 1820; Albany *Argus,* January 21, 1820. See also Andrew Miller, *New States and Territories, . . . in 1818* (n.p., n.d.), 25-26.

tionality of slavery restriction, (2) the question of slavery per se, and (3) the political significance of the Missouri Controversy.

The question of a liberal versus a strict construction of the Constitution was much discussed in the second Missouri debate. Though it cannot be said that all Southerners advocated a strict construction and all Northerners a loose one, there was certainly a tendency in that direction. From 1801 to 1819, with their own party in power and Virginians holding the presidency, Southern congressmen had shown a more nationalistic viewpoint than formerly. The Missouri Controversy sent them scampering back to the old strict constructionist, state rights standard. They now contended that Congress could not prohibit slavery in a new state unless specifically empowered to do so by the Constitution, and many of them seemed to think that they were fighting a holy battle to save the Constitution.[127]

While for the most part expressing respect for the rights of the states, Northern congressmen were forced, by their advocacy of restriction in Missouri, to favor a liberal constitutional interpretation. If there were doubt about whether or not a certain power had been conferred on the federal government, it should be assumed that it had been, said Representative Joshua Cushman of Massachusetts.[128] It even was claimed that Congress might abolish slavery in Missouri under the general welfare clause of the Constitution—a proposition which led Representative Christopher Rankin of Mississippi to remark that Caesar, Napoleon, and Cromwell all had justified their usurpations on the ground that they were required by the general welfare.[129]

"State rights are in danger" was proclaimed so lustily by the South that Ezra Gross of New York was reminded of the Eng-

[127] "I could not help wishing to be again in the midst of you, & to have had some humble share in the great battle you have fought for the Constitution." John J. Crittenden to James Barbour, April 3, 1820, James Barbour Papers, New York Public Library.

[128] *Annals of Congress*, 16 Cong., 1 Sess., 1297.

[129] *Ibid.*, 970-71, 1077, 1093, 1342.

lish cry, "the church is in danger."[130] Southerners stressed the great importance of the powers which had been reserved to the states, speaker after speaker quoting the tenth amendment on this point. John Scott of Missouri regarded the Union as a confederation or "alliance, offensive and defensive," between sovereign states, while James Pindall of Virginia called the Constitution "a national, or rather international compact" between the states themselves and between the states and the central government.[131]

The most forceful exposition of the state rights argument was that given by William Pinkney in his address of February 15, 1820. Pinkney discussed the constitutional provision that "New States may be admitted by the Congress into this Union." Conceding for the sake of argument that the congressional power of admission was discretionary and that Congress could refuse to admit Missouri, he still denied that conditions could be attached to its admission, since the power to refuse did not necessarily imply the existence of a power to exact terms. The power which Congress possessed in this instance was simply that of admitting a state "into this Union." Pinkney asked dramatically: "What is that Union?" He answered: "A confederation of States equal in sovereignty, capable of everything which the Constitution does not forbid, or authorize Congress to forbid. It is an equal Union between parties equally sovereign." No state, insisted Pinkney, could be deprived of powers exercised by the other states. For if a new state should come into the Union "shorn of its beams—crippled and disparaged beyond the original States, it is not into the original Union that it comes . . . it is a different sort of Union. The first was Union *inter pares:* This is a Union between *disparates,* between giants and a dwarf, between power and feebleness, between full proportioned sovereignties and a miserable image of power—a thing which that very Union has shrunk and shrivelled from its just size, instead of preserving it in its true dimensions."[132]

130 *Ibid.,* 1253.   131 *Ibid.,* 1265, 1495.
132 *Ibid.,* 397. Pinkney's phraseology closely resembled that used by the

The force of precedent was one of the most powerful arguments in favor of the constitutionality of Missouri slavery restriction. Of course, the principal precedent relied on was the Ordinance of 1787—"the immortal ordinance," as Northerners loved to call it.[133] Under the terms of this law, slavery was prohibited forever in the Old Northwest by a "compact" between the original states and the people and states of the Northwest Territory. The ordinance was originally enacted by the Continental Congress and was affirmed by the new Congress after the adoption of the Constitution.

The South denied on various grounds that the Ordinance of 1787 was a suitable precedent for interfering with slavery in the proposed state of Missouri. Congressman Pindall of Virginia maintained that the antislavery clause of the ordinance was meant to apply to the Old Northwest only during its territorial status, not after it was carved into states. Others declared that the ordinance was of illegal origin. John Scott derided the idea that there was a binding compact between the federal government and the people or states of the Northwest. There were in 1787 no states and few people in the Northwest with whom to make a compact, said Scott. Congress had therefore made "a compact with the mountains, the woods, and the lakes, who were personified and made to consent for inhabitants yet to come."[134] Northerners argued that however dubious might have been the origin of the ordinance, it yet afforded a precedent for excluding slavery from Missouri,

---

United States Supreme Court in the case of Coyle *v*. Oklahoma, when the Court held that " 'This Union' was and is a union of States, equal in power, dignity and authority, each competent to exert that residuum of sovereignty not delegated to the United States by the Constitution itself." The congressional enabling act of 1906 for the admission of Oklahoma placed the new state under certain restrictions in locating its seat of government, but the Court ruled that these were not binding after admission since they had the effect of changing the Union into one of unequal members. 221 *U. S.* 559 (1911). "The Supreme Court has repeatedly upheld the correctness of Pinkney's contention." Homer C. Hockett, *The Constitutional History of the United States* (2 vols., New York, 1939), II, 150.

[133] *Annals of Congress*, 16 Cong., 1 Sess., 243.
[134] *Ibid.*, 164, 293, 322, 1029, 1222, 1282-87, 1506.

since the mere fact that it had been acquiesced in universally for years almost gave it the character of legality. The South held, on the other hand, that Ohio, Indiana, and Illinois, after admission to the Union, were no longer bound by the anti-slavery clause of the ordinance and might become slave states if they so desired.[135]

Although a majority of the Southern members of Congress supported the Missouri Compromise of 1820, which forever prohibited slavery in the unorganized Louisiana Purchase north of 36° 30', many Southerners considered the word "forever" to be applicable only to territories and not to future states. This, according to William Lowndes and Louis McLane, was the correct interpretation of the compromise, though McLane pointed out that if slavery had been prohibited during the territorial stage, new states would have no reason for establishing it.[136]

The only constitutional concession that any Southern congressmen were willing to make was that Congress possessed the right to prohibit slavery in a territory. Apparently almost half of them were unwilling to concede even this as a matter of principle, although somewhat more than half would vote for it in the form of a "hoss trade" compromise. Charles Pinckney of South Carolina denied emphatically that Congress could exclude slavery from a territory. To do so, he said, would ultimately have the same result as abolishing it in a new state, since states formed from free territory were certain to be free also. William Lowndes thought Congress might prohibit sla-

[135] This position was later upheld by the Supreme Court. In the case of Escanaba Company v. Chicago, the Court declared that Illinois, after it became a state, could no longer be controlled by the provisions of the ordinance. 107 U. S. 678 (1883).

[136] *Annals of Congress*, 16 Cong., 1 Sess., 1111, 1167. Joseph Hemphill of Pennsylvania and Rufus King stated that the South would not consider the compromise binding on future states north of 36° 30'. *Ibid.*, 1134; King, *Rufus King*, VI, 290. *Niles' Register* was of the opinion that the compromise was as applicable to future states as to territories, but the Richmond *Enquirer* and Washington *Intelligencer* expressed uncertainty about how that part of the compromise should be interpreted. *Niles' Weekly Register*, XVIII (1820), 26; Washington *Daily National Intelligencer*, February 29, 1820; Richmond *Enquirer*, March 7, 1820.

very in unsettled but not in settled territories, while John Tyler of Virginia anticipated the Dred Scott case by arguing that it would be unconstitutional to forbid slavery even in an unsettled territory.[137]

The principle of popular (squatter) sovereignty or local self-government was the keystone of the South's entire constitutional defense system in 1819-1821. A South Carolina congressman wrote plaintively to a Northern newspaper that the South and West had never meddled in the municipal affairs of the Northern states, that "All *they* wish is to be let alone in the enjoyment of their own rights. *They* would disdain to legislate, not alone against the Constitution, but against the private rights, interests, and feelings of any Northern or Eastern *State or Territory*."[138] It was argued also that mankind had an "eternal and indefeasible right to self-government," that every ten square miles in the United States was "as competent as the whole collected wisdom of the nation to frame a constitution," and that, in accordance with the spirit of the federal Constitution and Declaration of Independence, every territory which contained the requisite population was entitled to statehood on equal terms with the other states.[139] Obviously these doctrines, if carried to their logical conclusion, would have precluded congressional interference with slavery in the territories as well as the states. The compromise of 1820 represented an attempt to solve the slavery question on the basis of popular sovereignty, since it permitted the Missourians to frame a constitution of their own choosing and prohibited slavery in an unsettled territory where there were few squatters to contest the decision of Congress.[140]

When the passage of the compromise tossed the responsibility for its constitutionality into the lap of President Monroe,

[137] *Annals of Congress*, 16 Cong., 1 Sess., 1326-27, 1391, 1481.
[138] Hartford *American Mercury*, March 7, 1820.
[139] *Annals of Congress*, 16 Cong., 1 Sess., 321, 355, 1073, 1525.
[140] William O. Lynch, "The Influence of Population Movements on Missouri Before 1861," in *Missouri Historical Review*, XVI (1922), 507. For a discussion of the Southern concept of local self-government, see Carpenter, *The South as a Conscious Minority*, 34-76.

he sought the advice of his cabinet members, asking them if Congress had the right to prohibit slavery in a territory and if the eighth section of the Missouri bill, interdicting slavery forever in the area north of 36° 30', applied to future states that might be formed there. According to John Quincy Adams, who was Secretary of State at the time, Monroe and all the cabinet agreed that Congress could prohibit slavery in a territory.[141] Neither Crawford, Calhoun, nor Wirt, however, could find any express power to that effect in the Constitution, and Wirt was strongly opposed to the use of implied powers. In interpreting the eighth section of the Missouri bill, all the cabinet except Adams decided that the word "forever" applied only to the territorial period.[142]

Another point of argument concerned slavery itself. Northern orators in the second Missouri debate laid great stress on the moral iniquity of slavery. Timothy Fuller of Massachusetts declared that the right to hold human beings in perpetual bondage was found only in barbarian and despotic codes. Jonathan Roberts of Pennsylvania asked where Southerners had derived their claim to be owners and masters. He answered: "From the violence of savage warfare; from the frauds and crimes of the man-stealer."[143]

Most Southern members of Congress conceded that slavery in itself was wrong. John Tyler called it a dark cloud.[144] Robert Reid of Georgia compared the South to a man with a cancer. "For my own part," said Reid, "surrounded by slavery from my cradle to the present moment, I yet

'Hate the touch of servile hands;
'I loathe the slaves who cringe around.' "[145]

141 Former President Madison was inclined to disagree with Monroe on this point. Madison to Monroe, February 23, 1820, Monroe Papers, Library of Congress.

142 For the discussion in the cabinet, see Adams, *Memoirs of J. Q. Adams*, V, 4-9, 14-15. For the written opinions given Monroe by the cabinet members regarding the compromise, see Ford, *Writings of J. Q. Adams*, VII, 1-2.

143 *Annals of Congress*, 16 Cong., 1 Sess., 344, 1474.

144 *Ibid.*, 1391.   145 *Ibid.*, 1025.

John Randolph was quoted as saying that all the misfortunes of his life were light in the balance when weighed against the single misfortune of being a slaveholder.[146] George Tucker of Virginia deplored any federal intervention in the affairs of Missouri but believed that it would probably be wise for the Missourians to take state action against slavery.[117]

While in general Southern congressmen stressed the impossibility of emancipation but declined to defend the "peculiar institution" as a positive good, there was a militant minority which undertook the latter task. Senator Freeman Walker of Georgia and Nathaniel Macon assured their colleagues that slaves were kindly treated, cheerful, apparently happy, and better cared for in old age than any poor in the world.[148] The most spirited defense of Negro servitude came from two South Carolinians, Senator William Smith and Representative Charles Pinckney.

Smith argued that it had always been the lot of men to serve one another. Ever since the flood, slavery had existed in all countries. Even Athens, seat of the Muses, possessed slaves. Smith could not agree with the passage in Jefferson's *Notes on Virginia* which Northerners were so fond of quoting that "The whole commerce between master and slave is a perpetual exercise of the most boisterous passions." Instead he felt that the whole commerce between master and slave was patriarchal. As for Jefferson's *Notes*, they had been written nearly forty years before, being "the effusions of the speculative philosophy of his young and ardent mind, and which his riper years have corrected." Smith went on to say that the chosen people of God were slaves and that slaveholding was sanctioned by Christ and the holy fathers.[149] Charles Pinckney denied Northern assertions that slavery was contrary to the will of God,

---

[146] *Ibid.*, 1429.   [147] *Ibid.*, 1531.   [148] *Ibid.*, 173, 226.

[149] *Ibid.*, 266-75; Thomas Jefferson, *Notes on the State of Virginia* (Philadelphia, 1788), 172. Southerners who were embarrassed by Jefferson's condemnation of slavery found consolation in quoting General Moultrie's account of the joyful greeting he received from his slaves when he returned to his South Carolina plantation during the Revolutionary War. William Moultrie, *Memoirs of the American Revolution* (2 vols., New York, 1802), II, 355-56.

declaring that there were hundreds of statements in the Old and New Testaments recognizing its existence and none which censured or forbade it. Of the slave's condition, Pinckney said: "The great body of slaves are happier in their present situation than they could be in any other, and the man or men who would attempt to give them freedom, would be their greatest enemies."[150]

Most of the Southern press and politicians were not yet ready to regard slavery as a blessing in 1820, though the addresses of Smith and Pinckney foreshadowed the proslavery argument of 1830-1860.

The political significance of the Missouri bill was apparent in congressional oratory. Like the first debate, the second one disclosed the fact that it was, in part, a struggle for political power between the North and South. This involved both the balance of power in the Senate and the three-fifths ratio.

When the Constitution was framed, there had been seven Northern and, counting Delaware, six Southern states. At the time the Tallmadge amendment was introduced, there were eleven free and ten slaveholding states, but the admission of Alabama in 1819 gave each section eleven states. Although the desire to maintain a balance of power between the North and South can be traced back to the Continental Congress, it was greatly intensified by the Missouri Controversy. When it became evident that only the Senate was preventing congressional action against Missouri slavery, the South evinced a great determination to maintain an equilibrium in the Senate, while the North was eager to win back the majority it had lost with the admission of Alabama.

According to Representative John Holmes, Southern congressmen were saying to the North: "We have yet a hope in the Senate of the United States—We will not let go this hope by adding another nonslaveholding state which will give you the preponderance and enable Congress to let loose our slaves to cut our throats." Holmes concluded that "The House therefore will not let in Missouri and the Senate will not let in a

150 *Annals of Congress*, 16 Cong., 1 Sess., 1323-25.

nonslaveholding state without a counterbalance."[151] Rufus King complained that Missouri's admission as a slave state would overturn the balance in favor of the South, and former Senator Lacock of Pennsylvania observed that "the possession of the western domain by either the one or the other [slave or free states] is expected to give them a lasting ascendancy in the government."[152] "It is political power that the northern folks are in pursuit of," wrote former Senator Tait of Alabama, who expressed a hope that the South and West "united, with a division of the North, may still keep the power with us."[153] John Quincy Adams aptly remarked that the political power motive operated about equally on both sides.[154]

The three-fifths ratio of slave representation was clearly a major issue in the second Missouri debate, being harped upon by Northern Democrats as well as Federalists. Senator David Morril of New Hampshire feared that if the principle of slave representation was extended into the vast area beyond the Mississippi, the Eastern states would be reduced to insignificance within twenty years in both branches of the government. Morril asked: "Why should Missouri come into the Union with this superior political power? What claim has she to these superabundant political rights?" John Sergeant of Pennsylvania was afraid that the free states would be ruined if the fifty thousand slaves in Louisiana were allowed to "blacken the country from the Mississippi to the Pacific." He said: "For every five slaves there are three votes, and the time may come when the voice of the slaves, in the councils of the nation will be louder than that of the freeman." Jonathan Roberts of Pennsylvania declared that the further expansion of slavery would inure to the benefit of "the slaveholding interest, pecuniarily and politically. The scale of political power will preponderate in favor of the slaveholding States. The effect of

---

[151] John Holmes to William King, February 23, 1820, William King Papers.

[152] *Annals of Congress*, 16 Cong., 1 Sess., 382-83; Abner Lacock to James Monroe, January 30, 1820, Monroe Papers, Library of Congress.

[153] Charles Tait to John W. Walker, January 5, 1820; Tait to Thomas W. Cobb, February 29, 1820, Walker Papers.

[154] Adams, *Memoirs of J. Q. Adams*, V, 15.

such an event is hardly problematical." James Burrill of Rhode Island stated that "if we proceed far, as we are going on, in a short period the slave representation must have a very controlling influence in our Government."[155]

It is said that the Missouri Controversy was the first occasion on which the South ever defended slave representation in Congress.[156] It now rested its defense on numerous grounds, arguing that representation for slaves was as reasonable as that for females and minors, who also had no political rights; that a Southern slave was more productive and hence more valuable to the federal government than the average Northern inhabitant; and that the South's share of direct taxes and imposts was greater than the North's. Furthermore, Nathaniel Macon hinted that it would be unwise of the North to insist on emancipation, for only three fifths of the slaves were represented, but if emancipated they would all be counted as part of the population.[157]

Thus, until it was finally concluded by the compromise of 1820, did the second Missouri debate rock along amid interminable discussions of constitutional and moral principles. The length and acrimoniousness of the debate became discouraging to the participants, who would have been still more despondent if they had known that even the compromise would not effect a permanent settlement of this vexatious issue.

[155] *Annals of Congress*, 16 Cong., 1 Sess., 153, 217, 337, 964-66, 1205, 1438.
[156] Simpson, "Significance of Slave Representation," 340-41.
[157] *Annals of Congress*, 16 Cong., 1 Sess., 229, 356-57, 1311-15, 1537.

"It was a federal movement. . . . When this . . . was perceived the Northern democracy became alarmed, and only wanted a turn or abatement in the popular feeling at home, to take the first opportunity to get rid of the question by admitting the State, and reestablishing party lines upon the basis of political principle."—THOMAS HART BENTON[1]

CHAPTER V

THE ISSUE IS REJOINED AND FINALLY LAID TO REST

*A*CCORDING TO nearly every historian who has written on the subject, the compromise of 1820 would have effected a permanent settlement of the Missouri Controversy if the Missourians had not attempted to insert in their constitution a provision which prevented free Negroes and mulattoes from immigrating to the new state. Actually, it was not the Missourians but the slavery restrictionists who first revived the controversy after the passage of the compromise, and this they did long before the meeting of the Missouri constitutional convention and before any issue relating to free Negroes and mulattoes had arisen. The leadership in the revival of the controversy was assumed by the same general group (though not in all cases the same individuals) which had organized the antislavery meetings in the fall of 1819—the Federalist and Clintonian philanthropists and politicians of the Middle states.

The compromise of 1820 admitted Maine to statehood on March 15, 1820, but did not specifically admit Missouri. It merely authorized the Missourians to form a constitution and state government, without requiring them to prohibit slavery.

It further provided that Missouri's constitution should be republican and not repugnant to the federal Constitution and that "the said State, when formed, shall be admitted into the Union, upon an equal footing with the original States, in all respects whatsoever."[2] This meant, it was generally assumed, that Missouri would draw up a constitution which sanctioned slavery and that Congress would perfunctorily accept it. Nevertheless, if recent precedent were adhered to, Missouri could not actually enter the Union until its constitution had been approved by both houses of Congress.

On March 21, less than three weeks after the adoption of the compromise of 1820, Representatives James Kelton and Abraham Baily of Chester County introduced resolutions in the lower house of the Pennsylvania legislature deploring the outcome of the Missouri question and requesting the Pennsylvania delegation in the next session of Congress to vote against the final admission of Missouri except on condition that its slave population should be gradually freed. While these resolutions were not approved by the legislature,[3] they did suggest a new line of attack to the antislavery diehards. They were promptly published by Theodore Dwight's New York *Advertiser* with the comment that "there is one chance left to wipe off the deep stain which was fixed upon our national character, by the vote on the Missouri bill. We hope this chance will not be lost." Similar views were expressed by anonymous writers in the Philadelphia *Aurora* and *Poulson's Advertiser* who pointed out that the question of whether Missouri's constitution was republican would arise when Congress met again and that it could be rejected as antirepublican if it tolerated slavery.[4]

[1] *Thirty Years' View*, I, 10.

[2] *Annals of Congress*, 16 Cong., 1 Sess., *Appendix*, 2555-59.

[3] By a vote of 81 to 10, the House decided to postpone the resolutions for the present and commend them to the attention of the next legislature, which would meet in December, 1820. Pennsylvania *House Journal*, 1819-1820, pp. 989-90, 1013-15.

[4] New York *Daily Advertiser*, March 28, 1820; Philadelphia *Aurora*, March 25, 1820; *Poulson's American Daily Advertiser* (Philadelphia), March 23, April 17, 1820.

On April 13 the New York *Advertiser* restated its hope that Missouri would not be permitted to sanction slavery. It declared that should the Senate be evenly divided on the question, the Vice-President would cast the deciding vote. For that reason it urged Northerners to elect a Northern man for Vice-President in 1820. On the same day that the *Advertiser* delivered itself of these sentiments, a meeting of the Pennsylvania Society for Promoting the Abolition of Slavery suggested that Missouri might voluntarily prohibit slavery. "If this hope shall fail," said the Society, "another remains. It will rest with the legislature of the United States, whether they will receive into their bosom a new member, who has neglected or disclaimed the opportunity and the honour of approaching the Union with a constitution truly republican."[5]

One of those who strove hardest to keep the Missouri Controversy alive was Robert Walsh, Jr., of Philadelphia, a gifted writer of Irish and Quaker descent and an ardent Federalist. Walsh had published a widely read pamphlet on the Missouri question in 1819,[6] and shortly after the enactment of the compromise he became editor of a new antislavery newspaper, the Philadelphia *National Gazette and Literary Register*. A group of gentlemen headed by Roberts Vaux, a prominent lawyer, philanthropist, Quaker, and Federalist, induced Walsh and William Fry, the bookseller, to form a partnership for the publication of the *Gazette*, whose first number appeared on April 5, 1820. It was believed that the dispute over Missouri had shown the need for such a newspaper in Philadelphia.[7]

The first issues of the *Gazette* devoted so much space to the Missouri question that the South became frightened, and the Richmond *Enquirer* warned Walsh and Theodore Dwight not to "sport upon the very edge of the barrel of gunpowder with the torch in their hands."[8] The *Gazette* contended that the

[5] *Poulson's American Daily Advertiser* (Philadelphia), April 28, 1820.
[6] *Free Remarks on the Spirit of the Federal Constitution* (Philadelphia, 1819).
[7] Ellis P. Oberholtzer, *The Literary History of Philadelphia* (Philadelphia, 1906), 193.
[8] Richmond *Enquirer*, April 18, 1820.

compromise was so unacceptable that it was, in itself, a strong incitement to a renewal of the controversy. It then went on to say that "The nature of the case is, moreover, such, that the next Congress cannot admit in its predecessor, a moral or constitutional competency to effect or allow the issue which is prematurely declared to be determined." The *Gazette* managed to find one saving loophole in that clause of the compromise which stipulated that Missouri's constitution should not be repugnant to the federal Constitution. It asked whether this did "not leave the whole question open, and raise a certain barrier to her [Missouri's] admission into the Union, until she has herself prescribed a definite term to the hideous institution which she can abolish, confessedly without danger to her safety or prosperity."[9]

An interesting side light on Walsh is the fact that he once wrote a book to defend America against the criticisms and attacks which were being directed against it by the British. In such an undertaking, of course, Walsh found it necessary to defend that American institution which British critics were most fond of harping upon—Southern slavery. He did not defend it in the abstract but by comparison with the same institution in other countries and as a necessary evil. Thus his argument was similar to that later used by Southerners to justify slavery in Missouri. A clever Southerner remarked that "to every thing advanced against the Southern States, upon the doctrines of abolition and emancipation, in the newspaper called the *National Gazette, will be found an answer* in the production of the same author, called '*an appeal*' [*An Appeal from the Judgments of Great Britain Respecting the United States of America*]."[10]

[9] Philadelphia *National Gazette and Literary Register*, April 5, 1820. See also Sister Mary F. Lochemes, *Robert Walsh: His Story* (New York, 1941), 107-17. Walsh wrote to Rufus King on December 1, 1820, that "The strongest objection against the Missouri Constitution is not the exclusion of free negroes, but the perpetuation of slavery." Rufus King Papers, New-York Historical Society.

[10] Charleston *Southern Patriot, And Commercial Advertiser*, January 16, 1821.

While Walsh and Fry were founding the Philadelphia *Gazette*, Baptist Irvine was attempting to establish an anti-slavery newspaper in Washington. Irvine was an Irishman who was characterized by John Quincy Adams as "one of the men with whom this age abounds—a fanatic of liberty for the whole human race—honest, but with a brain always in a snarl."[11] In a circular addressed to certain members of Congress regarding his proposed newpaper, Irvine denounced the Northern congressmen who voted with the South on the Missouri question, as well as the newspapers which "cheered the perpetrators with *mercenary* applause." He declared that honest newspapers were needed to prevent similar occurrences and that half a dozen such presses (possibly one) could have changed the outcome of the vote on Missouri. He concluded that *"long possession of power* by any section of the confederacy generates a *tone of arrogance"* and that Southern insolence *"must be curbed,* or the *north* must *passively* receive law from the *south.*"[12] Irvine's plans for setting up a new newspaper in Washington did not materialize, though he did become one of the editors of the Washington *Gazette.*

In May, 1820, an influential Democratic newspaper in Ohio joined the chorus of those who were seeking to reopen the Missouri dispute—the Steubenville *Western Herald*, published by James Wilson, grandfather of Woodrow Wilson. Editor Wilson noted hopefully that the next session of Congress could refuse to admit Missouri if its constitution permitted slavery. Congress, he said, must guarantee a republican form of government to every state, "and no slave holder can have the presumption to say, that any kind of government can be republican, under which one portion of the people can be held as slaves to the other portion. The constitution of Missouri cannot be valid without the assent of Congress—the friends of freedom have yet another chance—may they know how to use it."[13]

11 Adams, *Memoirs of J. Q. Adams,* IV, 444.
12 New York *National Advocate,* June 1, 1820.
13 Steubenville *Western Herald,* May 27, 1820.

By June, the news of the revival of the Missouri Controversy had reached William Dillwyn, Samuel Emlen's father-in-law, in England. Dillwyn wrote to Emlen to express his pleasure at the turn of events. Emlen himself hoped that the admission of Missouri could be staved off until the meeting of the Seventeenth Congress in 1821, when the antislavery forces might be stronger than in the Fifteenth and Sixteenth Congresses.[14]

In short, Dwight, Walsh, Wilson, Emlen, and others were attempting to do in 1820 what the South and its Northern allies actually did do thirty-four years later—repeal the Missouri Compromise. Certainly the refusal to admit Missouri as a slave state would have repealed the spirit, if not the letter, of the compromise and would probably have been as disastrous to the cause of sectional harmony as the Kansas-Nebraska Act was in 1854. The charge, however, which was made against such men as Dwight and Walsh by some of their contemporaries—that they were acting in violation of a solemn compact between the sections[15]—was obviously untrue. As has been shown, the parties to the Missouri compact, if the compromise could be called a compact, were the moderate men of the North and South. Since the antislavery extremists had never endorsed the compromise, they were under no moral obligation to regard it as a sacred and irrepealable statute.

In their efforts to keep the issue of Missouri slavery before the public, Dwight and his associates were aided by a series of unexpected events that played into their hands. In the first place, Missouri held a convention in the summer of 1820 to frame a state constitution, and some of the candidates for the convention were antislavery men who had opposed congressional interference with slavery but favored state action against its further introduction. Many Northerners who had the er-

---

[14] William Dillwyn to Samuel Emlen, Higham Lodge, England, June 20, 1820, William Dillwyn, Samuel Emlen, and Susanna Emlen Papers, Ridgway Branch Library, Philadelphia; Samuel Emlen to Roberts Vaux, February 19, 1821, Vaux Papers.

[15] [Mathew Carey?], *Considerations on the Impropriety and Inexpediency of Renewing the Missouri Question. By a Pennsylvanian* (Philadelphia, 1820), 41-42.

roneous impression that the antislavery ticket would be victorious in Missouri[16] were greatly angered by the news of its overwhelming defeat. Then, when the constitution was framed and published, it was found to contain two clauses which were especially obnoxious to the North. One clause made it illegal for free Negroes and mulattoes to enter Missouri. Another forbade the legislature to emancipate slaves without the consent of their owners.

Free Negroes and mulattoes were citizens in some of the states, and the federal Constitution provides that "The citizens of each State shall be entitled to all privileges and immunities of citizens in the several States." While Missouri's free Negro and mulatto clause was thus clearly unconstitutional, it must be said in justification of the Missourians that a number of other states had similar laws on the subject and that free Negro immigration was regarded with dread and abhorrence by a large part of the nation at this time.[17] The Anti-Missourianism of James Wilson's *Western Herald* had not prevented it from suggesting in 1819 that Ohio take steps to prevent the immigration of free Negroes from the South to its soil. Failing to do this, said Wilson, Ohio might as well erect a new penitentiary and, after the manner of Hamilton County, establish a judicial circuit in the middle of every Negro settlement.[18] The Clintonian press of New York censured Missouri's constitution, but a year before, one of its organs, the *Columbian*, sympathized with Ohioans who did not wish to receive certain liberated Negroes from Virginia. The people of Ohio, said the *Columbian*, were merely denying "the right of any state or individual to force an ignorant and depraved population upon them."[19]

[16] New York *Columbian*, May 10, 1820; Boston *Daily Advertiser*, May 20, 1820; Hartford *American Mercury*, May 23, 1820; Portland *Gazette*, May 30, 1820; Detroit *Gazette*, June 9, 1820.

[17] John H. Russell, *The Free Negro in Virginia 1619-1865* (Baltimore, 1913), 71-72; John C. Hurd, *The Law of Freedom and Bondage in the United States* (2 vols., Boston, 1858-1862), II, 77-78, 97, 117-18, 145-46; Franklin, *From Slavery to Freedom*, 231.

[18] Steubenville (Ohio) *Western Herald*, July 3, 1819.

[19] New York *Columbian*, July 17, 1819.

The Dwights, Walshes, Wilsons, and others were themselves partly responsible for that provision in the Missouri constitution which forbade the legislature to emancipate slaves without securing the consent of the owners or giving them full compensation. Thomas Hart Benton afterward claimed the credit for inserting this clause in the constitution, and his newspaper, the St. Louis *Enquirer*, predicted as early as May 3 that the constitution would contain such a clause as a result of "foreign interference in our affairs." Throughout the Missouri Controversy some Northerners were hopeful of delaying the admission of Missouri until the proslavery party there could be swamped, as they assumed it inevitably would be, by antislavery immigrants from the North.[20] Taking cognizance of this fact and of the continued agitation of the slavery question by Theodore Dwight and others, the *Enquirer* concluded that a constitutional provision guaranteeing slavery irrevocably in Missouri (rather than simply permitting its existence) would be the only means of preventing the state from being converted "into the most dreadful theatre of intrigue, bribery and corruption that ever was witnessed."[21] In other words, the *Enquirer* was determined that there should be no "Bleeding Missouri" in American history, that Missouri should not suffer the unenviable fate which later befell Kansas when uncertainty as to its future status turned it into a battlefield where Northern and Southern immigrants fought for supremacy.

The constitution of Missouri was vigorously denounced by the antislavery press of the Eastern and Middle states, with William Leete Stone, editor of the New York *Commercial Advertiser*, taking the role of chief critic. Stone was a Federalist who feared the political power of the South and an aristocrat who detested the white Northern proletarians who voted for Southern Democratic Presidents. (He was opposed to universal suffrage. "I am no Jacobin—no democrat," he said; "I hate the mob."[22]) Like so many Federalist aristocrats, he had a

20 *Ibid.*, February 19, 1820; Brown, *Missouri Compromises*, 32-33.
21 St. Louis *Enquirer*, June 14, 1820; Benton, *Thirty Years' View*, I, 8-9.
22 Fox, *Decline of Aristocracy in New York*, 429.

kindly feeling for racial minorities, which prompted him to serve as a delegate to antislavery conventions and to write biographies of the Indian chiefs Brant, Uncas, and Red Jacket. Though a controversialist in politics, he was amiable in private life and warmly sympathetic to all things religious and charitable.[23] Such a man was well qualified to carry the banner of Anti-Missourianism, and carry it he did, at this stage of the game, with gusto.

Even before Missouri's constitutional convention had completed its work and approved the new constitution, the *Commercial Advertiser* expressed a hope that the Missouri question would come up again at the next session of Congress and that "firmness enough will be found in the representatives from the northern, or free states, to contest every inch of ground, and if possible, reverse the unfortunate decision of the last session." When the Richmond *Enquirer* asked emphatically: "Will this *Missouri Question* never terminate? Shall we never hear the last of it?" Stone replied: "No, Mr. Enquirer, it will not 'terminate' very soon. You will not soon 'hear the last of it'—never, we hope, until Missouri is forced to adopt a *republican* form of government, in the pure and uncorrupted meaning of the term." An article in the Baltimore *Federal Republican* asserted that a refusal to admit Missouri would violate the compromise of 1820, which was an implied compact, and hence would constitute "a fraud in legislation." Stone answered this contention with prophetic foresight: "We suspect that in less than fifty years, if Missouri is suffered to retain the constitution she has made, in its present shape, that part of the 'compromise' which restricts slavery to 36 degrees 30 minutes north latitude will be altered, amended, or repealed, as shall best suit the views, interests, and ambition of the same class of men who triumphed over the free and hardy sons of the north, at the last session. Nor in this case should we hear a whisper about 'legislative fraud' from the south."[24]

[23] Samuel G. Goodrich, *Recollections of a Lifetime* (2 vols., New York, 1856), II, 109.
[24] New York *Commercial Advertiser*, July 13, September 5, October 16, 1820.

In September the *Commercial Advertiser* published five essays to prove that Missouri should not be granted statehood with the constitution which it had drawn up. Most of the essays were concerned with slavery and emancipation, though the free Negro and mulatto issue was also discussed. In October Stone reported that a memorial to Congress, protesting against the adoption of the constitution of Missouri in its existing form, was being prepared and would be signed by a large proportion of the young men of New York City. He recommended that the young men of other states imitate the example of New York and suggested that public meetings be called in all the cities and towns of the North to consider the subject. As for the changes which ought to be made in Missouri's constitution, Stone was specific. Let Congress say to the Missourians: *"You shall never enter the pale of the American Union, unless you turn your face against slavery, and enter as a free state."*[25]

Between the adjournment of the Missouri constitutional convention in July and the opening of the second session of the Sixteenth Congress on November 13, 1820, it became increasingly evident that the Missouri Controversy was to be fought all over again, although it would have been difficult to predict on what ground the restrictionists would make their main stand. An anonymous pamphlet published in Connecticut in October maintained that the compromise of 1820 was not binding on the North since it was a fraud and dealt with a subject on which no compromise could be made without violating principle and duty.[26] Shortly before Congress met, Governor De Witt Clinton, in an address to the legislature of New York, reiterated his opposition to the admission of new slave states but did not mention Missouri by name.[27] At the same time one of Clinton's friends, John C. Spencer, introduced resolutions in the legislature opposing Missouri's admission be-

25 *Ibid.*, September 13, 15, 20, 22, 28, October 16, December 4, 1820.

26 *A Caveat; or Considerations Against the Admission of Missouri, With Slavery, Into the Union* (New Haven, 1820), 36-37.

27 Albany *Statesman*, November 10, 1820; Albany *Argus*, November 10, 1820.

cause its constitution sanctioned slavery, made it difficult to emancipate slaves, and forbade free Negroes and mulattoes to enter Missouri. These resolutions were later amended. In the form in which they were finally passed it was not clear whether they favored the repudiation of the compromise. They did protest, however, against the formation of additional slave states from territory not included in the original boundaries of the United States and declared that Congress ought not to accept or confirm the constitution of a new state if it discriminated against any of the citizens of the existing states.[28] While the New York resolutions were ambiguous, the same could certainly not be said for those which the Vermont legislature passed on the same day as New York (November 15). Vermont urged its congressional delegation to vote against the admission of Missouri on the ground that its constitution was antirepublican, as evidenced not only by the clause relating to free Negroes and mulattoes but also by the mere fact that it legalized and perpetuated slavery.[29] The lower house of the Indiana legislature, by a vote of 22 to 5, took a stand similar to Vermont's, although the upper house did not concur.[30]

In the meanwhile, no sooner had the second session of the Sixteenth Congress convened at Washington than the North and South engaged in a contest for control of the speakership of the House. The chief candidates to succeed Henry Clay, who had resigned from this position, were John W. Taylor of New York, William Lowndes of South Carolina, John Sergeant

[28] Albany *Statesman*, November 14, 17, 1820; *Annals of Congress*, 16 Cong., 2 Sess., 23-24. "We did what we could at our last session [of the legislature] to help along the righteous cause, altho' not a few were of opinion that it did not become us again to interfere on the question." John A. King to Rufus King, December 4, 1820, Rufus King Papers.

[29] *Annals of Congress*, 16 Cong., 2 Sess., 78-80.

[30] Washington *Daily National Intelligencer*, February 7, 13, 1821. For additional information on the revival of the Missouri Controversy in the summer and fall of 1820, see *ibid.*, August 8, 1820; *Thomas's Massachusetts Spy* (Worcester), August 30, 1820; Canandaigua *Ontario Messenger*, September 12, 1820; Newark *Centinel of Freedom*, September 12, 1820; Carlisle (Pennsylvania) *Republican*, October 24, 1820; Richmond *Enquirer*, October 27, November 10, 1820.

of Pennsylvania, and Samuel Smith of Maryland. After protracted balloting, Taylor was finally victorious on the twenty-second ballot. The Missouri question was not the only issue in the election for the speakership, but it seems to have been the principal one, and Lowndes attributed his defeat to it.[31] Since 1801 the South had largely monopolized the office of Speaker, Southern men having held it in eight Congresses, a Northerner in but two. The Missouri Controversy had made the North more sectionally conscious and eager to reverse a situation like this.

Taylor's election was greeted with hosannas in the anti-slavery camp and correspondingly depressed the South. Former Congressman Salma Hale of New Hampshire declared jubilantly that "The sceptre is departing from the South."[32] Representative Solomon Van Rensselaer of New York wrote his wife that "we have received one great victory in the choice of Speaker, which like the Allies over Bonaparte, has given our ranks confidence; and I hope and believe we will put down the *Missouri Constitution.*"[33] "The South," Senator Walker of Alabama dolefully observed, "may write Ichabod on its banner— 'the glory is departed.' We shall have no more slaveholding Presidents: and henceforth we must be content to choose between the Clintons and the Tompkins—the Candidates whom the *free* States may deem fit to propose."[34] The Washington *Intelligencer* lamented that the Speaker should be chosen on a sectionalistic basis and would have preferred the old alignment of Federalist and Democrat. Robert Walsh gleefully

31 *Annals of Congress,* 16 Cong., 2 Sess., 434-38; William Lowndes to Mrs. Lowndes, November 14, 17, 1820, William Lowndes Papers, Library of Congress; Mrs. St. Julien Ravenel, *Life and Times of William Lowndes of South Carolina* (Boston, 1901), 208-209. Congressman William Eustis took a different view of the matter, holding that "Taylor's election was not decided by the Missouri question but by a pertinacity in the supporters of the other candidates." William Eustis to Caesar A. Rodney, November 25, 1820, Thomas and Caesar A. Rodney Papers, Library of Congress.

32 Salma Hale to John W. Taylor, November 28, 1820, Taylor Papers.

33 Catharina V. R. Bonney, *A Legacy of Historical Gleanings* (2 vols., Albany, 1875), I, 356.

34 John W. Walker to Charles Tait, November 20, 1820, Tait Papers.

translated the *Intelligencer*'s remarks as meaning, "ah! could we but retain those distinctions by means of which the South, Virginia particularly, our dearest Mother, has been enabled so long to sway the Union.—How unlucky that a point should have arisen which enlists on one side the moral feelings and may gradually set free the will and understanding, of the hitherto docile or insensible portion of the American people!"[35]

The slavery restrictionists would have been chagrined if they had known how little advantage they would derive from the outcome of the Speaker's election. Up to this point Taylor had acted as antislavery whip and floor leader, making the motions for his side, keeping in touch with absentees, and marshaling his forces at each roll call. He assumed an impartial attitude, however, as soon as he was chosen Speaker. Henceforth his policy closely resembled that of the Speaker of the British House of Commons, and he demonstrated his neutrality by appointing pro-Southern majorities to key committees which were entrusted with making reports on the Missouri constitution and compromise measures.[36] Moreover, when Henry Clay returned to Congress early in 1821 and, as in the preceding session, sought to secure a compromise by means of parliamentary juggling and stacked committees, Taylor did not lift a finger to upset his applecart, although he could easily have done so if he had wished.

With Taylor having soared away to Olympian heights of objectivity and disinterestedness, John Sergeant took his place, to some extent, as the leader of the antislavery party in the House of Representatives. Sergeant, a Federalist congressman from Philadelphia, was an eminent jurist, scholar, and gentleman, as well as an eloquent and persuasive speaker. Like many another Federalist, he greatly concerned himself with the welfare of Negroes and Indians. He was active in the work of

[35] Philadelphia *National Gazette and Literary Register*, November 20, 1820.
[36] De Alva S. Alexander, "John W. Taylor, New York's Speaker of the House of Representatives," in *Quarterly Journal of the New York State Historical Association*, I (1920), 28-29; John W. Taylor to Mrs. Taylor, February 20, 1821, Taylor Papers; Brown, *Missouri Compromises*, 33.

antislavery societies and, though as a lawyer he usually served vested interests, fought the legal battles of the Cherokee Indians for purely humanitarian reasons.[37] In common with his Anti-Missourian neighbors, Joseph Hopkinson and Roberts Vaux, he was a champion of good government and reforms[38]— provided the reforms were "safe" ones which would not interfere with the prerogatives of his own social class.[39] And what reform could be safer, from the standpoint of Northern Federalists, than the emancipation of slaves in the distant South and West? Of course, Sergeant's leadership in the last phase of the Missouri Controversy had one obvious drawback. The fact that he was a Federalist led some Northern Democrats to suspect his motives and made them more eager than ever to effect a final compromise with the South, lest the continued agitation over slavery should lead to a revival of the Federalist party.

The final attempt to keep Missouri out of the Union—by rejecting its constitution—forms the third Missouri debate in Congress. As soon as the debate began, it became apparent that the antislavery forces would make their main stand against the free Negro and mulatto clause of the Missouri constitution rather than on the question of slavery. This not only placed the opponents of Missouri on strong constitutional ground but was also good strategy. Subsequent events were to show that in spite of the compromise of 1820 approximately two thirds of the Northern congressmen would vote to reject any constitution that Missouri presented unless it provided for the gradual abolition of slavery. The free states would have to muster considerably more than a two-thirds majority, however, to outvote the Solid South. Only on the free Negro and mulatto issue was it reasonable to suppose that Northern opinion would be sufficiently unanimous to enable the restrictionists to achieve

[37] Adams, *Neglected Period of Anti-Slavery,* 259; *Dictionary of American Biography,* XVI, 589.
[38] Philip S. Klein, *Pennsylvania Politics 1817-1832* (Philadelphia, 1940), 116.
[39] Vaux was not as conservative as Sergeant and Hopkinson in his choice of reforms. In later years, after he had become a Jackson supporter, he was ostracized by the aristocracy of Philadelphia because of his opposition to the National Bank. Joseph J. McCadden, *Education in Pennsylvania 1801-1835 and its Debt to Roberts Vaux* (Philadelphia, 1937), 145-47.

their immediate goal—the rejection of Missouri's constitution and the postponement of a settlement of the controversy until the meeting of the Seventeenth Congress in 1821.

The third Missouri debate centered chiefly in the House of Representatives, since there could be no doubt that the Senate would be favorable to the immediate admission of Missouri. All of the Southern senators would vote for admission, as well as three Northwestern senators who were natives of the South: Edwards and Thomas of Illinois and Taylor of Indiana. Moreover, the friends of Missouri could count on the support of the two senators from the new state of Maine, John Holmes and John Chandler. Holmes, who had voted for the compromise of 1820 while a member of the lower house of Congress, said that he now felt bound by a solemn compact to admit Missouri.[40] Both Holmes and Chandler were stanch Democrats who were inclined to follow the Southern leadership of the party and to distrust the antislavery motives of their Northern Federalist neighbors. As for the rights of free Negroes and mulattoes, that was a matter which rested lightly on the consciences of the Maine senators. Holmes wrote sarcastically that "The simpathy now it seems is turned from *Slaves* to free negroes." Chandler thought that it was foolish and unnecessary for Missouri to insert a provision on this subject in its constitution but that the antislavery men were only looking for a pretext anyway and "if this had not been in [the constitution] something else would have been seized on as an objection."[41] It was ironical that the senators from Maine and Illinois, the two free states most recently admitted to the Union, should have voted consistently with the South from the beginning to the end of the Missouri Controversy instead of joining with the North to maintain a sectional equilibrium in the Senate as they had been expected to do.

On December 12, 1820, after a lengthy debate, the Senate passed a resolution for the final admission of Missouri. With a touch of the Pontius Pilate technique, the resolution declared

[40] *Annals of Congress*, 16 Cong., 2 Sess., 80-81.
[41] John Holmes to William King, November 17, 1820; John Chandler to King, December 17, 1820, William King Papers.

that "nothing herein contained shall be so construed as to give the assent of Congress to any provision in the constitution of Missouri, if any such there be, which contravenes that clause in the Constitution of the United States which declares that 'the citizens of each State shall be entitled to all privileges and immunities of citizens in the several States.'" John H. Eaton of Tennessee was responsible for the Pontius Pilate proviso, which he introduced in the form of an amendment to the admission resolution.[42] The Senate passed the resolution, as thus amended, by a vote of 26 to 18. The only Southerner who voted against it was Nathaniel Macon of North Carolina, who opposed it because it contained the Eaton amendment. As an extreme state rights man, Macon was determined to admit Missouri without any provisos or insinuations. Six Northern senators voted in favor of the resolution: Edwards, Thomas, and Taylor from the Northwest; Holmes and Chandler of Maine; and John F. Parrott of New Hampshire. Parrott, a Democrat, had no sympathy for the antislavery movement, regarding it as a Federalist plot to undermine the Democratic party.[43]

While the Senate had spoken in Missouri's favor, the House of Representatives was yet to be heard from. A copy of the Missouri constitution had been presented to the House on November 16, 1820, and had been referred to a select committee of three. In accordance with his policy of showing no

[42] *Annals of Congress*, 16 Cong., 2 Sess., 41, 100, 102, 116, 118-19.

[43] Brown, *Missouri Compromises*, 12-13. The vote by states on the Senate admission resolution was as follows (*Annals of Congress*, 16 Cong., 2 Sess., 116):

STATE	for	against	STATE	for	against
Maine	2		Delaware	2	
New Hampshire	1	1	Maryland	2	
Vermont		2	Virginia	2	
Massachusetts		1	North Carolina		1
Rhode Island		2	South Carolina	2	
Connecticut		2	Georgia	2	
New York		2	Kentucky	2	
New Jersey		2	Tennessee	2	
Pennsylvania		2	Alabama	2	
Ohio		2	Mississippi	2	
Indiana	1	1	Louisiana	2	
Illinois	2		TOTAL	26	18

favoritism to his own section of the country, the Speaker, Taylor, gave two of the three places on the committee to Southerners. From the committee on November 23, Lowndes of South Carolina reported a resolution declaring Missouri's admission on an equal footing with the original states. He also presented a report which recommended that any question concerning the constitutionality of the free Negro and mulatto clause of Missouri's constitution should be left to the judiciary for determination. On December 13, after a prolonged debate in which the Missouri constitution was severely criticized as being incompatible with the federal Constitution, the House rejected Lowndes' admission resolution by a vote of 93 to 79. Only one representative from a slave state, Willard Hall of Delaware, voted against the resolution, while only five Northerners supported it.[44]

[44] *Annals of Congress,* 16 Cong., 2 Sess., 440, 453-55, 669-70. The five Northerners were Henry Shaw of Massachusetts, Henry Meigs of New York, Joseph Bloomfield and Bernard Smith of New Jersey, and Henry Baldwin of Pennsylvania. The vote by states on the admission resolution was recorded thus:

STATE	for	against
Maine		7
New Hampshire		6
Vermont		6
Massachusetts	1	11
Rhode Island		1
Connecticut		7
New York	1	22
New Jersey	2	4
Pennsylvania	1	21
Ohio		5
Indiana		1
Illinois		1
Delaware	1	1
Maryland	8	
Virginia	23	
North Carolina	11	
South Carolina	8	
Georgia	6	
Kentucky	9	
Tennessee	6	
Alabama	1	
Mississippi	1	
Louisiana		
TOTAL	79	93

It was now clear to everyone that the Missouri question, far from being settled, would dominate the second session of the Sixteenth Congress as effectively as it had the preceding one. Missouri was faced with the prospect of being kept out of the Union indefinitely, and the relations between Northern and Southern representatives were once more strained to the breaking point. Where formerly there had been much intimacy, "little more than speaking terms" remained.[45]

It will be recalled that the compromise of 1820, though it did not specifically admit Missouri to statehood, authorized the Missourians to form a constitution and state government. This they had promptly done, casting aside all the trammels of their territorial status, electing a governor and state legislature, and in every respect constituting themselves a *de facto* state. They elected John Scott to the lower house of Congress and sent David Barton and Thomas H. Benton to the Senate. Throughout the third Missouri debate, Barton, Benton, and Scott were in Washington, claiming seats in Congress and insisting that Missouri was already a state. It was rumored periodically that the Senate was planning to admit Barton and Benton to full membership, in defiance of the House of Representatives.[46] Actually they were admitted at once to seats on the floor, were allowed to frank letters, and exercised all the privileges of members except that of voting.[47] In the House, the Speaker and the Northern majority were willing to recognize Scott as Missouri's territorial delegate, but that title he spurned "because [he wrote] I take the ground that we are a STATE." Each morning the Speaker would call upon the "Delegate from the Territory of Missouri" to present petitions, etc., though no one would answer to that designation.[48]

As Maine had long since been granted statehood under the terms of the compromise of 1820, Southerners accused the

45 James Thomas to William King, December 25, 1820, William King Papers.
46 Nashville *Whig*, January 3, 1821; St. Louis *Enquirer*, January 27, 1821.
47 St. Louis *Enquirer*, December 23, 1820; William M. Meigs, *The Life of Thomas Hart Benton* (Philadelphia, 1904), 125-26.
48 St. Louis *Enquirer*, January 27, 1821; Richmond *Enquirer*, February 13, 1821.

Northern representatives of foul play in refusing to admit Missouri. They also wanted to know whether the North considered Missouri's present status to be that of a state, territory, or former territory; and they sought unsuccessfully, by various motions and stratagems, to make their opponents commit themselves. When the House received three memorials purporting to come from the legislature of "the State of" Missouri, Speaker Taylor deleted the words "the State of" so that the entry in the House *Journal* would merely refer to memorials from the legislature of Missouri. Taylor was accused of insulting the sovereign state of Missouri by this act, though it is obvious that he was only attempting to be neutral and noncommittal.[49]

On January 24, 1821, the House considered a compromise resolution presented by William Eustis, a Massachusetts Democrat. Eustis' resolution, which provided for the admission of Missouri on condition that it expunge the objectionable free Negro and mulatto clause from its constitution, was overwhelmingly defeated.[50] On January 29, on motion of Henry Clay, who had recently returned to Washington after a long absence, the House turned its attention to the Senate resolution admitting Missouri but withholding approval from any provision in its constitution, if there were such, which was in violation of the federal Constitution. After hours and days of futile wrangling it was decided, at Clay's suggestion, to refer the Senate's resolution to a committee of thirteen members. On February 10 Clay reported the resolution back to the House, amended to admit Missouri "upon the fundamental condition, that the said State shall never pass any law preventing any description of persons from coming to and settling in the said State, who now are or hereafter may become citizens of any of the States of this Union." If its legislature assented to the condition prior to the fourth Monday of November, 1821, Missouri was to be admitted by proclamation of the President without any further action on the part of Congress.[51]

[49] *Annals of Congress*, 16 Cong., 2 Sess., 735-42, 841-57, 859-63.
[50] *Ibid.*, 942-44.
[51] *Ibid.*, 982, 1027, 1078-80. In addition to Clay, the following served on

Once more Clay was cast in the role of public compromiser number one. With dramatic eloquence, he called upon the spirit of harmony to preside over the deliberations of the House. Turning to the Northern representatives, he is said to have begged, entreated, adjured, supplicated, and beseeched them to have mercy on the people of Missouri. Clay's oratorical efforts at this time drew tears from many of his listeners and were a source of amazement both to the members of Congress and the audience in the gallery, who were "alike lost in astonishment and wonder at the almighty powers of this most astonishing man."[52]

Nevertheless, by a vote of 83 to 80, the House rejected the Senate's admission resolution as amended by Clay's committee.[53] Northerners opposed the amended resolution partly because it tolerated slavery and partly because it did not require Missouri to expunge the free Negro and mulatto clause from its constitution. On the other hand, three Southerners—John Randolph, Weldon Edwards of North Carolina, and William Terrell of Georgia—voted against the resolution because they were determined that Missouri should be admitted without any reservations.

Meanwhile, the members of the House had another opportunity of voting on the question of slavery restriction. Before the final rejection of the Senate-Clay resolution, Rollin C. Mallary sought to tack on it an amendment requiring Missouri to provide for the gradual abolition of slavery before entering the Union. Mallary was a Vermont representative who later

---

the committee: Josiah Butler of New Hampshire, William Eustis of Massachusetts, Gideon Tomlinson of Connecticut, William D. Ford and Aaron Hackley of New York, John Sergeant and Samuel Moore of Pennsylvania, John W. Campbell of Ohio, Samuel Smith of Maryland, William S. Archer of Virginia, William Lowndes of South Carolina, and Thomas W. Cobb of Georgia. The vote in the committee in favor of the amended resolution was close—seven to six. Brown, *Missouri Compromises,* 34.

[52] *Annals of Congress,* 16 Cong., 2 Sess., 1094; Brown, *Missouri Compromises,* 30-31; Coleman, *John J. Crittenden,* II, 52; Georgetown (D. C.) *Metropolitan,* February 15, 1821.

[53] *Annals of Congress,* 16 Cong., 2 Sess., 1116-17.

(1828) won distinction as chairman of the committee which wrote the "Tariff of Abominations." The Mallary amendment to the Missouri admission resolution was defeated by a vote of 107 to 61, with almost two thirds of the Northern representatives supporting it and the South solidly against it.[54] The vote of the Northern congressmen by states was:

STATE	for Mallary's motion	against it
Maine	4	3
New Hampshire	4	2
Vermont	6	
Massachusetts	10	3
Rhode Island		1
Connecticut	3	3
New York	15	8
New Jersey		4
Pennsylvania	15	6
Ohio	3	3
Indiana	1	
Illinois		1
TOTAL	61	34

Thus by a two to one majority the representatives from the free states repudiated the Missouri Compromise within less than a year after its adoption. It is not surprising that they should do this, however. They had never been in favor of the compromise and did not, like some of their descendants, regard it as sacrosanct. Rather, they considered it an undesirable piece of legislation which they would gladly repeal if they could.

Early in February, 1821, Representative William Plumer of New Hampshire wrote his father that he had attended a caucus of about twenty antislavery congressmen who met to chart a course of action on the Missouri question. Almost all of those present were weary of the controversy and believed that it was now too late to prevent the admission of Missouri as a slave state, but at the same time they agreed that they must not ap-

[54] *Ibid.*, 1094, 1114.

pear to relinquish their former doctrines. Evidently many votes were cast for the Mallary amendment as a matter of principle or from stubbornness and not with any hope of success. Of course, there were those who would not admit that success was no longer attainable. According to Representative Plumer, it was the opinion of well-informed people in the West that if Missouri could be kept out of the Union for two more years, it would be overrun with Northern immigrants and prohibit slavery of its own accord.[55] John Sergeant and other Pennsylvanians were said to have received letters from antislavery Missourians assuring them that if another election for a constitutional convention were held in Missouri, the antislavery party could win.[56] As a matter of fact, the antislavery men were definitely in the minority in Missouri and would remain so for the next forty years. As the Washington *Intelligencer* correctly observed, Sergeant and his friends were laboring "under the disadvantage of incorrect information."[57]

On February 16 there was another attempt to secure a compromise, this time in the Senate. Senator Jonathan Roberts of Pennsylvania introduced a resolution which provided for the admission of Missouri with the understanding that its constitution should be so amended that it would not discriminate against citizens of any of the states. Roberts' measure was defeated by a nonsectional vote of 24 to 19, partly because the senators thought that since they had already passed one admission resolution, it was up to the other house to make the next move.[58] Among those supporting Roberts were his colleague, Walter Lowrie of Pennsylvania, and David L. Morril of New Hampshire. Roberts, Lowrie, and Morril were strong

[55] Brown, *Missouri Compromises*, 29, 32-33.
[56] Nashville *Clarion*, March 14, 1821; St. Louis *Enquirer*, March 24, 1821. Charles King wrote to Rufus King from New York on February 17, 1821, that "There are two gentlemen here from Missouri, of some consequence in that part of the world, whom Jno Duer (who is with us) has seen—and who feel exceedingly anxious that the Missouri constitution should be referred back to a convention in Missouri for amendment, in the strong expectation, that the restrictionists will have a majority in the next convention." Rufus King Papers.
[57] Washington *Daily National Intelligencer*, March 9, 1821.
[58] *Annals of Congress*, 16 Cong., 2 Sess., 35₁-55, 362-64.

antislavery men whose remarks in the second Missouri debate had been offensive to the South. Until now inclined to oppose compromises, they found themselves driven to pursue a different course by the fear that an attempt was being made to rebuild the Federalist party on the Missouri issue.[59] Lowrie had the distinction of having been won over to the compromise of 1820 after its enactment. Though he voted against it, he was shortly afterward defending it on the ground that if either side to the dispute had won a complete victory, "the harmony, good will and confidence, which it is a national duty to cultivate, would have been much impaired, if not destroyed."[60]

The middle of February, 1821, found Congress deadlocked. One year after a major compromise supposedly had laid it to rest forever, the so-called "misery debate" was still going on and was now being referred to as "this distracting question," "this trying question," or "this ominous and ill-boding question."[61] Congressmen became accustomed to dining by candlelight, as the debates over Missouri often lasted from morning to night.[62] Once more frayed nerves led to threats of violence and secession. Southerners warned that Missouri might revolt against Northern oppression. Three hours after the House rejected Missouri's constitution by a vote of 93 to 79, Representative Francis Jones of Winchester, Tennessee, wrote to a friend in his state that "I am sorry to tell you, that in my opinion, in fact the Union is now almost dissolved. I declare to you, that when the result of the vote was announced, my feelings were inexpressible."[63] In the course of an address to the House, Benjamin Hardin of Kentucky remarked that "Gentlemen think that if Missouri falls, she will fall alone; but, sir, I will go with her, and so will her sister states, who have blood and treasure." Several cries from the galleries were heard to add, "and we'll go with you Hardin." Hardin was the man

[59] Benton, *Thirty Years' View*, I, 10.
[60] Boston *Patriot & Daily Mercantile Advertiser*, April 19, 182U.
[61] *Niles' Weekly Register*, XVII (1820), 441; *Annals of Congress*, 16 Cong., 2 Sess., 1101, 1124, 1128.
[62] Brown, *Missouri Compromises*, 36.
[63] Nashville *Clarion, and Tennessee Gazette*, January 2, 1821.

whom John Randolph compared to a butcher's knife sharpened on a brickbat, saying that he was "rough, and cut deep."[64]

On February 21, after all attempts to admit Missouri had failed, Representative William Brown of Kentucky proposed the repeal of the eighth section of the enabling act of March 6, 1820, excluding slavery from the unorganized Louisiana Purchase north of 36° 30'. In refusing to admit Missouri with slavery, said Brown, the North had violated the compromise adopted at the preceding session of Congress. It was only fair, then, that the South should be released from the obligations which the compromise imposed on it.[65]

The topic of Missouri managed to wedge its way into any other subject that was under discussion. There was no getting away from it. It even fastened its tentacles firmly about the presidential election of 1820, and in order to rescue the latter, it was necessary for Clay to pilot another compromise through the House of Representatives. All agreed that President Monroe had been re-elected, but the whole Missouri Controversy was involved in the question of whether he had received 231 electoral votes or 228. Missouri had given him three votes, which the North was unwilling to count as part of the total and Southerners were determined should be counted.

Anticipating that there would be trouble when the two houses of Congress met together to canvass the electoral returns, a joint committee of the Senate and House met in advance to consider the problem. This committee recommended a compromise resolution which provided that if Missouri's votes were challenged and it was obvious that counting them would not alter the outcome of the election, the presiding officer should in that case announce two sets of returns. One set would include the votes of Missouri and the other would not, but it would be pointed out that in any event Monroe and Daniel D. Tompkins had been re-elected President and Vice-President. The Senate accepted the committee's recommenda-

64 Georgetown (D. C.) *Metropolitan*, February 3, 1821; John F. Darby, *Personal Recollections of Many Prominent People* (St. Louis, 1880), 34-35.
65 *Annals of Congress*, 16 Cong., 2 Sess., 1195-1209.

tion, though not without considerable grumbling. In the House it was approved by a vote of 90 to 67, this being one of the few occasions when a compromise proposal was supported by most of the Northern representatives and opposed by a majority of the Southerners. The joint committee which proposed the compromise was appointed at the suggestion of Senator James Barbour of Virginia. Clay was one of the House members on the committee, and it was he who reported the compromise to the House and served as its chief sponsor.[66]

When the Senate and House of Representatives assembled in the House Chamber on February 14, 1821, to make the official canvass of the electoral vote, the solemnity of the occasion was marred by strife and confusion in spite of the Barbour-Clay compromise. Arthur Livermore of New Hampshire objected to receiving the returns from Missouri; John Floyd of Virginia attempted to cry down Missouri's enemies "in a violent and frantic manner"; and John Randolph's shrill voice could be heard, though not always understood above the tumult, lashing out at compromises and hypothetical election results. When Representative Livermore interrupted the counting of the vote, the Senate left the House Chamber in a huff, but later it returned, and the re-election of Monroe and Tompkins duly was proclaimed.[67]

While the Barbour-Clay compromise ensured the re-election of Monroe, it did not of course end the Missouri Controversy. Indeed the stalemate over Missouri's admission now seemed almost hopeless. Representative Plumer of New Hampshire explained the dilemma of Congress in a letter to his father.

[66] *Ibid.*, 267, 288, 341-43, 1058-59, 1147-53. The exact wording of the Barbour-Clay resolution was: "*Resolved,* That, if any objection be made to the votes of Missouri, and the counting or omitting to count which shall not essentially change the result of the election; in that case they shall be reported by the President of the Senate in the following manner: Were the votes of Missouri to be counted, the result would be, for A. B. for President of the United States,—votes; if not counted, for A. B. as President of the United States, —votes; but in either event A. B. is elected President of the United States; and in the same manner for Vice President."

[67] *Annals of Congress,* 16 Cong., 2 Sess., 345-47, 1153-66; Brown, *Missouri Compromises,* 35-38.

The Southern people, wrote Plumer, "before they would vote for any [compromise] amendment were obliged to convince themselves that it meant nothing [would impose no real restraints on Missouri]—and this was enough to convince us that we ought not to vote for it."[68] Only a magician could be expected to pull a compromise rabbit from a parliamentary hat like this; yet, after all, there was a magician in Congress in 1821—Henry Clay.

On February 22, with the House on the verge of distraction, Clay proposed that a committee of twenty-three be appointed to confer with a Senate committee regarding some plan for Missouri's admission. This, said the Washington *Intelligencer*, was presumably the last attempt which would be made "to untie the Gordian knot" before the adjournment of the Sixteenth Congress.[69] It was customary for the Speaker to appoint committee members, but Taylor wanted to relinquish his prerogative in this instance. Therefore, on motion of Clay, the House chose twenty-three men by ballot to confer with seven from the Senate. Clay circulated through the House a list of those whom he would like to have with him on the committee, and for the most part these were the ones selected.[70] Thus the "Great Pacificator" had practically a free hand in dealing with

68 Brown, *Missouri Compromises*, 30.

69 Washington *Daily National Intelligencer*, February 23, 1821.

70 Letter from Representative William Brown in Frankfort (Kentucky) *Commentator*, March 15, 1821; *Annals of Congress*, 16 Cong., 2 Sess., 381-82, 1219-20, 1223-24; Benton, *Thirty Years' View*, I, 10; *Appendix to Congressional Globe*, 31 Cong., 1 Sess., 125; Van Deusen, *Henry Clay*, 146. In addition to Clay, the House members of the committee were: Mark L. Hill of Maine; Samuel Eddy of Rhode Island; James Stevens of Connecticut; William D. Ford, Aaron Hackley, Nathaniel Pitcher, and Henry Storrs of New York; Henry Southard of New Jersey; Henry Baldwin, William Darlington, Samuel Moore, and Thomas J. Rogers of Pennsylvania; John Sloane of Ohio; Thomas Culbreth of Maryland; William S. Archer, Philip Barbour, and John Randolph of Virginia; James S. Smith of North Carolina; Thomas W. Cobb of Georgia; William Brown of Kentucky; John Cocke of Tennessee; and Christopher Rankin of Mississippi. The seven senators on the committee were: John Holmes of Maine, David L. Morril of New Hampshire, Rufus King of New York, Jonathan Roberts of Pennsylvania, Samuel L. Southard of New Jersey, James Barbour of Virginia, and Richard M. Johnson of Kentucky.

the committee. The composition of Clay's compromise committees usually followed the same pattern. They contained a majority of moderate men and a substantial number of Northerners who had opposed a compromise up to then but who might, if subjected at close range to Clay's eloquence and persuasiveness, be won over to the idea.

At the meeting of the joint Senate-House committee (thirty members in all) Clay presented the resolution which was to constitute the second Missouri compromise or compromise of 1821:

That Missouri shall be admitted into this Union on an equal footing with the original States in all respects whatever, upon the fundamental condition, that the fourth clause of the twenty-sixth section of the third article of the constitution submitted on the part of said State to Congress shall never be construed to authorize the passage of any law, and that no law shall be passed in conformity thereto, by which any citizen of either of the States in this Union shall be excluded from the enjoyment of any of the privileges and immunities to which such citizen is entitled under the Constitution of the United States: *Provided,* That the Legislature of the said State, by a solemn public act, shall declare the assent of the said State to the said fundamental condition, and shall transmit to the President of the United States, on or before the fourth Monday in November next, an authentic copy of the said act; upon the receipt whereof the President, by proclamation, shall announce the fact: whereupon, and without any further proceeding on the part of Congress, the admission of the said State into this Union shall be considered as complete.[71]

The House and Senate branches of the committee voted separately on Clay's resolution. In both cases the vote was favorable. Clay afterward recalled the language that he used in addressing the House committeemen. "Now, gentlemen," he said, "we do not want a proposition carried here by a small majority, thereupon reported to the House, and rejected. I am for something practical, something conclusive, something decisive upon the question. How will you vote, Mr. A.? How will

[71] *Annals of Congress,* 16 Cong., 2 Sess., 1228.

you vote, Mr. B.? How will you vote, Mr. C.?" Clay found to his delight that if the Northerners continued to vote in the House as they did in the committee, the passage of a compromise was certain.[72]

On February 26 Clay reported the compromise resolution to the House of Representatives, noting with pride that the senators on the joint committee were unanimous in their approval of it and that the House committeemen were nearly so.[73] The House now moved with unusual rapidity and, by a vote of 87 to 81, passed the compromise on the very day that Clay reported it from the committee.[74] The only Southern representative who voted against the final passage of the resolution was

[72] *Appendix to Congressional Globe*, 31 Cong., 1 Sess., 125.

[73] *Annals of Congress*, 16 Cong., 2 Sess., 1236. Six of the seven senators on the committee favored the resolution. The seventh, Rufus King, did not attend the committee meeting. King took little interest in the last phase of the Missouri Controversy, believing that the main issue had been decided a year before. Brown, *Missouri Compromises*, 42; King, *Rufus King*, VI, 385.

[74] *Annals of Congress*, 16 Cong., 2 Sess., 1238-40. The following is the House vote by states on the final passage of the resolution:

STATE	for	against
Maine	1	6
New Hampshire		6
Vermont		5
Massachusetts	1	12
Rhode Island	1	
Connecticut	1	6
New York	6	17
New Jersey	4	1
Pennsylvania	4	19
Ohio		6
Indiana		1
Illinois		1
Delaware		
Maryland	8	
Virginia	18	1
North Carolina	12	
South Carolina	6	
Georgia	6	
Kentucky	10	
Tennessee	6	
Alabama	1	
Mississippi	1	
Louisiana	1	
TOTAL	87	81

John Randolph. As the protagonist of state rights, Randolph would not vote for any measure which did not admit Missouri unconditionally. For the same reason Robert S. Garnett and Severn Parker of Virginia refrained from voting. Most Southerners agreed with Representative Hugh Nelson of Virginia, who supported the compromise because he "thought it better to make some sacrifice to form, than to lose the substance."[75] Eighteen Northern congressmen voted for the compromise. They were: Mark L. Hill of Maine; Henry Shaw of Massachusetts; Samuel Eddy of Rhode Island; James Stevens of Connecticut; Robert Clark of New York (who felt bound by the compromise of 1820 to vote for Missouri's admission);[76] William D. Ford, James Guyon, Aaron Hackley, Henry Meigs, and Henry Storrs of New York; Ephraim Bateman, Joseph Bloomfield, Bernard Smith, and Henry Southard of New Jersey; and Henry Baldwin, Samuel Moore, Thomas J. Rogers, and Daniel Udree of Pennsylvania.

The tactics by which Clay secured a favorable vote in the House for the compromise of 1821 rivaled those which he had employed a year before and are thus described by a member of Congress:

It will be recollected that Mr. Clay . . . obtained the appointment of a committee of 13 which was considered large. The object undoubtedly was to have an opportunity of operating on the weak and timid. He succeeded in bringing over some New Yorkers—but still could not accomplish his object. On Thursday last he proposed the appointment *(by ballot)* of a committee of 23—in this he succeeded—and in order to play off his game with treble effect, he proposed going immediately into the balloting, but it was discovered that he and his partizans had their tickets ready cut and dry—and our side were totally unprepared. Their ticket had on it several leading southern men, and all those from the north who had evinced that their firmness was shaken. It was however postponed until next morning—still however we could not act with concert, and they in part succeeded—On Saturday the committee was filled up—and on

[75] Hugh Nelson to Charles Everette, February 26, 1821, Hugh Nelson Papers, Library of Congress.
[76] *Annals of Congress,* 16 Cong., 2 Sess., 1125.

that evening they met (together with a committee of 7 from the Senate.) I am told that during that evening's sitting they converted Mr. Southard of New Jersey, of the House of Representatives. They met again on *Sunday* evening, and agreed on their resolution, and converted Thomas J. Rogers and Dr. Samuel J. Moore of Pennsylvania.—During the night and this morning Mr. Clay got the resolution printed—and laid on the tables; and had it taken up. The previous question was called and properly for debate was absolutely useless. The resolution was adopted, ordered to be engrossed—and immediately the engrossed resolution, prepared before hand, passed. Such unexampled perseverance shews what some are capable of.[77]

On February 28, two days after Clay's success in the House, the compromise of 1821 was approved in the Senate by a vote of 28 to 14, and the third Missouri debate came to a close.[78]

[77] Letter from unnamed congressman in Harrisburg (Pennsylvania) *Chronicle*, March 5, 1821.

[78] *Annals of Congress*, 16 Cong., 2 Sess., 390. The vote in the Senate by states on the final passage of the Clay admission resolution was as follows:

STATE	for	against
Maine	2	
New Hampshire	2	
Vermont		1
Massachusetts		2
Rhode Island	1	1
Connecticut		2
New York		2
New Jersey	1	1
Pennsylvania	2	
Ohio		2
Indiana	1	1
Illinois	2	
Delaware	2	
Maryland	1	
Virginia	2	
North Carolina	1	1
South Carolina	1	1
Georgia	1	
Kentucky	2	
Tennessee	2	
Alabama	2	
Mississippi	2	
Louisiana	1	
TOTAL	28	14

Eleven Northern senators joined with the bulk of the Southerners to give the compromise its wide margin of victory. They were: John Holmes and John Chandler of Maine, John F. Parrott and David L. Morril of New Hampshire, William Hunter of Rhode Island, Samuel L. Southard of New Jersey, Jonathan Roberts and Walter Lowrie of Pennsylvania, Waller Taylor of Indiana, and Jesse B. Thomas and Ninian Edwards of Illinois. The only Southern senators who opposed the compromise were Nathaniel Macon of North Carolina and William Smith of South Carolina. These two, like John Randolph, insisted on an unconditional admission for Missouri.

First and last, as has been shown, the Missouri Controversy necessitated the enactment of three different compromises. Jesse B. Thomas was the author of the compromise of 1820, which is usually and properly designated as *the* Missouri Compromise. The arrangement for counting the electoral vote of 1820 may be called, for want of a better name, the Barbour-Clay compromise. Finally, the resolution for Missouri's admission in 1821 is known as the second Missouri compromise or compromise of 1821.[79]

Clay's role as peacemaker in 1821 helped to win for him the title of "Great Pacificator." At a public dinner in his honor shortly after the adoption of the second compromise, Thomas Hart Benton dubbed him the "Pacificator of ten millions of Brothers."[80] Other contemporaries were loud in their praise. Langdon Cheves wrote Clay that "you have accomplished all that was practicable. . . . The Constitution of the Union was in danger & has been saved." "I conscientiously believe," said a Pennsylvania congressman, "that *Henry Clay* of Kentucky saved that which *George Washington* of Virginia won—the United Independence of America." Even the anti-Southern and anticompromise Washington *Gazette,* edited by Jonathan Elliot and Baptist Irvine, grudgingly acknowledged admiration for Clay as a parliamentarian when it attributed the outcome

[79] For the full text of the resolution, as approved on March 2, 1821, see *Annals of Congress,* 16 Cong., 2 Sess., *Appendix,* 1830; 3 *U. S. Stat.* 645.
[80] St. Louis *Enquirer,* June 23, 1821.

of the Missouri question to "the very extraordinary exertions of an extraordinary man" and to his *"grand committees."*[81]

It is almost superfluous to say that the fear of Federalism played an important part in corralling eighteen Northern votes in the House for the compromise of 1821 and in rolling up a two to one majority in its favor in the Senate. Certain Northern Democrats had long feared that a Federalist plot was lurking beneath the surface of the attempted restriction on Missouri. During the winter of 1820-1821 many of them became convinced that the welfare of the Democratic party demanded a speedy and permanent compromise with the South. Thomas H. Benton, in his memoirs, gives a list of Northern Democrats who entertained this opinion and expressed it to him.[82] It will be recalled that Benton and David Barton, as the senators-elect from Missouri, had seats on the Senate floor at this time, although they were not yet allowed to vote. Barton voiced the sentiments of a host of Democrats when he declared, in a letter to a St. Louis editor, that he would not be surprised "after four years to see our next President riding into the City of Washington, not on a white horse, or an ass's colt, but on a free negro or mulattoe."[83]

John Sergeant, Federalist leader of the restrictionists, overplayed his hand and created displeasure in Democratic circles by an address that he delivered in the House on February 1. Though not recorded in the *Annals*, Sergeant's remarks can be reconstructed from the accounts of those who heard them. The gist of them was that no action regarding Missouri ought to be taken until the next session of Congress, at which time the questions of slavery restriction and free Negro immigration could both be reconsidered. Sergeant also stressed the necessity for a balance of power and, according to David Barton,

[81] Langdon Cheves to Henry Clay, March 3, 1821, Henry Clay Papers, Library of Congress; Wilmington (Delaware) *American Watchman*, March 6, 1821; Washington *Gazette*, February 27, 1821.

[82] Benton, *Thirty Years' View*, I, 10. Benton's list cannot be entirely accurate, since it contains the names of three Federalists: William Hunter, Outerbridge Horsey, and Nicholas Van Dyke.

[83] St. Louis *Enquirer*, December 30, 1820.

declared that Missouri was needed by the free states as a counterbalance to Florida, which would soon be ready to enter the Union as a slave state.[84] Representative Plumer noted in a letter to his father that Sergeant's address was not well received, although Plumer himself endorsed it heartily.[85]

In the meantime, a sensation had been created by Joshua Cushman, a Congregational minister and member of Congress from Maine. The press somehow got hold of a confidential circular letter that Cushman had prepared and distributed among a few intimate friends. Cushman was a Democrat, but a writer in the Portland *Argus* pointed out that his circular bore a close resemblance to those which the Federalists had been wont to circulate in 1809 and 1810.[86] The circular, which was aimed primarily at the leaders of the Democratic party in Maine, evidently was intended to promote Cushman's senatorial candidacy against John Holmes. It asserted, with considerable justification, that the leaders of the Maine Democracy were seeking to align the new state with the South against the anti-slavery forces of the North. Predicting that such a course was doomed to failure, it boldly declared that the signs of the times "do not augur perpetuity, or uninterrupted succession, to the southern dynasty" and that not "on the indiscriminate offerings of peace [compromises], but on the *balance of power,* depends the safety of our republic." The section of Cushman's letter that gave the greatest offense was that which dwelt upon the political unity of the South and called for a similar solidarity in the North. Apparently, though his meaning was not absolutely clear, Cushman desired a new alignment of political parties, based on geographical distinctions, with a union of Northern Democrats and Federalists in a common front against the South.[87]

[84] *Ibid.,* March 24, 1821; Washington *Daily National Intelligencer,* February 2, 1821; Brown, *Missouri Compromises,* 30.
[85] Brown, *Missouri Compromises,* 30.
[86] Portland *Eastern Argus,* January 9, 1821.
[87] For the full text of Cushman's circular, see Washington *Gazette,* February 19, 1821; Richmond *Enquirer,* January 25, 1821.

Obviously for the benefit of Northern Democrats, Southern congressmen made a great outcry over "Parson" Cushman's circular and Sergeant's balance of power address. William Brown of Kentucky in a long oration reviewed the story of the Hartford Convention and proved to his own satisfaction that the spirit which produced it was now active in the Missouri Controversy.[88] Perhaps more effective than the efforts of Southerners, however, was the attitude of the Democratic press. Never enthusiastic in their support of Anti-Missourianism, a large number of Northern Democratic journals were proclaiming by February, 1821, that Federalists were hoping to postpone Missouri's admission until the meeting of the Seventeenth Congress in order to create a new sectional party at the expense of the Democrats.[89]

The Pennsylvania congressional delegation was subjected to considerable pressure, in behalf of a compromise, from the press and party regulars at home. The necessity for a speedy and conciliatory settlement of the Missouri question was stressed by the two leading Democratic newspapers of Philadelphia, the *Democratic Press* and *Franklin Gazette*, and by many individuals.[90] Shortly after the adoption of the compromise of 1821, the *Franklin Gazette* published approvingly a letter from a correspondent in Washington which asserted that "The federal and factious prints may rail and rave; but the republicans of Pennsylvania, New York and New Jersey have unequivocally declared that the salvation of the great republican family demanded its [Missouri dispute] being put to rest forever. Letters were received here every day from different quarters to bring the subject to a close this session." The *Gazette* correspondent went on to describe a conversation with a Pennsylvania congressman who reported the receipt of letters from various parts of his state, particularly Harrisburg and

[88] *Annals of Congress*, 16 Cong., 2 Sess., 1105-1108. See also John Tyler's address in *ibid.*, 1022-24.

[89] See Chapter VI.

[90] Philadelphia *Democratic Press*, February 14, 21, 1821; Philadelphia *Franklin Gazette*, March 3, 1821.

Pittsburgh, urging the termination of the controversy.[91] The Washington *Intelligencer* published two letters from Pennsylvanians to members of Congress. One was from a Pittsburgh Democrat who feared that the failure to arrange a compromise would produce "the most dangerous political consequences." The other letter, written by a Philadelphian, voiced a suspicion that there was something concealed in the current antislavery propaganda—"something like a combination to divide, not the Union, but the *great Democratic family of the Union.*"[92]

Nicholas Biddle, the Philadelphia financier, was one of the Pennsylvanians who was writing letters to Washington in 1821 to urge the desirability of a compromise. As a patriotic American, Biddle was frightened by the sectional animosities which had been unleashed in Congress and resolved to do his bit to disperse them. He urged the Democratic newspapers of Philadelphia to work for a peaceful settlement and wrote letters to certain members of the Pennsylvania congressional delegation assuring them that their standing with their constituents would not be injured by voting for a compromise. It was Biddle's desire that Pennsylvania should "interpose between the conflicting parties, & close a breach which rash & violent spirits are daily evidencing." To Representative Thomas J. Rogers he wrote: "Rely upon it you have nothing to fear at home—The leading prints on the republican side in this city have come out in distinct approbation of the settlement. The principal persons of the party are decidedly favorable to it—and every days observation confirms my belief that the great anxiety of the sober men of our State is to close the dispute—to close it immediately—& above all to risk no great interest by urging to extremity doubtful pretensions."[93]

Philadelphians who favored the compromise of 1821 gave a supper in honor of the Pennsylvania members of Congress who

[91] Philadelphia *Franklin Gazette*, March 5, 1821.

[92] Washington *Daily National Intelligencer*, March 5, 1821.

[93] Nicholas Biddle to C. J. Ingersoll, February 18, 1821; Biddle to Senator Walter Lowrie, February 20, 1821; Biddle to Representative Thomas J. Rogers, February 22, 27, 1821; Biddle to Senator Jonathan Roberts, February 25, 1821, Biddle Papers.

supported it. The tenor of the gathering was reflected in one of the toasts given: "Our Guests—*They* deserve well of their country who preserve its harmony and union."[94] Later, in the summer of 1821, Biddle wrote to President Monroe to assure him that Pennsylvania had accepted the compromise with good grace and that those who voted for it had not suffered in the estimation of the country.[95]

On the day after the compromise passed the House of Representatives by the close margin of 87 to 81, a correspondent of the *Franklin Gazette* declared that greetings and congratulations were being offered on all sides in Congress, that many of those who voted against the compromise rejoiced over its success, and that everybody was happy *"except the Hartford Convention men."*[96] Clay and Plumer likewise reported that many who voted against the compromise secretly favored it. Clay pointed out that he could always secure large majorities for any collateral motion which was designed to promote a compromise.[97] Evidently, then, some anticompromise votes did not reflect the personal sentiments of those who cast them but were dictated by political considerations or the fear of appearing to be inconsistent.

The arguments advanced by both sides in the third Missouri debate ranged over the whole field of American politics, history, and race relations. Missourians and some Southerners held that the entire debate was a thing of supererogation—that Missouri was already a state and should be treated as such. Their argument was that when a territory complied with the terms of an enabling act for its admission, it automatically became a state. Northerners, on the other hand, contended that an enabling act alone would not confer statehood upon a territory but must

[94] Washington *Daily National Intelligencer*, March 12, 1821.

[95] Nicholas Biddle to James Monroe, June 14, 1821, Monroe Papers, Library of Congress; *Congressional Globe*, 30 Cong., 2 Sess., *Appendix*, 65.

[96] Philadelphia *Franklin Gazette*, March 2, 1821.

[97] Brown, *Missouri Compromises*, 43; *Appendix to Congressional Globe*, 31 Cong., 1 Sess., 125.

be supplemented by a final congressional resolution declaring the admission of the newly formed state into the Union.[98]

Ostensibly, at least, free Negro and mulatto citizenship was the main issue in the third debate, and the North was on strong ground as long as it did not wander away from this subject. The second section of the fourth article of the federal Constitution provides that "The citizens of each State shall be entitled to all privileges and immunities of citizens in the several States." It would be difficult to formulate a universally acceptable definition of the word "citizen," but, in accordance with any reasonable interpretation of the term, there were certainly Negro citizens in the United States at the time the Constitution was framed. Negroes served as soldiers in the Revolutionary War, and in 1787 they voted, in limited numbers, in some or all of the New England states, New York, New Jersey, Maryland, and, possibly, in North Carolina and elsewhere.[99]

That Negroes were citizens in some of the states in 1787 as well as in 1821 is more apparent to historians today than it was to a great many Americans at the time of the Missouri Controversy. Throughout the ante bellum period there was a widespread belief in all parts of the nation that the rights and privileges enumerated in the Constitution and Declaration of Independence were not applicable to Negroes and that there never had been a Negro in any state who was a citizen in the full sense of the word. This belief was rendered more plausible

[98] McLaughlin agrees with the Northern position. "The proper principle," he says, "would seem to be that the state does not exist as a member of the union until its admission is formally declared by Congress." McLaughlin, *Constitutional History of the United States*, 382.

[99] James T. Adams, "Disfranchisement of Negroes in New England," in *American Historical Review*, XXX (1925), 543-47; Franklin, *From Slavery to Freedom*, 158, 217; Marion T. Wright, "Negro Suffrage in New Jersey, 1776-1875," in *Journal of Negro History*, XXXIII (1948), 172-75; James M. Wright, *The Free Negro in Maryland 1634-1860* (New York, 1921), 119. In North Carolina, where the constitution of 1776 did not deny the franchise to free Negroes, the latter voted in considerable numbers in the early decades of the nineteenth century, though it is not certain that they were voting as early as 1787. See Guion G. Johnson, *Ante-Bellum North Carolina, A Social History* (Chapel Hill, 1937), 602.

by the fact that even in states where the Negro voted, he usually was discriminated against in some fashion.[100] David Daggett, Chief Justice of Connecticut, held in 1833 that "slaves, free blacks and Indians" could not be considered citizens within the meaning of the second section, fourth article, of the federal Constitution, and Chief Justice Taney expressed a similar opinion in the Dred Scott case.[101] It is not surprising therefore that Representative Louis McLane of Delaware should assert in the third Missouri debate that "the free negroes and mulattoes in the United States are not that description of citizens contemplated by the Constitution of the United States as entitled to Federal rights."[102] Even more dogmatic was Representative Charles Pinckney of South Carolina. Having served as a delegate to the Constitutional Convention of 1787, Pinckney now claimed that it was he who had written the second section of the fourth article of the Constitution. "I say," he declared, "that, at the time I drew that constitution, I perfectly knew that there did not then exist such a thing in the Union as a black or colored citizen, nor could I then have conceived it possible such a thing could ever have existed in it; nor, notwithstanding all that is said on the subject, do I now believe one does exist in it."[103]

In reply to the Southern contention that Negro citizenship was unknown in American law, Senator Morril of New Hampshire cited, by name, several distinguished mulatto citizens of

100 "The free Negro was known as 'free,' but in none of these states [the thirteen states of 1790] was he as free as the white man." Charles H. Wesley, "Negro Suffrage in the Period of Constitution-Making 1787-1865," in *Journal of Negro History,* XXXII (1947), 148.

101 Stephen B. Weeks, "The History of Negro Suffrage in the South," in *Political Science Quarterly,* IX (1894), 677; Dred Scott *v.* Sandford, 19 *Howard* 393 (1857).

102 *Annals of Congress,* 16 Cong., 2 Sess., 614.

103 *Ibid.,* 1134. The famous Pinckney Plan for a constitution apparently did provide for a community of citizenship privileges between the states, and a similar provision was to be found in the fourth article of the Articles of Confederation. It is quite possible that this provision entered the Constitution through the medium of Pinckney's plan. See Andrew J. Bethea, *The Contribution of Charles Pinckney to The Formation of the American Union* (Richmond, 1937), 53-55, 78.

Vermont, New Hampshire, and Massachusetts.[104] Representative William Eustis of Massachusetts spoke eloquently in defense of free Negro and mulatto rights, basing his appeal on the traditional American sympathy for the underdog. "If," he said, "their number be small, and they are feebly represented, we to whom they are known are proportionably bound to protect them. But their defence is not founded on their numbers; it rests on the immutable principles of justice. . . . I trust . . . that we will extend good faith even to the blacks."[105]

Southerners argued that it was the duty of the judiciary, rather than Congress, to determine whether any features of Missouri's constitution were incompatible with the federal Constitution, especially since a number of states denied admission to free Negroes. The answer most commonly given to this proposition was that Congress ought not to surrender its own responsibilities to the courts. Northerners also dwelt on the injustice of requiring a Negro to institute an expensive lawsuit to secure what he was entitled to without one—free ingress to every state in the Union.

It was surprising that Southern congressmen, especially the Virginians, should be willing to entrust the final settlement of the free Negro and mulatto issue to John Marshall and the Supreme Court. As the citadel of the state rights cause, Virginia was intensely anti-Marshall in 1821 and was vigorously opposing the Chief Justice's nationalistic decisions.[106] Nevertheless, without batting an eyelash, one Virginia state rights man after another—Philip P. Barbour, Alexander Smyth, William S. Archer, John Floyd—rose in the House of Representatives and insisted that the judiciary was the proper agency for determining the citizenship status of Negroes and mulattoes.[107]

Like its predecessor of 1820, the compromise of 1821 did not specifically admit Missouri to statehood. It empowered the President of the United States to do this by proclamation as

---

[104] *Annals of Congress*, 16 Cong., 2 Sess., 108-109.   [105] *Ibid.*, 639.

[106] William E. Dodd, "Chief Justice Marshall and Virginia, 1813-1821," in *American Historical Review*, XII (1907), 776-87.

[107] *Annals of Congress*, 16 Cong., 2 Sess., 553, 559, 592-93, 993.

soon as the Missouri legislature should promise that the new
state would never pass discriminatory legislation against the
citizens of any other state. There were those in the North who
predicted—and no doubt the wish was father to the thought—
that Missouri would refuse to make such a promise.[108] The
antislavery Edwardsville, Illinois, *Spectator* hoped that this
would be the case; for, said the *Spectator*, "A separation [from
the Union] is better than an incongruous connexion."[109] Two
months after the passage of the compromise, Theodore Dwight's
New York *Advertiser*, in whose breast hope sprang eternal,
opposed the candidacy of Churchill C. Cambreling for Congress on the ground that he was not a dependable antislavery
man. "Let it not be said in answer to this objection," continued
the *Advertiser*, "that the Missouri question is settled and fin-
ished. This cannot be known even as it regards that territory.
Should the legislature of Missouri neglect or refuse to pass the
act provided for in the resolution passed by Congress for the
purpose, things must stand in the same situation in which they
were at the commencement of the last session." Finally, said
the *Advertiser*, the same question would arise in the case of
other new states such as Florida, "as well as the boundless regions above and below 36 degrees and a half of latitude."[110]

In June, 1821, the Missouri legislature made the promise
which Congress desired but expressed it in such sarcastic and
defiant language that the ire of the antislavery press was again
aroused. Theodore Dwight could "hardly imagine a more cut-
ting satire" than the preamble to Missouri's act of assent, while
Robert Walsh's Philadelphia *Gazette* declared that the phraseology of the preamble exploded and stultified the second compromise. Missouri's language, said the *Gazette*, merited at least
a formal protest and rebuke from one branch of the national
government.[111] Of all the men in public life, Walsh was prob-

[108] St. Louis *Enquirer*, June 2, 1821.
[109] Edwardsville *Spectator*, April 3, 1821.
[110] New York *Daily Advertiser*, April 23, 1821.
[111] *Ibid.*, July 18, 1821; Philadelphia *National Gazette and Literary Register*,
August 13, September 6, 1821.

ably the most unwilling to turn his face away from Missouri and admit defeat. He did so only with the greatest reluctance and with many a fond backward glance at what might have been. Indeed, he took so many backward glances that he was accused, even in the North, of harboring disunion sentiments. "Mr. Walsh," said the Pittsburgh *Statesman*, "still talks occasionally of a dissolution of the Union, and hints as significantly as he dares, that it would be a clever thing. Let him speak out loudly—that the nation may execrate him, as it must if he thus deliberately wishes its ruin."[112] At last even Walsh had to admit, in the summer of 1821, that "nothing of a political nature, connected with Missouri, can be discussed now with the least chance of obtaining public attention."[113]

President Monroe, less squeamish than Dwight and Walsh and happy to be rid of a vexatious problem, proclaimed the final admission of Missouri on August 10, 1821. When the Seventeenth Congress began its first session in the next December, Missouri's senators and representatives were admitted to their seats with scarcely a ripple of protest. At the same time, in a contest for the speakership, John W. Taylor was defeated for re-election by Philip Barbour of Virginia. Although the memory of the Missouri Controversy prompted many Southerners to vote against Taylor, his defeat was due primarily to the Tammany or Bucktail faction in his own state of New York.[114] In any event, new alignments were in the offing, and it was clear that the attempt to prohibit slavery in Missouri by act of Congress finally had been relegated to the limbo of lost causes.

[112] Pittsburgh *Statesman*, March 10, 1821.

[113] Philadelphia *National Gazette and Literary Register*, July 6, 1821.

[114] John W. Taylor to Richard Taylor, December 12, 1821; John W. Taylor to William D. Ford, January 18, 1822, Taylor Papers. Taylor's quarrel with the Bucktails was not of his choosing. He was friendly to De Witt Clinton but did not wish to be regarded as either a Clintonian or Bucktail. John W. Taylor to E. Cowen, February 27, 1821, Taylor Papers.

"It is given out to be settled, but nothing is less true. Its influence will increase, its magnitude also."—
RUFUS KING[1]

CHAPTER VI

PUBLIC OPINION IN THE FREE STATES

*I*N EVALUATING the attitude of the public toward the Missouri Controversy, one salient fact must be kept in mind, namely, that the average person is always more interested in eating, earning a livelihood, and seeking entertainment than in any political issue. It follows then that Congress may debate some question until it mistakes the strident clamor of the Capitol for public opinion and imagines that the nation is more interested in its deliberations than it actually is. This was certainly the case in 1819-1821. There were, of course, many individuals throughout the land who shared the sentiments of the congressmen—men like Lewis Tappan of Boston, who declared that "During the [Missouri] contest in Congress people were in breathless suspense—and when the result was known, consternation and horror took possession of men's minds."[2]

While this was the effect which Missouri slavery had on Tappan and his limited circle of Boston acquaintances, it does not seem to have aroused a majority of the American people anything like so much. Martin Van Buren wrote Senator Rufus King that "notwithstanding the people of this state [New York] have felt a strong interest in the question, the excitement which exists in regard to it, or which is likely to arise from it, is not so great as you suppose."[3] In December, 1820, Northern and Southern members of Congress were said to be on little more than speaking terms because of Missouri, but at the same time

Albion K. Parris was writing from Portland, Maine, that he had scarcely heard the subject mentioned there.[4] Parris must have been a keen judge of public opinion, since he later served as governor of Maine for five terms. In this instance his views are substantiated by letters which Representative John Holmes of Maine received from his constituents. William P. Preble, a prominent Democratic politician of Portland, reported that the excitement over Missouri had never extended to Maine, and Barnabas Palmer wrote Holmes from Kennebunk that the people of his county had taken little interest in the matter aside from the embarrassment which it produced in the admission of Maine.[5]

Numerous statements in the press confirm the impression that the Missouri dispute meant more to Congress than to the average American. "Never," said the Philadelphia *Democratic Press*, "was representation less representative of the sentiment at home than in this affair. The country is as free from the political fever with which Congress is inflamed, as it is from the deadly distemper prevailing among the members." The Baltimore *Patriot* believed that the "violent commotion of the political atmosphere is almost confined to the capitol. The people do not yet participate in that unhappy heat of zeal and controversy, which has inflamed their Senators and Representatives." The Cincinnati *Inquisitor Advertiser* called the Missouri Controversy "the *black* question with which they have been so long agitated, and with which the country had become much disgusted." The Pittsburgh *Statesman* refused to publish a long essay on Missouri which it received from one of its subscribers. "Let the question be settled at Washington [said the

[1] King, *Rufus King*, VI, 318.

[2] Lewis Tappan to Benjamin Tappan, May 3, 1820, Benjamin Tappan Papers, Library of Congress.

[3] King, *Rufus King*, VI, 322.

[4] James Thomas to William King, December 25, 1820, William King Papers; Albion K. Parris to John Holmes, December 27, 1820, John Holmes Papers, Maine Historical Society.

[5] William P. Preble to John Holmes, January 16, 1820; Barnabas Palmer to Holmes, April 19, 1820, Holmes Papers.

Statesman]; God knows we have heard enough of it." The Washington *Intelligencer* expressed the opinion that the people did not realize how much excitement existed in Congress, adding: "We wish they may not hereafter realize it too powerfully."[6]

The Missouri Controversy was contemporaneous with the Panic of 1819, and the general public (as distinguished from Anti-Missourian zealots) would have been more than human if it had not been preoccupied primarily with the problem of staving off financial ruin rather than in worrying over the expansion of slavery in distant lands beyond the Mississippi. Some idea of how the depression forced the slavery issue into the background in most men's minds can be gleaned from a letter written by Thomas G. Percy, an exceedingly astute and observant Alabamian who lived near Huntsville and who, incidentally, was the great-grandfather of William Alexander Percy, author of *Lanterns on the Levee*.[7] In February, 1820, Percy wrote Senator John Walker that on his last visit to town "the Spanish relations—the more momentous Missouri question & the defective revenue, were not thought of or talked of by any one; every one had too much to occupy him in the deficiency of his own revenue." Percy concluded with charming candor: "I believe I had better keep away from Town for I shall be asked for money and it is what I have not got."[8]

The financial distress of the populace in 1819-1821 was real and quite sufficient to overshadow any disagreements regarding slavery. "Go where you will," wrote a New Jersey farmer at this time, "your ears are continually saluted with the cry of *hard times! hard times!*" "There never was," echoed the New York *Gazette*, "in the recollection of our oldest merchants, such a state of mercantile *embarrassment*." The West was especially

6 Philadelphia *Democratic Press*, February 24, 1821; Baltimore *Patriot & Mercantile Advertiser*, February 17, 1820; Cincinnati *Inquisitor Advertiser*, March 21, 1820; Pittsburgh *Statesman*, March 3, 1821; Washington *Daily National Intelligencer*, February 13, 1821.

7 Hester S. Ware, "A Study of the Life and Works of William Alexander Percy" (M.S. thesis, Mississippi State College, 1950), 2.

8 Thomas G. Percy to John W. Walker, February 8, 1820, Walker Papers.

hard hit. From Marietta, Ohio, came stories of lots which had been purchased for hundreds of dollars and now had to be sacrificed for thirty or forty dollars apiece. George Nixon wrote from Pearl River, Mississippi, that "the Scarcity of money, or the want of it, among the people Generally about here is beyond any thing of the like Since my first rememberance."[9]

Faced with a major depression, the people turned to Congress for some measure of relief. Among the remedies suggested were an increase in the tariff, a national bankruptcy law, and an extension of the time limit for meeting payments on lands purchased from the government. Though there might be much disagreement about the best method for combating the depression, there was considerable unanimity on one point —that Congress should act rather than debate and that it should not devote all of its time, in such an economically critical period, to a discussion of slavery. The congressmen, however, thought otherwise. In the first session of the Sixteenth Congress the Missouri Controversy delayed the passage of the annual appropriation bills. Even the Revolutionary veterans did not receive their pensions on time in some cases.[10] A year later the slavery issue was blamed for defeating the bankruptcy bill by delaying its consideration until it was almost time for adjournment.[11]

The Sixteenth Congress was not a popular one. Those Americans whose sense of humor exceeded their partisanship made merry over the pompous and redundant speeches delivered in the course of the Missouri debates.[12] The Wilmington, Delaware, *Watchman* regretted that the nation's lawmaking body should waste so much time on Missouri, thus sacrificing "other

[9] Trenton *True American*, April 24, 1820; New York *Gazette & General Advertiser*, February 28, 1821; New Bern (North Carolina) *Carolina Centinel*, January 15, 1820; George H. Nixon to David Holmes, October 8, 1819, Correspondence of Governor David Holmes, Series E, No. 2, Mississippi Department of Archives and History. See also Samuel Rezneck, "The Depression of 1819-1822, A Social History," in *American Historical Review*, XXXIX (1933), 30-33.

[10] *Niles' Weekly Register*, XVIII (1820), 33.

[11] Washington *Daily National Intelligencer*, March 5, 1821.

[12] Charleston *Courier*, March 18, 1820.

measures to which millions of sufferers are looking with the most agonizing solicitude for relief!"[13] One writer charged that the members of Congress did not wish to end the controversy until they had delivered the long addresses which they had already prepared.[14] The New York *Columbian* was distressed that "the important business of the session should be suspended to give place to this unprofitable and angry discussion."[15] The Boston *Patriot* asserted that Congress had been so long employed upon the "dry subject" of Missouri that it was useless to recur to its proceedings for anything of an interesting nature.[16] A writer in the Philadelphia *Democratic Press* complained that for two years Congress had distracted the country with a discussion of slavery and had neglected the "languishing interests of manufactures, of public lands, of the currency, of commerce."[17] On the eve of the third Missouri debate, a writer in the Baltimore *Federal Republican* declared that this subject had been exhausted and had become loathsome to all who were interested in the public good. Therefore, said the writer, congressmen should turn their attention to other matters of vital importance such as a bankrupt law.[18] After a study of editorial opinions, the Windsor, Vermont, *Republican* concluded that there were few editors who did not condemn long-winded speeches about Missouri as a waste of time.[19] Writers who were mathematically inclined took pleasure in calculating what the Missouri debates had cost the taxpayers, their estimates ranging from $42,790 to $75,000.[20] The New York *National Advocate* figured that the Missouri question had "cost the nation in debate nearly the value of the territory," and the Newport,

[13] Wilmington *American Watchman*, February 19, 1820.
[14] New York *National Advocate*, February 1, 1820.
[15] New York *Columbian*, February 3, 1820.
[16] Boston *Patriot & Daily Mercantile Advertiser*, March 2, 1820.
[17] Philadelphia *Democratic Press*, February 22, 24, 1821.
[18] Baltimore *Federal Republican*, quoted in Richmond *Enquirer*, November 28, 1820.
[19] Windsor *Republican & American Yeoman*, March 6, 1820.
[20] Portland *Eastern Argus*, March 14, 1820; Washington *Gazette*, May 19, 1820.

Rhode Island, *Republican* wondered whether it might not be well to have two Congresses, one for debating and the other for transacting business.[21]

From the preceding paragraphs it must not be inferred that the Missouri Controversy was merely a congressional tempest in a teapot, for it was more than that. Many people were interested in it, and anyone who had a speck of vision could hardly fail to recognize its potential significance. Still, the conclusion is unescapable that the mass of the people were not unduly alarmed. The thunder emanating from the Capitol might have led one to suppose that a dissolution of the Union was imminent. Actually, if there had been a civil war in 1819-1821 it would have been between the members of Congress, with the rest of the country looking on in amazement! The only other groups which were perhaps sufficiently aroused to take up arms were the Missourians (who obviously had more at stake than anybody else), the state rights squirearchy of eastern Virginia, and a few die-hard Federalists and Clintonians in the North. To be sure, the Union would almost certainly have broken up at some time in the 1820's if the advice of extremists like John Randolph and Theodore Dwight had been followed—that is, if there had been an absolute refusal to compromise, accompanied by a contest between Northern and Southern immigrants for the possession of Missouri. But this was a remote possibility, for a compromise to cover any eventuality was always a certainty as long as Henry Clay was around and as long as so many Northern Democrats were convinced that a Federalist dark lantern conspiracy was lurking somewhere behind the antislavery movement.

As has been indicated in an earlier chapter, there was one brief moment in which public apathy was partially overcome and considerable unanimity shown in the North in favor of congressional prohibition of slavery in Missouri. This was the period in the fall and winter of 1819-1820 when the antislavery

[21] New York *National Advocate*, December 12, 1820; Newport *Republican*, February 16, 1820.

meetings were being held throughout the free states and the Democratic press had not yet reached the conclusion that the meetings were of Federalist origin. It was at this same time that a number of Northern legislatures, either by unanimous vote or overwhelming majorities, passed resolutions in favor of congressional restriction. In December, 1819, Democratic Pennsylvania, by the unanimous vote of both houses of its legislature, declared that the extension of slavery beyond the Mississippi would "impede the march of humanity and freedom through the world, and would affix and perpetuate an odious stain upon the present race."[22] First and last, New Hampshire, Vermont, Massachusetts, New York, New Jersey, Pennsylvania, Ohio, and Indiana passed resolutions against the admission of Missouri, except with the exclusion of slavery.

The Northern solidarity of sentiment regarding slavery in Missouri—which only lasted from about November, 1819, to January, 1820—can be attributed partly to the work of antislavery pamphleteers. Senator Barbour of Virginia spoke facetiously of whole "go-carts" of pamphlets.[23] Many of the addresses made in Congress were put in pamphlet form and scattered over the country. One of Tallmadge's orations was published by the New York Manumission Society. It was also translated into German and had an extensive circulation in Germany.[24] The American Convention for Promoting the Abolition of Slavery printed one thousand copies of a pamphlet containing the speeches of Tallmadge, John W. Taylor, and Rufus King as well as other antislavery material.[25] As has been shown, a New York committee published the substance of two of

[22] Annals of Congress, 16 Cong., 1 Sess., 71.   [23] Ibid., 324.

[24] Speech of the Honorable James Tallmadge, Jr. of Duchess County, New-York, in the House of Representatives of the United States, on Slavery (New York, 1819); Poughkeepsie Dutchess Observer, February 23, 1820.

[25] Papers Relative to the Restriction of Slavery, Speeches of Mr. King, In the Senate, And of Messrs. Taylor & Talmadge . . . With a Report of a Committee of the Abolition Society of Delaware (Philadelphia, 1819); Minutes of the Seventeenth Session of the American Convention for Promoting the Abolition of Slavery, and Improving the Condition of the African Race (Philadelphia, 1821), 24.

King's addresses in the Senate.[26] Additional pamphlets came from the pens of Daniel Raymond of Maryland, Joseph Blunt of New York, William Hillhouse of Connecticut, and Robert Walsh.[27] Walsh's brochure, which made a great impression on his contemporaries, contained arguments that foreshadowed Seward's later doctrine of the "higher law."

Had the North been able to maintain for several years the solid and uncompromising antislavery front which it had established by December, 1819, the South and Southwest would probably have withdrawn from the Union in preference to perpetually being outvoted in Congress. It was the knowledge of that very fact which perhaps did more than anything else to undermine Northern solidarity. Former Governor Morgan Lewis of New York was speaking for a great many Northerners when he declared that while he had always been opposed to slavery, he did not believe that Congress had the constitutional right to prohibit it in Missouri and that should the attempt "be persisted in, it requires no Prophet to foresee that it will terminate in a Severance of Empire."[28] The other factors which soon wrecked all hope for Northern unity have already been mentioned. Victims of the depression insisted that Congress should give their woes priority over those of the slaves, while Northern Democrats became suspicious of the excessive antislavery zeal of certain Federalists and Clintonians.

As soon as a considerable body of Northern Democrats were convinced that the Federalists and Clintonians were seeking to

[26] Rufus King, *Substance of Two Speeches, Delivered in the Senate of the United States, on the Subject of the Missouri Bill* (New York, 1819). Another edition of this work was published at Philadelphia in 1819.

[27] Daniel Raymond, *The Missouri Question* (Baltimore, 1819); [Joseph Blunt], *An Examination of the Expediency and Constitutionality of Prohibiting Slavery in the State of Missouri. By Marcus* (New York, 1819); [Robert Walsh], *Free Remarks on the Spirit of the Federal Constitution* (Philadelphia, 1819). Hillhouse wrote at least three pamphlets on the Missouri question, all published at New Haven in 1820: (1) *Pocahontas; A Proclamation: With Plates;* (2) *The Crisis, No. 1, or Thoughts on Slavery, Occasioned by the Missouri Question;* (3) *The Crisis, No. 2, or Thoughts on Slavery, Occasioned by the Missouri Question.*

[28] Bonney, *Legacy of Historical Gleanings,* I, 339.

make political capital out of the Missouri question, a compromise with the South was inevitable. Because of the Southern leadership of the Democratic party, the Federalists had used slavery as an issue against the Northern Democracy for more than two decades, and the latter had grown accustomed to being denounced as tools of Virginia overlords. It is not surprising, therefore, that Democrats like Martin Van Buren should be inclined to make light of the antislavery movement in 1819-1821 on the ground that it was "old-hat" and Federalist inspired. Van Buren declared in his autobiography that he was forced to give nominal support to the movement to avoid injuring himself politically but that he did not sympathize "in the Missouri Agitation because I could not conceal from myself the fact, to which all we saw and heard bore testimony, that its moving springs were rather political than philanthropical." When Van Buren was asked to participate in the meeting held at Albany regarding Missouri, he replied that he was too busy to attend. He allowed his name to be used as one of the sponsors of the gathering but declined to sign the resolutions which it adopted.[29] Erastus Root, a former congressman and a power in the Bucktail faction of the New York Democracy, agreed with Van Buren. When the New York legislature was considering resolutions protesting against the admission of Missouri with slavery, Root tried to replace them with a substitute motion which, while strongly antislavery, was ambiguous on the Missouri question. The substitute, although the Assembly rejected it by a vote of 75 to 31, was more acceptable to many Democrats than the resolutions which were adopted.[30] H. A. S. Dearborn, Collector of the Port of Boston, declared that Northern Democratic congressmen "are stark, staring mad, if they think, an obstinate adherence to the restriction of Missouri, as connected with the compromise in the bill of the

29 John C. Fitzpatrick (ed.), The Autobiography of Martin Van Buren, in Annual Report of the American Historical Association for the Year 1918, II (Washington, 1920), 99-100, 140; Henry F. Jones to Martin Van Buren, January 19, 1820; Van Buren to Jones, January 21, 1820, Martin Van Buren Papers, Library of Congress.
30 New York Columbian, January 20, 21, 1820.

senate, will be agreeable to their constituents."[31] William P. Preble, one of the Democratic bosses of Maine, was afraid that the Federalists "have made 'cats paws' of *some* of our prominent republicans—men so anxious to appear before the public that they did not percieve they were merely *made use of*."[32]

There were rumors—so numerous that they could be had for a dime a dozen—that Rufus King hoped to rejuvenate the Federalist party and elevate himself to the presidency by means of the dispute over Missouri. Northern Democrats were so impressed by these rumors that, says Homer C. Hockett, "It may be found . . . when the subject is thoroughly investigated, that the passage of the famous compromise by which our commonwealth gained statehood was due to an erroneous belief in the personal ambition of an aged leader of a dead party."[33] As a matter of fact, the Democratic fear of King was only partly erroneous. There can be little doubt about King's views, for he was a forthright man who recorded his strong convictions in a voluminous correspondence which has been preserved. A study of his letters indicates that he was largely without personal ambition at this stage of his life and had no hope that the Federalist party would ever defeat the Democratic or, as it was still generally called, Republican party.[34] Nevertheless, King did fondly hope that the Missouri Controversy would result in a realignment of parties and secure the political predominance of the North in the national government. As the presidential election of 1824 drew near, he asserted that victory for John Quincy Adams would be a certainty if Maine, Rhode Island, and Massachusetts had done their duty in 1820. He went on to say that in 1820, for the first time, New York and Pennsylvania decidedly opposed the wishes of Virginia, "and had Massachusetts done as she ought to have done, (and for wh. omission she may be now & perhaps forever hereafter punished) the Govt. of the U. S. wd. have permanently been

[31] H. A. S. Dearborn to John Holmes, March 6, 1820, Holmes Papers.
[32] William P. Preble to John Holmes, January 16, 1820, *ibid.*
[33] Homer C. Hockett, "Rufus King and the Missouri Compromise," in *Missouri Historical Review*, II (1908), 220.
[34] King, *Rufus King*, VI, 300-303

placed in hands wh. ought to possess it, but which may never
again find as fair and honorable grounds of obtaining it."[35] It
is obvious that King's program could have been effected only
by a Northern sectional party similar to the Republican party
of the 1850's and 1860's, which was exactly the thing that a
great many Northern Democrats did not want. The political
power motive recurs again and again in the King correspondence. He professed to be interested in slavery solely because
of "its bearing and effects upon great political interests," and
predicted that if the South prevailed in Missouri, "we shall be
lost in political power or influence in the union. The slave
Legion will parcel out the great offices, will determine all
questions respecting the general & common welfare and, in a
word, will rule us as they have done in contempt of our rights."
According to King, the Northerners who voted for the compromise of 1820 had assisted in placing the free states "under a
Govt. of the privileged order of Men who are henceforth to be
& forever to remain our Masters."[36]

The Democrats' fear of King was no greater than their distrust of the motives of Governor De Witt Clinton of New York.
Nominally a Democrat, Clinton was never fully restored to the
good graces of party regulars after he accepted Federalist aid
in his campaign for the presidency against Madison in 1812.
At the time of the Missouri Controversy, he was at odds with
the Monroe administration and had accused officials of the
federal government of interfering in local New York politics.[37]
The rumors regarding Clinton and Missouri were reflected in
two toasts given at a Bucktail Democratic Fourth-of-July celebration at Poughkeepsie, James Tallmadge's home town, in
1820. Tallmadge, who had now become affiliated with the
Bucktails, was present and was complimented in one of the
toasts for his efforts to restrict slavery. At the same time, this
toast was aimed at Clinton: "*Slavery*—A foul stain upon our
national character; but a political adventurer shall not use it
for purposes of personal elevation."[38]

35 *Ibid.*, 501.   36 *Ibid.*, 278-79, 288, 324-25.
37 Albany *Argus*, January 23, 1821.   38 *Ibid.*, July 18, August 1, 1820.

Unlike Rufus King, Clinton did not wear his heart on his sleeve and was cagey about committing himself in writing.[39] It is therefore difficult to know exactly what his motives in the Missouri Controversy were. He was popularly regarded as one of the leaders of the movement to check slavery expansion and twice mentioned the subject in messages to the legislature. In January, 1820, he urged the legislators to give expression to the sentiments of the state on this important question, assuring them that "slavery is an evil of the first magnitude; and whatever may be the consequences, it is our duty to prohibit its progress in all cases where such prohibition is allowed by the constitution. No evil can result from its inhibition more pernicious than its toleration."[40]

Clinton's close friends and supporters were active in the campaign against Missouri slavery, particularly the following: Thomas Addis Emmet (brother of the Irish martyr, Robert Emmet); John Pintard, founder of the New-York Historical Society and Secretary of the New York Chamber of Commerce; Thomas Eddy, the Quaker philanthropist; Judge Ambrose Spencer; Representative John C. Spencer; Solomon Van Rensselaer, the Federalist congressman from the Albany district; Charles G. Haines; Ferris Pell; and Judge William W. Van Ness. Though Clinton and many of his friends were lifelong antislavery men, they were accused of harboring disunion views and of attempting to keep the Missouri issue alive as long as possible in order to use it as a vote-getting device. The letters written to Representative Van Rensselaer by leading Clintonians leave no doubt that in some cases these accusations were true. When Clinton was running against Daniel D. Tompkins, Vice-President of the United States and Democratic party regular, for governor of New York in 1820, Ambrose Spencer, Clinton's brother-in-law, wrote Van Rensselaer concerning Tompkins: "Is it true that he was against any restriction in regard to slavery in Missouri? It is very important that

[39] Missouri is scarcely mentioned in the Clinton letterbooks and manuscript correspondence, which are now in the possession of Columbia University.
[40] New York *Columbian*, January 7, 1820.

we should be able to fix that charge upon him if it be true—let me know as soon as possible."[41] In November, 1820, after the country at large had lost interest in Missouri, Charles G. Haines, who at one time was Clinton's private secretary, wrote Van Rensselaer apropos of the Missouri constitution: "For God's sake stand firm, and reject this odious and abominable instrument. . . . If Civil War and division of the Union come, so be it! Rather have these, than the extended horrors of Slavery. . . . If we do our duty, nothing can resist the tide of Northern feeling and Northern independence that has set in. The Bucktails stand mute and thunderstruck." It would be interesting to know exactly what Haines meant when he stated further on in his letter: "In all your operations at Washington, I hope nothing will be said of making Mr. Clinton our President. My feelings toward him you know and God knows; but we must embrace the whole ground, and this cannot be done, if we build upon the name and merits of any particular individual. This is Gov. Clinton's own opinion, as well as my own."[42] In December, 1820, Ferris Pell, a Clintonian, wrote Van Rensselaer that "All our friends hope the question on the *Missouri Bill* will be hard pressed."[43] In January, 1821, Judge William W. Van Ness, one of Clinton's Federalist supporters, wrote to exult over the rejection of Missouri's constitution, which event, he said, "has done more to restore the North to its just weight and influence in the National Councils than any event which has occurred for twenty years. Let us but be faithful to ourselves in the further progress of this question and we shall be redeemed from the contempt which was brought upon us by that miserable Sycophant who betrayed us to the lords of the South, to enable him to subserve his own purposes. I allude to that smallest of small men Daniel D. Tompkins."[44]

In the gubernatorial election of 1820, the Clintonians accused Tompkins, the candidate of the Bucktail or Tammany Democrats, of having sided with the South in the Missouri contest. Tompkins denied the charge, and his candidacy was supported

[41] Bonney, *Legacy of Historical Gleanings*, I, 344.
[42] *Ibid.*, 354-55.   [43] *Ibid.*, 359.   [44] *Ibid.*, 360.

by Rufus King, who had long disliked Clinton, and by James Tallmadge, who had fallen out with Clinton over patronage.[45] The Clintonians, however, continued to insist that Tompkins was pro-Southern. This was made the basis for an appeal to Negro voters in Clinton's behalf.[46] A pamphlet published at Canandaigua, entitled *The Advocates of Slavery in the State of New York, Exposed*, attributed the passage of the compromise of 1820 to Tammany's betrayal of the North.[47] Throughout the Missouri Controversy it was noticeable that while the Bucktail press in New York City and Albany was preaching moderation, the Clintonian papers were bitter against any suggestion for a compromise. Clinton was re-elected governor in 1820 in a close race. The Federalists, who held the balance of power, largely supported him in spite of the efforts of the King family on the other side.[48]

As for the Clintonians and a majority of the Northern Federalists, it can be said in conclusion that they were much more militant and uncompromising toward the South than the Democrats. There were, to be sure, certain exceptions such as Senator William Hunter of Rhode Island and Representative Henry Storrs of New York, who voted for both the first and second Missouri compromises. The general Federalist and Clintonian attitude, however, was expressed by an anonymous writer in a Federalist newspaper who exulted over "the weapon, which has at length placed itself in our hands" and over "the new parties, which this question is likely to produce."[49] Rufus King and other Federalists were eager to forget old labels and unite with Northern Democrats in a new sectional party that would assure Northern hegemony in the national government. Such a union would have been acceptable to some Democrats but was anathema to the party press and to many old-line regulars. These

[45] King, *Rufus King*, VI, 318-19, 322-23, 326-28, 336; Alexander, *Political History of New York*, I, 274. King received assurances from his son and from Van Buren that Tompkins was sound in his thinking on the Missouri question.
[46] New York *National Advocate*, April 5, 11, 12, 13, 21, 1820.
[47] *Ibid.*, April 3, 1820; Canandaigua *Ontario Messenger*, March 28, 1820.
[48] Fox, *Decline of Aristocracy in New York*, 198-200.
[49] Boston *Daily Advertiser*, March 2, 1820.

denounced the antislavery movement as a Federalist conspiracy and used their influence to secure a compromise with the South.

Right and wrong are often a matter of viewpoint, and only a dogmatic person would attempt to say whether Rufus King or the moderate Democrats were "right" in 1820-1821. From their viewpoint, the Democratic regulars were justified in clinging to the Virginia leadership of their party and spurning a union with antislavery Federalists. Though they ignored the fact that a Democrat, Tallmadge, had begun the contest over Missouri and though they erred in thinking that any Federalist cabal or conspiracy on the subject ever existed, they still appraised the antislavery movement correctly as far as it affected their own destiny. Here potentially was a weapon by means of which the Democratic party might be overthrown by conservative Federalists and by the Clintonians, who in New York had become the heirs of Federalism.[50] Rufus King's logical mind foresaw the rise of the sectional Republican party of 1854, and he erred only in supposing that the country was ripe for it in 1820. The course he favored was the same as that advocated by Lincoln when the latter wrote in 1860: "Entertain no proposition for a compromise in regard to the extension of slavery. The instant you do they have us under again: all our labor is lost, and sooner or later must be done over. . . . Have none of it. The tug has to come, and better now than later."[51] Those Northern Democrats who were as logical as King were unwilling to follow his leadership, since to do so required the repudiation of the Virginia Dynasty, under whose banner they had so long been enrolled. They could not forget that it was Virginia which had spoken out in resolutions against the Alien and Sedition Acts when Northern legislatures were silent or defended the Federalist "Reign of Terror." It was a Virginia senator, Stevens Mason, who had ridden to Vermont in 1799 to ransom Matthew Lyon, the scourge of aristocracy, from a Fed-

---

50 For the story of how Federalists became Clintonians in New York and Clintonians later turned into Whigs, see Fox, *Decline of Aristocracy in New York.*

51 John G. Nicolay and John Hay, *Abraham Lincoln A History* (10 vols., New York, 1886), III, 259.

eralist jail.[52] Anti-Missourian Federalists, reasoned many a Northern Democrat, were merely the same old reactionary group who had sponsored Hamiltonian aristocracy and later sympathized with Tory England against Republican America in the War of 1812. In 1819-1821 there were still many points of disagreement between Democrats and Federalists. As late as the great contest of 1817 in Connecticut, whose outcome paved the way for the transformation of that commonwealth into a modern state, the Federalists had defended the union of church and state and wished to retain Congregationalism as an establishment.[53] In the New York constitutional convention of 1821, Federalists and Clintonians opposed the extension of the suffrage and other reforms which a majority of the Democrats desired.[54] Thus the interests of Northern Democrats and Federalists were so incompatible that there was little chance of a permanent anti-Southern coalition between them in 1820.

In refusing to join wholeheartedly in the Anti-Missourian Crusade, the Northern Democracy was setting a precedent to which it would long adhere. When slavery became an issue in the thirties, Jacksonian Democrats were critical of antislavery men. They feared, says Schlesinger, that abolitionism was "a conservative plot" which would distract attention from the vital issues of banking and currency and disrupt the alliance between Northern and Southern liberals. Van Buren took the same stand which he had taken in 1820, while Churchill C. Cambreleng of New York branded the abolitionists as "almost exclusively, the old 'Church and State' faction."[55] Van Buren and Cambreleng later had a change of heart and became Free Soilers, but not until New Deal days did the national Democratic party embrace the principle of equal rights for Negroes. Woodrow Wilson, last pre–New Deal Democratic President, had the traditional Southern attitude toward the race question. His election in 1912 evidently was regarded in some circles as

[52] Claude G. Bowers, *Jefferson and Hamilton* (Boston, 1925), 388.
[53] Richard J. Purcell, *Connecticut in Transition 1775-1818* (Washington, 1918), 347-49.
[54] Fox, *Decline of Aristocracy in New York*, 238-69.
[55] Schlesinger, *Age of Jackson*, 424-25.

a victory for white supremacy, since it was followed by the introduction of a flood of anti-Negro legislation in Congress.[56]

From the time James Tallmadge introduced his amendment to the Missouri bill until the enactment of the last of the Missouri compromises, public opinion in most of the Northern states went through this cycle: indifference, temporary antislavery enthusiasm as a result of the Burlington–New York sponsored mass meetings, then more indifference and a determination on the part of Democratic leaders to lay the question forever at rest. New Hampshire provides a good illustration of this cycle of opinion.

On November 30, 1819, the Concord, New Hampshire, *Patriot* declared that "Whatever may be the public feeling *south* of the Potomac, there is but one sentiment *north* of the Chesapeake on this subject—and that is, if the evil which already exists cannot be prevented, at least that slavery shall not be permitted to spread beyond its present confines." If there was anyone who was qualified to speak for the Democracy of New Hampshire in 1819 it was Isaac Hill, publisher of the *Patriot*. He had made his paper the outstanding organ of the Democratic party in the state, and so great was his influence that he was said to "carry New Hampshire in his breeches pocket."[57]

On December 14, 1819, an antislavery meeting was held at Portsmouth. This gathering was well attended and, with only two or three dissenting voices, arrived at the conclusion that Congress possessed the power to prohibit slavery in Missouri and ought to exercise it.[58] Late in December, former Congressman Salma Hale, a Democrat, wrote to John W. Taylor to describe a similar meeting which had been held at Keene. "Our resolutions," said Hale, "express what is nearly, if not quite, the unanimous sentiment of the State."[59]

[56] Arthur S. Link, *Wilson, The Road to the White House* (Princeton, 1947), 502; Franklin, *From Slavery to Freedom*, 445-46.

[57] Everett S. Stackpole, *History of New Hampshire* (4 vols., New York, n.d.), III, 95.

[58] Portsmouth *Oracle*, December 18, 1819; Portsmouth *Gazette*, December 21, 28, 1819; George S. Hillard, *Memoir and Correspondence of Jeremiah Mason* (Cambridge, 1873), 231-32.

[59] Salma Hale to John W. Taylor, December 27, 1819, Taylor Papers.

The unanimity in New Hampshire which was so pleasing to Hale was surprisingly short-lived. As Hale admitted, opinion had never been entirely unanimous. Senator John F. Parrott had voted against the Missouri restriction in Congress, and his friends as well as a few party regulars made a slight attempt to prevent the calling of the Portsmouth meeting.[60] This group soon gained in strength, especially when Isaac Hill's Concord *Patriot* changed sides and charged that the object of those who were stirring up the slavery quarrel "is not so much to put a stop to slavery, as it is to create a Northern and a Southern interest; not so much to further the Union and happiness of this Republic, as to effect sinister and party purposes."[61] Early in 1820 former Governor William Plumer, an ardent slavery restrictionist, wrote his son, Congressman William Plumer, Jr., that the people of New Hampshire "are in general right—they condemn Parrot's vote." But he added that former Governor Jeremiah Smith, Judge Levi Woodbury, and Isaac Hill were on the other side and that former Senator Clement Storer feared the question would irritate the South.[62] Former Governor Smith was a Federalist, which emphasizes the fact that not even the Federalists were unanimous.

By the time the summer of 1820 arrived, public opinion in New Hampshire had moved a long way from its former solidarity on the Missouri question. When Governor Samuel Bell received resolutions from the Virginia legislature, upholding the position of Missouri and the South, it was doubtful whether New Hampshire would even answer them. Prodded by Jeremiah Mason, the New Hampshire legislature did issue a strong reply to Virginia, though only with reluctance and misgivings on the part of many of the legislators. Mason, one of the state's foremost lawyers and a Federalist, discussed the situation in a letter to Rufus King shortly before the legislature met. He feared, he wrote, that there would be considerable "difficulty in bringing our Legislature to the expression of any strong opinion with that degree of unanimity which is necessary to give it

[60] Hillard, *Jeremiah Mason,* 231.
[61] Concord *Patriot & State Gazette,* February 15, 29, 1820.
[62] William Plumer to William Plumer, Jr., February 21, 1820, Plumer Papers.

effect; the dominant [Democratic] party has been already greatly alarmed. Many of their influential leaders, among whom are the judges of our Superior Court, pretend to have doubts of the constitutional power of Congress to impose the restriction against slavery." Mason explained to King that "The true cause of the alarm is a fear that a schism may be produced in the party. The leaders are constantly recommending a peaceable acquiescence in the decision that Congress has made, and a careful abstaining from whatever may cause irritation, provoke local jealousies, etc."[63]

Historians have devoted much attention to the "dough face" Northern congressmen who supported the compromise of 1820, but they have largely overlooked a much more influential "dough face" element—the Northern Democratic press. From Philadelphia to Portland, leading Democratic journals lambasted the attempt to restrict slavery in Missouri as a Federalist "plot," applauded suggestions for a compromise, and destroyed all semblance of Northern unity. An analysis of press opinion in each state makes this quite apparent.

In Pennsylvania the two most important Democratic papers in 1819-1821 were the Philadelphia *Democratic Press,* published by the Irishman, John Binns, and the Philadelphia *Franklin Gazette,* published by John Norvell and Benjamin Franklin's grandson, Richard Bache.[64] The *Democratic Press* expressed little interest in the proposed Missouri restriction until November, 1820, when it vigorously denounced those who were seeking to revive the dispute. While conceding that such people were sincere in many cases, it believed that some of the more active on the same side were animated by the spirit

[63] Hillard, *Jeremiah Mason,* 245-46; King, *Rufus King,* VI, 348; *Niles' Weekly Register,* XVIII (1820), 337-40; Samuel Bell, *Message From His Excellency the Governor, Communicating Sundry Resolutions of the Legislature of Virginia on the Missouri Question* (n.p., 1820).

[64] William Duane's anti-Southern Philadelphia *Aurora* could hardly be called a Democratic newspaper in 1820. Though Duane considered himself the "father of democracy" in Pennsylvania, he had for years been a bitter opponent of both the national and state Democratic administrations. Klein, *Pennsylvania Politics,* 45.

of the Hartford Convention and moved solely by political motives. It concluded that "Those who have upon Christian Principles and the principles of Freedom, taken an active and zealous part, would do well to review their conduct and examine how far they have been lending themselves for political purposes." In February, 1821, the *Democratic Press* urged Pennsylvania congressmen to vote for Senator Roberts' proposed compromise, declaring that "They may assure themselves that such a vote will be most acceptable in Pennsylvania.—They will be hailed as honest patriots, who have taken the alarm and fled, when they saw the kind of men and motives and objects, which were combatting by their sides."[65]

The *Democratic Press* and *Franklin Gazette*, which were usually at each other's throats in local politics, saw eye to eye on the Missouri question. The *Franklin Gazette* was at first moderate in its attitude and condemned abusive language on either side, but in November, 1820, it took a much stronger stand and denounced the attempt being made to revive the controversy. "We sincerely believe," it stated, "that the agitators of the Missouri question *now* are actuated by a desire to sever the union, if they cannot otherwise obtain the reins of power. They hate the southern states, not for their slavery, but for their republicanism. It was with their aid we upset the fabric of federal folly and tyranny in 1800; and they never have and never will forgive them and us for it." Later, in February, 1821, the *Franklin Gazette* asserted that slavery in Missouri "has been made a stalking horse for the discomfited 'moral' traitors of the Hartford Convention."[66]

New Jersey had the distinction of being one of the few Northern seaboard states whose leading Democratic presses did not denounce Anti-Missourianism as a Federalist plot. The Newark *Centinel of Freedom* and Trenton *True American*, the

[65] Philadelphia *Democratic Press,* November 20, 1820, February 21, 1821. The *Democratic Press* published a number of letters from writers who condemned Northern agitation against Southern slavery. See for November 30, December 2, 4, 26, 30, 1820, February 22, 1821.

[66] Philadelphia *Franklin Gazette,* March 21, November 1, 1820, February 24, 1821.

party Bibles of good Jersey Democrats, consistently favored the congressional restriction of slavery in Missouri.[67] Both, however, were moderate in their antislavery views and threw open their columns to writers who took the other side. One such writer, "SENEX," wrote to the *Centinel of Freedom* to ask: "Has not the clamour raised on the Missouri question, originated almost wholly with the federal party? Who called the meeting at Trenton? Federalists. Who were the orators? Federalists. What papers were most clamorous? Federal."[68] To another writer who advanced similar arguments, Senator James J. Wilson's *True American* replied that it could not accept the view that all the Federalists who advocated restriction "were actuated by sinister views, nor that all the Republicans who supported it were the dupes of designing men."[69]

Those Jerseymen who thought they could detect the presence of a Federalist in the Missouri woodpile received editorial support from the New Brunswick *Fredonian,* which maintained that the contest was "introduced and agitated" by Federalists and supporters of Clinton "for the elevation of *this* man, or some other Catiline." And, said the *Fredonian,* the slavery controversy had "the same end to answer that the Hartford Convention had, to wit, *the acquisition of power.* Yes, this indeed is the secret spring, the moving principle, that actuates these hypocritical brawlers about *slavery,* when many of them would hardly give a crust of bread to a poor black, to save him from starvation."[70]

In New York state, press opinion toward the Missouri question was pretty much divided along party lines. A strong antislavery stand was taken by the principal Federalist papers: William Coleman's New York *Evening Post,* which had been

[67] Newark *Centinel of Freedom,* November 30, 1819, December 26, 1820; Trenton *True American,* June 21, 1819; Fee, *Transition from Aristocracy to Democracy in New Jersey,* 147.
[68] Newark *Centinel of Freedom,* August 15, 1820. For two similar letters, see *ibid.,* March 14, September 12, 1820.
[69] Trenton *True American,* September 9, 1820.
[70] New Brunswick *Fredonian,* August 17, 1820.

founded by Alexander Hamilton; Theodore Dwight's New York *Daily Advertiser;* William L. Stone's New York *Commercial Advertiser;* and the New York *American,* which was published by members of the King, Verplanck, and Hamilton families. Vying in restrictionist zeal with the Federalists were the chief Clintonian journals: the New York *Columbian,* Albany *Statesman,* and Canandaigua *Ontario Messenger.* On the other hand, the two main organs of the regular Democrats, the New York *National Advocate* and Albany *Argus,* were pro-Southern.

The pro-Southern attitude of the New York *National Advocate,* a Tammany paper, is partly explainable by the fact that its able and versatile Jewish editor, Mordecai M. Noah, had spent part of his life in Charleston. At first Noah was sympathetic toward the Tallmadge amendment and attended the meeting held in New York in November, 1819, to protest against the admission of new slave states. It was not long before he changed his mind and decided that "the shield of humanity" was being used to cover "the most envenomed and long pent-up political hostility." Soon the *National Advocate* was asserting that slavery restriction was unconstitutional. By August, 1820, it was sure that the whole Missouri Controversy was a plot instigated by Daniel Webster and involving Justice Joseph Story, Joseph Hopkinson, Theodore Dwight, Robert Walsh, and Peter Jay. "*It was,*" concluded Noah, "*a second Hartford convention business,* conducted under the garb of humanity, and thousands took an active part who now view the actors and their objects with indignation."[71]

Noah had often been vilified because of his race and religion. He now found himself saddled with the additional charge of being proslavery.[72] The Clintonian New York *Columbian* called him "the mouth piece of southern principles and southern dictation," and accused him of licking "the dust from the feet of southern slaveholders." Noah, who could give as good as he

[71] New York *National Advocate,* November 18, 1819, January 25, February 19, August 24, 1820.

[72] Isaac Goldberg, *Major Noah: American-Jewish Pioneer* (Philadelphia, 1936), 111-20, 155-58, 251-53.

received, censured his opponents for "shedding more crocodile tears" over the Negroes in order "to get the reins of power in their hands."[73]

The regular Democratic paper in Albany was the *Argus*, later renowned as the organ of the Albany Regency. Like the *National Advocate*, it had no enthusiasm for the antislavery cause, being more afraid of De Witt Clinton than of Southerners. It deplored the efforts of Federalists to "make the Missouri a sectional question," and charged Clinton with striving "to convert the unhappy controversy respecting the state of Missouri, into a foundation for *organizing* a northern confederacy, as a preparatory step to a severance of the Union."[74]

In Connecticut the Democratic editors had scarcely a good word to say for the advocates of congressional restriction. The power of Federalism had not been broken in the Nutmeg State until 1817, when Oliver Wolcott led a Democratic-Tolerationist coalition to victory by defeating John Cotton Smith, "last of the Puritan governors" of Connecticut. In 1818 the Democrats were able to present the state with a new constitution which disestablished the Congregational church and provided for other reforms.[75] The Missouri Controversy followed so closely on the heels of the "Revolution of 1817-1818" that Connecticut Democrats were hardly in a mood to unite with Federalists against the South. Governor Wolcott took a strong antislavery stand[76] but could not carry the party press with him.

The Federalists of Connecticut, led by the Hartford *Courant*, were excessively zealous in their support of slavery restriction. Edward Mansfield, who in this period was a young student at Farmington, wrote in his memoirs of the bitterness of his Federalist teacher and neighbors toward the South.[77] Burning in

[73] New York *Columbian*, December 2, 5, 1820; New York *National Advocate*, August 26, 1820.

[74] Albany *Argus*, January 28, 1820, March 23, 1821.

[75] Purcell, *Connecticut in Transition*, 346-51, 373-419; Jarvis M. Morse, *A Neglected Period of Connecticut's History 1818-1850* (New Haven, 1933), 1-7.

[76] Hartford *American Mercury*, May 9, 1820.

[77] Edward D. Mansfield, *Personal Memories Social, Political, and Literary with Sketches of Many Noted People 1803-1843* (Cincinnati, 1879), 86.

effigy was the order of the day. Because he voted for the compromise of 1821, Representative James Stevens was burned in
effigy at Litchfield while young Henry Ward Beecher and other
boys danced around the flames.[78] Senator James Lanman suffered a similar indignity at Hartford in 1820 as a result of one
of his votes on the Missouri bill. Lanman was a member of the
Democratic or, as it was then often called in Connecticut with
reference to its advocacy of religious freedom, Toleration party.
Consequently the burning of his effigy became a party issue.
According to the Federalist version, it was burned by a vast
assemblage of citizens, while a Democratic source insisted that
only a host of boys and a few Federalists were involved. Some
Federalists condemned the burning but were probably secretly
pleased.[79] In the state senatorial election of 1820 the Tolerationists (Democrats) were branded as "ADVOCATES FOR
SLAVERY!!!" Nevertheless, they won the election.[80]

The Democratic fear of antislavery Federalism in the "Land
of Steady Habits" is shown by this anonymous article that appeared in the Hartford *Times:*

That the Missouri question covers designs "dark and deep," is now
no longer doubted. At first, discerning men *suspected* mischievous
designs; finding it difficult to believe that such men as the notorious
Theodore Dwight felt their "bowels yearn with compassion" for the
Southern slaves; but these suspicions are now confirmed—what was
at first prophecy, is now history. The mask is completely thrown off.
The republicans in this community are not to be deceived by this
deep laid plot, and whilst they deeply lament the existence of
slavery, they also regret that there are men among us so depraved
as to attempt to make use of their "honest feelings" upon this subject for so wicked and detestable purposes.

The *Times* agreed with this writer, for it accused the Federalists of hoping "to inflame and mislead the public sentiment,
and to revive the old spirit of hostility to the Southern States,

[78] Paxton Hibben, *Henry Ward Beecher* (New York, 1927), 34.
[79] Hartford *American Mercury,* February 22, 1820; New Haven *Journal,* February 22, 1820; Washington *Daily National Intelligencer,* February 25, 1820.
[80] Hartford *Courant,* February 29, March 28, April 11, 1820.

which they hope will tend either to bring them into power or to dissolve the Union, a project which they have long cherished, and which they will never abandon."[81] The Hartford *American Mercury* agreed with the Federalists that resistance to slavery was the first principle of republicanism, but it believed that the New England congressmen who voted against the Missouri restriction had acted conscientiously, in accordance with their interpretation of the Constitution.[82] The New Haven *Columbian Register* opined that the Federalist press wished to turn the subject of Missouri "into a pure party question. The changes have been rung for this purpose from Theodore Dwight, down to our neighbour Sherman Converse [editor of the Federalist New Haven *Journal*]."[83] Even more emphatic was the New London *Republican Advocate*, which asked: "Who are they that at this time sympathize so deeply with the southern slaves?" It answered: "Most of them are the very men who, while thousands of our fellow-citizens, our friends, our kindred, were held in worse than slavery, on board the floating dungeons of Britain, never sighed for their fate—yea, declared '*it was no essential injury*'—they are also the very men who went heart and hand with the Hartford Convention federalists in their unholy attempts to dissolve the Union!!!"[84]

The Democratic press of Rhode Island was much of the same mind with that of Connecticut. The *Patriot*, largest paper in Providence, declared that Boston Federalists deprecated the amicable settlement of the Missouri dispute since "they hoped, by it, to establish sectional parties which should take the place of the present."[85] The Newport *Republican* resented the use of the word "dough face" to describe those who voted for the compromise of 1820. This term, said the *Republican*, was considered so clever "that the whole federal pack, (including Clintonians, and all others, who would rejoice in the division and destruction of the Republican party,) in their illiberal and

81 Hartford *Times, and Weekly Advertiser*, February 22, 1820.
82 Hartford *American Mercury*, March 28, 1820.
83 New Haven *Columbian Register*, February 12, 1820.
84 New London *Republican Advocate*, March 15, 1820.
85 Providence *Patriot*, March 11, 1820.

unmanly animadversions on that question, have tossed about this witty expression, with as much eagerness as little boys will bandy about a foot-ball."[86]

The leading Democratic journal of Massachusetts, the Boston *Patriot*, which was at first mildly favorable to the proposed congressional restriction of slavery in Missouri, soon began to waver. By January, 1820, it had decided that tolerating slavery was a lesser evil than placing the Union in jeopardy. It disapproved of the revival of the Missouri Controversy in the summer of 1820 and finally ended up by hailing it "as a most fortuitous circumstance, that so many of the *Hartford Convention journals* have come out on this question; as while they worked in secret we knew not the extent of danger to which the nation was exposed."[87] The Boston *Yankee* was both strongly Democratic and strongly Anti-Missourian, but its office was destroyed by fire in January, 1820, and it never resumed publication. The Democratic Pittsfield *Sun* followed the lead of the *Patriot* in deploring sectionalism and declining to take part in the antislavery crusade.[88] Likewise the Portland *Eastern Argus*, oldest and most influential Democratic organ in Maine, held aloof from the crusade. Though it noted that considerable heat had been generated on the subject, it thought that "a good deal of the excitement was artificial, and would in no degree tend an enlightened and dispassionate decision of the question by the constituted authorities."[89] Even in rock-ribbed antislavery Vermont, the Windsor *Republican*, after first endorsing congressional restriction, later concluded that it was a Federalist "plot." After the passage of the compromise of 1821, the *Republican* rejoiced that the Federalists "have been once more discomfited."[90]

[86] Newport *Republican*, September 27, 1820.

[87] Boston *Patriot & Daily Mercantile Advertiser*, January 10, September 29, October 20, 1820, March 2, 1821. The *Patriot* published a number of letters condemning antislavery agitation. See for December 10, 1819, January 11, February 2, March 15, 17, 18, 1820, March 29, 1821.

[88] Pittsfield *Sun*, February 16, 1820.

[89] Portland *Eastern Argus*, December 21, 1819.

[90] Windsor *Republican & American Yeoman*, February 14, 1820, March 12, 1821.

The attitude of the Northern Democratic press filled the anti-slavery forces with grief and dismay. The Clintonian New York *Columbian* observed that "The administration papers, at Washington, in Virginia, in the Carolinas, in Georgia, in Maryland, in Pennsylvania, in New-York, and in some of the eastern states are coming out hotter and hotter as the ADVOCATES OF SLAVERY. What is Republican America coming to? O, Mores! O, tempora!"[91] Said the Clintonian Canandaigua *Ontario Messenger:*

Are they afraid of having any question fairly met on its own merits? They have only, as they imagine, to bawl out, *federalism! British influence! Hartford convention! Blue lights!* and they deem the people of this country so besotted with party passion, and so ignorant, that the noise and bluster will turn their attention from the subject, or at least drown the voice of reason and truth. But they are mistaken. The citizens of this State will never be made to believe that the principles recorded in the Declaration of Independence, and enjoined by the Christian religion, are allied to those of the Hartford convention, or to treasonable plots for the dismemberment of the Union. And they will treat the insinuation that they are so connected, as an insult to their understandings.[92]

Various explanations were offered to account for the conduct of the Democratic newspapers. It was suggested that President Monroe was holding the patronage whiplash over them. Some newspapers derived much of their revenue from the privilege which they enjoyed of printing the laws of the United States. Federalists hinted that Monroe would withdraw the patronage from any paper that took a strong stand against Missouri slavery.[93] This charge will not hold water. Monroe was too undecided in his own mind about Missouri to bring pressure to bear on anybody else. Then, it was the Secretary of State, John Quincy Adams, who was in charge of the publication of the federal laws, and it is beyond imagination that this proud scion of Massachusetts would use his power to distribute pat-

91 New York *Columbian,* December 12, 1820.
92 Canandaigua *Ontario Messenger,* September 5, 1820.
93 New Haven *Journal,* February 29, 1820.

ronage for the purpose of dragooning the Northern Democratic press into the proslavery column.[94]

Where pressure was exerted on the press, it came from local party leaders rather than Monroe. It has already been pointed out that Nicholas Biddle urged the newspapers of Philadelphia to work for a compromise in 1821.[95] In the case of Maine, it is possible to discern the exact nature of the pressure to which the press was subjected. It came from no less a person than William King, first governor of Maine and most influential figure in the state. William was a half brother of Rufus King, but he was a Democrat, and his views on the Missouri question were as different from those of Brother Rufus as daylight from dark. Having heartily endorsed the compromise of 1820 and urged Representatives Hill and Holmes to vote for it, which they did, William was willing to share in the responsibility for its passage. He appealed to the press and presently wrote Holmes that "The gentlemen who contemplated a new party, the North against the South, will in this state I am sure be much disappointed, we are now taking measures to have all the Republican papers in Maine give such a direction to this business as will distroy their hopes here."[96] The Portland *Eastern Argus* was already in favor of the compromise and sympathetic toward Hill and Holmes, but the effect of King's admonition upon the Hallowell *American Advocate* became speedily apparent. Hitherto the *Advocate* had rivaled the Federalist Portland *Gazette* in its restrictionist zeal. Now the *Gazette* noted sorrowfully that the *Advocate* had changed its tune and wished to see the whole subject, including "the delusive compromise ... buried in oblivion."[97]

In contrast with their Democratic colleagues, many Federalist and Clintonian editors were militant against Missouri

[94] For Adams' motive in withdrawing patronage from the Canandaigua *Ontario Messenger,* see Adams, *Memoirs of J. Q. Adams,* V, 265-66.

[95] See Chapter V.

[96] William King to John Holmes, February 23, March 28, 1820, Holmes Papers; King to Mark L. Hill, March 6, 1820, William King Papers; Hatch, *Maine, a History,* I, 166.

[97] Portland *Gazette,* May 16, 1820.

slavery and filled their columns with articles advocating restriction. They also derived no end of pleasure from exchanging insults and threats of disunion with the Richmond *Enquirer* and Southern fire-eaters. A writer in the Salem, Massachusetts, *Gazette* declared that "Had I a choice, dreadful as the alternative would be, I should say with Mr. Lowry, of Pennsylvania, let the union be dissolved rather than extend Slavery." "Let them separate—," said a writer in *Poulson's Advertiser,* "with our Senator, we will exclaim—better separate, than extend Slavery—better separate, than torture the sublime principles of our free government into an authority for oppression." Dwight's New York *Advertiser* assured the South that "Of one thing, . . . you may rest assured—we cannot be browbeaten out of our rights, nor frightened out of our abhorrence of slavery."[98]

Yet, even the Northern Federalists were unable to maintain a solid front against the South. Mention has already been made of the fact that during the era of good feelings the leaders of Massachusetts Federalism, including Governor John Brooks, had embarked on a policy of co-operation with the Monroe administration. Massachusetts also wanted to secure a reimbursement from the federal government for the expenses incurred by the state militia in the War of 1812. Jonathan Mason, who was represented as the proper person *"to get our money,"* was elected to Congress from Boston in 1817 by a coalition made up of Democrats and certain Federalists. When the Missouri Controversy arose, Mason was afraid that the payment of the militia claims would be jeopardized if Massachusetts played too militant a role against slavery.[99] There were others who counseled caution: Harrison Gray Otis, John Lowell, Josiah Quincy. Otis thought that Democrats rather than Federalists should take the lead. Lowell, who had once made horrendous threats himself, was now frightened by Southern threats. The result of all this was that the Massachusetts legislature hesitated to

[98] Salem *Gazette,* March 10, 1820; *Poulson's American Daily Advertiser* (Philadelphia), March 11, 1820; New York *Daily Advertiser,* November 23, 1819.

[99] *Niles' Weekly Register,* XIII (1817), 209-10; King, *Rufus King,* VI, 274.

pass resolutions on the Missouri question. It finally did pass the resolutions, but not until Rufus King had been enraged by the vacillation of his native state and former Senator Christopher Gore had lamented that "Massachusetts cowers under the arrogant Pretentions of Virginia, and without a Struggle submits to have the Chains, under which she groans, rivetted and increased."[100] The Massachusetts appeasers were, of course, merely the exception that proved the rule, for in general it was the Federalists throughout the North who took the lead in the Anti-Missourian Crusade.

The difference in the attitude of Democratic and Federalist newspapers toward the compromise of 1820 was striking. For the most part the Democratic papers did not comment on the compromise at all. Those that did were usually in favor of it. Isaac Hill's Concord, New Hampshire, *Patriot* pronounced it "generally satisfactory, except indeed to the 'choice spirits' who wanted . . . an opportunity to fan wider the flame of party discord and sectional heart-burnings." The *Patriot* rejoiced that the "old Junto are wofully disappointed" and "the hopes of the Hartford Conventionists are again blasted." The Portland *Eastern Argus* approved of the compromise because it permitted Missouri to enter the Union on an equal footing with other states but prohibited slavery in at least four fifths of the Louisiana Purchase. The *Argus* was happy to see the end of a quarrel which had threatened the stability of the Union and happy to disappoint "the aspiring hopes of some ambitious demagogues." The Worcester, Massachusetts, *Aegis*, though it had favored congressional restriction, endorsed the compromise and was glad that so momentous a question had been terminated. The Boston *Patriot* was pleased that "The great evil of slavery, . . . will finally be eradicated from our country, and without the Eastern Junto being able to make use of it as a stepping-stone to lift themselves into power." The Portsmouth, New Hampshire, *Gazette*, an old Democratic paper, was dissatisfied with the compromise but confined its disappointment

[100] Morison, *Harrison Gray Otis*, II, 225-28; Hillard, *Jeremiah Mason*, 235-39; King, *Rufus King*, VI, 259-61, 272-73, 280, 292, 501.

to an expression of pride that New Hampshire's representatives "remained firm," in accordance with the wishes of their constituents. The Salem, Massachusetts, *Essex Register* was one of the few important Democratic newspapers in the entire country which made a spirited protest against the compromise. "We consider," it said, "the admission of Missouri as a slaveholding State, (notwithstanding the ádvantages of the admission of Maine, and the prohibition in the territory above-mentioned) as a partrial triumph of self-interest, over humanity, justice, and sound national policy."[101]

While Democratic editors greeted the compromise of 1820 with silence, approval, or mild disapproval, a veritable Niagara Falls of invective poured forth from the Federalist and Clintonian printers. Dwight's New York *Advertiser* called the compromise "a mere farce" which would deceive nobody "with sense enough to keep out of the fire." "The Slave States," said Dwight, "will henceforth maintain the perpetual ascendancy in the national councils, and the Free States, with numbers enough to assert and support all their rights and privileges, have voluntarily surrendered them." The New York *American* was afraid that the compromise would add five new states to the South and only one to the North. "Northern votes have contributed to extend and perpetuate slavery," said the New York *Columbian*. "Pity 'tis, 'tis true." The New Haven *Journal* called the compromise "MOST HORRIBLE AND DISGRACEFUL!!!" The Providence *Gazette* regarded it as "dishonourable" and "worse than nothing." The Providence *American* declared that "the Representatives from the free States have surrendered the vital principle they had so strenuously aimed to establish." The Boston *Daily Advertiser* observed that "a new wound is inflicted on the honour of our country, and the curse of slavery is extended over a tract of country nearly equal to the five original slave holding states of the Union." "MAINE," said the Salem *Gazette*, "has now, by the act of Congress, become a

101 Concord *Patriot & State Gazette*, March 14, 1820; Portland *Eastern Argus*, March 14, 1820; Worcester *National Aegis*, March 15, 1820; Boston *Patriot & Daily Mercantile Advertiser*, March 8, 1820; Portsmouth *Gazette*, March 14, 1820; Salem *Essex Register*, March 8, 1820.

separate State, of Freemen. MISSOURI, a State with *Slaves*, to rule Freemen." The Keene, New Hampshire, *Sentinel* thought that "something has been gained in the exclusion of Slavery from the territories. . . . But still we have suffered a disgraceful defeat. We had the power to prevent the *black torrent* from rolling one inch farther."[102]

The "dough face" congressmen who voted for the compromise of 1820 found themselves buried under a mountain of vituperation by the Federalist press. A writer in the New Haven *Journal* compared them to Judas. The *Journal* published a picture of a slaveholder flogging a slave and under it the caption: "Who, in *Connecticut*, are the advocates for SLAVERY [obviously a thrust at Democrats and Tolerationists]?"[103] A "Black List" of Northerners who voted against the Missouri restriction appeared in the Boston *Commercial Gazette*, Portsmouth *Oracle*, Keene *Sentinel*, and Hartford *Courant*.[104] The *Courant* placed its list under a picture depicting the horrors of the African slave trade.

There were some who regarded the "dough faces" as devils incarnate. Ferocious toasts were given against them by their enemies at various Fourth-of-July celebrations in 1820. To judge from such toasts, said the New Brunswick *Fredonian*, "there was hardly a chance for the *lives* of those gentlemen who voted for the *compromise*," much less a prospect of their being re-elected.[105] The only exhibition of rage remembered in the

[102] New York *Daily Advertiser*, March 7, 1820; New York *American*, March 8, 1820 (The *American* was anti-Clintonian and allied with the Bucktail Democrats in New York politics, but its editors, among whom were a son of Rufus King and a son of Alexander Hamilton, were Federalists. See Newburgh, New York, *Political Index*, February 8, 1820); New York *Columbian*, March 6, 1820; New Haven *Journal*, March 7, 1820; Providence *Gazette*, March 27, July 27, 1820; Providence *American, And General Advertiser*, March 10, 1820; Boston *Daily Advertiser*, March 8, 1820; Salem *Gazette*, March 10, 1820; Keene *Sentinel*, March 11, 1820.

[103] New Haven *Journal*, March 14, 1820.

[104] Boston *Commercial Gazette*, March 13, 1820; Portsmouth (New Hampshire) *Oracle*, March 11, 1820; Keene (New Hampshire) *Sentinel*, March 18, 1820; Hartford *Courant*, March 21, 1820.

[105] New Brunswick (New Jersey) *Fredonian*, August 3, 1820. The following toasts are typical: Worcester County, Massachusetts—" 'Dough Faces'—Unworthy

household of James Russell Lowell came when Lowell's father, who was a minister, lost his self-control on reading in the morning newspaper that the compromise had passed Congress.[106] Upon returning to his native state, a Northern senator who had voted against restriction was surprised when a distinguished gentleman refused to shake hands with him. He requested an explanation, to which the gentleman replied: *"I cannot shake hands with a man who has the blood of thousands on his head."*[107] In spite of such censure, and although they were assured by Joseph Story and Robert Troup that they had misrepresented the North and voted for "humbug" legislation,[108] the compromisers were not altogether in bad company. No less respectable a body than the Pennsylvania Society for Promoting the Abolition of Slavery declared that the compromise would check the spread of slavery in the West and was at least a partial victory for the abolitionist cause.[109]

One of the charges most commonly made against Northern compromisers was that they were hated even in the South, which looked upon them as foreign spies in its service. John Randolph's epithet, "dough faces," was cited as proof that Southerners "love the treason but hate the traitor."[110] Actually,

---

a residence north of 36° 30′ north latitude. May the frowns of freemen keep them in the *oven* of retirement until they are *baked* into a more thorough *consistency*." (Boston *Columbian Centinel,* July 19, 1820); Lyons, New York— "The advocates of Slavery—may they hang upon the rim of the moon with their fingers greased." (New York *Columbian,* July 19, 1820); Newville, Pennsylvania—"The members of the last congress who voted for slavery—May Cain's mark be set on their foreheads." (Philadelphia *Aurora,* July 25, 1820).

106 Edward E. Hale, *James Russell Lowell and His Friends* (Boston, 1901), 8.

107 Hartford *Courant,* June 20, 1820.

108 William W. Story (ed.), *Life and Letters of Joseph Story* (2 vols., Boston, 1851), I, 366; King, *Rufus King,* VI, 308.

109 *Minutes of the Seventeenth Session of the American Convention for Promoting the Abolition of Slavery,* 10. For an able defense of the compromise by a Northerner, see [Carey?], *Considerations on the Impropriety and Inexpediency of Renewing the Missouri Question,* 13-41, 63-64. John Quincy Adams professed to favor the compromise but seems to have secretly despised the Northern congressmen who voted for it. Adams, *Memoirs of J. Q. Adams,* IV, 530, V, 4, 12.

110 Hartford *Courant,* March 14, 1820.

the "dough faces" were heroes in the eyes of most Southerners. Jefferson gave them his warmest blessing.[111] When Jonathan Mason wrote a letter in defense of his vote, the Petersburg, Virginia, *Intelligencer* hailed him as "a moral Colossus, at whose feet the shafts of factious malice fall spent and harmless."[112] The St. Louis *Enquirer* summarized the general attitude of the slaveholding states toward the Northern representatives who voted for the compromise of 1820 when it requested that "Fame, with her brazen Trumpet, from the summit of the Allegany, proclaim their honored names thro'out the vast regions of the South and West."[113]

The second Missouri compromise or compromise of 1821 encountered far less opposition than that of 1820 for the simple reason that the country was now weary of sectional strife and ready to welcome peace at any price. The Federalist New York *Evening Post*, once enthusiastic for restriction, could only rejoice after the second compromise that an insurmountable barrier to all the other public business before Congress had at last been removed.[114] There still remained a few Federalist and Clintonian editors who saw fit to call upon the gods to avenge their wrongs. Theodore Dwight published another black list and was joined in his denunciation of the second compromise by William L. Stone, Robert Walsh, the Clintonian papers of New York and Albany, and a scattering of editors elsewhere.[115]

So far in this study there has been little mention of public opinion and the attitude of the press in Ohio, Indiana, and Illinois. There are two reasons why public opinion in this re-

[111] Ford, *Writings of Jefferson*, X, 157-58.
[112] Petersburg *Intelligencer*, quoted in Washington *Daily National Intelligencer*, April 10, 1820.
[113] St. Louis *Enquirer*, March 29, 1820.
[114] New York *Evening Post*, March 1, 1821.
[115] New York *Daily Advertiser*, March 2, 1821; New York *Commercial Advertiser*, March 6, 1821; New York *Columbian*, March 1, 1821; Philadelphia *National Gazette and Literary Register*, March 1, 1821; Albany *Statesman*, March 9, 1821; Portsmouth (New Hampshire) *Oracle*, March 10, 1821; Keene (New Hampshire) *Sentinel*, March 10, 1821; Harrisburg *Chronicle*, March 5, 15, 1821.

gion needs to be considered separately from that in the Northern seaboard states in 1819-1821. In the first place, it was still possible at that time to classify most of the newspapers along the seaboard according to party affiliation. In the overwhelmingly Democratic West, on the other hand, the old party labels had largely disappeared.[116] In the second place, a large percentage of the population of the Old Northwest was made up of Southern immigrants, which created a different situation from that existing in the East.

The gateway to the West in 1820 was Scotch-Irish Pittsburgh. This city had the distinction of being one of the few remaining Federalist strongholds in all the West, and its leading newspaper, the Pittsburgh *Gazette*, was dubbed the "lone outpost of Federalism in the West."[117] In the Missouri Controversy, however, the *Gazette* was no outpost of Federalism at all. It was as mild and conciliatory toward the South as any Democratic newspaper could be and defended its congressman, Henry Baldwin, when he voted for the compromise of 1820. Likewise the compromise was evidently acceptable to the Pittsburgh *Statesman*, which expressed happiness "that this all important subject has been decided forever."[118]

Beyond Pittsburgh lay Ohio, oldest state of the Northwest and first fruit of the Ordinance of 1787. If a straw vote had been taken in Ohio in 1820, it would undoubtedly have yielded a large majority in favor of congressional restriction of slavery. The Southern influence was not as strong here as in Illinois, and many of those who had come from the South were antislavery. Indeed, Quakers and other Southerners who disliked

116 "It is true the old division of parties are but little known in this quarter." Cleveland *Herald*, July 25, 1820; "Ohio—The elections in this state have just taken place. The political divisions of Federal and Democratic, seem here to be unknown. Yet parties exist, and as much zeal is exhibited, as in any state where the old party names still prevail." West Chester (Pennsylvania) *Village Record*, November 10, 1819.

117 Klein, *Pennsylvania Politics*, 11; Russell J. Ferguson, *Early Western Pennsylvania Politics* (Pittsburgh, 1938), 64.

118 Pittsburgh *Gazette*, March 16, 1820; Pittsburgh *Statesman*, March 15, 1820.

slavery had long been in the habit of moving north of the Ohio River in order to rear their families in free territory.[119]

In January, 1820, both houses of the Ohio legislature unanimously passed resolutions against the admission of Missouri as a slave state.[120] In Congress some Ohioans voted with the South in the first Missouri debate, but none supported the compromises of 1820 and 1821, thus making possible a proud boast at Steubenville's Fourth-of-July celebration in 1820: "The delegation of Ohio in congress; good men and true—not one *dough faced traitor* amongst them."[121]

Nevertheless, while Ohio was predominantly in favor of the Missouri restriction, it contained a substantial minority on the other side, including William Henry Harrison, afterward President of the United States. Harrison was a member of the Fifteenth, though not of the Sixteenth, Congress and voted against restriction in Missouri as well as in Arkansas in the first Missouri debate. This became an issue against him and helped to cause his defeat when he ran for Congress in 1822.[122]

The press of Ohio was far from unanimous on the Missouri question. The Cincinnati *Liberty Hall* disliked slavery but maintained that Congress did not have the constitutional power to prohibit it in new states.[123] The Cincinnati *Inquisitor Advertiser* showed little interest in the controversy and made no comment on the compromise of 1820, though it did denounce the burning in effigy of Senator Lanman by an antislavery mob at Hartford. "Much as we abhor slavery," it said, "we abhor such transactions still more."[124] The Chillicothe *Scioto Gazette*, edited by John Bailhache, seems to have favored the Missouri restriction at first. Of the compromise of 1820, it said: "This

[119] Beverley W. Bond, *The Civilization of the Old Northwest* (New York, 1934), 474; Barnhart, "Southern Influence in the Formation of Ohio," 36, 42.
[120] Steubenville *Western Herald*, January 29, 1820.
[121] Philadelphia *Aurora*, July 18, 1820.
[122] Freeman Cleaves, *Old Tippecanoe, William Henry Harrison and His Time* (New York, 1939), 252-55; Dorothy B. Goebel, *William Henry Harrison A Political Biography* (Indianapolis, 1926), 235-37.
[123] Cincinnati *Liberty Hall*, February 18, 1820.
[124] Cincinnati *Inquisitor Advertiser*, March 14, 1820.

result, although not altogether equal to our wishes, is, considering the great difference of opinion and interest which existed on the subject, perhaps the most satisfactory that could have been expected." In November, 1820, Bailhache followed the lead of various Eastern editors in professing to discern a political motive behind the antislavery movement. He assured his readers that he would be happy to oppose slavery by every constitutional means but that he did not wish to have the question "used as a stepping-stone, for the purpose of hoisting certain aspiring demagogues into office." He feared that "such is the design of the 'master-spirits,' which are now engaged in stirring up the prejudices of the people of the free states against our southern brethren. Their object evidently is, to disturb our political tranquility, that they might ride into office on the wings of the tempest." Editor Bailhache also deplored any attempt to represent the Southern people "as bloodthirsty wretches, who care nothing for the life of a slave, and think it no crime to spill his blood." To show the injustice of such charges, he pointed out that a white man had recently been executed in Raleigh, North Carolina, for the crime of murdering a slave.[125] The views of the Cleveland *Herald* were rather similar to those of Bailhache's *Scioto Gazette*. In commenting on the compromise of 1820, the *Herald* said: "Submission to the will of the majority is the duty of every citizen; and as this 'distracting question' is now settled by the competent tribunal, we sincerely hope the angry discussions to which it has given rise, and the sectional excitement it has unhappily engendered, will be permitted to sink to oblivion." The *Herald* warned that "No parties are so dangerous to the Union, and against none are we so solemnly cautioned by the illustrious Washington, as geographical ones."[126]

The Columbus *Monitor* and the Mount Pleasant *Philanthropist* felt differently from the newspapers whose opinions

125 Chillicothe *Scioto Gazette, and Fredonian Chronicle*, March 16, November 16, December 14, 1820.
126 Cleveland *Herald*, March 21, 1820.

have just been cited. The restrictionist *Monitor* was filled with "grief and . . . astonishment" by the passage of the compromise of 1820. Since the *Philanthropist* was nationally known as an antislavery organ, it was not surprising that it should say of the compromise that "the man who regards the prosperity of his country and the happiness of his species, will long have occasion to lament this decision."[127]

The Gibraltar of Anti-Missourianism in Ohio was not the Western Reserve, as one might expect, but the town of Steubenville. Here it was that James Wilson, grandfather of Woodrow Wilson, edited his Democratic and militantly anti-Southern *Western Herald*. While at first the *Western Herald* accepted the compromise of 1820 with good grace, it was not long before it was calling it "a disgraceful compromise—a compromise, the advantages of which are all on one side." Wilson joined Theodore Dwight and the Federalist diehards in repudiating the spirit of the compromise and attempting to reopen the whole issue of restriction even before Missouri had framed its constitution. The people of Steubenville doubtless approved of this extreme stand, for a public meeting in the town in 1819 had declared that it deprecated the introduction of slavery into new states more than it did "the horrors of war or even of intestine or civil commotion." Wilson himself, though he did not believe the Union was in danger of dissolution, felt sure that more than two thirds of the American people would prefer to risk such a calamity rather than have slavery spread over the West.[128]

Indiana, like Ohio, was predominantly in favor of the Missouri restriction but had an influential minority which espoused the opposite side. Southern immigrants had played an im-

---

[127] Columbus *Monitor*, quoted in R. Carlyle Buley, *The Old Northwest Pioneer Period 1815-1840* (2 vols., Indianapolis, 1950), II, 18; Mount Pleasant *Philanthropist*, March 18, 1820.

[128] Steubenville *Western Herald*, December 18, 1819, March 18, May 27, July 1, 1820; Francis P. Weisenburger, "The Middle Western Antecedents of Woodrow Wilson," in *Mississippi Valley Historical Review*, XXIII (1936), 375-85; Eugene H. Roseboom and Francis P. Weisenburger, *A History of Ohio* (New York, 1934), 202.

portant part in the early history of Indiana, and 58 per cent of the delegates in the convention which framed the first constitution of the state were natives of the South.[129] Many of these ex-Southerners were hostile to slavery. Others were not, however, and Indiana had long had a proslavery party.[130] Its congressional delegation in 1819-1821 consisted of Representative William Hendricks, a native of Pennsylvania, and Senators James Noble and Waller Taylor, both of whom had been born in Virginia. While Hendricks and Noble voted consistently to prohibit slavery in Missouri, Taylor's position was ambiguous. According to the Vincennes *Centinel,* published in his home town, he was proslavery.[131] In the Fifteenth Congress he supported the first clause of the Tallmadge amendment, opposed the second one, and voted to admit slaves to Arkansas. In the Sixteenth Congress he aligned himself first with one side, then the other. On two different occasions he was censured by the legislature for voting against restriction.[132]

The press of Indiana was as badly divided as in the other Northern states. The Brookville *Enquirer* was strongly restrictionist and disapproved of the compromises of 1820 and 1821. The Vincennes *Centinel* was at first of the same opinion as the *Enquirer.* Later it reversed its position and argued that Missouri was entitled to an unrestricted admission. The *Centinel* endorsed the compromise of 1820, saying that the latter ended *"the possibility of a dissolution of the Union . . . it is over*—each party has gained as much as it expected, and none can be dissatisfied with the result." The compromise of 1820 was also acceptable to the antislavery Vincennes *Western Sun,* which felt "a degree of pleasure in observing that an understanding now exists, which we hope will not be forgotten, that

[129] John D. Barnhart, "The Southern Influence in the Formation of Indiana," in *Indiana Magazine of History,* XXXIII (1937), 271.

[130] For the story of the struggle between the proslavery and antislavery parties in Indiana, see J. P. Dunn, *Indiana A Redemption from Slavery* (Boston, 1905).

[131] Vincennes *Centinel,* February 26, 1820.

[132] *Niles' Weekly Register,* XVII (1820), 344; *ibid.,* XIX (1821), 415.

the right of extending slavery north of 36 degrees and thirty minutes of north latitude, is not, hereafter, to be contended for."[133]

Montgomeryville, located in Gibson County, Indiana, was apparently the only town in all the Northern states which held a mass meeting for the purpose of defending the right of Missouri to enter the Union as a slave state. This gathering applauded Senator Taylor's record and condemned Senator Noble and Congressman Hendricks for voting to reject Missouri's constitution. Colonel John W. Maddox, who was conspicuous at the meeting, was subsequently accused of owning eight or ten slaves, kept within the state in violation of its laws. In answer to attacks made upon him by the editor of the Corydon *Gazette*, Colonel Maddox, who was more Southern than he was literate, replied that "you talk of my negro pride I very much Exult in it   you must recollect Sir that this part of the State is mostly Settled (or inhabited) by Virginians and Kentuckyans which you certainly know are the better kind of people." As for Montgomeryville, concerning which uncomplimentary remarks had been made, the colonel declared that it was a respectable town with "good building of hughed loggs and frame houses with good Shingled rooff Brick Chimneys Store houses and a potharcaries Shop."[134]

Men like Colonel Maddox were more numerous in the neighboring state of Illinois than in Indiana. Illinois had a slavery contest of its own, rivaling the Missouri Controversy and closely connected with it. This topic, however, will be discussed in a later chapter.

Although universal suffrage did not yet prevail throughout the whole country in 1820, an inkling concerning public opinion may be had from the fate, at the hands of the voters, of the

[133] Brookville *Enquirer*, March 23, April 13, 1820, March 20, 1821; Vincennes *Centinel*, February 12, 26, April 1, 1820; Vincennes *Western Sun & General Advertiser*, April 1, 1820.

[134] Brookville *Enquirer*, March 6, April 24, 1821; Washington *Daily National Intelligencer*, February 5, 1821.

eighteen "dough faces." These, it will be recalled, were the Northern congressmen who made possible the passage of the compromise of 1820—fourteen by voting with the South and the remaining four by being absent when the crucial vote was taken on March 2. The antislavery forces had left no stone unturned to bring the pressure of public opinion to bear on Congress. That had been the object of the mass meetings held at the request of the Trenton and New York correspondence committees. In January, 1820, when fresh pressure was needed, Representative John Sergeant, the Pennsylvania Federalist leader, wrote to Roberts Vaux of Philadelphia to appeal for aid. In a letter marked "Confidential," he informed Vaux that "You are not ignorant of the influence which the sentiments of our Constituents have upon our deliberations. At this moment we stand in need of it all, . . . on our side it is obvious that there is wavering and irresolution." Sergeant requested Vaux "to direct your exertions to certain points, where by the means of correspondence you may perhaps have it in your power to do something—I would particularly request your attention to New York State, the District of Maine, and the Western parts of Pennsylvania. If you can do any there, pray exert yourself."[135] Judging by the results achieved, whatever Vaux was able to do was not sufficient to accomplish Sergeant's object.

When congressional elections were held in 1820 and early in 1821, only five of the eighteen compromisers were returned to the House of Representatives. This does not mean that public opinion was against the compromise of 1820 by a ratio of thirteen to five. The compromisers who were re-elected probably won in spite of their support of the compromise rather than because of it. On the other hand, some of those who were defeated would not have won even if they had voted consistently for restriction.

One of the first "dough faces" to feel the wrath of his constituents was David Fullerton, a Democrat, of Greencastle, Pennsylvania. Soon after the passage of the compromise, he was burned in effigy by a crowd at Carlisle, a town in his dis-

[135] John Sergeant to Roberts Vaux, January 20, 1820, Vaux Papers.

trict. A feature of the burning was a large transparency bearing the words, "FULLERTON AND SLAVERY." A number of newspapers denounced the action at Carlisle. The editor of the Baltimore *Federal Gazette* called Carlisle *"Mobville,"* and similar opinions were expressed by the editors of the Westmoreland, Pennsylvania, *Republican* and Chambersburg, Pennsylvania, *Republican*. The Carlisle *Republican* defended the burning, however, asserting that it was the work of "Honest citizens of all parties, enraged to see their country tricked out of her liberty and a certain part of the human race groaning under the most ignominious servitude." The Carlisle paper concluded: "Let the advocates of slavery and all its concomitant miseries make their best of it [the burning]." In April, 1820, when Fullerton angered his constituents by voting against an increase in the tariff, it was rumored that he might be burned in effigy again. In May he resigned from Congress, feeling no doubt that popular sentiment was against him. Eventually his neighbors seem to have forgiven him, since he later served in the Pennsylvania Senate for many years.[136]

After sweeping Fullerton out of public life, antislavery men turned their attention to Pennsylvania's other compromising congressman, Henry Baldwin of Pittsburgh. Baldwin had once been a radical Democrat. Later, after becoming more conservative, he was elected to Congress on the Federalist ticket, although he was rated as neutral in party affiliation at the time of the Missouri Controversy.[137] As the nation's leading advocate of a high protective tariff, he was the darling of the manufacturing interests, whose feelings toward him are shown by a Fourth-of-July toast given at Pittsburgh in 1820: *"Henry Baldwin, Esq*—The nation looks to him as the champion of her industry; and England dreads his tariff more than our ships of battle."[138] Baldwin's vote for the compromise became an issue

---

[136] Carlisle *Republican*, March 14, 28, May 16, 1820; James L. Harrison (ed.), *Biographical Directory of the American Congress 1774-1949* (Washington, 1950), 1187.

[137] Ferguson, *Early Western Pennsylvania Politics*, 165-66, 242, 260; Washington *Gazette*, December 4, 1819.

[138] New York *Columbian*, July 18, 1820.

against him when he was opposed for re-election in 1820 by William Marks, President of the Pennsylvania Senate. There was scant likelihood of his defeat. The Pittsburgh *Gazette* and Pittsburgh *Mercury* rushed to his defense, and it was in vain that editor James Wilson, from nearby Steubenville, thundered antislavery imprecations at the "luminary, whose effulgence has dazzled the eyes of the manufacturers" and "put a *spell* upon all the types and lampblack within the goodly city of Pittsburgh." Baldwin's district, which consisted of Allegheny and Butler counties, re-elected him by a majority of 1,315 votes. In Allegheny County (Pittsburgh) he received 2,075 votes to 1,344 for Marks.[139]

Not so fortunate as Baldwin were the three New Jersey compromisers: Joseph Bloomfield, Charles Kinsey, and Bernard Smith. These three gentlemen had definitely displeased a large part of the electorate, nor did the leading Democratic journals come to their aid, as would have been the case in some places. Senator James J. Wilson, Democratic stalwart and editor of the Trenton *True American,* wrote from Trenton in May, 1820, that "Bloomfield has paid a visit to this place; and Mr. Kinsey spent three or four days here on his way home. But I cannot find that they have made any proselytes to their opinions; or softened the resentment every where felt and expressed."[140]

It is surprising that Joseph Bloomfield should have voted with the South in the Missouri dispute, for he had been a lifelong antislavery man and president of the New Jersey Abolition Society.[141] Moreover, he lived in Burlington, the fountainhead of Anti-Missourianism, and was on intimate social terms with the Boudinots and Griffiths.[142] It seems, however, that he was predestined to be always in political disagreement with his neighbors. While the Boudinots and Griffiths remained with

---

[139] Pittsburgh *Gazette,* March 16, April 6, October 9, 16, 23, 1820; Steubenville (Ohio) *Western Herald,* June 10, July 15, 22, 1820; *Niles' Weekly Register,* XIX (1820), 142.

[140] James J. Wilson to William Darlington, May 29, 1820, Darlington Papers, Library of Congress.

[141] *Poulson's American Daily Advertiser* (Philadelphia), March 22, 1820.

[142] Fee, *Transition from Aristocracy to Democracy in New Jersey,* 126-27.

"the virtuous few" in the party of "wealth and talent," Bloom-field forsook Federalism and became the first Democratic governor of New Jersey. Later, when Elias Boudinot and William Griffith launched their crusade against Missouri slavery, Bloomfield again held different views. He must have known that his stand would not be popular in Burlington, as he himself told John Quincy Adams that he had received a letter from a respectable and sober neighbor who asked him whether a civil war would not be more desirable than the extension of slavery.[143]

In 1820 New Jersey chose its congressmen by state-wide vote rather than by districts. Democratic nominations, which were tantamount to election, were made by a state convention. Bloomfield, Kinsey, and Smith were candidates for the Democratic nomination. The Missouri question was used as an issue against them, and they were both defended and denounced in numerous letters published in the press.[144] The convention did not see fit to renominate any of them.[145] According to the New Brunswick *Fredonian*, which vigorously supported Smith, the convention thought it unwise to renominate the latter because of the unpopularity which he incurred by voting for the compromise.[146] Doubtless this consideration applied equally to Bloomfield and Kinsey.

The five New York "dough faces" were Henry Meigs and Henry R. Storrs, who supported the compromise, and Walter Case, Caleb Tompkins, and Harmanus Peek, who were absent when the decisive vote was taken on March 2, 1820. Not one of these men was re-elected, but it must not be assumed that they were all defeated by the slavery issue. Harmanus Peek missed so many roll calls during his single term in Congress that his absence on March 2 probably had no significance except as evidence of illness or chronic absenteeism. In the case of the other compromisers, it must be borne in mind that

[143] Adams, *Memoirs of J. Q. Adams*, IV, 529.
[144] Newark *Centinel of Freedom*, August 8, 29, September 12, 19, 26, 1820; Trenton *True American*, September 9, 16, 23, 1820.
[145] Newark *Centinel of Freedom*, October 10, 1820.
[146] New Brunswick *Fredonian*, October 12, 1820.

New York's congressional turnover was so high in this period that it was not even customary for representatives to be re-elected. Of the twenty-seven men who represented the state in the Sixteenth Congress, only six were re-elected; and of these six, only one, John W. Taylor, had been a member of the Fifteenth Congress.[147] Not Missouri but "Clinton" and "anti-Clinton" were the catchwords in the New York congressional election of 1821, with the Clintonians polling 71,726 votes to 71,848 for their opponents.[148] Under such circumstances it is difficult to tell just what effect the Missouri question had on the fate of each candidate. The names of Meigs, Storrs, Tompkins, Case, and Peek did not appear in the general election returns, from which it would appear either that they were not candidates or else that they could not persuade any party or faction to nominate them.[149] Meigs, who was from New York City, believed that he had offended the voters by supporting a compromise; and it was almost certainly for this reason that Storrs, a Federalist who represented the Oneida County district, was retired from Congress for one term.[150] Neither Meigs nor Storrs was ruined politically. Storrs served in Congress again from 1823 to 1831, while Meigs was later president of the board of aldermen in New York City.[151]

The three Connecticut "dough faces" were Henry W. Edwards, who did not vote on March 2, 1820, and Samuel A. Foot and James Stevens, who backed the compromise. Like New Jersey, Connecticut chose its congressmen by state-wide vote instead of separate districts. Edwards insisted that he was not really a "dough face" and that he failed to vote solely because he was hungry and had sneaked home to get a bite to eat. Evidently this explanation was satisfactory to the voters. Edwards was renominated by the Democratic state convention in

---

147 New York *Commercial Advertiser*, May 22, 1821; Harrison, *Biographical Directory of Congress*, 119, 125, 132.

148 *Niles' Weekly Register*, XX (1821), 239.

149 Albany *Statesman*, May 29, 1821.

150 *Annals of Congress*, 16 Cong., 2 Sess., 532-33, 1169; Adams, *Memoirs of J. Q. Adams*, V, 228, 314.

151 Harrison, *Biographical Directory of Congress*, 1554, 1873.

1821 and encountered little opposition in the general election.[152] The convention did not renominate Foot and Stevens. Instead, Foot was a successful candidate for the state legislature. Subsequently he was a congressman, United States senator, and governor of Connecticut. Stevens held only minor offices for the remainder of his career.[153]

In Rhode Island strenuous but unsuccessful efforts were made to defeat another compromiser, Samuel Eddy. Eddy was renominated by the Democratic state convention in June, 1820. Those who disagreed with his Missouri vote nominated Samuel W. Bridgham to oppose him in the general election.[154] At first the movement against Missouri slavery had worn a nonpartisan aspect in Rhode Island and was encouraged by Dutee J. Pearce and other prominent Democrats.[155] Later the Democratic press became critical of the antislavery campaign, and the Eddy-Bridgham contest tended to revive the old hostility between Democrats and Federalists. The Federalist newspapers called loudly for Eddy's repudiation. The Providence *American* hoped that the friends of freedom would be "united and indefatigable in their laudable exertions to rescue the State from the reproach which a sanction of Mr. Eddy's vote would entail upon it to the latest generation." The Providence *Gazette* predicted that Eddy would be defeated "nor again give a Southern slave-holder an opportunity to include a Rhode-Island Representative among those '*whose principles are bounded by 36 degrees and 30 minutes North Latitude.*'" Similar opinions were voiced by the Newport *Mercury*.[156] Two Democratic papers, the Providence *Patriot* and Newport *Republican*, took up the cudgels in Eddy's behalf, accusing his opponents of be-

[152] Hartford *Courant*, March 28, 1820; Hartford *American Mercury*, March 13, April 24, 1821.

[153] Hartford *American Mercury*, March 13, April 10, 1821; Harrison, *Biographical Directory of Congress*, 1170, 1862.

[154] Providence *Patriot*, July 8, 1820, Providence *American, And General Advertiser*, August 15, 1820.

[155] Newport *Mercury*, December 18, 1819; Newport *Republican*, December 22, 1819.

[156] Providence *American, And General Advertiser*, August 18, 1820; Providence *Gazette*, July 20, 27, 1820; Newport *Mercury*, August 19, 1820.

ing Federalists.[157] The election was a heated one. Newspaper columns were filled with letters written by partisans on both sides, with some of Eddy's opponents claiming to be Democrats.[158] Eddy was re-elected, receiving 2,891 votes to 2,773 for Bridgham. The Federalist stronghold of Providence gave Bridgham a large majority.[159]

As will be shown in a later chapter, John Holmes and Mark L. Hill, the two Maine representatives who voted for the compromise of 1820, returned in triumph to the next Congress. In Maine's mother state, Massachusetts, the electorate felt differently, and Congressmen Jonathan Mason of Boston and Henry Shaw of Lanesboro were severely censured for supporting the compromise. At Stockbridge, in Shaw's Berkshire district, Fourth-of-July toasts proclaimed that "He who would make others slaves, ought himself to be a slave" and that citizens of the free states "who would *convert the National domain* into plantations for the *propagation of slaves*, are aliens and not sons."[160] Politically speaking, Shaw was said to have been "killed by the negroes."[161] He was not a candidate for re-election in 1820, though he did serve in later years as a member of the state legislature.[162]

Jonathan Mason, who represented a Boston district, had once been a Federalist but was not affiliated with either of the old parties in 1820.[163] His vote for the Missouri Compromise was vigorously defended by the Democratic Boston *Patriot*, and the Boston *Commercial Gazette* conceded that he was not guilty of

157 Providence *Patriot*, August 12, 1820; Newport *Republican*, September 27, 1820.
158 Providence *American, And General Advertiser*, August 11, 1820.
159 Providence *Patriot*, November 11, 1820.
160 Stockbridge *Berkshire Star*, July 13, 1820. For anti-Shaw letters, see *ibid.*, March 9, 23, April 20, July 20, August 24, 1820. The *Berkshire Star* was a Federalist paper.
161 William C. Fowler, *The Sectional Controversy* (New York, 1863), 83.
162 Stockbridge *Berkshire Star*, August 3, 1820. Shaw was a Democrat and not (as stated in Harrison, *Biographical Directory of Congress*, 1801) a Federalist. See Washington *Gazette*, December 4, 1819.
163 Washington *Gazette*, December 4, 1819. For evidence that Mason did not regard himself as a Federalist in 1820, see his letter to William Eustis, January 29, 1820, Eustis Papers.

corruption or intrigue.[164] Otherwise, not much was said in his favor. The Boston *Intelligencer* observed that while he was probably conscientious, his conduct was "a lasting reflection upon the judgment of those who selected him."[165] The Boston *Daily Advertiser* suggested that it might have been proper for Mason to resign when he found that his views were so different from those of his constituents. At length he did resign,[166] but not until he had voted for an increase in the tariff. His stand on the tariff was almost as unpopular in free trade and mercantile Boston as his vote for the Missouri Compromise. Lewis Tappan referred to him as "our slave & tariff representative," and Christopher Gore did not believe that he could get fifty votes if he ran for Congress again.[167]

In conclusion, a study of the congressional election of 1820-1821 throughout the Northern states indicates that a congressman who was chiefly interested in pleasing the public would have done well to vote against the compromise of 1820. The vast amount of popular indifference toward the compromise and the support given it by certain powerful groups did not alter the fact that a vote for it made many enemies without securing a corresponding number of friends. Such a vote, however, did not necessarily doom a congressman to political oblivion, especially if the local press and party leaders saw fit to come to his defense. It is not possible to determine the reaction of the voters to the second compromise or compromise of 1821. Some of the representatives who voted for it had already been defeated in the previous year, while others did not come up for re-election until 1822, by which time the Missouri question had been largely forgotten. Likewise, the public had a few years in which to cool off before it was time to pass judgment on several of the senators who advocated the two compromises.

[164] Boston *Patriot & Daily Mercantile Advertiser*, March 21, 27, 29, 1820; Boston *Commercial Gazette*, March 27, 1820.

[165] Boston *Intelligencer & Evening Gazette*, March 11, 1820.

[166] Boston *Daily Advertiser*, March 28, August 31, 1820.

[167] Lewis Tappan to Benjamin Tappan, August 30, 1820, Tappan Papers; King, *Rufus King*, VI, 347.

"It would seem as if all the Devils incarnate, both in the Eastern & Northern States, are in league against us."—James M. Garnett to John Randolph[1]

CHAPTER VII

PUBLIC OPINION
IN THE SLAVEHOLDING STATES

*T*HE MISSOURI Controversy was a topic which was always more interesting to Southern congressmen than to a majority of their constituents. It might be supposed that the introduction of the Tallmadge amendment in February, 1819, and the sulphurous debate that followed would have electrified the whole South. Instead, only the Southern members of Congress were electrified! During the summer of 1819, after the first Missouri debate, Southerners appeared to be blissfully unaware of the fact that they were engaged in a mighty sectional contest. Nowhere was popular indifference more marked than in Charleston, the future citadel of secession. Charles Pinckney, who represented Charleston in the Sixteenth Congress, departed from South Carolina in time to reach Washington when Congress convened in December, 1819. He afterwards declared that "At the time I left, or sailed, from the city I here represent, scarcely a word was said of the Missouri question; no man there ever supposed that one of such magnitude was before you."[2] Not until antislavery meetings were called in the free states and Northern legislatures and pamphleteers became active did the South begin to evince anything remotely resembling public interest in the Missouri question.

Naturally, a large part of the South ceased to be indifferent after the Anti-Missourian Crusade had been blown up to its maximum proportions in the North in the fall and winter of 1819-1820. Such proceedings in the North, said the Richmond *Enquirer,* could only bring "regret and heart-burning" to the South and West.[3] The Milledgeville, Georgia, *Journal* was distressed that Southerners did not hold meetings of their own to counteract those in the free states, and it admonished Georgians to "Come forward and speak boldly your sentiments; declare to the world that you will manfully resist all encroachments on your rights and your property."[4] Nathaniel Macon felt called upon to explain the absence of pro-Missouri mass meetings in the South. "Our people do not petition much;" he said, "we plume ourselves on not pestering the General Government with our prayers. Nor do we set the woods on fire to drive the game out."[5] Nevertheless, many public meetings were held in the South in this period to discuss such subjects as the tariff, banking, and relief for Savannah fire sufferers. In the very month that New Yorkers and Philadelphians expressed their sentiments against Missouri slavery, the citizens of Charleston met to petition Congress to establish a uniform system of bankruptcy throughout the nation.[6] It was a tribute to the self-confidence of the Southerners that they did not deem it necessary to hold meetings in Missouri's behalf. They took it for granted that their section was united, that no artificial stimulation of public opinion was necessary, and that the Southern congressional delegation could be counted upon to vote against the Missouri restriction until the end of time.

Regardless of whether they favored or opposed congressional restriction of slavery, many Southerners believed that the question had been magnified beyond its true importance. The

1 February 22, 1820, Randolph-Garnett Correspondence.
2 *Annals of Congress,* 16 Cong., 1 Sess., 1310.
3 Richmond *Enquirer,* November 23, 1819.
4 Milledgeville *Journal,* March 7, 1820.
5 *Annals of Congress,* 16 Cong., 1 Sess., 99.
6 New York *Daily Advertiser,* December 2, 1819.

Clarksville, Tennessee, *Gazette* complained that "Congress has already taken up so much time, on this, as we conceive, unimportant subject, that we fear subjects of great interest to the community will be laid over—or at least that that attention will not be paid to them which they merit."[7] "We cannot believe," said the Natchez *Republican*, "for we have never discovered, that the excitement among the people has kept any pace with that of their representatives."[8] The Frankfort, Kentucky, *Commentator* regretted that "The great and interesting concerns of commerce manufactures, &c. are suspended, and may possibly have the *go by*, to give place to windy debates, on a question magnified to greater importance than it deserves."[9] Shortly after the passage of the compromise of 1821, former Senator Charles Tait, who was then residing in south Alabama, wrote to Senator John Walker and expressed concern over the outcome of the Missouri dispute but added that "it is the relief bill [for the relief of those who could not meet payments on public land purchases] at wch. we have been looking with the most intense anxiety from this quarter."[10] In October, 1820, a Tennessean wrote to the Washington *Intelligencer* that "I take your paper, and (was it not for your giving so many of those long, killing speeches on the Missouri question,) believe it to be the best." After requesting a renewal of his subscription, this Tennessean touched upon the matter which was probably closest to the hearts of most Americans in the depression years from 1819 to 1822—the problem of how he could pay for a newspaper subscription or anything else. "God only knows," he said, "how you are to get your pay, for 'silver and gold we have none; but such as we have we will give unto thee.' "[11] For the

7 Clarksville *Gazette*, March 18, 1820.
8 Natchez *Republican*, March 28, 1820.
9 Frankfort *Commentator*, March 9, 1820.
10 Charles Tait to John W. Walker, March 5, 1821, Walker Papers. On October 16, 1820, Tait had written Walker: "I believe it is generally understood that we here [in Alabama] cannot pay for our lands if the present laws are enforced—They must be generally forfeited."
11 Washington *Daily National Intelligencer*, November 8, 1820.

most part, the letters which were written to Southern newspapers in 1819-1821 showed more interest in such topics as hard times, banking, and internal improvements than in Missouri slavery.

While there was a minority in the upper South which advocated the congressional restriction of slavery, it did not constitute an impressive percentage of the total population except in Delaware, Maryland, and the western Virginia panhandle. There was a considerable diversity of opinion in Delaware, as was to be expected, since that state was neither entirely Southern nor entirely slaveholding. Slavery was not profitable in the Chesapeake latitude, and in 1820 three fourths of Delaware's Negro population was free.[12] The state also had an active abolition society and counted many antislavery Quakers among its population.

In January, 1820, citizens of New Castle County, Delaware, at a meeting held in Wilmington, unanimously passed resolutions declaring that it was constitutional and highly expedient to prohibit the extension of slavery. Judge James Booth presided over the gathering, and Caesar A. Rodney was one of the speakers.[13] It was later charged that the meeting was "packed" with Pennsylvanians who were imported for the occasion.[14]

The press of Delaware never fully made up its mind regarding the best course to be pursued toward Missouri. The Democratic Wilmington *American Watchman* noted that the leading Democratic newspapers of New England looked upon the whole controversy as a Federalist plot to get votes; but, said the *Watchman*, it was not able either to confirm or deny such

[12] The decline of slavery in Delaware is illustrated by the following figures (*Seventh Census: 1850*, 211):

NEGRO POPULATION OF DELAWARE

	Free	Slave
1790	3,899	8,887
1800	8,268	6,153
1810	13,136	4,177
1820	12,958	4,509

[13] Wilmington *American Watchman*, January 19, 1820.
[14] Wilmington *Gazette*, March 11, 1820.

accusations. The editor deplored any attempt to array the North against the South, saying: "Those are seeds of dissention, which, if continued to be sown, will, like the fabled dragon's teeth, produce, in North and South, *Men* of Blood! I wash my hands of the consequences. I wish not to be for the North or the South alone. I wish to be for my country."[15] The attitude of the ardently Federalist Wilmington *Gazette,* which claimed to be the only Federalist newspaper in Delaware, was most interesting. Although it was published only a few miles south of the Mason and Dixon line, those few miles made a great deal of difference, for the *Gazette* reflected none of the anti-slavery zeal of the Eastern Federalist press. It advocated gradual emancipation in Delaware and seemed at first to favor the Missouri restriction but accepted the compromise of 1820 as "the best that could be done." During the third Missouri debate the *Gazette* asserted that those who sought to block Missouri's admission because of the alleged objectionable clause in its constitution were "influenced by other motives than the ostensible ones. . . . It is difficult to know what they wish, if it is not to produce as much difficulty and excitement as possible, with a view to their own aggrandisement." The *Gazette* complained of "all the racket which some of the eastern editors keep up on the subject," adding: "If they continue their din a little while longer, *no* one will regard it."[16]

The Quakers—especially the Bringhurst family of Wilmington—left no stone unturned to place Delaware in the antislavery column.[17] A great furor arose when President Monroe suddenly removed the Wilmington postmaster, Joseph Bringhurst, from office. The Clintonian Philadelphia *Aurora* averred that the dismissal of this "respectable *Quaker postmaster . . .* is something like an offering to *Moloch*—it is a *black business.*" Actually, Bringhurst's removal appears to have been recommended

15 Wilmington *American Watchman,* February 19, March 11, 1820, February 2, 1821.

16 Wilmington *Gazette,* February 26, March 22, 1820, January 19, 23, February 16, 1821.

17 D. Bringhurst to William Darlington, January 19, 1820, William Darlington Papers, New-York Historical Society.

by the state's entire congressional delegation and to have been decided upon before the Missouri Controversy began.[18]

After public opinion had been prodded for a month by the abolition society of Wilmington and the Quakers, the state legislature, which was predominantly Federalist, unanimously passed resolutions in favor of the congressional restriction of slavery in all new states.[19] A curious situation now developed. Willard Hall, a native of Massachusetts, was the only Democrat in the Delaware congressional delegation. He was also the only representative from the slaveholding states who voted consistently with the North (when he voted at all) on the Missouri question. Delaware's Federalist congressman, Louis McLane, and its two Federalist senators, Nicholas Van Dyke and Outerbridge Horsey, were pro-Southern. Being men of strong convictions, these three promptly wrote to inform the legislature that they respected its judgment but could not follow its advice, since they considered the proposed Missouri restriction unconstitutional.[20]

The Democrats made an issue of the fact that McLane, Van Dyke, and Horsey voted contrary to the legislature's wishes. To this the Wilmington *Gazette* replied that the Democratic representative, Willard Hall, spent his time in Delaware rather than Washington and did not answer roll call during much of the Missouri Controversy.[21]

When McLane ran for re-election in 1820, his opposition to the Missouri restriction was used against him, and he was bitterly "persecuted" for it, according to the Wilmington *Gazette*.[22] Two congressmen were chosen, by state-wide vote, from a field of four candidates. McLane was re-elected and Hall defeated, but the candidate polling the highest number of votes was Caesar A. Rodney, an antislavery Democrat who had taken a conspicuous part in the restrictionist meeting at

[18] Philadelphia *Aurora*, June 6, 21, 1820.

[19] Wilmington *American Watchman*, January 22, 1820; *Poulson's American Daily Advertiser* (Philadelphia), January 20, 1820.

[20] Wilmington *American Watchman*, February 19, 1820.

[21] Wilmington *Gazette*, March 11, 1820.

[22] *Ibid.*, September 22, 29, October 10, 1820.

Wilmington in January.[23] From the election returns, it is clear that public opinion in Delaware was strongly divided on the subject of congressional restriction—a view that is further substantiated by public letters defending both sides of the question.[24]

While Delaware probably had a substantial restrictionist majority and certainly had a numerous antirestrictionist minority, the exact reverse ratio prevailed in Maryland. The center of Anti-Missourianism here was the border city of Baltimore, which was said to abound in emancipation societies in 1820.[25] The restrictionists may have been in the majority in Baltimore, though not in the state as a whole. It is surprising that most Marylanders were not restrictionists. About half of the state's electorate was Federalist, and its large free Negro population testified to the unprofitableness of slavery and the antislavery convictions of many masters.[26]

On December 28, 1819, a group of citizens in Baltimore began an almost endless local controversy by assembling together to discuss the Missouri question. Presiding over the gathering was Mayor Edward Johnson, a man noted for his benevolence.[27] Elisha Tyson, a Quaker businessman and philanthropist, took the lead in calling the meeting. It was he who placed an advertisement in the newspapers inviting the public to attend. While a free expression of opinion was permitted,

23 *Niles' Weekly Register*, XIX (1820), 111. The vote by counties was:

	Rodney	McLane	Hall	Mitchell
New Castle	1,682	1,002	1,462	824
Kent	986	913	1,006	947
Sussex	1,358	2,002	1,061	1,730
TOTAL	4,026	3,917	3,529	3,501

24 Wilmington *Gazette*, March 4, 8, 11, 15, 22, 25, 1820.
25 Baltimore *American & Commercial Daily Advertiser*, January 3, 1820.
26 See *Seventh Census: 1850*, 222, as follows:

NEGRO POPULATION OF MARYLAND

	Free	Slave
1790	8,943	103,036
1800	19,587	105,635
1810	33,927	111,502
1820	39,730	107,397

27 J. Thomas Scharf, *The Chronicles of Baltimore* (Baltimore, 1874), 440.

Tyson made arrangements to have the restrictionist viewpoint presented by several talented speakers. The meeting passed resolutions in favor of congressional restriction in Missouri, though only after a warm debate and against the vigorous opposition of Reverdy Johnson, H. M. Brackenridge, and others. A committee of five was appointed to prepare a restrictionist memorial to Congress and present it to the citizens of Baltimore for their signatures. The committee consisted of James Kemp, Episcopal bishop of Maryland; Thomas Kell; Hezekiah Niles, editor of *Niles' Register;* Paul Allen, editor of the Baltimore *Morning Chronicle;* and Daniel Raymond, a political economist. The memorial, which was signed by more than two thousand people, stressed the fact that the signers were "citizens of a slave holding state, and consequently not liable to that prejudice on this subject, which citizens belonging to non-slave holding states are often supposed to possess."[28]

The conduct of the Baltimore meeting was widely criticized as well as praised. It was charged that it was gotten up by surprise, that only forty or fifty people voted for the resolutions, that the entire audience probably did not own a dozen slaves, and that many of the participants were Quakers and Northerners.[29] It was true that Elisha Tyson, Paul Allen, Hezekiah Niles, and Daniel Raymond were born in the North and that Bishop Kemp was a native of Scotland. A friend of the meeting estimated that more than two hundred people were present (out of Baltimore's total population of 62,000). He asserted that John Hoffman and Thomas Kell, who spoke in favor of restriction, probably owned more slaves than the five gentlemen who spoke on the other side.[30]

The press of Baltimore was divided. The *American* and the *Patriot* were mildly pro-Southern, while *Niles' Register* and the

[28] Baltimore *Patriot & Mercantile Advertiser,* December 30, 31, 1819; Baltimore *American & Commercial Daily Advertiser,* January 1, 1820; [John S. Tyson], *Life of Elisha Tyson, the Philanthropist* (Baltimore, 1825), 103; Philadelphia *Friend,* I (1828), 349.

[29] Baltimore *American & Commercial Daily Advertiser,* January 1, 3, 1820; Richmond *Enquirer,* January 6, 1820.

[30] Baltimore *American & Commercial Daily Advertiser,* January 1, 1820.

Morning Chronicle advocated restriction. Two Baltimoreans entered the contest as pamphleteers. Daniel Raymond's pamphlet upheld restriction, and that written by Joseph D. Learned was, in part, an attempt to refute Raymond's arguments.[31]

In the first Missouri debate, Congressman Samuel Smith of Baltimore supported one clause of the Tallmadge amendment. Otherwise, the Maryland congressional delegation voted steadily with the South. Shortly after Senator Robert H. Goldsborough voted against Tallmadge's proposition, he wrote privately to Rufus King to explain that his sympathies were altogether with the North.[32] He evidently did not vote his convictions for fear of injuring himself or the cause of Federalism in Maryland. The state legislature, by large majorities in both houses, passed strong resolutions against restriction.[33] Among the minority which opposed the resolutions was State Senator Roger B. Taney, afterwards Chief Justice of the United States Supreme Court. Apparently Taney, who seems to have been an anti-restrictionist, believed that the legislature had no right to issue resolutions instructing congressmen how to vote.[34] Robert Goodloe Harper, another state senator, was one of the few prominent Southerners who maintained that Congress had the constitutional power to prohibit slavery in new states, though he did not deem it expedient to exercise the power in Missouri's case.[35] In general, party affiliation appeared to have no effect on the attitude of Marylanders toward Missouri. All of the members of the state senate were Federalists at this time.[36]

Since Washington was a Southern city in 1820, the weight of public opinion in the District of Columbia was enlisted in the South's behalf. The Washington *Gazette* pointed out that

31 Daniel Raymond, *The Missouri Question* (Baltimore, 1819); Joseph D. Learned, *A View of the Policy of Permitting Slaves in the States West of the Mississippi* (Baltimore, 1820).

32 King, *Rufus King*, VI, 342.

33 Washington *Daily National Intelligencer*, January 12, 1820.

34 Carl B. Swisher, *Roger B. Taney* (New York, 1935), 99. According to tradition, Taney opposed the Missouri Compromise in 1820. Thirty-seven years later, after he became Chief Justice, he declared it unconstitutional.

35 *Niles' Weekly Register*, XVII (1820), 434-35.

36 Washington *Gazette*, October 12, 1819.

Southern congressmen had "great advantages as it regards the public ear; for they speak in the midst of a slave[holding] population, and the *buz,* of course, is in their favor."[37] The people of Washington never seemed to tire of the Missouri question. In January, 1821, the *Gazette* expressed amazement that people should still line the galleries of the Capitol to listen to debates on so threadbare a topic.[38]

The Washington *Daily National Intelligencer* was America's leading newspaper in the period of the Missouri Controversy, occupying the place which is now filled by the New York *Times* and *Herald Tribune.* The *Intelligencer* could be pardoned, perhaps, if it boasted now and then of its news coverage. In 1820 it reported with pride that it received regularly about three hundred newspapers from all parts of the United States and Canada as well as letters from such distant places as Sierra Leone, Malaya, Manila, and Liverpool, "each transmitting something of which we can make use for the advantage of our readers."[39] Joseph Gales, Jr., and William W. Seaton, publishers of the *Intelligencer,* were also the official reporters of the debates and proceedings of Congress. The *Intelligencer* was sometimes called the "Court Gazette" because of its intimacy with the Monroe administration, and its editorials were widely copied by editors who were too lazy to do their own writing. Though moderate and conciliatory toward what it called "the most dangerous question that has ever arisen in the Republic,"[40] the *Intelligencer* was definitely pro-Southern and used all of its immense prestige to defeat the Missouri restriction. It did not of course defend slavery as an abstract principle but relied on the stock Southern argument that the condition of the slaves would be improved by spreading them over a larger area.[41]

The ardently restrictionist Washington *Gazette* did not have as much prestige as the *Intelligencer.* The press of Georgetown, D. C., was pro-Southern. The Georgetown *Metropolitan,* referring to the matter of free Negro immigration, urged Mis-

---

[37] *Ibid.,* February 8, 1820.   [38] *Ibid.,* January 30, 1821.
[39] Washington *Daily National Intelligencer,* August 2, 1820.
[40] *Ibid.,* March 9, 1821.   [41] *Ibid.,* January 29, 1820.

souri to remain a territory, declare her independence, or fight her way into the Union rather than "suffer herself to be bullied out of a *positive right*, and which right is so highly essential to her well-being, that without it she would be a cypher."[42] The Georgetown *Messenger* at first advocated congressional restriction but later had a change of heart.[43] This was not an unusual course of procedure in the slaveholding states. When a Northern newspaper came out against restriction, it usually stuck by its guns. On the other hand, the Southern newspapers which defended restriction frequently became frightened by their own boldness and beat a hasty retreat from so advanced a position.

In Kentucky a large majority of the people seem to have sympathized with the Missourians in their fight against congressional restriction. There were, however, some dissenting voices.[44] According to the Edwardsville, Illinois, *Spectator*, three Kentucky newspapers approved of restriction—the Georgetown *Patriot*, Louisville *Western Courier*, and Frankfort *Commentator*.[45] Eventually the *Commentator* shifted to the opposite side when it decided that it was "the *blue-light* men" who were blocking Missouri's admission to the Union.[46] Amos Kendall's Frankfort *Argus*, while not upholding congressional restriction, was displeased by the vehemence with which Missourians resisted it. "It is curious," said the *Argus*, "to observe how anxious *freemen* are to perpetuate *slavery!!*"[47]

Notwithstanding its restrictionist minority, Kentucky was, on the whole, more militantly pro-Missourian than some of the states further south. There were several reasons for this. Kentuckians had a tradition of self-assertiveness, dating back to the Virginia-Kentucky Resolutions and the bumptiousness of "War Hawk" days. Moreover, it was generally supposed that restric-

[42] Georgetown *Metropolitan*, February 8, 1821.
[43] Georgetown *National Messenger*, November 22, 1819, February 23, 28, 1821.
[44] Asa E. Martin, *The Anti-Slavery Movement in Kentucky Prior to 1850* (Louisville, 1918), 34.
[45] Edwardsville *Spectator*, March 7, 1820.
[46] Frankfort *Commentator*, January 20, 27, March 9, 1820, February 8, 1821.
[47] Frankfort *Argus of Western America*, June 4, 18, 1819.

tion was an Eastern Federalist move, engineered by Rufus King and De Witt Clinton and designed to retard the growth of the West or secure a dissolution of the Union. Joseph Cabell Breckinridge bespoke the thoughts of many a Kentuckian when he wrote that "Clinton is the master moving spirit. He had rather be first in a Northern confederation, than second in the American empire. . . . The Hartford Convention was an innocent measure, compared to the present project."[48]

The Kentucky legislature passed vigorous antirestrictionist resolutions, avowing "its solemn conviction that the States already confederated under one common Constitution, have not a right to deprive new States of equal privileges with themselves."[49] The leading journals of Lexington and Louisville, with the exception of the Louisville *Western Courier*, were emphatically pro-Southern. The Louisville *Public Advertiser* blamed the Missouri Controversy on Eastern capitalists who were seeking "an opportunity of monopolizing the lands for which the western people have toiled and fought and bled."[50] The Lexington *Western Monitor* conceded that slavery was evil but asserted that "The slave-holding states will not brook an invasion of their rights. They will not be driven by compulsion to the emancipation, even gradually, of their slaves."[51] The Lexington *Gazette* accused "Yankees" of committing nearly every sin in the Decalogue. "Their *pecuniary interest*," said the *Gazette*, "whether in peace or war, seems to be the sole rule of their conduct. It is high time we should adopt some policy towards the Yankees . . . and if they desire to be our tinkers, pedlars, and carriers on the ocean, they must respect our rights." The *Gazette* warned that Missouri would demand admittance to the Union on an equal footing with the original states regardless of whether Congress enacted a law for that purpose and that "If she does so against the consent of congress, she will of course be prepared to protect her conduct, and her sister ter-

[48] Joseph Cabell Breckinridge to Robert J. Breckinridge, December 19, 1820, Breckinridge Family Papers, Library of Congress.
[49] *Annals of Congress*, 16 Cong., 1 Sess., 236.
[50] Louisville *Public Advertiser*, March 4, 1820.
[51] Lexington *Western Monitor*, March 20, 1821.

ritory will join her, heart and hand. It would be well for the eastern members of congress to make a solemn pause, before they invite such awful extremities." The *Gazette* concluded that the final decision of the Missouri question "must affect the interests, power, political weight and destinies of the *southern* and *western states;* and either make us, as we have too long been, dependents on Atlantic or *Yankee* notions and views—or the Independent members of Independent governments. In this subject the die is cast—and we must win or lose by the event."[52] Some Kentuckians were not even willing to compromise with the North. The Louisville *Public Advertiser* called the compromise of 1820 "humiliating"; and a Kentucky postrider, who was not a slaveholder, declared that the South had been "yankied" into "giving up the restriction on the Territory [above 36° 30'], for a right to which Missouri was entitled without it."[53]

The leader of Tennessee's restrictionist minority was Elihu Embree, an East Tennessean of Pennsylvania Quaker descent. In 1819-1820 Embree edited an antislavery newspaper at Jonesboro, the *Manumission Intelligencer.* In April, 1820, he discontinued this paper and replaced it with a monthly abolitionist magazine called *The Emancipator.* When the third number of the latter was issued, it was estimated that 2,600 copies would be needed to satisfy circulation demands. Embree remarked with pride that "less than twenty years ago a man would have been mobbed, and the printing office torn down, for printing and publishing any thing like the Emancipator; whereas it now meets the approbation of thousands, and is patronized perhaps at least equal to any other paper in the State."[54]

Embree was an active worker in the Manumission Society of Tennessee, whose convention memorialized Congress in 1819

[52] Lexington *Gazette*, January 7, March 10, 1820.
[53] Louisville *Public Advertiser*, March 11, 1820; *Annals of Congress*, 16 Cong., 2 Sess., 1206-1207.
[54] Brigham, *History and Bibliography of American Newspapers*, II, 1058; Philadelphia *National Gazette and Literary Register*, July 22, 1820; Jonesboro *Emancipator*, June 30, 1820. All references to the *Emancipator* in the footnotes of this book are taken from the reprint of it by B. H. Murphy, Nashville, 1932. See also E. E. Hoss, *Elihu Embree, Abolitionist* (Nashville, 1897).

against the further extension of slavery in Missouri.[55] The Washington branch of the society, meeting at Jonesboro in January, 1820, unanimously passed resolutions favoring congressional prohibition of slavery in new states and thanking Rufus King for his efforts to abolish it in Missouri.[56] It is impossible to say just how many Tennesseans shared the views of the Manumission Society. Andrew Jackson denounced the restrictionists as hypocrites,[57] while the principal newspapers of the state showed little interest in the subject one way or the other.

In North Carolina the Raleigh *Minerva,* which represented the local remnants of Federalism, espoused the cause of congressional restriction and threw open its columns to antislavery writers, some of whom were college students. No doubt the *Minerva* was voicing the views of a respectable minority of North Carolinians, including Quakers, Moravians, mountaineers, and the state Manumission Society.[58] However, just as in Tennessee and Kentucky, the minority was not strong enough to control the vote of its representatives in Congress.

In Virginia Anti-Missourian toasts were drunk at a Fourth-of-July celebration in the panhandle in 1820, and *Niles' Register* claimed that it had received "numerous" letters from the western parts of the state upholding the same viewpoint.[59] When the legislature passed resolutions against restriction, two legislators from Rockingham County objected vigorously. Daniel Bryan of Rockingham was the only state senator who voted against the resolutions. He spoke feelingly of the evils of slavery, assuring his fellow lawmakers that the law of nature gave no right to one man to sell another. In the state House

[55] *Annals of Congress,* 16 Cong., 1 Sess., 829.

[56] New York *Daily Advertiser,* March 6, 1820. See also Asa E. Martin, "Anti-Slavery Activities of the Methodist Episcopal Church in Tennessee," in *Tennessee Historical Magazine,* II (1916), 104.

[57] Bassett, *Correspondence of Andrew Jackson,* III, 21.

[58] Henry M. Wagstaff, *State Rights and Political Parties in North Carolina—1776-1861* (Baltimore, 1906), 41-42; Jonesboro (Tennessee) *Emancipator,* October 31, 1820.

[59] Steubenville (Ohio) *Western Herald,* August 12, 1820; *Niles' Weekly Register,* XVII (1820), 363.

of Delegates, John S. Herring of Rockingham also lifted his voice in behalf of "degraded, and enslaved man." In order to show his opposition to the proposed resolutions, Herring moved to postpone the consideration of the whole subject, but his motion was rejected by a vote of 172 to 9.[60]

The weakness and futility of western Virginia's antislavery protest in 1820 is rather remarkable. The Clarksburg *Republican Compiler*, published in the heart of what is now the state of West Virginia, advocated the abolition of slavery by constitutional methods and was willing to support an amendment to the Constitution which would grant this power to Congress. Pending the ratification of such an amendment, however, the *Compiler* regarded the proposed Missouri restriction as unconstitutional.[61] Most of the Virginia congressmen who represented districts west of the Blue Ridge Mountains were not even willing to prohibit slavery in the unorganized territories north of 36° 30'. All of them except John Floyd of the Abingdon district voted against the Thomas proviso.[62]

The scattered and ineffectual opposition to the westward expansion of slavery which manifested itself here and there in the Old Dominion was completely drowned out by a mighty pro-Missourian clamor in the eastern section of the state. In 1820 the Virginia squires and party leaders fancied themselves to be the particular guardians of state rights and Southern interests. Whenever they supposed that these were in danger, they could make as much noise as Theodore Dwight, the Quakers of Burlington, or anybody else. The leader of the state rights noisemakers was Thomas Ritchie's Richmond *Enquirer*, the journal of which Jefferson wrote: "I read but a single newspaper, Ritchie's Enquirer, the best that is published or ever has been published in America."[63] The *Enquirer* was one of the

[60] Richmond *Enquirer*, January 27, February 3, 10, 15, 17, 29, 1820.

[61] Clarksburg *Republican Compiler*, February 4, 1820.

[62] Charles H. Ambler, "Life of John Floyd," in *John P. Branch Historical Papers of Randolph-Macon College*, V (1918), 31, 43.

[63] Henry S. Randall, *The Life of Thomas Jefferson* (3 vols., New York, 1858), III, 495.

first to take a stand on the Missouri question. In May and July, 1819, it urged Missourians not to be guilty of rash or violent conduct but at the same time never to yield "one jot of their rights of state sovereignty." Missouri was assured that Virginia "will be the last either to abandon one atom of her own sovereign power, or any other state in the assertion of *her* rights."[64] The *Enquirer* insisted that its concern was for state rights and not slavery, which it called "an evil . . . we know not how to get rid of." Nevertheless, abolition by the federal government must not be tolerated. It was necessary to meet the violator of the Constitution at the threshold. "Shrink now," warned the *Enquirer*, "and we shall hear of abolitions—of the extinction of the slave representation feature in the Congress of the U. States."[65] Ritchie did not mince words in paying his respects to Rufus King and De Witt Clinton. He asserted that King, whom he formerly respected, now stood "exposed in the eyes of his countrymen, goaded by an unholy ambition, attempting to clutch the office, which we forever trust will elude his grasp." As for "De Witt Clinton," said the *Enquirer*, "we have never concealed our opinion. Ambitious, intriguing, grasping in his designs, careless of his means—such is one of those who aspire to 'lord it over Venice.' "[66]

Ritchie believed in freedom of the press and opened the columns of the *Enquirer* to writers on both sides of the Missouri question, although there were few in the latitude of Richmond who cared to defend the restrictionist side. Of antirestrictionist writers there was, of course, no shortage. Exclaimed one of these: "Let not . . . a disgraceful supineness possess us: Let not 'the fatal Coma,' . . . overcome us longer with lethargic slumber; . . . when the enemies of our institutions are throwing up outworks which at a period not remote, may be used for the subversion of our sovereignty and independence."[67] Most Virginia newspapers were not as militant as the *Enquirer*. Indeed, many of them, as in other states, made no editorial comment

---

[64] Richmond *Enquirer*, May 14, July 9, 1819.
[65] *Ibid.*, January 6, February 10, 1820.
[66] *Ibid.*, February 19, 1820.   [67] *Ibid.*, December 23, 1819.

on the Missouri question. The Norfolk and Portsmouth *Herald* was inclined to favor restriction until, evidently becoming frightened by its own temerity, it suddenly changed tack and began to out-Herod Herod (or perhaps we should say, out-Ritchie Ritchie).[68]

Richmond was probably the most overwhelmingly pro-Missourian town in America. In December, 1819, Ritchie declared that he had met only one man who favored congressional restriction.[69] Even Chief Justice Marshall seems to have been disturbed by Northern antislavery agitation, for he expressed a fear that it might prevent President Monroe's re-election.[70] Early in 1820 Charles Yancey wrote from Richmond that excitement was intense "& many feel as though they have on their Armour & orders to March to N. england; in great haste."[71] With only one or two dissenting votes, the lower house of the legislature adopted resolutions stating that Virginia was "united in a common cause with the people of the Missouri Territory, and bound to interpose for their defence." These resolutions were toned down before being accepted by the state senate but even then were forcibly worded.[72]

Virginia hotspurs were immensely displeased by the compromise of 1820, which was received with as much disdain in Richmond as in Eastern Federalist circles. President Monroe, who was more conciliatory than other Virginians, found himself on the horns of a dilemma. He realized that the compromise was as advantageous to the South as any settlement that could be obtained, and he was sympathetic with those Northern Democrats who were jeopardizing their political careers to

[68] Norfolk and Portsmouth *Herald*, December 20, 1819, January 26, 28, 1820.

[69] Richmond *Enquirer*, December 21, 1819.

[70] Lyon G. Tyler (ed.), "Missouri Compromise. Letters to James Barbour, Senator of Virginia in the Congress of the United States," in *William and Mary College Quarterly*, X (1901), 15.

[71] "Original Letters," *ibid.*, XXI (1912), 76.

[72] *Preamble and Resolutions on the Subject of the Missouri Question, Agreed to by the House of Delegates of Virginia, and the Amendment of the Senate, Proposed Thereto* (Richmond, 1820); *Niles' Weekly Register*, XVII (1820), 343-44, 416-17.

support it.[73] Monroe's course of action throughout the entire dispute over Missouri was cautious and vacillating. He did not believe that Congress could legally prohibit slavery in a new state and at first was not certain that it could do so even in the territories.[74] He attempted to be neutral[75] but, becoming thoroughly alarmed by the excitement prevailing in Washington, finally decided to put out feelers regarding a compromise. Accordingly he wrote to his son-in-law, George Hay, who was then attending a meeting of the Virginia legislature at Richmond, proposing that Hay and Charles Johnson come to Washington and help arrange a compromise.[76] He also suggested to Senator James Barbour that it would be wise to separate the Maine and Missouri bills and let each stand on its own merit.[77] Meanwhile the President's daughter, Mrs. Hay, was beseeching her husband to exert himself in behalf of a compromise. Hay wrote to his wife in February, 1820: "You distress me beyond measure by your solicitations to go to Washington. . . . I could do no good, if I was there. The mere circumstance of my departure from my post . . . would excite every sort of suspicion and animadversion."[78]

Monroe's deference to the Virginia legislature was amazing. He even suggested that a group of the legislators come to Washington and act as a liaison between the legislature and Congress in working out a compromise.[79] As he made the mistake of supposing that the entire country was as excited as Washington and Richmond, he feared that the Union was in

[73] "We have induced the President to *think*, & advise his Southern friends to be cautious. it is every day becomeing more important to put this question at rest." Mark L. Hill to William King, February 9, 1820, William King Papers.

[74] *Congressional Globe*, 30 Cong., 2 Sess., *Appendix*, 67.

[75] James Monroe to George Hay, January 10, 1820, Monroe Papers, New York Public Library.

[76] James Monroe to George Hay, January 5, February 6, 1820, *ibid.*

[77] James Monroe to James Barbour, February 3, 1820, Barbour Papers.

[78] George Hay to Mrs. Hay, February 12, 1820, Monroe Papers, Library of Congress.

[79] Letter from Monroe to an unnamed person, Washington, January or February, 1820, published in Columbus (Ohio) *Crisis*, December 14, 1864. Date of letter given incorrectly in *Crisis*.

dire peril. In Richmond on February 9, 1820, a legislative caucus was held to nominate presidential electors. The caucus was reluctantly informed by Charles Yancey that he had received a letter from Senator James Barbour stating that Monroe and the cabinet favored a compromise which would permit slavery in Missouri but abolish it in the territories north of 36° 30′.[80] The effect of this pronouncement was startling. Being unwilling to re-elect Monroe if he was a compromiser, the caucus indignantly adjourned without selecting nominees for electors. One aged member of the legislature was so upset that he shed tears and exclaimed: "Would to god we had war with England, France, Spain, or any other nation, which would unite the People, rather than that civil war with the Northern States, which must inevitably take place if any restriction is made on our right to hold Slaves, and to transport them where we please."[81]

Said the Richmond *Enquirer* of the proposed compromise:

But what do we do by acceding to it? Yield to a panic; give way to a sort of duresse practised on us by other states? No; no: . . . don't encourage them to go on with their demands. Don't persuade them, that if they take similar ground again; if they talk of putting us under the ban of the constitution, they may again succeed—that they may tax *us* to raise up their hot-bed manufactures:—or abolish the slave representative feature in our constitution.—If we yield now, beware.—They will ride us forever. No; we at the South have been empty boasters if we now betray that high spirit, that fearlessness about consequences, by which we flattered ourselves we were so much distinguished. . . . As to disunion, if our Eastern brethren have made up their minds to it, deeply, solemnly as we should regret it, we must bow to their resolution—but let us adhere to justice and the constitution. They may outvote us;—but let us not bind ourselves by our own votes.[82]

The Norfolk and Portsmouth *Herald* was hopeful that Monroe did not really approve of the compromise, though it had no

[80] Tyler, "Missouri Compromise. Letters to James Barbour," 10; Richmond *Enquirer*, February 10, 1820.

[81] Boston *Columbian Centinel*, February 19, 1820.

[82] Richmond *Enquirer*, February 10, 1820.

hesitancy in saying that if he did, "well may the legislature of this state, and the people of all the southern states unite their voices in indignant opposition to his re-election."[83]

Soon a torrent of censorious letters was pouring into Washington from Richmond. Henry St. George Tucker wrote Barbour that he was unable to describe the sensation created "by your letter. A compromise which gives up the fairest & largest portion of the Western territory & leaves to us a narrow slip intersected with Mountains in one direction, destroyed by Earthquakes in another and interspersed in a third with swamps & bayous & infested with mosquitos & bilious diseases— never can be grateful to us." Tucker asked if the object of the compromise was to re-elect Monroe. He added: "We are unwilling to purchase his service at such a price: still less willing to support him if *he* can with a view to his own Election thus surrender the valuable rights of the South."[84] Equally emphatic was Judge Spencer Roane, who wrote Monroe that Virginia "will, at least, not sign the instrument of her own degradation. She will say, with the revered patriots of 1776, 'we have counted the cost of this contest, & find nothing so intolerable as *voluntary* slavery.'" Roane told Monroe further that in spite of rumors to the contrary, Virginians were still counting upon him to oppose restriction both in the states and in territories which would shortly become states.[85]

Not all Virginians were as generous as Roane in interpreting Monroe's motives, and the President became so incensed at the criticisms directed against him by his native state that he wrote to his son-in-law: "As to the preservation of this office, I hope that I am too well known not [to] be understood, to be ready to withdraw from it, without regret. The principles, on which,

[83] Norfolk and Portsmouth *Herald*, February 14, 1820.

[84] Henry St. George Tucker to James Barbour, February 11, 1820, Barbour Papers.

[85] Spencer Roane to James Monroe, February 16, 1820, Monroe Papers, New York Public Library; "Letters of Spencer Roane, 1788-1822," in *Bulletin of the New York Public Library*, X (1906), 174-75. Letters expressing opposition to a compromise were also written by Andrew Stevenson, William F. Gordon, and Charles Yancey. Tyler, "Missouri Compromise: Letters to James Barbour," 13, 19; "Original Letters," 75.

238 THE MISSOURI CONTROVERSY

I have, & shall invariably act, place me, above all attempts to preserve it, by measures of concession, either here or elsewhere. If the legislators prefer any one else, let them declare it." Noble words, but belied by the additional statement, in this very communication, that Monroe had written a letter to Dr. Charles Everett which could be shown in Richmond if Hay and Everett thought proper.[86] They must have thought it proper, since Charles Yancey wrote soon afterwards that he had seen a letter from Monroe to Everett in which the President stated that he would resist restriction in any form, "even to the hazard of the Union."[87]

On February 17 the caucus reassembled and nominated Monroe supporters as candidates for the electoral college. Some members of the caucus realized that they had been too precipitate in condemning their representatives in Washington. Moreover, they were now under the impression that Monroe intended to veto the compromise—an impression based on Monroe's letter to Everett and Judge Roane's letter to Monroe.[88] Not shown to the caucus was a last minute letter from Monroe to Roane, sent by way of George Hay, in which the chief executive again expressed doubt and hesitation. Hay was careful to return this letter to his father-in-law without showing it to Roane or anyone. Hay hinted in his reply that it might be possible to arrange a compromise after the caucus had been gotten safely out of the way.[89] As for Monroe, he toyed with the idea of vetoing the compromise and even prepared a rough draft of a veto message.[90] Subsequently, however, he not only signed the compromise legislation but warmly defended it in a letter to Jefferson.[91]

[86] James Monroe to George Hay, February 11, 1820, Monroe Papers, New York Public Library.

[87] Tyler, "Missouri Compromise. Letters to James Barbour," 16-17.

[88] George Hay to James Monroe, February 17, 1820, Monroe Papers, Library of Congress.

[89] Ibid.

[90] Congressional Globe, 30 Cong., 2 Sess., Appendix, 67.

[91] Stanislaus M. Hamilton (ed.), The Writings of James Monroe (7 vols., New York, 1898-1903), VI, 122-23. Two letters "from a gentleman in Wash-

Many Virginians remained unreconciled to the compromise. The Richmond *Enquirer* could "scarcely ever recollect to have tasted of a bitterer cup," and the Norfolk and Portsmouth *Herald* would "rather the question should have remained forever unsettled than to have seen the constitutional guarantee of state rights set at nought by congressional usurpation."[92] As has been seen, eighteen Virginia congressmen voted against the Thomas proviso, while only four supported it.

Though grieved by the passage of the compromise of 1820, the Richmond *Enquirer* declared that the Union was too dear to be torn asunder and that it had never really been in danger during the Missouri Controversy.[93] In truth it had not been. There were some, to be sure, who advocated disunion. The Petersburg *Intelligencer* published a letter from an unnamed Virginia congressman who asserted that the Union, as then constituted, was worthless and that unless it was reformed, to protect the South against Northern aggression, he would abandon it with as much indifference as he would an association of pickpockets, swindlers, and cutthroats.[94] Usually, however, threats of disunion, whether in the North or South, went no further than daring the other side to start something. Thus Dwight's New York *Advertiser* said of Virginian braggadocio: "As for dividing the Union, that is out of the question—THEY DARE NOT DO IT."[95] Writing in similar vein but from a point of view of a Southerner, Archibald Stuart contended that the North would not risk a division of the Union for fear of losing the Southern carrying trade. This consequence, said Stuart, was "too obvious to escape The attention of a Cunning

---

ington" to a friend in Richmond, which appeared in the *Enquirer* on February 17, apparently were written by Monroe or at his suggestion. They contained an able defense of the compromise.

[92] Richmond *Enquirer*, March 7, 1820; Norfolk and Portsmouth *Herald*, March 10, 1820.

[93] Richmond *Enquirer*, March 7, 1820.

[94] Petersburg *Intelligencer*, quoted in Baltimore *Patriot & Mercantile Advertiser*, March 11, 1820.

[95] New York *Daily Advertiser*, February 24, 1820

240   THE MISSOURI CONTROVERSY

pelf loving people from which I conclude their proceedings are intended for Temporary and ambitious purposes."[96]

The vehemence with which Virginians defended Southern and Missourian rights attracted nationwide attention. Harrison Gray Otis remarked that they were "reviving the system of intimidation by which they have always governed the Union," and Theodore Dwight called Virginia "the customary haughty dictatrix."[97] In the opinion of a Connecticut pamphleteer, William Hillhouse, Virginians had been so long accustomed to beating and domineering over their slaves that they considered themselves entitled to treat the rest of mankind in the same manner. Hillhouse published a satirical pamphlet in 1820 which purported to be a proclamation to the free states from the "lords of that very soil, known and acknowledged to be the ancient dominion; the land of opossums, . . . and . . . the descendants of Pocahontas." The proclamation, dated *at our imperial City of Richmond, the first year of the crusade for unlimited slavery,*" insisted that Virginia alone should select Presidents for the United States and admonished Northerners to bow every neck and bend every knee in token of submission![98]

So great was the Northern outcry against Virginian intransigence and against the influence which the Old Dominion wielded in the national government, that John Randolph called the words, "Virginia Influence," the "999th stave of the Yankee doodle doo."[99] Some Northerners thought that they could detect in the conduct of the Virginians toward the Missouri question "a despicable effort *to preserve to them selves the de-*

96 Archibald Stuart to James Monroe, December 8, 1820, Monroe Papers, Library of Congress. For similar arguments, see Lexington (Kentucky) *Gazette,* March 17, 1820; Charleston *Southern Patriot, And Commercial Advertiser,* February 19, 1820.
97 Morison, *Harrison Gray Otis,* II, 226; New York *Daily Advertiser,* January 19, 1820.
98 [Hillhouse], *Pocahontas: A Proclamation.*
99 John Randolph to James M. Garnett, January 29, 1820, Randolph-Garnett Correspondence. "Virginia! Virginia influence!—the starling's cry was not more monotonous nor less incessant, than this hacknied watchword, but just about as significant." Washington *Daily National Intelligencer,* August 15, 1820.

parting sceptre of national dominion."[100] It is true that the political power motive recurred as often in the columns of the Richmond *Enquirer* as in the correspondence of Rufus King or the editorials of Theodore Dwight. The exclusion of slavery from the western territories meant that eventually that area might be occupied by states which would vote with the North against Virginia. "That is to say," observed the *Enquirer,* "you are to restrict them when *territories* that you may regulate them, according to Eastern principles, when they become . . . [states].—You cramp the foot of the Chinese child that when old it may hobble as you please. You take all that immense region North of Missouri, its lands and its political power to yourselves and your children."[101]

One explanation of the Old Dominion's belligerence in the Missouri Controversy is that it was a manifestation of Virginian nationalism as distinguished from American nationalism. In 1820 many Virginians could remember the day when their state had been an independent nation extending from the Atlantic to the Great Lakes and including Kentucky and Illinois among its counties. "When I speak of my country," said John Randolph, "I mean the Commonwealth of Virginia."[102] Nathaniel Beverley Tucker, afterward famous as a fire-eater and author, was deeply imbued with Virginian nationalism in 1820. At that time he was temporarily domiciled in Missouri, where he was a picturesque local figure. At his farm in the Florissant valley he had set up a law office in a large hollow sycamore tree which he had cut off ten feet above the ground and covered with a roof.[103] Tucker's hatred of the North was so great that he advised the framers of Missouri's first constitution to prohibit "Yankees" from crossing the Mississippi River. When asked how this could be accomplished, he replied that passengers

[100] Hartford *Courant*, February 29, 1820.

[101] Richmond *Enquirer,* February 8, 1820. See also for December 14, 16, 23, 1819.

[102] Garland, *John Randolph,* II, 103.

[103] Walter B. Stevens, *Centennial History of Missouri (the Center State)* (6 vols., St. Louis, 1921), I, 14.

presenting themselves at the ferry on the Illinois side should
be required to pronounce the word "cow." If they said "keow,"
they should be turned back.[104]

Though Tucker was judge of the Northern Circuit Court of
Missouri Territory, one would suppose from the letters which
he wrote to the Richmond *Enquirer* that he was the ambassador
to Missouri from the sovereign state of Virginia. He was afraid
that congressional restriction would make the trans-Mississippi
lands north of the thirty-sixth parallel "a Yankee country, governed by the snivelling, sanctimonious doctrines in politics and
religion which, as a Virginian, I early learned to abhor." He
spoke of the hundreds of Virginians who had settled in Missouri
and pointed out that "It would surely be grateful to every Virginian to see an important country rising in the west that
would reflect the true image of his parent state." Tucker af-
fectionately used the term "southrons" to designate all Southerners, and at times his Southern patriotism was not distin-
guishable from loyalty to Virginia.[105] However, he was probably not yet disloyal to the Union. To be sure, he declared in
1851 that he realized at the time of the Missouri Controversy
that the Union was a curse and vowed then never to rest until
it was "shattered into fragments."[106] Nevertheless, in an address to a St. Louis grand jury in December, 1820, he paid
eloquent tribute to "the laws and institutions of our common
country." He added that, "In contemplating our connection
with the government of the United States, in our late subordinate relation we may see some things to complain of, but many
more which deserve our acknowledgments."[107]

While not disloyal to the Union, Virginia in 1820 was a nation
within a nation, eager to maintain its prestige and prerogatives.

[104] *Ibid.;* Maude H. Woodfin, "Nathaniel Beverley Tucker," in *Richmond
College Historical Papers,* II (1917), 21.

[105] Anonymous letters in Richmond *Enquirer,* May 21, December 11, 1819.
For evidence that Tucker was the author of the letters, see Edwardsville (Illinois) *Spectator,* February 15, 1820.

[106] William P. Trent, *William Gilmore Simms* (Boston, 1895), 183; Carl
Bridenbaugh (ed.), *The Partisan Leader,* by Nathaniel Beverley Tucker (New
York, 1933), xii-xiii.

[107] St. Louis *Enquirer,* December 23, 1820.

These appeared to be threatened by the antislavery movement, the rising "American System" of Henry Clay, and the judicial decisions of John Marshall. Feeling in Virginia against the Supreme Court was running high. This was the period in which Chief Justice Marshall rendered some of his greatest nationalistic decisions—Martin v. Hunter's Lessee, McCulloch v. Maryland, Cohens v. Virginia.[108] Virginia wanted none of Marshall's brand of American nationalism and resented his decisions so bitterly that Spencer Roane launched a movement to strip the Court of a portion of its powers.[109] It was in 1820 that John Taylor published *Construction Construed* and that Jefferson denounced the national judiciary as "the subtle corps of sappers and miners constantly working under ground to undermine the foundations of our confederated fabric."[110] Virginia's opposition to slavery restriction, then, was only one phase of a campaign which it was conducting against the centralization of power in the federal government.[111]

But whatever the motives of Virginians may have been, their position in the Missouri Controversy was too militant and uncompromising to suit the rest of the South. The Natchez *Republican* accused "the Virginian dynasty" of seeking "to swallow in the stupendous vortex of its ambition, the whole political influence of the confederation." The Baltimore *Patriot* felt that "Virginians will yet blush at the advocacy of principles, on which *their* pride and *our* boast, Washington, taught them to frown." The Georgetown, D. C., *Messenger* reminded its neighbors across the Potomac that "The spirit of compromise was necessary in forming the Union: and, however long the Union may continue, the spirit of compromise will always be found necessary to preserve it." The New Orleans *Gazette* asserted that it made no difference whether slavery was tolerated or

[108] According to Beveridge, Marshall's opinion in Cohens v. Virginia was, in part, an answer to Southern threats of secession during the Missouri contest. Albert J. Beveridge, *The Life of John Marshall* (4 vols., Boston, 1916-1919), IV, 340-43.
[109] Dodd, "Marshall and Virginia."
[110] Ford, *Writings of Jefferson*, X, 170.
[111] Richmond *Enquirer*, July 16, December 7, 1819.

prohibited in Missouri but that Louisiana was "deeply, vitally interested in conserving the union of the states entire, and . . . her citizens . . . are not to be made the dupes of any scheme, which has the slightest tendency to disunion, whether it originate in Virginia or New York, Massachusetts or Missouri: they will resist it with their voices, and if necessary, with their arms!"[112]

While Virginia's delegation in the lower house of Congress cast eighteen votes against the Thomas compromise proviso and only four in its favor, the representatives from the remainder of the South supported the proviso by a vote of thirty-five to nineteen. Moreover, except in Virginia, the leading Southern newspapers hailed the passage of the compromise with satisfaction. The Washington *Intelligencer* rejoiced that the question "is SETTLED." "Thank God, it is, at last, decided; and, as we believe, decided right," said the Baltimore *Patriot*. The Charleston *Southern Patriot* believed that such a settlement "must be accompanied by the most gratifying emotions in the mind of every temperate citizen of the Republic, whether he be an inhabitant of the North, South, East or West." The Augusta, Georgia, *Chronicle* viewed "this decision as a constitutional triumph" and felt "a proud satisfaction in recording it." The St. Stephens, Alabama, *Halcyon* remarked that "the Missouri question is at length settled, entirely consonant to the hopes and wishes of a large majority of the people of the United States." The Natchez *Republican* rejoiced because it considered "any thing preferable to a state of civil discord and confusion." The Frankfort, Kentucky, *Argus of Western America* maintained that Southerners would receive by the compromise all that nature would ultimately have given them anyway. The Lexington, Kentucky, *Gazette* was at first fearful of "*a Yankee trick*" but later decided that the "*Yankees*" had been defeated.[113] Additional support for the compromise came from

112 Natchez *Republican,* July 27, 1819; Baltimore *Patriot & Mercantile Advertiser,* February 15, 1820; Georgetown *National Messenger,* February 14, 1820; New Orleans *Orleans Gazette and Commercial Advertiser* (Country Edition), March 17, 1820.

113 Washington *Daily National Intelligencer,* March 3, 1820; Baltimore *Patriot*

the Raleigh *Star* and Salisbury *Western Carolinian* in North Carolina and from the Nashville *Clarion* and Clarksville *Gazette* in Tennessee.[114]

In 1861 the deep South regarded Virginia as an old lady who was slow to make up her mind and would probably never make it up unless South Carolina sprinkled blood in her face.[115] Conditions were different in 1820. Virginia was then a vigorous middle-aged matron whose belligerence distressed her more conciliatory Southern sisters. Georgia was the only state of the deep South which was anything like so uncompromising as Virginia in 1820. A young Northerner visiting in Savannah at the time was impressed by the indignation which the attempt to prohibit slavery in Missouri had aroused among Georgians.[116] The press of the state strongly condemned restriction, the legislature unanimously passed resolutions against it,[117] and the delegation in the national House of Representatives opposed the Thomas proviso by a two to one majority. Elsewhere in the lower South there was little inclination to follow Virginia's leadership in the Missouri Controversy. The compromise of

---

& Mercantile Advertiser, March 4, 1820; Charleston *Southern Patriot, And Commercial Advertiser*, March 11, 1820; Augusta *Chronicle & Georgia Gazette*, March 16, 1820; St. Stephens *Halcyon, And Tombeckbe Public Advertiser*, April 3, 1820; Natchez *Republican*, April 11, 1820; Frankfort *Argus of Western America*, March 9, 1820; Lexington *Gazette*, March 3, 31, 1820.

[114] Wagstaff, *State Rights in North Carolina*, 43; Nashville *Clarion, and Tennessee Gazette*, March 21, 1820; Clarksville *Gazette*, April 15, 1820. There was little opposition to the compromise of 1821 in the South. It was apparently acceptable to the Richmond *Enquirer* (March 1, 3, 1821) and was specifically endorsed by the Washington *Daily National Intelligencer* (February 28, 1821), the Baltimore *American & Commercial Daily Advertiser* (March 2, 1821), the Georgetown, D. C., *National Messenger* (February 28, 1821), the Charleston *Southern Patriot, And Commercial Advertiser* (March 10, 1821), the Louisville *Public Advertiser* (March 21, 1821), the Lexington *Western Monitor* (March 20, 1821), and the Natchez *Republican* (March 27, 1821).

[115] See speech of Roger A. Pryor, quoted in Robert W. Winston, *High Stakes and Hair Trigger, The Life of Jefferson Davis* (New York, 1930), 185.

[116] Barck, *Letters from John Pintard*, I, 352-53.

[117] Washington *Gazette*, November 30, 1820. However, most of Georgia's leaders did not yet defend slavery in the abstract as a positive good. Ruth Scarborough, *The Opposition to Slavery in Georgia Prior to 1860* (Nashville, 1933), 179-80, 184-85.

1820 was quite acceptable in north Alabama, if we are to judge from Thomas G. Percy's statement that "Very little has been said here about the settlement of the Missouri question. All that I have heard speak of it rejoiced that it was disposed of."[118] At about the same time, Charles Tait was writing from south Alabama that "the Compromise is entirely satisfactory here. At any rate I have never heard a remark in disapprobation of it."[119] It is especially interesting to contrast the bellicosity of the Virginians in 1820 with the comparative moderation of two states in the deep South which later became the happy hunting grounds of secessionists and Dixiecrats—South Carolina and Mississippi.

In 1820 South Carolina was by no means the citadel of nullification and strict construction that it would someday be. In fact, Governor James Hamilton, Jr., afterward estimated that nineteen twentieths of the state's citizens had approved of a loose interpretation of the Constitution as late as 1821.[120] Calhoun, foremost son of the Palmetto State, was still an ardent American nationalist in this period of his life. He professed to be "no advocate for refined arguments on the constitution," believing that the latter "was not intended as a thesis for the logician to exercise his ingenuity on. It ought to be construed with plain, good sense."[121] According to Representative Plumer of New Hampshire, Calhoun told him early in 1822 that "his education had been northern, his politics, his feelings, his views, & his sympathies were all northern."[122] Though doubtless an exaggeration, Plumer's statement was partially true. Such was Calhoun's reputation that in 1824 he felt called upon to deny the charge that he was an enemy of state rights or had ever endeavored to weaken them.[123]

[118] Thomas G. Percy to John W. Walker, April 5, 1820, Walker Papers.
[119] Charles Tait to John W. Walker, May 20, 1820, *ibid.*
[120] Sydnor, *Development of Southern Sectionalism*, 177.
[121] Wiltse, *John C. Calhoun Nationalist*, 134-35.
[122] Brown, *Missouri Compromises*, 72.
[123] J. Franklin Jameson (ed.), *Correspondence of John C. Calhoun*, in *Annual Report of the American Historical Association for the Year 1899*, II (Washington, 1900), 221.

Naturally Calhoun heartily endorsed the compromise of 1820, declaring that "all sober statesmen became anxious for the compromise, which happily for the country was effected, as I hope, and sincerely believe, forever." Calhoun was inclined to pooh-pooh the suggestion that a premeditated struggle for supremacy between the North and South had begun. "We to the South," he wrote, "ought not to assent easily to the belief, that there is a conspiracy either against our property, or just weight in the Union. . . . Nothing would lead more directly to disunion with all of its horrows [than this belief]." Rather, said Calhoun, "Our true system is to look to the country; and to support such measures and such men, without a regard to sections as are best calculated to advance the general interest."[124] Calhoun's views were shared by the Charleston *Southern Patriot*, which expressed the hope that more frequent contacts between Northerners and Southerners would aid in correcting mutual prejudices and in binding the Union more firmly together.[125]

In the lower house of Congress, five South Carolina representatives voted for the Thomas proviso, and four opposed it. Both of the South Carolina senators, John Gaillard and William Smith, opposed it. However, when the compromise of 1820 (including the Thomas proviso) came before the Senate, Gaillard voted for the whole measure and Smith against it. Thus Smith was as uncompromising as John Randolph and Thomas Ritchie. This did not help his candidacy when he ran for re-election in 1822. Calhoun, who regarded him as "narrow minded," thought that he did not fairly represent the state.[126] One of Smith's supporters contended that his conduct in the Missouri Controversy entitled him to re-election. To such arguments, Henry L. Pinckney, who did not dream that he himself would eventually become a Nullifier, replied that the nation was founded on compromise and that no one deserved a re-

[124] John C. Calhoun to Charles Tait, October 26, 1820, October 1, 1821, Tait Papers. See also Thomas M. Owen (ed.), "Letters from John C. Calhoun to Charles Tait," in *Gulf States Historical Magazine*, I (1902), 99, 103-104.
[125] Charleston *Southern Patriot, And Commercial Advertiser*, March 11, 1820.
[126] Jameson, *Correspondence of Calhoun*, 204.

ward for risking the horrors of disunion. When the balloting took place in the legislature, Smith received only seventy-four votes to ninety-one for Robert Y. Hayne.[127] While Smith's defeat was not due primarily to the Missouri question, it does seem to indicate that the Charleston *Patriot* was speaking for a majority of the voters of South Carolina when, shortly after the enactment of the compromise of 1821, it praised "that spirit of diffusive patriotism that takes in the welfare of the Union, in opposition to the strength of local attachments."[128]

The failure of Mississippi to play an important role in the Missouri Controversy can be attributed partly to its small population and isolated location. It was not admitted to the Union until 1817, and in 1819-1821 most of its people and wealth were concentrated in the southwestern counties, especially in the old Natchez district. Natchez, which retained political and economic leadership in the state until 1821,[129] could hardly be expected to hoist the state rights banner. With a conservative population, including many Northerners and Federalists, it was destined to be in later years a stronghold of Unionism and Whiggery.[130] Neither of its newspapers showed any pro-Southern spirit in 1820. The *State Gazette* appeared to be indifferent toward the Missouri question, while the *Republican*, edited by Richard C. Langdon, was one of the few newspapers in the lower South which upheld congressional restriction. Such a measure, said the *Republican*, was necessary for national defense and domestic tranquillity. Moreover, it believed that the attitude of Northerners on the subject was "founded only on principles of humanity—on a deep interest for the honor and character of the nation and regard for the future safety of the

[127] Theodore D. Jervey, *Robert Y. Hayne and His Times* (New York, 1909), 137-47.

[128] Charleston *Southern Patriot, And Commercial Advertiser*, March 10, 1821.

[129] Robert C. Weems, Jr., "The Bank of the Mississippi, A Pioneer Bank of the Old Southwest 1809-1844" (Ph.D. dissertation, Columbia University, 1951), 326-28, 434-36.

[130] John K. Bettersworth, *Confederate Mississippi* (Baton Rouge, 1943), 15-16.

Southern States—What other motives can they have?" Later the *Republican* began to waver, fearing that restriction might be unconstitutional.[131]

Mississippi's entire congressional delegation—two senators and one representative—supported the compromise of 1820, although Senator Thomas H. Williams voted against the Thomas proviso when it was considered separately from the remainder of the compromise. The nearest thing to a fire-eating leader in Mississippi in 1820 was Governor George Poindexter, who announced that he could view the movement to prohibit slavery in Missouri "in no other light, than as a bold attempt by a dominant party, to prostrate the barriers, by which, the rights of the States are guarded and protected, from the arbitrary encroachments, of the General Government."[132] When Elihu Embree sent Poindexter several numbers of his abolitionist magazine, the *Emancipator,* the governor replied that every true Christian looked forward with patient hope to the remote day when slavery would disappear[133] but that in the meantime publications like Embree's could only serve to excite prejudice and passion. Besides, wrote Poindexter, *"you represent an association of individuals, in another section of the United States, who bear the expense of the work you have undertaken,* and reward your labours; . . . I cannot, therefore subscribe, even one cent for your paper, and have no wish to receive it on any terms."[134]

The negative role of the deep South in the Missouri Controversy was to be in marked contrast with its aggressive leadership of the state rights cause a few decades later. With memo-

[131] Natchez *Republican,* January 11, February 15, 1820.

[132] Message to the General Assembly, no date, Correspondence of Governor George Poindexter, Series E, No. 4, Mississippi Department of Archives and History.

[133] Poindexter's biographer believes that statements such as this were mere sophistry and that Poindexter was really proslavery. Mack Swearingen, *The Early Life of George Poindexter* (New Orleans, 1934), 162-63. Prior to 1832, it was not popular in Mississippi to defend slavery as an abstract principle. See Charles S. Sydnor, *Slavery in Mississippi* (New York, 1933), 239-41, 245.

[134] Jonesboro (Tennessee) *Emancipator,* September 30, 1820.

ries of 1861 still in mind, it is hard to believe today that Charleston and Mississippi should have been relatively placid in 1820 while Richmond and St. Louis were "agitated as if affected by all the Volcanic Eruptions of Vesuvius."[135] It seems strange that Thomas Ritchie and Thomas Hart Benton should ever have heaped fuel on the fires of sectionalism, while Calhoun sought to quench them. On one point, however, the upper and lower South were in agreement in 1820. They were both opposed to the congressional restriction of slavery in the new state of Missouri. After making allowances for those who were indifferent and for the South's restrictionist minority, the fact remains that the slaveholding states were more united in opposition to the Missouri restriction than the North was in its favor. There was a Solid South as early as the Confederation period.[136] Certainly there was one in 1820. Southerners might disagree on the wisdom of a compromise but not on the main issue. The solidarity of the South filled many Northerners with envy. "Verily," said a writer in the Portland *Gazette*, " 'they manage these things better' in Virginia. In that as well as in every other slave-holding state their members are on this great slave question *true to a man.* . . . What a contrast to the self-destroying councils of the North and the East, where our demagogues so often raise themselves to consequence by playing off faction against faction."[137]

By uniting the Southern states in a common defense for two years, the Missouri Controversy made the Solid South more solid. It also promoted a spirit of Southern nationalism as opposed to American nationalism. There is an old story about an Indian chief who put a chip in his pouch every time that he was insulted. When the pouch became full, he went to war. The Missouri question gave the South a number of chips for its pouch. When it was over, Langdon Cheves was of the opinion

---

[135] King, *Rufus King*, VI, 286. For a detailed account of the transfer of the state rights leadership from the upper to the lower South, in the decade after the Missouri Controversy, see Sydnor, *Development of Southern Sectionalism*, 177-202.

[136] See Chapter I.   [137] Portland *Gazette*, March 14, 1820.

that it had done, "irremediably, much evil, and the disease can never be completely eradicated. . . . The whole Idea of restriction was a wicked Conception which though it may be forgiven ought not to be forgotten." "Hereafter," said Charles Tait, "the North can expect no act of liberality on this subject from the South. Touching this matter the Sword has been drawn & the Scabbard thrown away."[138]

The South could not have achieved comparative unity in 1819-1821 if certain groups which might have been expected to support restriction had not failed to do so. One of these was the Southern Federalists, who, as it turned out, generally opposed restriction with as much vigor as the Southern Democracy. All nine of the Federalist congressmen from Delaware, Maryland, Virginia, and North Carolina voted with the rest of the South on March 2, 1820, when the restrictive amendment to the Missouri bill was finally killed.

Another group in the South which failed signally to support the cause of restriction was the surviving liberal statesmen of the Revolutionary period. These men had been reared in the Age of Enlightenment and consequently were more tolerant than later generations in their ideas about slavery and religion. Clement Eaton lists nine men as illustrative of the broad-minded and philosophical type of statesmen who were bred on the Southern plantations of the eighteenth century: George Mason, George Washington, Thomas Jefferson, Charles Carroll, James Madison, James Monroe, John Randolph of Roanoke, Christopher Gadsden, and Willie Jones.[139] Five of Eaton's list of "aristocrats with liberal views" were still living in 1820: Jefferson, Carroll, Madison, Monroe, and Randolph. As the liberal Southern aristocrats had always been against slavery, it was supposed in the North that they would be in favor of congressional restriction in Missouri. The meeting held in Boston

[138] Langdon Cheves to Henry Clay, March 3, 1821, Clay Papers; Charles Tait to John W. Walker, May 20, 1820, Walker Papers. For similar remarks, made by William H. Crawford, see W. H. Sparks, *The Memories of Fifty Years* (Philadelphia, 1870), 228-30.

[139] Eaton, *Freedom of Thought in the Old South,* 62.

to discuss the Missouri question was confident that its efforts to prevent the extension of slavery were "countenanced and supported by characters most venerable in those states in which it is not yet abolished."[140] The Bostonians were mistaken, actually, for the surviving Southern "aristocrats with liberal views" were bitterly opposed to congressional restriction. Though they hated slavery, they could never consent to have it abolished by act of Congress at the request of Rufus King and De Witt Clinton.

It has already been shown that of all Southerners, John Randolph was the most implacable in his opposition to the Missouri restriction. President Monroe was willing to compromise with the North as far as unsettled territories were concerned but never in the case of a new state like Missouri. Nor did he doubt that restriction was "an effort for power, on the part of its authors, which is to be wielded, in every direction, for their benefit, without regard, to its consequences in the southern states." In Monroe's eyes, Rufus King was the archfiend who hoped to use Missouri as a lever either for dismembering the Union or securing an ascendancy to the North over the South.[141] Former President Madison was of the same opinion as Monroe, to whom he wrote that the idea was fast spreading that the object of the restrictionists was not to improve the condition of the slaves but "as you intimate, to form a new State of parties founded on local instead of political distinctions; thereby dividing the republicans of the North from those of the South, and making the former instrumental in giving the opponents of both an ascendancy over the whole."[142] At this time Madison wrote an allegorical treatise, *Jonathan Bull and Mary Bull*, in defense of the South's position on the Missouri question, but for some reason it was not published until many

[140] *Niles' Weekly Register*, XVII (1819), 242.

[141] James Monroe to George Hay, January 5, 1820, Monroe Papers, New York Public Library; letter from Monroe to an unnamed person, published in Columbus (Ohio) *Crisis*, December 14, 1864.

[142] James Madison to James Monroe, February 10, 1820, Monroe Papers, Library of Congress.

years later.[143] Another Southern statesman of the Revolutionary period who showed scant sympathy for congressional restriction was the aged Charles Carroll of Carrollton. Being a Federalist, Carroll could not condemn Anti-Missourianism on the ground that it might injure the Democratic party. Nevertheless, he regarded the Missouri question as unimportant, expressed impatience at Northern antislavery agitation, and observed that "The ardor and perseverance with which the debate is pursued give room to suspect that something else than the exclusion of slaves from the Missouri State is at the bottom."[144]

To no one was congressional restriction less appealing than to the dean and mentor of all Southern "aristocrats with liberal views," Thomas Jefferson. The Sage of Monticello was immensely distressed at the thought that the Federalists might, by this issue, regain "the ascendency from which their sins had hurled them." The Missouri dispute, he wrote, "is a mere party trick. The leaders of federalism, defeated in their schemes of obtaining power by rallying partisans to the principle of monarchism, . . . have changed their tack, and thrown out another barrel to the whale." Jefferson felt that "King is ready to risk the union for any chance of restoring his party to power and wriggling himself to the head of it, nor is Clinton without his hopes nor scrupulous as to the means of fulfilling them."[145] Aside from the Federalist angle, Jefferson had a horror of Northern interference in Southern race relations, and he regarded the proposed Missouri restriction as a flagrantly unconstitutional invasion of state rights.[146]

Jefferson's last years were filled with sorrow by the animosities that the Missouri Controversy unleashed. He considered this question more ominous than any that had confronted the

[143] James Madison, *Jonathan Bull and Mary Bull, An Inedited Manuscript* (Washington, 1856).

[144] Kate M. Rowland, *The Life of Charles Carroll of Carrollton 1737-1832* (2 vols., New York, 1898), II, 320-21.

[145] Ford, *Writings of Jefferson*, X, 162, 192; Thomas Jefferson to James Monroe, March 3, 1820, Monroe Papers, Library of Congress.

[146] Ford, *Writings of Jefferson*, X, 158, 177.

American people from the battle of Bunker Hill to the Treaty of Paris and regretted that the fruits of the Revolution were now to be lost in the fury of sectional strife. Though sectionalism was temporarily quieted by the compromise of 1820, he was sure that it would be revived, since "A geographical line, coinciding with a marked principle, moral and political, once conceived and held up to the angry passions of men, will never be obliterated; and every new irritation will mark it deeper and deeper." Jefferson feared that America would be divided into Athenian and Lacedaemonian confederacies. His predictions included another Peloponnesian war or a servile war.[147]

Believing that a war between the states was highly probable, Jefferson sought to prepare the South for the day of reckoning. One solution lay in emancipating the slaves and expatriating them to Haiti. Jefferson was hopeful that the Virginia legislature would take steps looking toward that end.[148] Another source of protection could be looked for in the extension of education, which with Jefferson was always the universal panacea. In this case, the South must educate its youth in the proper state rights doctrine. "All the States but our own," wrote Jefferson, "are sensible that knowledge is power. The Missouri question is for power. The efforts now generally making through the States to advance their science, is for power; while we are sinking into the barbarism of our Indian aborigines, and expect, like them, to oppose by ignorance the overwhelming mass of light and science by which we shall be surrounded."[149]

Jefferson was afraid that the Southern youths who were attending Northern colleges would imbibe "lessons of Anti-Missourianism." It was no longer wise, he thought, for Southerners to patronize these institutions. The South could not trust those who were against it "in position and principle to fashion to their own form the minds and affections" of the younger gen-

147 *Ibid.*, 152, 157-58, 186.   148 *Ibid.*, 173, 178.

149 Nathaniel F. Cabell (ed.), *Early History of the University of Virginia, as Contained in the Letters of Thomas Jefferson and Joseph C. Cabell* (Richmond, 1856), 178.

eration. The number of Virginians who received their education in the North appalled Jefferson. He was told that more than half of the students at Princeton were Virginians. No doubt, he said, they would return home "deeply impressed with the sacred principles of our holy alliance of Restrictionists."[150]

If Virginians were to go begging elsewhere for their education, Jefferson preferred that it should be to Kentucky rather than any other state, "because she has more of the flavor of the old cask than any other."[151] However, the University of Virginia, just nearing completion, was his main reliance. At first he had hoped that the new university would be the future bulwark of the human mind in the western hemisphere. Soon, as a result of the Missouri question, he began to regard it as a bulwark of the South against Northern aggression.[152] For that reason, he urged the legislature to grant adequate funds for its maintenance. In 1822 he reported that he had received letters from nearly every state south of the Potomac, the Ohio, and the Missouri, indicating that all of these were looking forward anxiously to the opening of the University of Virginia as an event which was to relieve them from sending their sons to the Northern universities.[153]

According to Clement Eaton, one reason for the disaster which befell the South in the 1860's was its change of leadership. When the liberal statesmen of the Revolutionary and Jeffersonian periods passed away, their places were taken by men of narrower outlook such as Rhett, Yancey, and Davis.[154] Nevertheless, one wonders whether Eaton's "aristocrats with liberal views" would have been any more successful than Davis

[150] *Ibid.*, 201, 202; Roy J. Honeywell, *The Educational Work of Thomas Jefferson* (Cambridge, 1931), 150-51.

[151] Cabell, *Early History of the University of Virginia*, 178.

[152] Charles H. Moffat, "Jefferson's Sectional Motives In Founding the University of Virginia," in *West Virginia History*, XII (1950), 61-69; Honeywell, *Educational Work of Thomas Jefferson*, 153; Frank L. Owsley, "Two Agrarian Philosophers: Jefferson and Du Pont de Nemours," in *Hound & Horn*, VI (1932), 170-72.

[153] Cabell, *Early History of the University of Virginia*, 201, 202, 239.

[154] Eaton, *Freedom of Thought in the Old South*, 62-63.

and his colleagues in coping with the abolitionists. The Missouri Controversy brought Randolph, Monroe, Madison, Carroll, and Jefferson as close to the smoke and battle of the Civil War as they would ever get, and it is significant that they reacted to the situation not as liberals, not as apostles of the Enlightenment, but as *Southerners.*

Writers in recent times have deplored the tendency in the ante bellum South between 1830 and 1860 to repudiate the equalitarian philosophy of Jefferson.[155] It is only fair to add that Jefferson himself became more conservative on the race question in his old age. In 1784 he had sought unsuccessfully to abolish slavery in all the western country, south as well as north of the Ohio River,[156] by congressional ordinance. In 1820 he still loved gradual emancipation but, loving state rights more, opposed the Missouri restriction. In 1776 he had maintained that all men are created equal and endowed with the unalienable right of liberty. In 1820, alarmed by the implications of his own doctrine, he expressed a fear that if Congress undertook to regulate the condition of the inhabitants of each state, it might "next declare that the condition of all men within the United States shall be that of freedom; in which case all the whites south of the Potomac and Ohio must evacuate their States, and most fortunate those who can do it first."[157] If, after 1820, the South followed a "road from Monticello," the conclusion is unavoidable that Jefferson helped to place it on that road by his attitude toward the Missouri Controversy and his efforts to sectionalize Southern education.

Jefferson was not the only Southerner who was afraid of Northern educators. When the Kentucky legislature was considering a bill in 1820 which was directed against New England peddlers, one legislator took advantage of the occasion to utter

155 Joseph C. Robert, *The Road From Monticello, A Study of the Virginia Slavery Debate of 1832* (Durham, 1941), 55-56; W. G. Bean, "Anti-Jeffersonianism in the Ante-Bellum South," in *North Carolina Historical Review,* XII (1935), 103-24.

156 Ford, *Writings of Jefferson,* III, 430; Stone, "Ordinance of 1787," 327.

157 Ford, *Writings of Jefferson,* X, 177.

anathemas against New England peddlers in general and particularly against Horace Holley, president of Transylvania University, who was described as a "spiritual pedlar."[158] At the
same time there were vacancies on the faculty of South
Carolina College. A correspondent of the Columbia, South
Carolina, *Telescope* suggested that it would be wise to fill these
positions with natives of the state, as far as possible. He pointed
out, with reference to the Missouri contest, that "if our selection
of Teachers and Principal is made from those quarters of the
union which usually supply the demand, we shall incur the
risk of having sentiments inculcated in the minds of our youth
extremely dangerous to the interests and prosperity of the
Southern States." There was considerable discussion on this
subject in the press of Charleston and Columbia. The Charleston *Southern Patriot* was partial to instructors from the North,
contending that residence in the South would make them pro-
Southern and that they would strengthen the bonds of union
between the North and South.[159]

Half of the *Southern Patriot's* prophecy (the pro-Southern
half) proved to be correct in the case of Dr. Thomas Cooper,
formerly of Pennsylvania and England, who arrived at Columbia in the midst of the trouble over Missouri to take the chair
of chemistry at South Carolina College. Though in his youth
he had been ardently antislavery, Dr. Cooper had already
sided with the South on the Missouri question before leaving
Pennsylvania.[160] Later he became a distinguished protagonist
of slavery and nullification.

[158] Washington *Gazette*, February 15, 1820.

[159] Charleston *Southern Patriot, And Commercial Advertiser,* August 5, September 2, 1820.

[160] See article signed "T. C." in Philadelphia *Democratic Press,* December 22,
1819. For evidence that Cooper was the author of the article, see the *Democratic Press* for January 6, 1820. Regarding the change in Cooper's attitude
toward slavery, see Dumas Malone, *The Public Life of Thomas Cooper 1783-
1839* (New Haven, 1926), 19-22, 76, 284-85.

"It is a question in which Congress have no right to interfere, and to which we as the people will never submit."—FRANKLIN (MISSOURI) INTELLIGENCER.[1]

CHAPTER VIII

SPECIAL PARTIES TO THE MISSOURI CONTROVERSY: MISSOURI, MAINE, AND ILLINOIS

*Q*UITE NATURALLY, the Missouri Controversy created more excitement in Missouri than anywhere else.[2] Long before most Southerners had taken any interest in the question and even before Burlington and New York had bestirred themselves, the Missourians were already holding mass meetings and issuing grand jury pronouncements against congressional restriction.

Missourians in 1819-1821 regarded themselves as Westerners rather than Southerners. Nevertheless, as they were overwhelmingly of Southern origin,[3] their attitude toward the race question was entirely Southern. Taking slavery for granted and assuming that it could not safely be abolished within the foreseeable future, even though many conceded that it was a theoretical evil, they deeply resented "Yankee" meddling in their affairs. A resident of St. Charles, Missouri, wrote in 1820 that "yankees . . . are generally very abnoxious to the good citizens of Missouri."[4] At this time a large majority of Missourians felt that they constituted one people with the older slave states, where they or their ancestors had formerly resided, in opposition to "Yankees" and Northerners.

In 1820 St. Louis could trace its cultural development back to the days of the French occupation, and elsewhere in the territory brick buildings and other signs of civilization were beginning to appear. The town of Franklin, far up in the Boon's Lick country, could boast that it possessed a newspaper and a fire department.[5] Still, Missouri was essentially a frontier area, where a large percentage of the population was said to "live somewhat in the stile of the savages, on venison and bare meat, in little smoky huts exposed to thé changes of the climate, and the inclemency of the weather."[6] Like the good frontiersmen they were, such people could be counted upon to have a perennial chip on their shoulder against the seaboard states. In fact they combined the South's touchiness on the race question with the frontiersman's traditional distrust of the East and always insisted that slavery restriction was an Eastern attempt to check the growth of the West.[7]

Unlike the people of the older slave states, the Missourians were never quite sure that they possessed internal unity in the fight against restriction. Their population contained a minority of Northerners and restrictionists. Furthermore, there was always the possibility of an inundation of new settlers from the

[1] Quoted in St. Louis *Enquirer*, June 2, 1819.

[2] Missouri's attitude toward the controversy has been treated here as briefly as possible, since this subject has already been exhaustively discussed in Floyd C. Shoemaker, *Missouri's Struggle for Statehood 1804-1821* (Jefferson City, 1916). See also Harrison A. Trexler, *Slavery in Missouri 1804-1865* (Baltimore, 1914), 100-12; Frank H. Hodder, "Side Lights on the Missouri Compromises," in *Annual Report of the American Historical Association for the Year 1909* (Washington, 1911), 151-61.

[3] James F. Ellis, *The Influence of Environment on the Settlement of Missouri* (St. Louis, 1929), 71-97; Hattie M. Anderson, "Missouri, 1804-1828: Peopling a Frontier State," in *Missouri Historical Review*, XXXI (1937), 174-80; Lynch, "Influence of Population Movements on Missouri," 506.

[4] James Devore to J. Cabell Breckinridge, December 23, 1820, Breckinridge Papers.

[5] Jonas Viles, "Missouri in 1820," in *Missouri Historical Review*, XV (1920), 42.

[6] James Devore to J. Cabell Breckinridge, December 23, 1820, Breckinridge Papers.

[7] St. Louis *Enquirer*, June 2, 1819; Shoemaker, *Missouri's Struggle for Statehood*, 302-303.

North. Hence it was thought necessary to arouse the public in Missouri against restriction by means of mass meetings, grand jury declarations, and editorial exhortations. Nathaniel Beverley Tucker was one of those most active in these proceedings. In his capacity as territorial judge, he was in a position to influence public opinion, and he made the most of his opportunity.[8]

Every newspaper in Missouri was opposed to congressional restriction,[9] but the noisiest in its opposition was the St. Louis *Enquirer,* which was edited by Thomas Hart Benton and Isaac N. Henry. In 1820 Benton was partial to the Southern way of life.[10] Indeed, if we are to judge by the editorials in his newspaper, he was an anti-Northern fire-eater in this period. Using language that the Charleston *Mercury* could hardly have improved upon in the 1850's, the *Enquirer* asserted on March 31, 1819, that

there seems to be no ground whatever for apprehending the passage of the bill clogged with the odious restriction which New England policy engrafted upon it. But suppose the worst came to the worst and Congress actually passed the law to suit the views of the New England politicians, would the Missouri submit to it? No! never! and those who suppose her capable of such pusillanimous submission, know nothing of the enlightened and energetic population which now fill this magnificent region. Every man here knows that the Congress have no right to read a state constitution, except to see that its character is Republican, and enough are here to make a constitution in the plenitude of State power, and to defend it after it is made; and if the bill had passed as framed in the House of Representatives at the late session, the people of the United States would have witnessed a specimen of Missouri feeling in the indignant contempt with which they would have trampled the odious restriction under their feet, and proceeded to the formation of a Republican constitution in the fulness of the peoples power.

[8] Chauncey S. Boucher and Robert P. Brooks (eds.), "Correspondence Addressed to John C. Calhoun 1837-1849," in *Annual Report of the American Historical Association for the Year 1929* (Washington, 1930), 258-59.

[9] Shoemaker, *Missouri's Struggle for Statehood,* 100.

[10] William N. Chambers, "Young Man from Tennessee, First Years of Thomas H. Benton in Missouri," in *Missouri Historical Society Bulletin,* IV (1948), 208.

Later the *Enquirer* remarked that the Northern congressmen who voted for the Tallmadge amendment "wish to expel *our* slaves, that *their* brothers, and sons, and nephews, and cousins, may enter upon the possession of this magnificent country."[11] The *Enquirer*, as well as other Missouri newspapers, published numerous letters from Missourians who objected to congressional restriction. One such writer, who styled himself "HAMPDEN," urged his fellow citizens to bear in mind that "the question now before you is not whether slavery shall be permitted or prohibited in the future state of Missouri; but whether you will meanly abandon your rights, and suffer any earthly power to dictate the terms of your constitution."[12] By March, 1820, the *Enquirer*, having either become hysterical or desirous of creating that impression, warned that Missouri was in danger of conquest by the North. In that event, said the *Enquirer*, the balance of power would be overturned, the Negro population would be emancipated, and "lighted torches & poisoned daggers will be put into the hands of slaves to rouse their sleeping masters from their beds amidst the flames of their houses and the cries of their slaughtered children."[13]

Quite as militant as the St. Louis *Enquirer* in its opposition to congressional restriction, the Franklin *Intelligencer* gave notice to Eastern congressmen that "As well might they arrest the course of the ocean that wash their barren shores, as to check our future growth."[14] Not so clear-cut was the course pursued by the St. Louis *Gazette* and its publisher, Joseph Charless, a native of Ireland. The *Gazette* professed to be strongly opposed to congressional restriction but printed the letters which it received on both sides of the question, including a number of communications written by restrictionists.[15] Those Missourians who were unwilling to have the restrictionist view-

---

[11] St. Louis *Enquirer*, May 12, 1819.
[12] *Ibid.*, April 7, 1819.   [13] *Ibid.*, March 25, 1820.
[14] Franklin *Intelligencer*, quoted in St. Louis *Enquirer*, June 2, 1819.
[15] For letters written by anonymous restrictionists, see St. Louis *Gazette & Public Advertiser*, April 28, May 26, June 2, 9, August 11, September 8, 1819, January 5, February 23, 1820. Opponents of restriction were especially angered by the letters from "A Farmer of St. Charles County," which appeared in the *Gazette* for April 7, 21, May 5, 19, June 9, 30, August 4, 1819.

point presented at all discontinued their subscriptions to Charless' paper, claiming that its policies would "ruin the country." Rumors of an organized attempt to boycott the *Gazette* did not deter the latter from carrying out its motto, "TRUTH WITHOUT FEAR," and maintaining what it called "the liberty of the press."[16] While Charless showed bravery in this instance, he was not as tolerant as his highly commendable motto would indicate. He had been known to suppress news which was disagreeable to him,[17] and his tolerance toward the advocates of congressional restriction may well have been due to the fact that, in spite of protestations to the contrary, he was secretly in favor of the Tallmadge amendment.[18]

On May 15, 1819, an antirestrictionist mass meeting was held in the courthouse at St. Louis. Alexander McNair presided over the gathering, David Barton acted as secretary, and Thomas Hart Benton was the principal speaker. The meeting was of the unanimous opinion that the abolition of slavery in Missouri by Congress would be "equally contrary to the rights of the state and to the welfare of the slaves themselves."[19] Similar meetings were held in the counties of Montgomery, Howard, Washington, Ste. Genevieve, and New Madrid.[20] The New Madrid meeting declared that Missouri would refuse to enter the Union except on an equal footing with the original states.[21] The Montgomery countians viewed restriction as an unprecedented and unconstitutional "usurpation of our most

16 St. Louis *Gazette & Public Advertiser*, May 12, 1819.

17 William N. Chambers, "Pistols and Politics, Incidents in the Career of Thomas H. Benton, 1816-1818," in *Missouri Historical Society Bulletin*, V (1948), 17.

18 Charless went out of his way to write a confidential letter to the Northern antislavery leader, John W. Taylor, to assure him that the St. Louis *Enquirer's* "intemperate language" was not representative of public opinion in Missouri. Joseph Charless to John W. Taylor, April 29, 1819, Taylor Papers.

19 St. Louis *Gazette & Public Advertiser*, May 19, 1819; St. Louis *Enquirer*, May 19, 1819.

20 St. Louis *Gazette & Public Advertiser*, May 19, August 4, 1819; St. Louis *Enquirer*, May 12, July 28, August 4, 25, October 6, 1819; Jackson *Herald*, September 18, 1819.

21 Jackson *Herald*, September 18, 1819.

sacred rights."[22] Antirestrictionist remonstrances also came from the Mount Pleasant Association of Baptist Churches, meeting at Mount Zion in Howard County,[23] and from grand juries in St. Louis, St. Charles, Jefferson, Washington, and Montgomery counties.[24]

Between 1819 and 1821, Missourians drank antirestrictionist toasts at public dinners and patriotic celebrations until they must have been blue in the face. The following Fourth-of-July toasts in 1819 were typical: *"The Territory of Missouri*—With a population of near 100,000 souls demands its right to be admitted into the union on an equal footing with the original states." *"The people of Missouri*—They want no Congressional provision in forming their constitution, they will provide for themselves." *"Messrs. Talmadge and Taylor*—Politically insane, may the next Congress appoint them a dark room, a straight waistcoat and a thin water gruel diet." *"The Territory of Missouri*—May she be admitted into the Union on an equal footing with the original States, or not received in any other way."[25]

A public gathering in St. Ferdinand township of St. Louis County endorsed the Tallmadge amendment, but this seems to have been the only meeting in the territory which took such a stand.[26] In the city of St. Louis a man was apt to have a fight on his hands if he championed restriction.[27] Even a large part of the Northern minority was antirestrictionist. Benjamin Lundy, who was in Missouri at the time, afterward testified that some of those who were loudest in favor of slavery had migrated to Missouri from the free states.[28] That an overwhelming majority of Missourians were against the Tallmadge amendment there can be no doubt. An antislavery man who

---

[22] St. Louis *Gazette & Public Advertiser*, May 19, 1819.

[23] *Niles' Weekly Register*, XVII (1819), 200-201.

[24] St. Louis *Gazette & Public Advertiser*, April 14, July 14, August 11, 1819; St. Louis *Enquirer*, August 4, 25, 1819.

[25] St. Louis *Enquirer*, July 14, 21, 1819.

[26] St. Louis *Gazette & Public Advertiser*, June 23, 1819.

[27] *Ibid.*, January 5, 1820.

[28] Mount Pleasant (Ohio) *Genius of Universal Emancipation*, December, 1821.

visited the territory during the admission controversy was impressed by the vehemence with which the people expressed opposition to congressional interference with slavery. He further reported that "The most boisterous on the subject here, as elsewhere, we soon discover to have been *overseers, grocers, &c.* who have invested their capital in property (so called) of this description, and make vehement declarations as to their right by *purchase*."[29]

Because of their announced intention of refusing to submit to congressional restriction, Missourians were accused of being advocates of disunion. Actually they were primarily concerned with fighting their way into the Union rather than out of it. Regarding restriction as unconstitutional, they repeatedly stressed the fact that they meant to resist it "by every possible constitutional means."[30] The chief organ of the hotspurs, the St. Louis *Enquirer*, was intensely pro-American and waxed eloquent in describing the "grand outline" which nature had "marked out" for the republic.[31]

If the first session of the Sixteenth Congress had adjourned without passing an enabling act for Missouri's admission, the people of the territory would probably have taken the matter into their own hands and organized a state government without waiting for congressional sanction. They would then have demanded admittance to the Union when Congress reconvened. As it turned out, this procedure, contemplated by Benton and others,[32] was unnecessary, for on March 25 the news of the passage of the compromise of 1820 reached St. Louis. Four days later the *Enquirer* carried exultant headlines at the top of its editorial page: "Gratifying news from Washington.—King and Clinton defeated.—The Senate triumphant.—Final passage of the Missouri State Bill without restriction."

29 Frankfort (Kentucky) *Commentator*, March 30, 1820.
30 St. Louis *Gazette & Public Advertiser*, May 19, 1819. See also *ibid.*, April 14, July 14, 1819.
31 St. Louis *Enquirer*, August 11, 1819.
32 *Ibid.*, May 19, 1819, March 25, 1820; St. Louis *Gazette & Public Advertiser*, May 19, August 4, 1819.

The passage of the compromise, which was popular in Missouri, was celebrated with the ringing of bells, the firing of cannon, illuminations, and transparencies. One transparency represented a Negro in high spirits, rejoicing that Congress had permitted slaves to be brought to so fine a land as Missouri.[33]

Early in May, 1820, under the authority granted by Congress, delegates were elected to a convention to frame a constitution for the new state. This produced another heated contest over slavery, and some people who had opposed congressional restriction now advocated state restriction. In St. Louis Joseph Charless presided over a meeting held by those who believed that Missouri should establish a definite date beyond which the further importation of slaves would not be permitted. No interference with the existing slave property in the state was intended.[34] Benjamin Lundy served as secretary of a similar meeting at Herculaneum in Jefferson County. The Herculaneum group issued an address to the voters, admonishing them that "THIS PERHAPS, WILL BE THE ONLY TIME THAT YOU WILL EVER HAVE IT IN YOUR POWER TO OPPOSE THE HORRIBLE SYSTEM WITH EFFECT."[35] Judge John B. C. Lucas of St. Louis, one of the candidates for the convention who opposed the further importation of slaves, explained that he was "much alarmed at the idea of great slaveholders coming amongst us with their gangs of plantation slaves: assuming airs of nabobs; superciliously looking upon our plain and unassuming farmers."[36] Lucas was a native of France who had formerly resided in Pennsylvania and whose son had been killed in a duel by Thomas H. Benton.

[33] St. Louis *Enquirer*, March 29, April 1, 1820; St. Louis *Gazette & Public Advertiser*, April 5, 1820.

[34] St. Louis *Gazette & Public Advertiser*, April 5, 12, May 3, 10, 1820.

[35] *Ibid.*, April 26, 1820. The restrictionists in Missouri in 1820 drew much of their strength from antislavery Baptist sects, such as the "Friends of Humanity," which had early secured a foothold in the counties of St. Louis, Jefferson, and Cape Girardeau. Benjamin G. Merkel, "The Abolition Aspects of Missouri's Antislavery Controversy 1819-1865," in *Missouri Historical Review*, XLIV (1950), 234-35.

[36] St. Louis *Gazette & Public Advertiser*, April 12, 1820.

Benton's *Enquirer* denounced state action against the future admission of slaves as vigorously as it had formerly condemned congressional restriction, contending that such a policy would stop immigration from the South and cause the "satellites" of King and Clinton to pour into Missouri. Among the epithets which the *Enquirer* applied to advocates of state restriction were "preachers who have arrived from the North," "relation of John Cotton Smith who was the Federal Governor or Lieut. Gov. of Connecticut," "northern confederates," and "candidates to frame our constitution . . . furnished from New York."[37]

The election resulted in a complete victory for the proslavery party. In St. Louis County the proslavery David Barton received the highest number of votes (892) given to any candidate, while John B. C. Lucas, the leading restrictionist candidate, received but 400. One of the successful proslavery candidates in St. Louis was Edward Bates, later attorney general in Lincoln's cabinet. Altogether the antirestrictionist candidates polled 7,265 votes in St. Louis County to 2,026 for their opponents. Elsewhere in the territory the outcome was the same. At Mine a Burton the antirestrictionists garnered 1,147 votes to 61 for manumission men. After a careful study of all available election returns, Shoemaker concludes that the restrictionist voters of Missouri were outnumbered at least seven to one and possibly ten to one.[38] Apparently no avowed restrictionist was elected to the convention.[39]

Some writers have ascribed the overwhelming victory of the proslavery party to the fierce resentment that had been bred in Missourians by the attempt of Congress to dictate the terms of their constitution.[40] There were, however, more important

[37] St. Louis *Enquirer*, April 8, 12, 29, 1820.

[38] Shoemaker, *Missouri's Struggle for Statehood*, 131. For the election returns in St. Louis County and at Mine a Burton, see St. Louis *Enquirer*, May 6, 10, 1820; St. Louis *Gazette & Public Advertiser*, May 10, 1820.

[39] According to tradition, there was one restrictionist in the convention— Benjamin Emmons of St. Charles, who was a Northerner by birth. Actually, he does not seem to have been a restrictionist. See Trexler, *Slavery in Missouri*, 103; St. Louis *Enquirer*, May 6, 1820.

[40] Hodder, "Missouri Compromises," 155; Louis Houck, *A History of Missouri from the Earliest Explorations and Settlements until the Admission of the State into the Union* (3 vols., Chicago, 1908), III, 250.

factors involved. As Shoemaker and Trexler point out, "reasons of dollars and self-interest" were a major consideration. The slaves of Missouri constituted a great vested interest with which their owners were determined to brook no interference.[41] If cornered in an argument, educated Missourians would generally admit that slavery was a theoretical evil, but this did not mean that they would consent to any form of manumission. Most Missourians were not slaveholders (only one sixth of the population was Negro). Nevertheless, having lived all their lives in slave territory, the nonslaveholders were no more likely to legislate against slavery than against the wind and the rain. Many had slaveholding relatives and neighbors in the older states whom they would like to see move to Missouri. The exclusion of slaveholders would discourage Southern migration and bring an influx of the hated "Yankees." Finally, it was thought that slave labor was needed to clear the land and open up the territory.[42]

The constitutional convention met in St. Louis in June and July, 1820.[43] The constitution which it drew up contained many good features, including universal white male suffrage and a guarantee of protection for the lives and persons of slaves. The state legislature was required by the constitution to enact legislation to "oblige the owners of slaves to treat them with humanity, and to abstain from all injuries to them extending to life or limb." In criminal cases slaves were to have the benefit of trial by jury and, if convicted of a capital offense, should receive the same punishment meted out to white people under similar circumstances. Likewise any person who maliciously killed or dismembered a slave should suffer the same punishment that would be inflicted for committing such a crime against a white person.[44]

[41] Shoemaker, *Missouri's Struggle for Statehood*, 132-34; Trexler, *Slavery in Missouri*, 104.

[42] St. Louis *Gazette & Public Advertiser*, April 12, 1820.

[43] For the official proceedings of the convention and the provisions of the constitution that it framed, see *Journal of the Missouri State Convention* (St. Louis, 1820); *Constitution of the State of Missouri* (St. Louis, 1820). A facsimile reprint of the convention *Journal* was published by the Statute Law Book Company of Washington, D. C., in 1905.

[44] Article III, Sections 26-28.

As has already been shown, the constitution contained two provisions which were obnoxious to certain elements in the North. One of these attempted to guarantee the perpetuity of slavery,[45] and the other made it mandatory upon the legislature to enact laws "To prevent free negroes and mulattoes from coming to, and settling in this state, under any pretext whatsoever."[46] While Northerners regarded the free Negro and mulatto clause as an expression of defiance, it really seems to have been put in the constitution largely because the framers found similar provisions in the codes of other states.[47]

Missouri not only framed a constitution in the summer of 1820 but proceeded, under it, to elect a governor, state legislature, and members of Congress. For their first governor the people chose Alexander McNair, a native of Pennsylvania and stanch antirestrictionist.[48] Governor McNair was duly inaugurated, the territorial government was superseded, and Missouri became a *de facto* state.

At least one newspaper in Missouri and a number of Northerners and Southerners who had hitherto been friendly to Missouri believed that its constitution contained "some foolish and unnecessary clauses, which will cause trouble."[49] Cause trouble

[45] Article III, Section 26. The reason for incorporating this provision in the constitution was discussed in Chapter V. Its exact wording was: "Sec. 26.—The general assembly shall have no power to pass laws, First, For the emancipation of slaves without the consent of their owners; or without paying them before such emancipation, a• full equivalent for such slaves so emancipated; and Second, To prevent bona-fide emigrants to this state, or actual settlers therein, from bringing from any of the United States, or from any of their territories, such persons as may there be deemed to be slaves, so long as any persons of the same description are allowed to be held as slaves by the laws of this state."

[46] Article III, Section 26.

[47] Frankfort (Kentucky) *Argus of Western America*, March 8, 1821.

[48] According to Timothy Flint, who was in Missouri at the time, no Northerner could hope to be elected to public office unless he declared himself unequivocally against restriction. Timothy Flint, *Recollections of the Last Ten Years* (Boston, 1826), 214.

[49] Senator John W. Walker of Alabama to Charles Tait, November 20, 1820, Tait Papers. The Missouri newspaper that agreed with Walker was the *Missourian* of St. Charles, which see for July 1, December 23, 1820. See also letter from John Scott in St. Louis *Enquirer*, December 16, 1820; New York *National Advocate*, December 18, 1820; Nashville *Clarion, and Tennessee Gazette*, January 9, 1821.

they certainly did. As has been seen, the free Negro and mulatto clause became a pretext for reopening the whole subject
of slavery restriction in Congress. From November, 1820, until
the latter part of February, 1821, the Northern majority in the
House of Representatives prevented the final admission of
Missouri.

During this period the people of Missouri suffered increasingly from a persecution complex and vowed that never before
had free citizens been treated so unjustly as they. To make
matters worse, the numerous atrocity stories about Missouri
which appeared in the Northern antislavery press convinced
many Americans that all Missourians were uncouth savages.
The first such story had to do with an obscure individual,
Humphrey Smith, a native of New Jersey, who fled from Missouri when a grand jury in Howard County indicted him for
attempting to incite a slave insurrection. According to Smith,
his offense consisted of advocating congressional restriction and
asking a Methodist how he could own slaves when the dis-
cipline of the church forbade it. The St. Louis *Enquirer* told a
different story, accusing Smith of "overt acts and criminal conduct among the slaves at Boonslick."[50]

Before the Smith story had been fully forgotten, Isaac Henry,
one of the editors of the St. Louis *Enquirer,* made a physical
assault upon Joseph Charless, editor of the St. Louis *Gazette.*[51]
Neither man was seriously injured but Missouri's reputation
was. Thereafter Missouri became the target of many a gibe
and witticism. When it was proposed to name the capital of
the new state Missouriopolis, the Cadiz, Ohio, *Telegraph* suggested that a more appropriate title might be Slave-opolis or
Black-opolis, meaning the black city or city of slaves.[52] Federalist and Clintonian newspapers regaled their readers with hair-
raising stories of Missouri mob violence and lawlessness—accounts of duels, personal encounters with dirk and pistol, St.

[50] St. Louis *Enquirer,* September 1, October 20, 1819; Edwardsville (Illinois)
Spectator, September 18, 1819; Boston *Columbian Centinel,* November 20,
1819.
[51] St. Louis *Gazette & Public Advertiser,* May 17, 1820.
[52] Cadiz (Ohio) *Telegraph,* quoted in Steubenville (Ohio) *Western Herald,*
September 2, 1820.

Louis ladies who wore and wielded dirks, fights between boat-
men, broken bones, noses bitten off, attacks by slaveholders on
ministers, floggings, and Negro mistresses (one of whom went
on a rampage and flogged her white paramour, who thereupon
committed suicide in humiliation).[53] A resident of Pittsburgh
who had been considering moving to Missouri took the pre-
caution to write first to the editor of the St. Louis *Gazette* to
ask if it was true that the people of St. Louis wore dirks and
pistols, "and consequently, a man's life is in continual danger."[54]

No doubt some of the atrocity stories were true and others
false or exaggerated; but even if they were all true they only
added up to one self-evident fact, namely, that Missouri in 1820
was a typical lusty American frontier community, possessing
all the virtues and vices usually associated with such an area.
It was natural that the people of Missouri should become more
and more sensitive about outside criticism. A Missourian who
was visiting in the North complained that "When I answer the
question that is frequently put to me—'where are you from?'
I can at once see an alteration of the countenance of the askers;
with Missouri goes suspicion, mistrust, and disrespect, and on
further acquaintance they are surprised to find me civil and
something like themselves."[55]

One of the greatest fears of many Missourians was that the
agitation over restriction would discourage immigration from
the South. At first this fear seemed groundless. In June, 1819,
several months after the introduction of the Tallmadge amendment, a resident of St. Charles County wrote an interesting
description of the caravans of Kentuckians and Tennesseans
"flowing through our town with their men servants and maid
servants, their flocks and their herds." He added that "The
tinkling of bells, the cloud of dust, the throng of hogs and cat-

[53] For various Northern atrocity stories about Missouri, see St. Louis *Enquirer*,
July 5, August 2, 19, 1820; New York *Daily Advertiser*, November 25, 1819;
Boston *Columbian Centinel*, November 27, 1819; Portland *Gazette*, June 29,
1820; New York *American*, June 20, 1820; New York *Commercial Advertiser*,
September 5, 1820.
[54] St. Louis *Gazette & Public Advertiser*, November 29, 1820.
[55] New York *Columbian*, July 21, 1820.

tle, the white headed children, the curly headed Africans, smiling infancy, blooming virgins, athletic manhood and decrepid age, altogether form groups too interesting to be painted but by the pencil of Teniers."[56] In October, 1819, the St. Louis *Enquirer* reported that the immigration to Missouri continued to be astonishingly great. It estimated that from thirty to fifty wagons daily crossed the Mississippi at the various ferries, bringing in an average of from four to five hundred new settlers each day. "The emigrants," said the *Enquirer*, "are principally from Kentucky, Tennessee, Virginia, & the states further south. They bring great numbers of slaves, knowing that congress has no power to impose the agitated restriction, and that the people of Missouri will never adopt it."[57] After continuing at full tide in the spring of 1820, immigration to Missouri finally came to a temporary halt in the latter part of the year. Whether this was due to the slavery dispute or to the depression it would be difficult to say.[58]

During the last phase of the contest over their admission, in the winter of 1820-1821, Missourians stoutly maintained that they were already a state and insisted that they would never consent to return to a territorial status.[59] This attitude was widely approved throughout the South. The Richmond *Enquirer* asserted that Missouri "will never be again a territory. She will never receive another Governor from the federal government, unless he is supported by 30,000 bayonets."[60] In the opinion of Andrew Jackson, Missouri would *"not retrograde, or humble herself,"* but might *"seize the public property and funds within her limits."*[61] Obviously Jackson did not want the Missourians to humble themselves. Jefferson predicted that should Congress employ force against Missouri, "there would be a

[56] St. Louis *Gazette & Public Advertiser,* June 9, 1819.
[57] St. Louis *Enquirer,* October 30, 1819.
[58] Dorothy B. Dorsey, "The Panic of 1819 in Missouri," in *Missouri Historical Review,* XXIX (1935), 80-81.
[59] St. Louis *Enquirer,* January 20, 1821; Washington *Daily National Intelligencer,* January 29, 1821; St. Charles *Missourian,* January 13, 1821.
[60] Richmond *Enquirer,* December 12, 1820.
[61] *Congressional Globe,* 30 Cong., 2 Sess., Appendix, 65.

secession of the members south of the line, and probably of the three Northwestern States, who, however inclined to the other side, would scarcely separate from those who would hold the Mississippi from its mouth to its source."[62]

Though at this time there was some talk among Missourians of establishing an independent country,[63] the St. Louis *Enquirer* and others urged continued loyalty to the Union.[64] At length Congress passed the compromise of 1821, authorizing President Monroe to proclaim the final admission of Missouri if its legislature would promise that the free Negro and mulatto clause in the constitution of the state should never be so construed as to exclude citizens of any other state from the benefit of the privileges and immunities granted them by the federal Constitution.

The legislature of the *de facto* state of Missouri met in special session at St. Charles to make the promise or declaration which Congress required of it. In sullen mood, the legislature pointed out that it did not possess the power to alter the operation of Missouri's constitution except in the manner prescribed by that constitution. It only agreed to make the promise that Congress desired, it said, because such a declaration "will neither restrain, or enlarge, limit or extend the operation of the constitution of the United States, or of this state, but the said constitutions will remain in all respects as if the said resolution had never passed, and the desired declaration was never made, and because such declaration will not divest any power or change the duties of any of the constituted authorities of this state, or of the United States, nor impair the rights of the people of this state, or impose any additional obligation upon them."[65]

Though President Monroe proclaimed the final admission of Missouri on August 10, 1821, loyal Missourians continued for

[62] Ford, *Writings of Jefferson*, X, 178.

[63] James Devore to Robert Breckinridge, December 19, 1820; Devore to J. Cabell Breckinridge, December 23, 1820, Breckinridge Papers.

[64] St. Louis *Enquirer*, December 23, 1820, February 3, 1821; Richmond *Enquirer*, February 20, 1821.

[65] Shoemaker, *Missouri's Struggle for Statehood*, 360-62. Henry S. Geyer was the author of this declaration or "solemn public act" of the Missouri legislature. It "was a wonderful document charged with satire. Mark Twain could not have done better." Stevens, *Centennial History of Missouri*, I, 57.

years to regard 1820 as the correct admission date.[66] Like the compromise of 1820, that of 1821 was destined eventually to be repudiated. In 1847 the Missouri legislature passed an act providing that "No free negro or mulatto shall, under any pretext, emigrate to this State, from any other State or territory."[67]

The status of Maine during the Missouri Controversy was similar to that of Missouri. While the latter's entrance into the Union was being blocked in the House of Representatives by a Northern majority, the admission of Maine was being delayed in the Senate by the South.

Prior to 1820, the "district" of Maine was a part of the state of Massachusetts. It was natural that the people of Maine, in 1819-1820, should wish to separate from the parent state and organize a government of their own, for they had a total population of nearly 300,000 and were not contiguous to Massachusetts proper. Moreover, Maine was predominantly Democratic, while Federalism still held sway in Massachusetts.

It will be recalled that Massachusetts consented to Maine's separate statehood by an act of June 19, 1819.[68] In accordance

[66] Jonas Viles, "The Territorial Period [of Missouri], 1804-1820," in *The South in the Building of the Nation* (13 vols., Richmond, 1909-1913), III, 214.

[67] *Laws of the State of Missouri, Passed at the First Session of the Fourteenth General Assembly, 1847*, 103-104. The condition of admission imposed upon Missouri did not specifically refer to free Negroes and mulattoes. It merely provided that the fourth clause of the twenty-sixth section of the third article of the constitution of Missouri should never be construed to exclude citizens of another state from the benefit of the privileges and immunities granted them by the federal Constitution. In the copy of the Missouri constitution which Congress had in its possession, the fourth clause of the twenty-sixth section of the third article was the provision regarding the migration of free Negroes and mulattoes. As the constitution was printed in Missouri, however, the fourth clause of the twenty-sixth section of the third article referred to something else. Because of this fact, some Missourians thought that Congress had made an error and had designated the wrong clause. They were willing to agree to the condition of admission, since they considered it to be meaningless as stated by Congress. Shoemaker, *Missouri's Struggle for Statehood*, 311-16; St. Louis *Gazette & Public Advertiser*, June 13, 1821; Lucien Carr, "An Error in the Resolution of Congress admitting Missouri into the Union," in *Proceedings of the Massachusetts Historical Society*, Second Series, XIII (1900), 448-54.

[68] For a full account of the separation of Maine from Massachusetts, see Hatch, *Maine, a History*, I, 107-72; Edward Stanwood, "The Separation of

with this act, Maine held a convention, drew up a state constitution, and petitioned Congress for admission to the Union. The people of Maine had every reason to believe that they would be admitted without any difficulty. Great, therefore, was their dismay when the Senate made their admission dependent on the admission of Missouri as a slave state. Almost immediately, without realizing it, they developed something in common with the Missourians—a persecution complex. A citizen of Washington County, Maine, complained that the members of the United States Senate were "attempting to make a jack ass of the State of Maine, to carry their surplus negro population into the Missouri Territory."[69] James Hooper observed that linking Maine and Missouri was "Like a man going to Market with a turkey and crow and he will not sell the turkey unless they will by the crow."[70] "We protest," wrote Judge Daniel Cony from Augusta, "solemnly protest, against coupling the destiny of Maine, the civilized populous State of Maine, (300000 free inhabitants) with the trackless regions, the dreary wastes, the sable tribes of the Missouri beyond the Mississippi."[71] The Hallowell *American Advocate*, a Democratic newspaper, declared that "Missouri has set up the idol of Slavery, and Maine must be sacrificed to this modern Moloch, feasting on human flesh, and thirsting for human gore."[72]

The union of the Maine and Missouri bills by the Senate created a difference of opinion in Maine. There were some who would rather have Maine denied statehood indefinitely than be the means of securing Missouri's admission as a slave state. To that group belonged the Portland *Gazette*, leading Federalist newspaper of the district, which maintained that it was better

---

Maine from Massachusetts," in *Proceedings of the Massachusetts Historical Society*, Third Series, I (1907), 125-64; L. F. Schmeckebier, "How Maine Became a State," in *Collections and Proceedings of the Maine Historical Society*, Second Series, IX (1898), 146-72.

[69] Portland *Gazette*, March 14, 1820.

[70] James Hooper to William King, January 29, 1820, William King Papers.

[71] King, *Rufus King*, VI, 268.

[72] Hallowell *American Advocate*, quoted in New York *Daily Advertiser*, February 12, 1820.

that Maine "should forfeit her right of admission into this Union, than that the dark and portentous tide of slavery, which is now ready to burst its barriers, should roll upon the west."[73] As a part of Massachusetts, Maine already had seven members in the national House of Representatives, and all but two of these were willing to jeopardize Maine's own chances of acquiring statehood in preference to aiding the cause of Missouri slavery. In taking such a stand, the congressmen had the support of many of their constituents.[74] The people of Vassalboro held a meeting in January, 1820, at which they unanimously declared that they preferred "remaining forever in their present situation to being admitted on ignominious terms, or giving the semblance of a sanction to the violation of the rights of humanity."[75]

On the other hand, there were many in Maine who would rather come into the Union coupled with the slave state of Missouri than not come in at all. The Portland *Eastern Argus,* oldest and most influential Democratic journal in the district, was the editorial spokesman for this group. The *Argus* condemned the coupling of the Maine and Missouri bills as an act of "Manifest injustice." Nevertheless it wanted the South to know that most of the people of Maine were taking no part in the campaign to abolish slavery in Missouri. It believed that two thirds of the people of the district were willing to forego the restriction on Missouri in order to secure statehood for themselves, and it thought that those who were opposing this course were people who had never really favored the separation of Maine from Massachusetts.[76]

The act of Massachusetts for Maine's separate statehood provided that Maine should revert to its old status as part of Massachusetts unless Congress consented to its admission before March 4, 1820. As the second Missouri debate dragged along, it began to look as if the time limit would expire with-

[73] Portland *Gazette,* March 7, 1820.
[74] Hatch, *Maine, a History,* I, 163-64.
[75] Boston *Columbian Centinel,* February 5, 1820.
[76] Portland *Eastern Argus,* January 11, 18, February 8, 1820.

out any action having been taken by Congress. What would Maine do in that event? It would, thought William King, with the consent of Massachusetts, set up a separate state government without waiting any longer for congressional approval.[77] Maine would then (like Missouri at a later date) occupy the anomalous position of a state outside the Union. Such a prospect did not appear to disturb William D. Williamson, who afterward served as acting governor of the state. Williamson wrote in January, 1820, that "we are about as willing to risk the untried consequences of sovereignty, separate from the confederation of the States, as to have slavery indelibly graven on the frontlet of that bill, which shall make Maine a *member* of the great American Empire."[78]

Maine's plight attracted much sympathy throughout the North. The Hartford *Courant* called the uniting of the Maine and Missouri bills "an unfair and disgraceful artifice," and the Worcester *National Aegis* denounced it as "one of the most dishonourable *tricks* (for it deserves no better name) that ever disgraced any deliberative assembly in America."[79] "Maine! ill-fated Maine! The story of her woes would make the angels weep!" exclaimed Representative Joshua Cushman.[80] Six of the Massachusetts congressmen who represented Maine districts presented a petition to Congress, protesting against the delay in admission.[81] Massachusetts extended the time limit for congressional action to two years, but the compromise of 1820 rendered this unnecessary.[82]

Despite the fact that so many citizens of Maine favored the congressional restriction of slavery in Missouri and bitterly re-

[77] King, *Rufus King*, VI, 256.   [78] *Ibid.*, 259.

[79] Hartford *Courant*, January 25, 1820; Worcester (Massachusetts) *National Aegis*, January 26, 1820.

[80] *Annals of Congress*, 16 Cong., 1 Sess., 1292.

[81] John Holmes, Martin Kinsley, Mark L. Hill, James Parker, Joshua Cushman, and Ezekiel Whitman, *Representation of the Members of the House of Representatives, from That Part of Massachusetts Hitherto Known as the District of Maine* (Washington, 1820).

[82] Hatch, *Maine, a History*, I, 165. For a memorial from prominent citizens of Maine requesting Massachusetts to extend the time limit, see *To the Honorable Senate, and the House of Representatives, of the Commonwealth of Massachusetts, in General Court Assembled* (n.p., 1820).

sented the attempt to make their own admission to the Union dependent on the perpetuation of Missouri slavery, there was still probably more pro-Southern and procompromise sentiment in Maine than in any other Northern state. The advocates of compromise included the Portland *Eastern Argus* and its able editor, Ashur Ware; William King, first governor of Maine; William P. Preble of Portland, one of the Democratic "bosses"; John Holmes and John Chandler, who were Maine's first United States senators; and Congressman Mark L. Hill.

The *Eastern Argus* early endorsed the idea of a compromise and censured those Federalists who were seeking, by means of the Missouri Controversy, to create a geographical alignment of political parties.[83] William King, Maine's most outstanding political figure in this period, was an ardent supporter of the compromise of 1820. At first he had assured his half brother, Rufus King, that the people of Maine disapproved of Congressman John Holmes' pro-Southern attitude and that they would not consent to "bargain their way" into the Union, "let the consequence be what it may."[84] Soon, however, the temptation to "bargain" for admission was too much for William King. By February 23, 1820, he was writing to John Holmes that he presumed a compromise would be necessary and offering to share responsibility with Holmes in enacting one.[85] On March 6, 1820, before it was known in Maine that Congress had passed the compromise, King and other political leaders wrote to Congressman Mark Hill to urge him to vote for it. They were hopeful that all of the Massachusetts congressmen who resided in Maine would do likewise. They advised Hill that "The best informed people in Boston, as well as all the people of this section of the state of all parties with whom we have conversed are agreed in opinion that a compromise on those principles would be highly proper, and more interesting to the North than any thing which the most sanguine had ever contemplated."[86]

[83] Portland *Eastern Argus*, March 7, 14, 1820.
[84] King, *Rufus King*, VI, 255, 265.
[85] William King to John Holmes, February 23, 1820, Holmes Papers.
[86] Portland *Eastern Argus*, October 24, 1820. Besides King, those signing the letter were: J. Wingate, Jr., Benjamin Ames, Samuel Winter, J. B. Swanton,

In the decisive vote of March 2, 1820, five of the Massachusetts congressmen from Maine districts opposed the Missouri Compromise and only two—John Holmes of Alfred and Mark Langdon Hill of Phippsburg—supported it. Both Holmes and Hill were widely criticized for the stand they had taken. The Federalist Portland *Gazette* regretted that they had given aid "to a system of increasing evil," while various writers in the *Gazette* stigmatized them as demagogues, parasites, and allies of Southern slave drivers.[87] They did not lack for defenders, however. William King brought pressure to bear on the Democratic press in their behalf, and the *Eastern Argus* assured the writers in the *Gazette* that no "howlings," be they ever so noisy, would turn Maine against the two men to whom it owed its admission to statehood.[88]

In February, 1820, one of Holmes' friends, R. C. Vose, made a careful survey of public opinion in Boston and Maine. He reported that in predominantly Federalist Boston the leading Democrats were decidedly in sympathy with Holmes' position on the Missouri question. He also told Holmes that he had talked with many of the representatives from York County, Maine, in the Massachusetts legislature and that "they all approved of your course & I beleive many would be willing to go farther,—as I returned in York & Saco, I found them alive to the subject; and that they were highly gratified with your course, and in Portland I beleive, with Mr [Ashur] Ware, that a large majority of our friends here are against restricting Missouri."[89]

J. F. Wingate, Thomas Robinson, N. Weld, P. H. Greene, Joseph Sewall, Jr., J. Crooker, William Pettingill, Nathaniel Groton, N. G. Allen, Luke Lambert, James McLellan, and David Stinson. For what is evidently a copy of this letter, see William King to Mark L. Hill, March 6, 1820, William King Papers.

[87] Portland *Gazette*, March 14, May 23, 30, 1820. See also George Thacher to John Holmes, January 16, 1820, Holmes Papers.

[88] William King to John Holmes, March 28, 1820, Holmes Papers; Portland *Eastern Argus*, April 25, 1820. For expressions of approval of the Missouri Compromise by Maine citizens, see also Ashur Ware to William King, March 11, 1820, William King Papers; Barnabas Palmer to John Holmes, April 19, 1820, Holmes Papers.

[89] R. C. Vose to John Holmes, February 20, 1820, Holmes Papers.

After the passage of the compromise of 1820, four of the Maine congressmen who had opposed it—Martin Kinsley, Joshua Cushman, Ezekiel Whitman, and Enoch Lincoln—issued an address to the people of Maine in explanation of their attitude. The address characterized the compromise as a "bitter draught," deplored the solidarity and political power of the South, and charged that the interests and welfare of Maine had been sacrificed to secure a balance of power for the slaveholding states. The Portland *Eastern Argus* accused the authors of the address, all of whom except Whitman were Democrats, of attempting "to rekindle the old jealousy of southern influence." Later the *Argus* published and recommended to its readers an article by "a highly valued correspondent" which sought to refute the four congressmen. To the charge made by the latter that the South was an "impenetrable phalanx" united for the purpose of acquiring political power, the *Argus'* correspondent replied that for years there had been an "impenetrable phalanx" in the North whose main object "has been to transplant power from the south to the north, and judging from the address, this would seem still to be the object."[90]

Feeling that their motives had been impugned, Representatives Holmes and Hill published pamphlets in self-defense.[91] Hill asserted in his pamphlet that it would have taken a civil war to abolish slavery in Missouri and that without a compromise Maine could not have secured statehood for at least four more years. Holmes declared that the Senate would have uncoupled the Maine and Missouri bills and admitted Maine much sooner if several senators who had made up their minds in favor of such a course had not been frightened by the doctrines "advanced by a Senator [evidently Rufus King] in the second debate" and by "the avowal that it was a contest for political power." Like Hill, Holmes deplored sectional rancor.

[90] Martin Kinsley, Joshua Cushman, Ezekiel Whitman, and Enoch Lincoln, *An Address to the People of Maine* (Washington, 1820); Portland *Eastern Argus*, March 28, April 4, 1820.

[91] John Holmes, *Mr. Holmes' Letter to the People of Maine* (Washington, 1820); Mark L. Hill, *Fellow Citizens of the State of Maine* (Washington, 1820).

If he had erred, he said, it was "from an excessive zeal for the preservation of the Constitution and a superabundant solicitude for the harmony and safety of the Union."

Neither Holmes nor Hill was punished by the voters of Maine for his support of the Missouri Compromise. Hill was re-elected to the Seventeenth Congress, defeating Joshua Head in a close contest.[92] Holmes, instead of being defeated, was promoted to a higher office, being chosen by the legislature of Maine in 1820 as one of the new state's first United States senators. In 1821 he was re-elected to the Senate. In the lower house of the legislature in 1821 he received ninety-two votes to forty-seven for all of his opponents combined, while in the state senate he was given fifteen votes to three for the opposition. The Portland *Eastern Argus* exultingly interpreted Holmes' two victories as a rebuke to the Federalist newspapers and as evidence that public opinion in Maine coincided with the moderate views expressed by the *Argus* in the Missouri Controversy.[93] Yet, at the same time that Holmes and Hill were being vindicated, three (Cushman, Whitman, and Lincoln) of the four congressmen who published the address against the compromise of 1820 were also re-elected. Thus it is clear that Maine was divided in its attitude toward the slavery issue. It had a militant restrictionist element in its population as well as a large pro-Southern and procompromise group.

During the third Missouri debate in Congress Maine was a member of the Union and had no more at stake in the contest than any other Northern state, but many of its leaders continued to sympathize with Missouri and the South. When Representative Joshua Cushman issued his famous circular letter, advocating the creation of a Solid North to counteract the influence of the Solid South, the *Eastern Argus* dubbed him "a new convert to federalism." A number of members of the state legislature issued a formal reply to Cushman, assuring him that "sectional distinctions do not accord with the sentiments of your constituents."[94] The pro-Southern sentiment in Maine in

92 Portland *Eastern Argus*, January 12, 1821.
93 *Ibid.*, August 15, 1820, February 2, 1821.
94 *Ibid.*, January 26, 30, 1821.

1820 can be partially accounted for by the fact that the leaders of the Maine Democracy distrusted their Federalist neighbors and had long looked to Virginia and the South for inspiration and protection. This is only part of the story, however, for there was also a considerable number of Federalists in Maine who were favorably disposed toward the Missouri Compromise of 1820.[95]

Although its destiny was not coupled with that of Missouri by act of Congress, Illinois was, like Maine, a special party to the Missouri Controversy. In 1820 its population, largely of Southern extraction, was concentrated in the southern end of the state and surrounded on two sides by slaveholding territory. Furthermore, slavery still existed in Illinois itself. The Ordinance of 1787, which theoretically abolished slavery throughout the Northwest, did not affect the slaves in old French settlements like Cahokia nor did it, in practical operation, prevent the holding of Negroes as indentured servants.[96]

The political atmosphere of Illinois was Southern indeed in 1820. The governor, both United States senators, and the representative in the lower house of Congress were all natives of the slave states. "Yankees" were highly distasteful to the average Illinoisan. In the legislature of 1822-1823, a state senator even opposed the project for a canal to unite the Illinois River with Lake Michigan on the ground that it would be an inlet for swarms of "blue-bellied Yankees" from the East.[97] An idea of the spirit of the times may be gleaned from the fact that those who wished to make Illinois a slave state sought to overcome the prejudices which many Illinoisans had against the "peculiar institution" by "exciting still greater prejudices against our eastern brethren, who, they say, will soon be the

[95] William King to John Holmes, March 28, 1820, Holmes Papers. Holmes himself was an ex-Federalist who had been nicknamed the "Duke of Summersetts" because of his sudden conversion to Democracy in 1811. *Dictionary of American Biography*, IX, 166.

[96] Barnhart, "Southern Influence in the Formation of Illinois," 366, 378; Theodore C. Pease, *The Frontier State 1818-1848* (Springfield, 1918), 49.

[97] Edwards, *History of Illinois*, 259.

majority if slavery be not admitted; contending, at the same time, that it is better for our present population '*to have Negro slaves, than Yankee masters.*'"[98]

As was pointed out in a previous chapter, Senators Jesse B. Thomas and Ninian Edwards of Illinois were both slaveholders. Thomas owned five servants or slaves in 1820.[99] Edwards, who was the owner of many Negroes, defended himself for not freeing them in language that today it is hard to believe an Illinois official should ever have used. He had no doubt, he wrote to a critic, that "you & others honestly believe our negroes are all entitled to their freedom. . . . But, . . . I feel confident that this opinion is the result of too limited a view of the question, and that however strong your present conviction I could satisfy you, in a personal interview, that it is erroneous, and that instead of bettering, it is calculated, by its obvious consequences, to deteriorate the condition of these unfortunate people."[100] Joseph M. Street, a prominent slaveholder of Gallatin County, further contributed to the Southern atmosphere of Illinois in 1820 by advertising for a runaway Negro ("Run away from the subscriber . . . a likely young negroe man named London. . . . A generous reward . . . to any person who will apprehend said boy and deliver him to me at Shawanoe Town or secure him in any Jail so that I get him.—Owners of ferries are requested not to put him over.—").[101]

To many Illinoisans indentured servitude seemed like a poor substitute for outright Negro slavery, and for years there was a more or less perpetual contest between those who wished to make Illinois a slave state and their opponents. The former held that the antislavery clause of the Ordinance of 1787 applied only to the territorial period and that Illinois, once statehood was acquired, could legalize slavery if it desired. Most

98 Edwardsville *Spectator*, July 18, 1820.

99 See receipts for Negroes purchased by Thomas, August 7, 1813, June 21, 1814, Thomas Papers; also Norton, *Illinois Census Returns 1820*, 153.

100 Ninian Edwards to an unnamed person, n.d., Edwards Papers (Autograph Letters, Vol. 51, pp. 287-92).

101 Joseph M. Street, Manuscript notice of runaway Negro named London, August 15, 1820, Chicago Historical Society.

of the Northern minority in Illinois and many—probably a substantial majority—of the Southern immigrants as well were opposed to the legalization of slavery in their new home. On the other hand those Southern elements in the population which were proslavery were numerous and influential. In 1819 Hooper Warren began the publication of a new weekly newspaper, the *Spectator*, at Edwardsville. In the prospectus of the paper he congratulated Illinois on being a free state. To his surprise, he found that his remarks against slavery had antagonized many people who, in consequence, refused to subscribe to the *Spectator*.[102] A Madison County farmer wrote in March, 1819, that "The people of this state are divided into two parties; one in favor of freedom—the other in favor of slavery."[103]

The Missouri Controversy swiftly brought the long smoldering contest over slavery in Illinois to the surface. At this time Illinois was only entitled to one representative in the lower house of Congress. Its first congressman, John McLean, who was a native of North Carolina and a proslavery man, voted against both clauses of the Tallmadge amendment in February, 1819. In August of the same year he was defeated for re-election by Daniel Pope Cook, who was a native of Kentucky but strongly opposed to slavery. McLean's vote on the Missouri bill was used as a major issue against him. A writer in the Kaskaskia *Intelligencer* doubtless summarized the attitude of most of the voters when he declared that he wanted a congressman "who will represent us and not the people of Missouri."[104] McLean received 1,558 votes and carried nine counties, while Cook polled 2,191 votes, winning ten counties.[105]

The victor, Daniel P. Cook, for whom Illinois' most populous county today is named, was an interesting and strong-willed character. According to Duff Green, whose wife was related to Cook's wife, Cook stated in 1817 that he was going to Illinois

---

[102] Edwardsville *Spectator*, May 29, 1819.

[103] Kaskaskia *Intelligencer*, March 31, 1819.

[104] *Ibid.*, March 31, June 30, July 7, 14, 21, 28, 1819; Edwardsville *Spectator*, July 31, 1819.

[105] Theodore C. Pease (ed.), *Illinois Election Returns 1818-1848* (Springfield, 1923), 1-2.

to become a candidate for Congress with a view to agitating the slavery question, since John Quincy Adams had convinced him that the antislavery forces would soon gain complete control of the Northwest as a result of heavy immigration from the free states.[106] In 1817 Cook wrote two antislavery letters, which were published in a Washington newspaper, and by 1818 he was on the stump in Illinois, jabbing away at the "slavemen."[107]

Partly as a result of Cook's election to Congress, the politics of Missouri and Illinois became so entwined that for a time it seemed as if they could never be separated. Resenting the efforts of Cook and other Illinoisans in behalf of congressional restriction for Missouri, the Missourians did all they could to aid the proslavery party in Illinois. They even toyed with the idea of establishing a proslavery newspaper at Edwardsville as a counterpoise to Hooper Warren's Edwardsville *Spectator*.[108] The St. Louis *Enquirer* accused the *Spectator* of being the source of the atrocity stories regarding Missouri that appeared in the Northern press. "That paper," said the *Enquirer*, "is certainly a most impartial liar . . . and the sympathetic presses which copy its filth, have hardly time to take down their types from one lie, before they have to set them up for another."[109] The *Spectator*, which was fully capable of holding its own with its opponents, asserted in July, 1820, that it had uncovered a great conspiracy among Missourians and holders of indentured Negroes to make Illinois a slave state. Included in the plot, it was alleged, were plans for the purchase of the *Illinois Gazette*

106 Duff Green, *Facts and Suggestions Relative to Finance and Currency, Addressed to the President of the Confederate States* (Augusta, Ga., 1864), 30. Green also made the charge (p. 33) that Rufus King stated, as early as 1817, that the Federalist party hoped to recover power on the slavery issue and that one of his sons had moved to Ohio and a son of Alexander Hamilton had gone to Illinois to profit thereby. This statement does not seem as plausible as the one regarding Cook. Edward King and William S. Hamilton did move to Ohio and Illinois respectively. However, Rufus King advised Edward to keep out of politics. King, *Rufus King*, V, 496, VI, 26.

107 Washington *National Register*, IV (1817), 161-62, 177-78; Elihu B. Washburne (ed.), *The Edwards Papers* (Chicago, 1884), 145. For sketches of Cook's life, see Edwards, *History of Illinois*, 253-73; Josephine E. Burns, "Daniel P. Cook," in *Journal of the Illinois State Historical Society*, VI (1913), 425-44.

108 Kaskaskia *Intelligencer*, August 5, 1820.

109 St. Louis *Enquirer* (Country Edition), October 27, 1819.

of Shawneetown and for the establishment of a new paper, under the editorship of Joseph M. Street, at Edwardsville.[110]

In 1820 Cook was a candidate for re-election to Congress and was opposed by Elias K. Kane, who, though a Northerner by birth, was generally regarded as pro-Southern. The Edwardsville *Spectator* accused Kane of having "partialities for the southern interest, and a desire that this state should give a *black vote* for President at the great trial in 1824."[111] Cook was denounced by his enemies as a Federalist—a charge which he denied—and was censured for being too friendly with Rufus King and John Quincy Adams.[112] Cook won the election by a large majority, receiving 4,493 votes to 2,445 for his opponent. During the campaign, Cook gave the voters to understand that he would accept the compromise of 1820 as a final settlement and, in accordance with its intent, vote to receive Missouri with a constitution of its own choosing. Later, he made himself temporarily unpopular by voting to reject the constitution of Missouri. This was used as an issue against him in 1822, in which year he was re-elected but received only 55 per cent of the votes cast, as compared with 65 per cent in 1820 and 58 per cent in 1819.[113]

While Cook's repeated victories leave no doubt that most of the voters of Illinois were antislavery, the proslavery element continued for years to be dominant in the state legislature. Resolutions censuring Senators Jesse B. Thomas and Ninian Edwards for their votes on the Missouri question were introduced in the state House of Representatives, but of course they were not passed.[114] Edwards remained in the Senate until his resignation in 1824. Thomas was re-elected in 1823.

Between 1821 and 1824, hopes of making Illinois a slave state persisted in some quarters and continued to be influenced by the existence of slavery in Missouri. Many Illinoisans who

[110] N. Dwight Harris, *The History of Negro Servitude in Illinois* (Chicago, 1904), 27-29.

[111] Edwardsville *Spectator*, August 1, 1820.

[112] *Ibid.*, July 25, 1820; Kaskaskia *Intelligencer*, July 22, 1820.

[113] Pease, *Illinois Election Returns*, 4-5, 11-12; Edwards, *History of Illinois*, 256-59.

[114] Edwardsville *Spectator*, January 16, February 6, 1821.

wanted to sell farm lands to wealthy slaveholding immigrants from the South were distressed when they beheld the latter passing through Illinois on their way to Missouri. These lordly immigrants were said to take a malicious pleasure in professing to regret the shortsighted policy of Illinois which discouraged slaveholders from settling there.[115] In some cases, even "the poor immigrant from the slave-states, with his one old horse hitched to a broken-down wagon, in which was contained his worldly all, with his 'old woman' and tow-headed children, and not enough 'plunder' to buy a cat—who never owned a slave, nor expected to be able to do so, would talk in the same way." One such illiterate and poverty-stricken Southerner, upon being asked why he did not remain in Illinois, answered, "well sir, your *sile* is mighty *fartil,* but a man can't own niggers *here;* gol durn you."[116]

A Southern slaveholder who did not pass through Illinois on his way to Missouri was James Madison's former private secretary, Edward Coles. Instead, Coles moved from Virginia to Illinois for the purpose of liberating his slaves. In July, 1819, he wrote to inform Madison that the liberated Negroes were behaving themselves remarkably well and that he had taken steps to educate the younger ones.[117] Subsequently Coles became governor of Illinois and leader of the antislavery party in the state, although many Illinoisans of Southern birth regarded him with the same contempt that Southerners felt for carpet-baggers during the Reconstruction era.[118]

Finally, in 1823, the legislature authorized the holding of a referendum on the question of calling a constitutional convention. This produced one of the most significant political contests in the history of the Old Northwest, since it was generally supposed that the object of the proposed convention was to legalize slavery. The referendum was preceded by an eighteen

115 Thomas Ford, *A History of Illinois* (Chicago, 1854), 51-52.
116 John Moses, *Illinois, Historical and Statistical* (2 vols., Chicago, 1889-1892), I, 323.
117 Edward Coles to James Madison, July 20, 1819, Edward Coles Papers, Chicago Historical Society.
118 Snyder, "Forgotten Statesmen of Illinois," 520.

months canvass which, for tumult and violence, has seldom been surpassed.[119] Many of those who had been prominent in the Missouri Controversy once more appeared upon the stage to play leading roles. Among the advocates of a convention were Jesse B. Thomas, author of the Missouri Compromise; former Congressman John McLean; and Elias K. Kane. Governor Coles, the leader on the other side, received aid and advice from Nicholas Biddle of Philadelphia, who had been one of the compromisers of 1820 and 1821, and from Roberts Vaux, the Philadelphia philanthropist who had striven so valiantly to make Missouri a free state. Vaux and his Philadelphia Quaker friends secretly furnished Coles with antislavery literature for use in the campaign.[120] The election was held on August 2, 1824, and resulted in a substantial victory for the antislavery forces, the vote being: for a convention, 4,972; against it, 6,640.[121] Thus Illinois definitely cast its lot with the free states in 1824.

Of the special parties to the Missouri Controversy, Missouri itself clearly had the most at stake. Fifty-five thousand Missourians (or a majority of that number) demanded the right to enter the Union with a constitution of their own choosing. After they had thundered at the gates of Congress for two years, this privilege was at last granted. The 300,000 inhabitants of Maine were equally insistent in demanding what they regarded as their inalienable right to self-government, although there was never much likelihood that Maine's development would be permanently affected by its involvement in the problem of Missouri slavery. Next to Missouri, Illinois was more concerned in the events of 1819-1821 than any other state. Had the principle of congressional restriction of slavery been successfully applied to Missouri, the future status of Illinois could not have been in doubt. Likewise, the admission of Missouri as a slave state probably made the referendum contest of 1824 in Illinois inevitable.

[119] Burke A. Hinsdale, The Old Northwest (Boston, 1899), 351.
[120] Alvord, Governor Edward Coles, 120-34.
[121] Pease, Illinois Election Returns, 27-29.

CHAPTER IX

RACE RELATIONS, DEMOCRACY, AND STATE RIGHTS

MANY OF THOSE who advocated congressional restriction in 1819-1821 were moderate in their denunciation of slavery and avoided lurid details. There were others, however, who lashed out at the "peculiar institution" with all the fury and invective used by the abolitionists a decade later. Never was the finger of condemnation to be pointed more accusingly at the South than by a poem published in the Boston *Columbian Centinel* in 1820 which began:

Hark! heard ye not that piercing cry,
Which shook the waves and rent the sky!
   E'en now, e'en now, on yonder western shores
Weeps pale Despair, and writhing Anguish roars:
In dark *Missouri* now, with hideous yell,
Fierce SLAVERY stalks, and slips the dogs of hell;

.   .   .   .

Hear . . . ye SENATES! hear this truth sublime,
"HE WHO ALLOWS OPPRESSION SHARES THE CRIMES."[1]

Withering blasts against slavery came from the pens of various pamphleteers and pulpiteers. Asa Cummings, a tutor of Bowdoin College, exclaimed in a sermon in 1820: "O, how unnatural to enslave and mangle our *brethren!* What flagrant cruelty, to bind, beat, torture those, who are *bone of our bone and flesh of our flesh!* The voice of our brothers' blood cries to heaven from the ground. How shall we meet them at the bar of God?"[2] According to Joseph Blunt, "The foundation stones of our planters' palaces are cemented with the sweat, mingled with the blood, of negroes; while we, with this charge of injustice and cruelty branded on our fronts, dare to raise our hands to heaven, and beseech the God of justice and mercy to preside over the destinies of the nation."[3] Blunt, William Hillhouse, and others also raised the issue of miscegenation and accused the planters of immorality.[4] A writer in the Boston Yankee declared that "The intercourse between white men and female slaves has become so frequent, as to appear to be rather a subject of glorying than of shame."[5]

As has been pointed out in preceding chapters, most Southern congressmen did not defend slavery as an abstract principle at the time of the Missouri Controversy but contented themselves with stressing the difficulties in the way of emancipation. The same attitude was taken by the Southern press. The Lexington, Kentucky, Western Monitor asserted that "We deprecate as much as any of our eastern brethren the existence of an evil which has been entailed upon us. But we deny the possiblity of suddenly removing it by legislative acts." The Norfolk and Portsmouth Herald conceded that human bondage was "a national evil." The Augusta Chronicle readily admitted that "slavery is an eye-sore upon the great charter of our rights," though it added that "A plan of abolition, gradual and almost imperceptible in its effects, can only be safely resorted to." Said the Richmond Enquirer: " 'Thou cans't not say that we did it.' It is an evil entailed upon us without our consent; against the protestations of our ancestors; and we know not how to get rid of it."[6]

[1] Boston Columbian Centinel, August 26, 1820.

[2] Asa Cummings, A Discourse Delivered at Brunswick, (Maine,) April 6, 1820, the Day of the Annual Fast in Maine and Massachusetts (Brunswick, 1820), 27.

[3] [Blunt], Examination of the Expediency and Constitutionality of Prohibiting Slavery, 6.

[4] Ibid., 9; [Hillhouse], The Crisis, No. 1, 10-11.

[5] Boston Yankee, May 27, 1819.

[6] Lexington Western Monitor, January 18, 1820; Norfolk and Portsmouth Herald, January 26, 1820; Augusta Chronicle & Georgia Gazette, January 6,

It is clear that in 1820 most educated Southerners and most of the South's leaders professed to regard slavery as intrinsically evil. In many cases these professions were undoubtedly sincere. The Richmond *Enquirer's* sincerity was demonstrated twelve years later when it advocated emancipation by state action during the great slavery debate of 1832 in the Virginia legislature.[7] As proof that Southerners were opposed to slavery in spite of their hostility to congressional restriction, the Washington *Intelligencer* cited the fact that Southern congressmen took the lead in 1819 in securing the enactment of more stringent legislation against the African slave trade. Later the *Intelligencer* published a letter from an unnamed Virginian who was so pleased by the new measures taken to break up the slave trade that he said: "I do not know that my American pride was ever more highly excited."[8]

Since nearly all Northerners and most of the South's leaders were willing in 1820 to acknowledge that slavery per se was an evil, it seems strange that strenuous efforts were not made to agree on some feasible plan of emancipation, based on cooperation between Congress and the states. Being violently opposed by so large a part of the nation, congressional restriction could hardly be regarded as feasible. Numerous proposals for a program of general but gradual emancipation were advanced during the years 1819-1821. Even the St. Louis *Enquirer,* chief antirestrictionist organ of Missouri, devoted considerable space to specific suggestions for nationwide emancipation of the slaves and compensation for their owners.[9]

1820; Richmond *Enquirer,* February 10, 1820. See also Georgetown (D. C.) *Metropolitan,* February 15, 1820; Warrenton (Virginia) *Palladium of Liberty,* January 7, 1820.

[7] Eaton, *Freedom of Thought in the Old South,* 168-69.

[8] Washington *Daily National Intelligencer,* March 12, 15, 1819. The chief sponsors of this legislation were Representatives Henry Middleton of South Carolina and Charles F. Mercer of Virginia. *Annals of Congress,* 15 Cong., 2 Sess., 442, 540, 1430-31. In 1820, largely through the efforts of Mercer, participation in the slave trade was made punishable with death. *Ibid.,* 16 Cong., 1 Sess., 2210-11; Du Bois, *Suppression of the African Slave-Trade,* 120-23.

[9] St. Louis *Enquirer,* August 23, 26, October 21, 1820.

Rufus King proposed in one of his congressional addresses that the nation's slave population be colonized eventually in Africa and in the meantime be protected from the domestic slave trade by being bound to the soil under a system resembling medieval villenage.[10] Other plans called for compensating the owners by means of a general tax on property or individuals and for colonizing the Negroes in Africa, California, or Haiti. Representative Henry Meigs of New York, one of the "dough faces" who supported the compromise of 1820, suggested that five hundred million acres of public land west of the Mississippi be used as a fund to annihilate the slave trade, compensate the slaveholders, and remove the slaves to Africa.[11]

There were many reasons why no plan of emancipation could hope to meet with general approval in 1819-1821. The country's leading antislavery advocates had developed a fixation on the subject of abolishing slavery in the new state of Missouri and were inclined to ridicule any other emancipation projects. Hence Robert Walsh's Philadelphia *Gazette* called the Meigs proposal "chimerical," while the New York *Columbian* asserted that it was "as feasible as it would be to gain possession of the island of Great Britain in exchange for 500 million acres of our western lands."[12] Most of the projects for manumission emanating from the South contemplated the removal of the freedmen to Africa. On the other hand, many Negroes were unwilling to leave America, nor were all the whites willing to see them go. John Quincy Adams believed that expatriation would injure the Negro while at the same time depriving America of a valuable labor force. "We could spare them as *slaves*—but not as *men*," said the Mount Pleasant, Ohio, *Philanthropist*.[13]

10 Richard O. Peters, Jr., to Roberts Vaux, February 12, 1820, Vaux Papers.

11 For Meigs' plan, see *Annals of Congress*, 16 Cong., 2 Sess., 1169-70. For various other emancipation plans, see Washington *Daily National Intelligencer*, May 29, December 20, 1819, September 2, 9, 1820, March 17, 1821; Washington *Gazette*, June 14, 1819, February 22, August 15, 1820; Philadelphia *Aurora*, January 25, 1820.

12 Philadelphia *National Gazette and Literary Register*, February 19, 1821; New York *Columbian*, February 21, 1821.

13 Franklin, *From Slavery to Freedom*, 237; Adams, *Memoirs of J. Q. Adams*, IV, 356; Mount Pleasant *Philanthropist*, April 24, 1819.

Finally, there was a large proslavery element in the South, especially in Georgia and South Carolina, that would have opposed any scheme of emancipation which human ingenuity could devise. Whether a majority of the Southern people belonged to this group it would be impossible to say. Charles Pinckney and William Smith of South Carolina, as has been seen, presented elaborate defenses of slavery in Congress at this time. Most of the South's leaders, still deeply imbued with the natural rights philosophy of the eighteenth century, declined to follow suit. It is doubtful, however, whether the mass of the Southern people were concerned with anyone's natural rights except their own. When Humphrey Smith denounced slavery at a Missouri camp meeting in 1819, his remarks caused great resentment and brought from several slaveholders the reply that "God had made negroes for slaves, and white men for masters, or he would not suffer it to be so."[14] While in the nation as a whole those who considered slavery an unmixed blessing were greatly in the minority, they derived strength from the lack of unity among their opponents. The antislavery majority of 1819-1821 reminds one of the chorus in a Greek tragedy, lamenting injustice and predicting disaster but seemingly powerless to avert it.

Liberal Southerners like Jefferson who sought an excuse for opposing congressional restriction laid great stress on the "diffusion" argument. The admission of Missouri as a slave state, they insisted, did not involve an extension of slavery but would merely diffuse the existing slave population over a larger area. This, said Jefferson, would lighten the burden of the slaves' future liberation "by bringing a greater number of shoulders under it."[15] The Washington *Intelligencer* denied that the Missouri Controversy had any relation to the multiplication of slaves in America. "Once for all," said the *Intelligencer*, "no such question is presented to the consideration of Congress,

---

[14] Boston *Columbian Centinel*, November 20, 1819. During the Missouri Controversy a considerable number of letters in defense of slavery appeared in Southern newspapers. See Washington *Daily National Intelligencer*, July 9, September 3, 14, October 25, November 23, 1819.

[15] Ford, *Writings of Jefferson*, X, 177.

or of the nation. The question concerns only the *diffusion* or the *concentration* of the slaves now in the country."[16] The restrictionist reply to the advocates of diffusion was that ultimately the size of the slave population would be determined by the means of subsistence, which would be increased by opening new areas to slavery. Malthus was cited as proof for this assertion. *"Diffusion,"* said Daniel Raymond, "is about as effectual a remedy for slavery as it would be for the small pox, or the plague."[17]

Whether for or against slavery, Southerners resented what they regarded as Northern meddling in their affairs. The South, it was said, had done much to ameliorate the condition of the slaves and outside interference could only provoke a reaction and delay emancipation.[18] "This Missouri Question," said the Warrenton, Virginia, *Palladium of Liberty,* "has been produced by the intermedling of our Northern Brethern. They have long dealt in lavish abuse of us, for the prevlency of an evil which we can not mend."[19] Henry Clay reminded Northerners that "there are delicate subjects, exclusively appertaining to the several States, which cannot be touched but by them, without the greatest hazard to the public tranquillity. They resemble those secluded apartments in our respective domicils, which are dedicated to family privacy, into which our nearest and best neighbors should not enter."[20]

The South's touchiness in any matter regarding slavery or the race question was strikingly illustrated by an unpleasant

[16] Washington *Daily National Intelligencer,* January 29, 1820. See also Learned, *View of the Policy of Permitting Slaves in States West of the Mississippi,* 15-20. Diffusion is advocated by some today as a solution for the American race problem. Gunnar Myrdal, while not regarding it as a solution, declares that "migration to the North and West is a tremendous force in the general amelioration of the Negro's position." *An American Dilemma, The Negro Problem and Modern Democracy* (2 vols., New York, 1944), I, 200.

[17] Boston *Daily Advertiser,* February 15, 1820; [Walsh], *Free Remarks on the Spirit of the Federal Constitution,* 93-96; Daniel Raymond, *Thoughts on Political Economy* (Baltimore, 1820), 456.

[18] Lexington (Kentucky) *Western Monitor,* March 20, 1821; Washington *Daily National Intelligencer,* November 27, 1819.

[19] Warrenton *Palladium of Liberty,* January 7, 1820.

[20] *Annals of Congress,* 16 Cong., 2 Sess., 1295.

episode in Savannah at the time of the Missouri Controversy. On January 11, 1820, Savannah was swept by a fire which destroyed more than 460 houses and buildings and four million dollars' worth of property. So great was the distress in the city that Mayor Thomas Charlton appealed to the rest of the country for assistance.[21] The entire nation responded generously, and contributions for relief poured in from North and South. The city of New York contributed more than $10,000. The committee in New York which supervised the collection of the $10,000 requested that it be "applied exclusively to the relief of all indigent persons, without distinction of color, who are dependent on their own industry for support, and who have been sufferers by the late fire." The reference to "distinction of color" seemed to the people of Savannah to be an unwarranted interference in their concerns and another appearance of "the Missouri matter . . . in the most unexpected form." Accordingly the mayor and aldermen decided, by unanimous vote, to return the money to New York, which they proceeded to do.[22] A storm of criticism followed. The Clintonian New York *Columbian* expressed astonishment "at this *insult* from a distant city."[23] The Pennsylvania legislature had passed an act appropriating $10,000 for the relief of the Savannah sufferers, but some of the legislators wished to repeal the act when they learned of the rejection of the New York contribution. Nevertheless, a repeal motion in the lower house was defeated.[24] The people of Newark, on hearing of the rebuff to New York, actually held a meeting and decided to return their contribution to the individual donors rather than forward it to Savannah.[25]

[21] Savannah *Daily Republican*, January 14, 17, 1820.
[22] *Ibid.*, February 25, March 2, 1820; E. Merton Coulter, "The Great Savannah Fire of 1820," in *Georgia Historical Quarterly*, XXIII (1939), 16-24.
[23] New York *Columbian*, March 15, 1820.
[24] Pennsylvania *House Journal*, 1819-1820, pp. 903-904.
[25] Newark *Centinel of Freedom*, March 21, 1820. There were some in Newark who wished to aid Savannah in spite of the rejection of the New York contribution. *Ibid.*, March 21, May 16, 1820. In Savannah itself there was a difference of opinion over whether the New York donation should have been rejected. Boston *Daily Advertiser*, April 5, 11, 1820.

One of the most widely discussed topics at the time of the Missouri Controversy was the possibility of a great slave revolt in the South similar to the one which had devastated San Domingo.[26] Northerners were fond of warning the South that this was the fate in store for it unless steps were taken to prevent the extension of slavery. Southerners retorted that Northern interference in their affairs was the event most likely to produce such a revolt.[27] The Missouri contest, wrote Andrew Jackson, "will excite those who is the subject of discussion to insurrection and masacre."[28] Southerners were especially afraid that Rufus King's speeches would create unrest among the slaves. Spencer Roane was fearful that "King & Co." might incite the slaves to rebel, and Senator William Smith of South Carolina asserted that the slaves of San Domingo had received less provocation than King had given to those of the South.[29] As it turned out, the slaveholders' fear of King was well founded. In the summer of 1822 the authorities of Charleston uncovered a plan for a slave uprising which, had it not been nipped in the bud, would probably have been the most extensive of its kind in the history of the Old South. During the trials that followed, it was disclosed that the leader of the proposed revolt, Denmark Vesey, who was an ex-slave, had been influenced by the Missouri Controversy and had read one of Rufus King's speeches to his followers.[30]

[26] For a full account of the slave insurrection in San Domingo, see T. Lothrop Stoddard, *The French Revolution in San Domingo* (Boston, 1914); C. L. R. James, *The Black Jacobins, Toussaint Louverture and the San Domingo Revolution* (New York, 1938).

[27] Raymond, *Missouri Question*, 21-24; [Blunt], *Examination of the Expediency and Constitutionality of Prohibiting Slavery*, 9-12; Taylor, *Construction Construed*, 300-301.

[28] Bassett, *Correspondence of Andrew Jackson*, III, 21.

[29] Spencer Roane to James Monroe, February 16, 1820, Monroe Papers, New York Public Library; *Annals of Congress*, 16 Cong., 1 Sess., 378.

[30] John M. Lofton, Jr., "Denmark Vesey's Call to Arms," in *Journal of Negro History*, XXXIII (1948), 405; James Hamilton, Jr., *An Account of the Late Intended Insurrection Among a Portion of the Blacks of This City* (Charleston, 1822), 42; Joseph C. Carroll, *Slave Insurrections in the United States 1800-1865* (Boston, 1938), 88-89; Herbert Aptheker, *American Negro Slave Revolts* (New York, 1943), 81.

In spite of sensitiveness to criticism and fears of a servile rebellion, Southerners were obviously more open-minded on the subject of their "peculiar institution" in 1819-1821 than they were to be several decades later. A Charleston newspaper, the *Times*, showed surprising open-mindedness in 1819 in a discussion of the slave code of its state. The South Carolina code, which was based on that of the West Indies island of Barbados, contained a number of harsh provisions.[31] The heaviest penalty that could be inflicted on a white person for the murder of a slave was the payment of a large fine or, if the defendant could not raise the money, seven years' imprisonment at hard labor. When a bill to make the murder of a slave punishable by death failed to pass in the legislature, the *Times*, after correcting a previous misstatement which it had made, declared that the situation "remains thus: if a white man *steal* a negro, the law will hang him; but if he *murder* one, he will only have to pay a fine. The injustice of this is too palpable, let it be viewed in whatever light it may, to need a single remark. We regret that *truth* obliges us to correct our statement; for we wished the world should not know that such laws existed in *South Carolina*."[32]

In 1821 South Carolina at last made it a capital offense to kill a slave unless the deed was committed in sudden heat and passion.[33] In the meantime, however, another defect in the state's Barbadian code had been revealed. In 1820 a slave in the Edgefield district was burned alive for the murder of his

[31] Edward McCrady, "Slavery in the Province of South Carolina, 1670-1770," in *Annual Report of the American Historical Association for the Year 1895* (Washington, 1896), 644-50; Howell M. Henry, *The Police Control of the Slave in South Carolina* (Emory, Va., 1914), 4.

[32] Charleston *Times*, quoted in Washington *Daily National Intelligencer*, June 12, 1819.

[33] Henry, *Police Control of the Slave in South Carolina*, 66-68. The law of North Carolina provided (1817) that "the offence of killing a slave shall be homicide and shall partake of the same degree of guilt, when accompanied with the like circumstances, that homicide does at common law." Hurd, *Law of Freedom and Bondage*, II, 85. In 1820 the governor of Virginia offered a reward of $500 for a man who had deliberately murdered one of his own slaves. Washington *Gazette*, August 4, 1820.

master, and this sentence was executed not by a mob but by due process of law.[34] Under the law such sentences could be meted out by a local court consisting of two justices of the peace and several freeholders, from whose verdict no appeal to a higher court was permitted prior to 1833.[35] South Carolina was widely condemned for the Edgefield burning, nor did the South as a whole rush to its defense. Though the Augusta *Chronicle* seemed to think the sentence justifiable,[36] the Norfolk and Portsmouth *Herald* spoke for many Southerners when it asserted that South Carolina had committed an act which "would do honor to the days of gothic barbarity."[37] The Mount Pleasant, Ohio, *Philanthropist* noted with dismay that while many Americans had recently been considering the advisability of abolishing capital punishment even in its mildest form, the South Carolinians were using it in a manner "which the 'inquisition' itself cannot exceed."[38]

The charge of hypocrisy was bandied around as freely as that of inhumanity during the Missouri Controversy. Northerners were reminded that their own ships had brought to America the slaves whose welfare was now a matter of so much concern. Senator William Smith of South Carolina presented several pages of names and figures to indicate the role which Rhode Island and Great Britain had played in supplying his state with slaves in the years 1804-1807.[39] Ironically, New-

[34] Augusta *Chronicle & Georgia Gazette*, February 1, 1820.

[35] Henry, *Police Control of the Slave in South Carolina*, 58-59, 64.

[36] Augusta *Chronicle & Georgia Gazette*, February 1, 1820. Perhaps the *Chronicle* was influenced by the fact that less than a year before, a slave conspiracy, having armed insurrection as its object, had been discovered in the Augusta-Edgefield section of Georgia and South Carolina. The leader was Coco or Coot, a veteran of the San Domingo uprising. *Ibid.*, May 10, 1819; Aptheker, *American Negro Slave Revolts*, 263; Carroll, *Slave Insurrections in the United States*, 76.

[37] Norfolk and Portsmouth *Herald*, February 4, 1820.

[38] Mount Pleasant *Philanthropist*, March 18, 1820. In justice to South Carolina it must be said that the courts of the state sometimes went out of their way to befriend the Negro by interpreting the law liberally in his behalf. See Helen T. Catterall (ed.), *Judicial Cases Concerning American Slavery and the Negro* (5 vols., Washington, 1926-1937), II, 267-69.

[39] *Annals of Congress*, 16 Cong., 2 Sess., 73-77. Elizabeth Donnan points out

port, Rhode Island, which had grown rich off of the slave trade in the eighteenth century, was one of the Northern cities which held a meeting to protest against the westward expansion of slavery in 1819.[40] Moreover, in 1820 the Rhode Island legislature elected to the United States Senate James De Wolf, who had formerly been engaged in the slave trade. De Wolf's defense against his critics was that he had not taken part in the trade for "*many, many years*."[41] His severest critics turned out to be Northerners. The West Chester, Pennsylvania, *Village Record* observed that "*Wolf* is certainly an appropriate name for a man-stealer." The Mount Pleasant, Ohio, *Genius of Universal Emancipation* suggested that "D'Tiger" would be an even more appropriate name for the senator.[42]

Southerners never wearied of protesting that they "smelt a rat" in the Missouri Controversy—the rat being a Northern quest for political ascendancy disguised under the mask of humanity. Actually, as has been previously indicated, the Anti-Missourians had a variety of motives for opposing the westward expansion of slavery. Jealousy of the South's political power was, in many cases, as powerful a motive as the humanitarian one. Certainly it was stressed in the memorials which Congress received from Northern mass meetings and legislatures. The Boston meeting raised the issue of slave representation "with a deep and earnest feeling of its importance."[43] The Vermont legislature warned that the creation of new slave states " 'will have a tendency to form a combination of power

---

a number of inaccuracies in Smith's list. Nevertheless, she declares that the part played by the Southern colonies in transporting Negroes from Africa "was insignificant as compared with that of the northern colonies or with the volume of trade which entered their ports." Elizabeth Donnan (ed.), *Documents Illustrative of the History of the Slave Trade to America* (4 vols., Washington, 1930-1935), IV, 235, 504-506.

40 Newport *Mercury*, December 18, 1819; Newport *Republican*, December 22, 1819.

41 Providence *American, And General Advertiser*, November 10, 1820.

42 West Chester *Village Record*, November 22, 1820; Mount Pleasant *Genius of Universal Emancipation*, February, 1822.

43 *A Memorial to the Congress of the United States, on the Subject of Restraining the Increase of Slavery*, 19-20.

which will control the measures of the General Government,' and which cannot be resisted, except by the physical force of the nation."[44] The legislature of New Hampshire expressed a fear that the further extension of slavery would "soon produce such a combination of political power, as may be sufficient permanently to control all the measures of the national councils."[45]

None of these memorials failed to give due emphasis to the humanitarian aspect of the contest over Missouri. "As connected with the rights of humanity," said the legislature of Massachusetts, "this question swells into one of immense magnitude."[46] Pennsylvania urged her sister states "to refuse to covenant with crime" by spreading the "cruelties of slavery from the banks of the Mississippi to the shores of the Pacific."[47] The legislature of Vermont hoped that Congress would never "plant the standard of the Union in Missouri, to wave over the heads of involuntary slaves, 'who have nothing they can call their own, except their sorrows and their sufferings,' and a life beyond the grave, and who can never taste the sweets of liberty, unless they obtain it by force or by flight."[48]

It was good strategy for Southerners to minimize the humanitarian side of the Missouri Controversy and play up its political angles. This they promptly did. "The balance of power vibrates;" said the Washington *Intelligencer,* "and the feelings of our politicians vibrate in sympathy." Said the Louisville *Public Advertiser:* "Missouri is at present the *object* of persecution, and the horrors of slavery constitute the popular tune, so pathetically sung by all the non-slave-holding states, for the purpose of obtaining the *'balance of power'* in Congress." In the opinion of the Norfolk and Portsmouth *Herald,* the Northern newspapers had "boldly displayed the cloven foot which marks their real design in advocating restriction.—Power, power —the preponderance of political power is the great desidera-

[44] *Annals of Congress,* 16 Cong., 2 Sess., 79.
[45] *Niles' Weekly Register,* XVIII (1820), 339.
[46] Boston *Columbian Centinel,* February 26, 1820.
[47] *Annals of Congress,* 16 Cong., 1 Sess., 71.   [48] *Ibid.,* 2 Sess., 80.

tum." The Charleston *Southern Patriot* pronounced the Missouri contest "nakedly a question of political power and management, and not of right and humanity." " 'Tis now as clear as the radiance of the noon-day sun," said the Milledgeville, Georgia, *Journal*, "that the restriction of slavery is but a secondary object—the mighty contest is for power—political power." Likewise the Huntsville, Alabama, *Republican* regarded the Missouri question "merely as a political manoeuvre" and "the Hobby Horse on which the ambitious men of the north hope to ride into power."[49]

The restrictionists were vexed no end that Southerners should attempt to dismiss the antislavery movement as a political plot. After receiving a letter from a young friend who was visiting in Georgia, John Pintard of New York wrote his daughter that "The Georgians are outrageous about the Missouri & impute every thing but justice & humanity, with conscious scruples of an outrageous violation of the national constitution, to us Northerns, as tho' we were actuated by unworthy motives."[50]

Since Northerners had interested themselves in the plight of the Southern slave, Southerners countered by inquiring into the condition of white laborers and free Negroes in the North. Using arguments which were to be elaborated in later years by William J. Grayson and George Fitzhugh, a writer in the Petersburg, Virginia, *Intelligencer* in 1820 compared the status of the Southern black slave with that of the Northern wage earner or "white slave." He concluded that the indigent white laborer was the slave of every man who possessed wealth, that he was virtually condemned to perpetual servitude, and that his only reward was subsistence. Finally, he argued, a black slave was cared for by his master in old age, but frequently the white

[49] Washington *Daily National Intelligencer*, January 29, 1820; Louisville *Public Advertiser*, February 14, 1821; Norfolk and Portsmouth *Herald*, January 28, 1820; Charleston *Southern Patriot, and Commercial Advertiser*, February 19, 1820; Milledgeville *Journal*, March 7, 1820; Huntsville *Republican*, February 26, 1820. See also Fredericksburg (Virginia) *Herald*, February 16, 1820; Lexington (Kentucky) *Gazette*, January 7, 1820.

[50] Barck, *Letters from John Pintard*, I, 352-53.

slave changed masters so often that he became old and infirm without securing the protection or friendship of any of his masters.[51]

In 1820, as always, the treatment accorded to the Negro population of the free states constituted proof, in the eyes of the South, that Northern professions of concern for the welfare of Southern slaves were hypocritical. There were, of course, Negroes in the North who had acquired wealth and standing in their communities. William Plumer cited the case of Wentworth Cheswell of Newmarket, New Hampshire, whose color did not prevent him from owning considerable property and serving as a justice of the peace.[52] In New York some Negroes were sufficiently well-to-do to vote in spite of high and discriminatory property qualifications imposed upon them by the constitution of 1821.[53] After due recognition is given to the prosperous element among the free Negroes, however, the fact remains that the great body of the race in the North in 1820 was an oppressed and underprivileged minority.[54] The indignities to which it was subjected were noticed and commented upon by English travelers.[55] Some idea of its housing can be had from a letter written by Dr. David Hosack of New York. "Our city," wrote the doctor, "is still healthy with exception of 2 or 3 streets divided with negroes and drunken Irishmen whose filth and mode of life render them at all times liable to fever but especially in these warm months."[56] Even

[51] Petersburg *Intelligencer,* quoted in New York *Daily Advertiser,* March 18, 1820.

[52] William Plumer to William Plumer, Jr., December 11, 1820, Plumer Papers.

[53] Fox, *Decline of Aristocracy in New York,* 269. See also Carter G. Woodson, *Free Negro Heads of Families in the United States in 1830* (Washington, 1925), xxxiii-xlv.

[54] On this point, see Franklin, *From Slavery to Freedom,* 231, 238; Edward R. Turner, *The Negro in Pennsylvania* (Washington, 1911), 142, 205; Frank U. Quillin, *The Color Line in Ohio, A History of Race Prejudice in a Typical Northern State* (Ann Arbor, 1913), 21-34, 44-59; Harris, *History of Negro Servitude in Illinois,* 226-27.

[55] Adams, *Neglected Period of Anti-Slavery,* 72-73.

[56] David Hosack to Col. Trumbull, September 11, 1820, David Hosack Papers, New-York Historical Society.

Governor De Witt Clinton, a friend of the Negro and a recipient of his vote, stated in an address to the New York legislature in 1819 that "The strong propensity of this race to congregate in our great towns, where they are peculiarly exposed to the contagion of bad example, and the degraded light in which they are contemplated by public opinion, must not lead us to expect from them many exhibitions of extraordinary virtues or talents."[57] The New York *American*, one of whose editors was a son of Rufus King, attributed much of the wretchedness and petty crime that existed in New York to "the ignorance, debauchery, and idleness of the lower class of blacks."[58] Visitors to Northern penitentiaries were impressed by the number of Negro inmates. In overwhelmingly white Pennsylvania 113 Negroes were sent to the Philadelphia penitentiary in 1821 and only 197 whites. As victims of popular prejudice, Negroes were often put in prison for slight offenses for which a white man would not have been penalized.[59]

The condition of the North's Negro population provided an abundance of ammunition for all those who did not wish to participate in the Anti-Missourian Crusade. New Jersey and Pennsylvania were reminded that under the operation of gradual emancipation acts, their citizens still possessed slaves. A writer in a Philadelphia newspaper urged the North to clean its own back yard before seeking to emancipate Southern slaves.[60] Said another Pennsylvanian, writing anonymously: "Of what advantage can it be to a *negro* to obtain his freedom, even in Pennsylvania. . . . With whom is he allowed to associate? With none but the most profligate and abandoned amongst the *whites*. Should he acquire property and demean himself with the utmost propriety, still he is *black*. . . . The *name of a negro* is a by-word, a reproach and a bug-bear. . . . Such are the

57 New York *Daily Advertiser*, January 8, 1819.
58 New York *American*, August 24, 1820.
59 Turner, *The Negro in Pennsylvania*, 155; Woodson, *Free Negro Heads of Families*, xlv.
60 Philadelphia *Democratic Press*, December 2, 26, 1820; Newark *Centinel of Freedom*, March 14, 1820.

feelings discovered, and such the conduct of Pennsylvanians towards this unfortunate race of beings—for whom their representatives affect such commisseration."[61]

The Missouri Controversy led to an interminable discussion of the conflicting principles which were later to be known as "gradualism" and "immediatism." The Tallmadge amendment provided for the gradual abolition of slavery in Missouri, and most of the restrictionists were careful to promise that they would never interfere in the internal affairs of the existing states. A meeting at Middlebury, Vermont, spoke for 99 per cent of the nation's restrictionists when it recognized the necessity for the temporary existence of slavery in a large portion of the country and acknowledged the dangers inherent in immediate and universal emancipation.[62] Nevertheless, Southerners insisted that immediatism was an issue, since they regarded the Missouri restriction as merely an entering wedge for the attainment of nationwide emancipation.[63] They were also alarmed over the contention, made by a few of the restrictionists, that slavery was unconstitutional and ought to be declared so by the United States Supreme Court.[64]

Jefferson was one of those who objected most vigorously to immediatism. He was willing, he said, to co-operate in any practical and gradual plan of emancipation, provided it was to be accompanied by the expatriation of the liberated slaves. "But as it is," he added, "we have the wolf by the ears, and we can neither hold him, nor safely let him go. Justice is in one scale, and self-preservation in the other." The real question, thought Jefferson, "is, are our slaves to be presented with freedom and a dagger?"[65] Another interesting protest against immediatism came from a border state Federalist newspaper, the Wilmington, Delaware, *Gazette*. While sympathetic to the idea

[61] Pittsburgh *Statesman,* January 26, 1820.

[62] Middlebury *National Standard*, January 11, 1820. See also Boston *Daily Advertiser,* January 7, 1820; Philadelphia *National Gazette and Literary Regis ter,* December 9, 1820.

[63] John W. Walker to Charles Tait, December 8, 1819, Tait Papers.

[64] New York *Columbian,* January 20, 21, 1820.

[65] Ford, *Writings of Jefferson,* X, 157-58, 186.

of gradual emancipation, the *Gazette* complained that the Missouri dispute had "led people with warm feelings, but upright intentions, to brand, with opprobrious epithets, those who refused to go all lengths in the crusades in favour of the black population of our country." The *Gazette* declared that it had been accused of being inhuman and unfeeling simply because it would not agree to the proposition that slavery should be abolished at all hazards, without regard to property rights, and that the Negro population, the moment it was made free, should have the privilege of moving and residing where it pleased, regardless of its idleness or ignorance.[66]

The discussion of immediatism inevitably raised the issue of equality and amalgamation. Joseph D. Learned, the Maryland pamphleteer, expressed a fear that the slaves, if freed, would demand the right of suffrage.[67] Nathaniel Macon wished to know if Northerners were willing to have Negro congressmen.[68] Charles Pinckney of South Carolina summarized the sentiments of most Southerners when he argued that the civilized world had always observed a distinction between the black and white races and that Negroes "certainly must have been created with less intellectual powers than the whites."[69] Louis McLane of Delaware asserted that he held no brief for slavery but could never agree "to put the white and black population upon an equality, or to destroy the features of both, by the vain attempt to amalgamate one with the other!"[70] The St. Louis *Enquirer* used an argument against amalgamation which was to be repeated, in varying forms, for thousands of times during the next century. This was the story of an abolitionist preacher who sought to convert a Missouri farmer to his equalitarian beliefs. The farmer professed conversion and offered to emancipate one of his intelligent male slaves on condition that the latter should be permitted to unite in marriage with the

[66] Wilmington *Gazette*, January 19, 1821.
[67] Learned, *View of the Policy of Permitting Slaves in States West of the Mississippi*, 39.
[68] *Annals of Congress*, 16 Cong., 1 Sess., 227.   [69] *Ibid.*, 2 Sess., 1136.
[70] *Ibid.*, 621.

preacher's daughter. Thereupon, the preacher, insulted, departed instantly without the formality of taking leave.[71]

Had there been no question of slavery—only the issue of equality and amalgamation—most Northerners would have been in hearty agreement with the South in 1820. Indeed, dislike and contempt for the Negro were partly responsible for the failure of many Northerners to join in the Anti-Missourian Crusade. The Albany *Argus,* speaking for this group, declared that "we feel an insurmountable repugnance to mix and associate with them [free Negroes] as equals; no white person of any character or standing, could think of forming a connexion with a black, as husband or wife."[72] Likewise many of the restrictionists were anti-Negro and were as anxious to keep the Negro race out of the trans-Mississippi country as they were to prevent the institution of slavery from expanding. The strongly restrictionist Washington *Gazette* called intermarriages between the races "vile intermixtures."[73] Former Congressman Ebenezer Sage of New York, a stanch restrictionist, referred to the Southern states as "sable" states and expressed a fear that if slavery was extended to Missouri, "we shall have a party coulored, pyed population, through all shades from the Japan to the white lilly; spread from the Mississippi to the pacific Ocean."[74] The restrictionist New York *American* was apprehensive that the aftermath of slavery's extension might someday be a "sable President" for America.[75]

It must not be supposed, however, that all Americans trembled at the thought of a "sable" President. Though very much in the minority, there were those in 1820 who defended the Negro against the charge of inferiority and were eager to see him integrated fully into American society. The Boston *Intelligencer* quoted Montesquieu in derision of the idea that Africans were inferior to whites merely because they had a

---

[71] St. Louis *Enquirer,* February 10, 1821.
[72] Albany *Argus,* August 25, 1820.
[73] Washington *Gazette,* February 9, 1820.
[74] Ebenezer Sage to John W. Taylor, January 24, 1820, Taylor Papers.
[75] New York *American,* January 5, 1820.

"dingy skin" and "wool upon the head" and "prefer a glass neclace to that of gold, which polished nations more highly value."[76] According to Joseph Blunt, the free Negroes who had come under his observation were as industrious and more provident than the lower class of white people.[77] At a mass meeting held in Cincinnati to discuss the Missouri question, one of the speakers was loudly applauded when he denied that Negroes were inferior and vindicated their right to all the privileges of citizenship.[78] A writer in the Steubenville *Western Herald* speculated on the possibility that the genius of a Newton or a Rittenhouse, the talents of a Chatham or an Eames, or the philanthropy of a Howard or a Penn might often have been planted in the breast of a slave where, because of man's inhumanity, it had no chance for expression.[79] Theodore Dwight's New York *Advertiser* asserted that "there is no material defect of bodily or mental powers and capacities, in the inhabitants of Africa," and the Philadelphia *Aurora* maintained that "there is no faculty which the colored man does not possess in equal power and perfection with those who enslaves him."[80] When it was proposed in the New York constitutional convention of 1821 to disfranchise Negroes on the ground that they were a "degraded" race, the aristocratic Peter A. Jay, son of John Jay, made a moving speech against the proposition. "I hoped," he said, "this old excuse for slavery would not have been repeated here. I did not believe it would be asserted at this time of day, that the God who made all the nations of the earth of one blood, has created one race for degradation. Sir, their bodies, their brains are not differently constructed from ours."[81] In the Missouri debates, friends of the Negro stressed his military services to the nation during the Revolu-

[76] Boston *Intelligencer & Evening Gazette*, March 11, 1820.

[77] [Blunt], *Examination of the Expediency and Constitutionality of Prohibiting Slavery*, 9.

[78] Boston *Daily Advertiser*, January 8, 1820.

[79] Steubenville (Ohio) *Western Herald*, December 16, 1820.

[80] New York *Daily Advertiser*, April 14, 1820; Philadelphia *Aurora*, January 4, 1820.

[81] Hammond, *History of Political Parties in New-York*, II, 17.

tionary War. One of the arguments used against the free Negro and mulatto clause of the Missouri constitution was that it might prevent Negro veterans from occupying the bounty lands granted them by the federal government.[82] In a letter to the Mount Pleasant, Ohio, *Philanthropist*, Ephraim Brookens of Chester Creek, Pennsylvania, suggested that Southern whites could solve the slavery question by intermarriage with the Negroes. This, he observed, was "a measure so easy that nothing but prejudice, unworthy of philosophical and liberal minds, prevents its adoption." The editor of the *Philanthropist* acknowledged that he was not an enthusiastic supporter of Brookens' proposal but added that, as a result of miscegenation, the South was rapidly becoming a nation of mulattoes anyway.[83]

Throughout the course of the Missouri debates, both the North and South invoked the concept of natural law and the most famous American document which expounded it—the Declaration of Independence—to sustain their respective positions. Robert Walsh and Rufus King emphasized the principle of "the higher law," though not calling it by that name. This principle, while it antedated the slavery controversy, was not popularized until Senator Seward made his well-known speech of March 11, 1850. With reference to the government of the territories, Seward stated that "there is a higher law than the Constitution [the law of God], which regulates our authority over the domain, and devotes it to the same noble purposes."[84] Using similar language, Robert Walsh advanced a theory of "dispensation from the letter of the Constitution." If, he said, the Constitution denied to the federal government the power of restricting slavery in a new state, "still I would contend that, in an extreme case like the present, never contemplated nor imagined, that government would be at liberty to consult the national interests, and minister to the ends of Eternal Justice

---

[82] *Annals of Congress*, 16 Cong., 2 Sess., 574, 636, 646.

[83] Mount Pleasant *Philanthropist*, February 17, 1821.

[84] Benjamin F. Wright, Jr., *American Interpretations of Natural Law* (Cambridge, 1931), 220-21.

and Benevolence."[85] Rufus King's address on natural law is not recorded in the *Annals of Congress*. According to a memorandum in his private papers, he asserted on that occasion that "I have yet to learn that one man can make a slave of another— if one man cannot do it, no number of individuals can have any better right to do it, and I hold that all laws or compacts imposing any such a condition upon any human being are absolutely void because contrary to the law of nature, which is the law of God, by which he makes his way known to man, and is paramount to all human control."[86] King always insisted that he did not advocate immediate emancipation in the existing slave states. Nevertheless, one wonders how his doctrine could have any validity if exceptions were to be made to it. Moreover, as an aristocratic Federalist who opposed universal suffrage in his own state,[87] King was hardly in a position to employ arguments based on the natural rights philosophy against the South.

If Southerners were unwilling to free the slaves, perhaps their most logical course would have been to repudiate the Declaration of Independence altogether. There were in fact a few who showed a tendency in such a direction. William Pinkney declared that the self-evident truths proclaimed by the Declaration were neither truths, if interpreted literally, nor originally designed to be so received.[88] John Randolph was said to have ridiculed the Declaration and to have dubbed its doctrine of equal rights an absurd "fanfaronade of metaphysical abstractions."[89] The St. Louis *Enquirer* remarked that if all men were born equal, every slave was entitled to instant freedom. But, said the *Enquirer*, "necessity, policy, expediency, &c. forbid— and what becomes then of the maxim that all men are entitled to equal rights?"[90] Most of the South's congressmen had no

---

85 [Walsh], *Free Remarks on the Spirit of the Federal Constitution*, 56-57.

86 Extract from Rufus King's speech on the Missouri question, Box 18 A, Item 217, Rufus King Papers. See also *Annals of Congress*, 16 Cong., 1 Sess., 380-81; John W. Walker to Charles Tait, February 11, 1820, Tait Papers.

87 King, *Rufus King*, VI, 406.

88 *Annals of Congress*, 16 Cong., 1 Sess., 405.

89 [William Darlington], *Desultory Remarks on the Question of Extending Slavery into Missouri* (West Chester, Pa., 1856), 24.

90 St. Louis *Enquirer*, February 10, 1821.

intention of unequivocally repudiating the natural rights philosophy of the Declaration of Independence. In general they expressed profound respect for the Declaration as an abstract truth, while at the same time denying that it was applicable to their own slaves. Just why it did not apply to the latter was not made clear.[91] Certain Southerners attempted to bend the Declaration to their own purposes by arguing that it gave Missouri the right to enjoy an unrestricted state sovereignty.[92] John Scott, Missouri's territorial delegate, read lengthy quotations from Vattel, the Swiss natural rights philosopher, to prove the same point.[93] A St. Louis grand jury contended that Missouri's right to statehood, without any restriction regarding slavery, did not depend upon the will of Congress "but was virtually and essentially secured to us by the original declaration of American Independence, as set forth in our bill of rights, and secured to us by the Constitution of the United States."[94]

The doctrine of state rights, whose special guardian the South fancied itself to be, rested ultimately upon a supposed fundamental or natural law in accordance with which each local area was entitled to self-government. The Missouri Controversy led Southerners and Missourians to take an extreme stand in behalf of local self-government. Though Missourians regarded themselves as a part of the federal Union, their first constitution began with the statement that "We, the people of Missouri, . . . do mutually agree to form and establish a free and independent republic, by the name of the 'State of Missouri.'" Thomas H. Benton maintained in 1819 that the proper role for Congress in the admission of new states was merely that of a master of ceremonies.[95]

It is axiomatic that those who advocate state rights are often guilty of inconsistencies,[96] and this was certainly the case in

[91] *Annals of Congress*, 16 Cong., 1 Sess., 301, 350, 1154-55, 1384.
[92] *Ibid.*, 350, 1073, 1155, 1522.
[93] *Ibid.*, 1493-98.
[94] St. Louis *Gazette & Public Advertiser*, April 14, 1819.
[95] St. Louis *Enquirer*, May 19, 1819.
[96] See Arthur M. Schlesinger, *New Viewpoints in American History* (New York, 1926), 220-44.

1819-1821. The St. Louis *Enquirer* was noted for the vehemence with which it resisted federal encroachments in the matter of slavery restriction, which it called "simply and nakedly a question of *state sovereignty*."[97] At the same time, however, the *Enquirer* was loud in its demands for an extensive program of federal internal improvements which, if carried out, would undoubtedly have strengthened the central government at the expense of the states.[98] On the other hand, the Clintonians, while championing the right of the general government to prohibit slavery in a new state, suddenly raised the state rights banner in New York and accused the Monroe administration of interfering in local politics by using its patronage to defeat Clinton in his campaign for governor.[99] Ohio favored congressional restriction for Missouri, but in the "Ohio Controversy," which was contemporaneous with the Missouri Controversy, Ohioans flouted federal authority in no uncertain terms. Ignoring Chief Justice Marshall's decision in the case of McCulloch *v.* Maryland, the state of Ohio forcibly collected a tax of $100,000 from the Chillicothe branch of the United States Bank and enacted legislation (which was not repealed until 1826) outlawing the Bank from its borders.[100]

One of the most hotly debated topics in the Missouri debates was the charge made by Northerners that Southern society and government were aristocratic, undemocratic, and antirepublican. The Reverend Josephus Wheaton stated the case for restrictionists with the assertion that "The phrase *republican slave holder* is a solecism. The Emperor Nero whose despotism and cruelty have long been proverbial . . . in my opinion had as good a claim to be called a republican, as any man who traffics in slaves or unnecessarily holds them in bondage."[101] The Washington *Gazette* declared that "there is no *middle class* in

[97] St. Louis *Enquirer*, November 10, 1819.

[98] *Ibid.*, June 16, 1819.

[99] New York *Columbian*, February 8, 12, 1821.

[100] Roseboom and Weisenburger, *History of Ohio*, 131-35; Washington *Daily National Intelligencer*, November 6, 1819.

[101] Josephus Wheaton, *The Equality of Mankind and the Evils of Slavery, Illustrated: A Sermon* (Boston, 1820), 22.

the slave-holding states. The white man who labors there is degraded to the level of a slave, and treated with equal contempt."[102] "The owners of slaves," said Governor Oliver Wolcott of Connecticut, "must necessarily be the chief owners of the soil; and those labourers who are too poor to own both, though nominally free, must be dependent on an artistocratical order, and remain without power or political influence in the state."[103]

Southerners vociferously denied the accusation that their government or way of life was undemocratic. From the fervor with which they proclaimed their devotion to the abstract principles of liberty and democracy, one would never guess that they were slaveholders. At the same time that the St. Louis *Enquirer* was breathing dire threats against anyone who attempted to prevent Missourians from holding slaves, it carried a forceful editorial applauding the South Americans for revolting against Spanish tyranny and rejoicing over the spread of republicanism throughout the world.[104] Charles Pinckney of South Carolina, though a proslavery man, proudly boasted of the fact that America was "the ark, in which alone, amidst all the deluges of despotism, the seeds and principles of freedom have been, and are still safely, preserved."[105] In no part of America, said Senator Freeman Walker of Georgia, were the "pure principles of democracy" so much cherished as in the slaveholding states.[106] Congressman George Strother of Culpeper, Virginia, described himself as a Republican and a representative of hardy yeomen.[107]

To the Northern contention that manual labor was considered disgraceful in the South, the Washington *Intelligencer* replied that masters often labored beside their slaves and that no people in the world worked harder than four fifths of the white men in the slaveholding states.[108] According to Senator

[102] Washington *Gazette*, February 10, 1820.
[103] Hartford *American Mercury*, May 9, 1820.
[104] St. Louis *Enquirer*, September 11, 1819.
[105] *Annals of Congress*, 16 Cong., 2 Sess., 1141.
[106] *Ibid.*, 1 Sess., 162.   [107] *Ibid.*, 1059.
[108] Washington *Daily National Intelligencer*, December 20, 1819.

William Smith of South Carolina, Southerners, whether slave-holders or nonslaveholders, were as industrious as any people in America.[109] Rupert B. Vance has recently raised the question of whether, since the Negro slave constituted the proletariat in the Old South, the existence of slavery had the effect of pushing the plain white people to a higher level than they would otherwise have occupied.[110] A similar thesis was advanced during the Missouri Controversy by two Kentuckians— Senator Richard M. Johnson and Congressman William Brown. Both Johnson and Brown regarded servant and valet duties as too menial to be performed by a self-respecting white man. In Kentucky, they said, such chores were done by slaves, leaving the more honorable and dignified labor of agriculture and the mechanic arts to the whites. Consequently there were no class distinctions among the whites of Kentucky as there were in the North. Brown asserted that he could enumerate the names of many nonslaveholding acquaintances who had been elected to public office in the South, and Johnson declared that he was delighted to entertain honest laborers and mechanics, however poor, at his table.[111]

[109] *Annals of Congress*, 16 Cong., 1 Sess., 420.

[110] Rupert B. Vance, book review in *Journal of Southern History*, XVI (1950), 547.

[111] *Annals of Congress*, 16 Cong., 1 Sess., 348-49; *ibid.*, 2 Sess., 1203-1206. See also Leland W. Meyer, *The Life and Times of Colonel Richard M. Johnson of Kentucky* (New York, 1932), 212; Washington *Daily National Intelligencer*, September 3, 1819. Recent historical scholarship substantiates the contention that the Southern nonslaveholder was neither degraded nor excluded from politics. Fletcher Green, Charles Sydnor, and others have shown that the existence of slavery did not prevent the South from broadening the basis of suffrage and moving steadily in the direction of democracy, as far as the whites were concerned, between 1820 and 1860. In the case of the Negroes, however, there was a reverse trend, and free Negroes in the same period were disfranchised in North Carolina and elsewhere. For a discussion of political democracy in the Old South, see Fletcher M. Green, "Democracy in the Old South," in *Journal of Southern History*, XII (1946), 3-23; Fletcher M. Green, *Constitutional Development in the South Atlantic States, 1776-1860* (Chapel Hill, 1930), 296, 302-304; Sydnor, *Development of Southern Sectionalism*, 275-93.

In the economic realm, a whole school of writers, sometimes called the Vanderbilt group, has shown that the ante bellum South contained a large middle class of respectable small farmers and nonslaveholders. See especially Frank L.

Some Southerners apparently saw nothing incompatible between republicanism and slavery. John Lindsey, a candidate for the Missouri constitutional convention of 1820, informed the voters that "My political principles, I believe are well known to be republican, and as to slavery, I shall be in favor of it."[112] Lindsey's reasoning enraged Dr. Nathaniel Ames, that Massachusetts Yankee of Yankees and Jacobin of Jacobins. "Such ignorant apes," said the good doctor, "ought to be chained, blacked and taught. No wonder Western emigrants are ranked below savages."[113] Southerners had no hesitancy in claiming that the South was more republican than the North. With pride, they quoted Edmund Burke's statement that the Southern colonists appreciated the blessings of liberty more than their Northern brethren.[114] Colonel John W. Maddox, a Southerner who was residing in Indiana at the time of the Missouri contest, stated to an antislavery editor that he was "begotten by a republican Suck.d the paps of one and I hope to live and dy one and its not all your free negroe pride will turn me."[115] Noting Southern claims to a superior brand of republicanism, Rufus King sarcastically referred to the slavehold-

Owsley, *Plain Folk of the Old South* (Baton Rouge, 1949); Blanche H. Clark, *The Tennessee Yeomen 1840-1860* (Nashville, 1942); and Herbert Weaver, *Mississippi Farmers 1850-1860* (Nashville, 1945). Certain conclusions of the Vanderbilt writers have been challenged by Fabian Linden on the ground that they exaggerate the size and well-being of the middle class yeomanry and minimize economic inequalities and class stratification. Nevertheless, Linden concedes that no one "will protest the general thesis which is argued by the Vanderbilt group that 'the old planter–poor-white stereotype of southern society' is an outmoded fiction." "Economic Democracy in the Slave South: an Appraisal of Some Recent Views," in *Journal of Negro History*, XXXI (1946), 140-89.

It is interesting to note that a majority of white Southerners have earned a livelihood by manual labor from colonial times to the present day. After a study of this topic, Gustavus W. Dyer concluded that only one type of labor—household and valet duties performed for hire—was discredited by slavery. *Democracy in the South Before the Civil War* (Nashville, 1905), 48-49.

[112] St. Louis *Gazette & Public Advertiser*, April 12, 1820.
[113] Charles Warren, *Jacobin and Junto* (Cambridge, 1931), 323-24.
[114] Edmund Burke, *Speech of Edmund Burke, Esq. on Moving His Resolutions for Conciliation with the Colonies* (London, 1775), 32-33.
[115] Brookville (Indiana) *Enquirer*, April 24, 1821.

ing states as those "which call themselves, and are spoken of by others as the truly republican States and the peculiar friends of liberty."[116]

Whether they lived in the North or South, most Americans in 1820 were theoretical devotees of the principle of equalitarian democracy.[117] In politics as well as religion, both sections of the country professed to worship the same god.[118] In neither section, however, was democracy fully practiced. Nearly everywhere it stopped short of the color line and several other lines.

One of the most effective arguments employed by the restrictionists was that slavery was an anachronism and contrary to "the spirit of the age."[119] The Missouri Controversy began within less than five years after the Congress of Vienna, at a time when Americans believed that two great forces were struggling for possession of the world's soul—American democracy and European absolutism. Should America extend slavery, said the restrictionists, it would play into the hands of the "legitimates" of Europe and enable them to assert that liberty was but a name in the world's greatest republic.[120] There was also the problem of American missionaries abroad. The Missouri Compromise would be a source of discouragement to them, said the Concord *Observer,* a religious newspaper.[121]

In so far as there was a world opinion on the Missouri question, it was against the South. Southerners were replying to

[116] King, *Rufus King*, VI, 329.

[117] The leaders of Southern thought had not yet shifted their allegiance from Jeffersonianism to the ancient Greek type of democracy based upon slavery, although several quotations in this chapter reveal the beginnings of a tendency in that direction. For the later Southern ideal of a Greek democracy, see Vernon L. Parrington, *The Romantic Revolution in America 1800-1860* (New York, 1927), 99-108; Merle Curti, *The Growth of American Thought* (New York, 1943), 442-43.

[118] According to Ralph H. Gabriel, this was still the case in 1861-1865. "Paradoxically," he says, "the general outlines of the thought-patterns of Northern and Southern leaders [regarding the American democratic faith] were the same." *The Course of American Democratic Thought* (New York, 1940), 114.

[119] *Annals of Congress*, 16 Cong., 1 Sess., 255.

[120] Pennsylvania *House Journal*, 1819-1820, p. 989.

[121] Concord (New Hampshire) *Observer*, March 20, 1820.

the English critics of slavery at the same time that they were opposing the Missouri restriction.[122] Northern newspapers published articles in favor of restriction taken from the London *Times*, Liverpool *Advertiser*, and Montreal *Herald*.[123] When one of James Tallmadge's addresses was circulated in Germany, the Germans expressed amazement at the necessity for such a speech in a country which boasted of so much liberty and equality.[124] An American who in this period made a tour of England, France, Germany, and Russia declared that he was compelled to cease all remarks on the oppressed condition of the poor in those countries, since the universal answer was: "*Americans* should not speak of *Oppression!—Look at home at your Slaves!!!*"[125]

The arguments that were used in 1820 in discussions of the race question were in many cases identical with, or quite similar to, those which one still hears in the middle of the twentieth century. They were, of course, not original in 1820. Most of them had been pressed into service in 1804 in the debate on the Breckinridge Bill for the government of Louisiana.[126] In fact, they were quite old even then. Frank J. Klingberg has shown that nearly all the problems of relationships between the white and Negro races that have arisen at any time since were uncovered and discussed in South Carolina in the colonial period in connection with the work of the English Society for the Propagation of the Gospel in Foreign Parts—"the original interventionist" in the deep South.[127]

---

[122] See *Letter to the Edinburgh Reviewers: by "An American."* First Published in the *National Intelligencer* of November 16, 1819 (n.p., n.d.); John Wright, *A Refutation of the Sophisms, Gross Misrepresentations, and Erroneous Quotations Contained in 'An American's' 'Letter to the Edinburgh Reviewers'* (Washington, 1820).

[123] New York *American*, February 9, 1820; New York *Daily Advertiser*, March 14, 1820; Washington *Gazette*, December 17, 1819.

[124] Poughkeepsie *Dutchess Observer*, February 23, 1820.

[125] D. Bringhurst to William Darlington, January 19, 1820, Darlington Papers, New-York Historical Society.

[126] Brown, *Constitutional History of the Louisiana Purchase*, 108.

[127] Frank J. Klingberg, *An Appraisal of the Negro in Colonial South Carolina* (Washington, 1941), 123.

But if the arguments used were similar to those of the present day, the political alignment was not. The principal champions of the Negro in 1820 were the Federalist and Clintonian aristocrats of the Eastern and Middle states. Northern mechanics and laborers, with whom the Negro was a competitor in the economic world, opposed any favors to him.[128] This produced strange inconsistencies from the present day point of view. Although the victory of the Democrats in Connecticut in 1817 resulted in an extension of popular government, the new constitution which they gave the state in 1818 disfranchised the Negro.[129] The New York constitutional convention of 1821, led by radicals like Erastus Root—of whom it was said that "He would have graced the Mountain thirty years before in France" —greatly extended the elective franchise. Opposing the radicals at every step in the convention were the Federalists, now reduced to a small company but still as determined as ever "to impede the onward movement to a government of all men by all men."[130] Nevertheless, when the question of Negro suffrage arose, the roles of the two parties in the convention were suddenly reversed, and it was only with the greatest difficulty that the Democratic majority was persuaded not to disfranchise the Negro altogether. A spokesman for those favoring such a course, Erastus Root, who incidentally was pro-Southern in his attitude toward the Missouri question,[131] argued that "there was some cause for alarm, when a few hundred Negroes of the city of New York, following the train of those [aristocratic Federalists] who ride in their coaches, and whose shoes and boots they had so often blacked, shall go to the polls of the election and change the political condition of the whole state." The Federalists, in their turn, while vigorously opposing universal white suffrage, strenuously condemned the curtailment of Negro voting. Against Federalist opposition, the convention finally adopted a compromise measure which established stricter

128 Fox, *Decline of Aristocracy in New York*, 269-70.
129 Adams, "Disfranchisement of Negroes in New England," 545.
130 Fox, *Decline of Aristocracy in New York*, 240-41, 248-69.
131 New York *Columbian*, January 21, 1820; Albany *Argus*, January 21, 1820.

voting qualifications for Negroes than for whites.[132] James Tallmadge, Jr., who was a delegate to the convention, supported the compromise and also stated that he was not in favor of universal suffrage.[133]

In conclusion, it is evident that the present day alignment of "liberalism" versus "conservatism" on the race question did not exist in 1819-1821. Many of those who were active in the campaign to prohibit slavery in Missouri were Sabbatarians, advocates of the union of church and state, opponents of universal suffrage, and protagonists of various types of special privilege. Conversely, many of those most strongly opposed to the Missouri restriction would be classified today as liberal in everything except their attitude toward slavery and the race issue. One more illustration should be sufficient. Richard M. Johnson of Kentucky was one of the most determined opponents of congressional restriction. "Yet," says the leading New Deal historian, "during the eighteen-twenties, Johnson stood out as the one Senator who consistently advocated the rights of the common man."[134]

[132] Fox, "Negro Vote in Old New York," 258-63.

[133] L. H. Clarke (ed.), *A Report of the Debates and Proceedings of the Convention of the State of New-York; Held at the Capitol, in the City of Albany, on the 28th Day of August, 1821* (New York, 1821), 141, 180, 183, 186.

[134] Schlesinger, *Age of Jackson,* 141.

CHAPTER X

AN ECONOMIC BASIS FOR SECTIONALISM

*T*HE MOST OBVIOUS economic interpretation of the Missouri Controversy is that many owners of slaves throughout the South were unalterably opposed to any measure which might ultimately deprive them of their labor force and livelihood. Speaking in behalf of those who, for economic reasons, objected to congressional interference with slavery in Missouri or anywhere else, the Savannah *Daily Republican* addressed a significant question to Northerners in 1820. "How," it asked, "are our slaves to be emancipated? Will the northern people, in case we consent to give them up, bear an equal proportion of this loss of property, as in justice they ought? And will they send annually their proportion of laborers to cultivate our swamp lands and rice fields, or shall we let them lay waste, and will they bear their proportion of this loss also?"[2]

Some historians have attributed the vehemence with which the South condemned the proposed Missouri restriction to the increasing profitableness of slavery after the invention of the cotton gin.[3] Right here, however, one runs into a paradox. With certain exceptions, the deep South, where slavery was most profitable, was less militant and more amenable to a compromise in 1820 than Virginia, where slavery was certainly not profitable. Not that Anti-Missourians were at a loss to discover an economic motive for Virginian intransigence. The Virginians, they said, had become slave breeders for the states in which slave labor could be used to advantage. An anonymous writer in the Washington *Gazette* was no doubt hitting at Virginia when he referred to "the people who keep breeding farms, and wish an extensive market for the surplus of the black warrens."[4] Dwight's New York *Advertiser* thought that it could detect in the attitude of the Virginians "*a fearful apprehension . . . that a boundless market for the disposal of human beings, would not be opened in the vast regions beyond the Mississippi, for the supply of which the old slave states may rear live-stock at a great profit.*"[5] It is true that Virginians derived considerable revenue by selling surplus slaves for shipment to the lower South. Virginia and Maryland had become a second Guinea in this respect.[6] Just how much that fact influenced their position on the Missouri question, it would be difficult to say, but it must have carried some weight.

In 1819-1821 two rival economies were struggling for the possession of the western country, each bent on colonization and exploitation. Southern planters who hoped to escape eventually from the worn-out lands of the seaboard states by migrating westward with their slaves were naturally opposed to the Missouri restriction. On the other side of the picture, some Northerners were resentful of the fact that the slaveholding states had monopolized all the lands in the nation which were best adapted for the cultivation of tobacco, cotton, and sugar.[7] Northern immigrants, it was argued, could hardly be expected

[1] New Brunswick (New Jersey) *Fredonian*, July 27, 1820.

[2] Savannah *Daily Republican*, February 29, 1820.

[3] James A. Woodburn, "The Historical Significance of the Missouri Compromise," in *Annual Report of the American Historical Association for the Year 1893* (Washington, 1894), 292-93.

[4] Washington *Gazette*, February 1, 1820.

[5] New York *Daily Advertiser*, January 27, 1820.

[6] Frederic Bancroft, *Slave-Trading in the Old South* (Baltimore, 1931), 67-74; Richmond *Enquirer*, February 27, 1821; Charles Tait to James A. Tait, October, 1819, Tait Papers.

[7] *Annals of Congress*, 15 Cong., 2 Sess., 1222-23; *Minutes of the Seventeenth Session of the American Convention for Promoting the Abolition of Slavery*, 48.

to settle in Missouri and compete with slave labor,[8] not to mention the probability that slaveholders would run up the price of Missouri lands to a point where poor men could not afford to purchase them.[9]

A further economic interpretation of the Missouri Controversy is to be found in the disagreement between the slaveholding and free states over the tariff. This subject produced a sectional alignment as early as the first Congress after the adoption of the Constitution, when Senator Pierce Butler of South Carolina threatened "a dissolution of the Union, with regard to his State, as sure as God was in his firmament!"[10] For a brief moment after the War of 1812 it seemed that the South might get on the protectionist band wagon, and, had it done so, the subsequent course of American history would have been profoundly different. Although a majority of the Southern congressmen did not vote for the tariff of 1816, so large a minority of them did that the country was not aware of any North-South cleavage in the voting of that year.[11] Protectionist sentiment in the South rapidly diminished after 1816, however, and by 1820 it was clear that the slave states were the chief obstacle in the way of further tariff increases.

The Panic of 1819 led to insistent demands from the manufacturers as well as the laboring class of the Middle states for higher protective duties. Nicholas Biddle told the story of a laboring man who argued that since, during the Revolution, cargoes of tea were thrown into the river, so now foreign manufactured goods should be treated in the same manner.[12] In May, 1819, the Philadelphia Society for the Promotion of National Industry, attributing the depression to the importa-

[8] Canandaigua *Ontario Messenger*, December 21, 1819.

[9] Kaskaskia (Illinois) *Intelligencer*, July 14, 1819.

[10] John G. Van Deusen, *Economic Bases of Disunion in South Carolina* (New York, 1928), 17; Carpenter, *The South as a Conscious Minority*, 29-30; James C. Ballagh, "Southern Economic History: Tariff and Public Lands," in *Annual Report of the American Historical Association for the Year 1898* (Washington, 1899), 228.

[11] Babcock, *Rise of American Nationality*, 238.

[12] Nicholas Biddle to Jonathan Roberts, March 16, 1820, Biddle Papers.

tion of foreign goods, launched a nationwide campaign to secure an upward revision of the tariff.[13] A meeting held at Philadelphia in August, 1819, resolved to support no one for public office who was known to be unfriendly to the principle of protection for domestic manufactures.[14]

The protectionist demands of the Northern states brought immediate and strenuous protests from the South. Virginians, holding a Fourth-of-July celebration on the banks of the James in 1819, drank an uncomplimentary toast to the manufacturing interests. "Their leading object," the Virginians concluded, "is to empty our pockets and fill their own—and they pursue it 'with a step as steady as time, and an appetite as keen as death.' "[15] John Randolph called the manufacturers "the 'Caitiff Dogs' that would make us 'Cornplanters' & Tobacco Planters their hewers of wood & Drawers of water."[16] James M. Garnett, the Virginia agriculturist, wrote Randolph that "unless you Rulers of the land defeat the schemes of our Manufacturers, 'the plough,' in a short time, will prove as unprofitable an occupation as the pen."[17] The Charleston *Southern Patriot* accused the protectionists of seeking a monopoly at the expense of their own countrymen and wondered what would become of the South's cotton fields under such a program.[18] "If," said the Milledgeville, Georgia, *Journal,* "we can furnish the raw material to foreigners and purchase from them the fabric into which it is manufactured cheaper than that manufactured at home, we say, let us be at liberty to do so."[19]

Southern opposition to protection was so much greater in 1820 than in 1816 as to arouse speculation that the South might be seeking, by this means, to secure revenge for the attempted

[13] Washington *Gazette,* May 19, 1819.
[14] *Poulson's American Daily Advertiser* (Philadelphia), August 25, 1819.
[15] Richmond *Enquirer,* July 16, 1819.
[16] John Randolph to James M. Garnett, February 22, 1821, Randolph-Garnett Correspondence.
[17] James M. Garnett to John Randolph, March 31, 1820, *ibid.*
[18] Charleston *Southern Patriot, And Commercial Advertiser,* April 30, May 26, 1819.
[19] Milledgeville *Journal,* February 1, 1820.

Missouri restriction. A writer in the Baltimore *Federal Gazette* asserted that the North was now reaping its reward for meddling in the domestic concerns of the South.[20] The debate and vote on the proposed tariff increases in the Sixteenth Congress took place in April and May, 1820, after the passage of the Missouri Compromise and at a time when the slavery issue had supposedly been laid to rest. However, long before the enactment of the compromise, it was known that the Southern congressional delegation would vote overwhelmingly against any move to raise the tariff.[21] The tariff bill of 1820 was introduced in the House by Representative Henry Baldwin of Pittsburgh.[22] It was frankly protectionist in character and, according to *Niles' Register*, would cover the nation with smiles in less than six months after its adoption.[23]

While the slaveholding states were largely responsible for the defeat of the Baldwin bill, there were of course some Southerners who favored it. Among the protectionist petitions sent to Congress was one from certain citizens of Hampshire County, in western Virginia.[24] In the Natchez district of Mississippi a number of cotton planters had been won over to the idea of protection, and in 1819 the Natchez *Republican* strongly advocated an increase in the tariff to protect American manufactures.[25] In the same year protectionist toasts were drunk at a Fourth-of-July celebration in Jefferson County, Mississippi.[26] Congressman Eldred Simkins of South Carolina complained that some Southern newspapers had been enlisted in the cam-

20 Baltimore *Federal Gazette*, quoted in Richmond *Enquirer*, November 30, 1819. See also Frank W. Taussig, *The Tariff History of the United States* (New York, 1931), 73.

21 Pittsburgh *Gazette*, February 18, 1820.

22 *Annals of Congress*, 16 Cong., 1 Sess., 1663-69, 1913-16. The debate on the bill, which fills many pages of the *Annals*, is summarized in Edward Stanwood, *American Tariff Controversies in the Nineteenth Century* (2 vols, Boston, 1903), I, 180-94.

23 *Niles' Weekly Register*, XVIII (1820), 81.

24 Knoxville *Register*, February 20, 1821.

25 Natchez *Republican*, June 22, 1819; *Niles' Weekly Register*, XVI (1819), 384.

26 Natchez *State Gazette*, July 17, 1819.

paign to raise the tariff and that only a few of them were opposing it.[27] In Kentucky the advocates of a high tariff seem to
have been in the majority. Lexington had factories which were
as desirous of protection from foreign competition as those of
Pittsburgh. There was, for instance, the extensive establishment of Messrs. Brand, Postlethwait, & Co. near Lexington
which operated one thousand spindles, spun "twenty hundred
dozen of cotton" weekly, and, for good measure, had a Sunday
school that was personally superintended by the owners of the
factory.[28] When the Lexington *Gazette* learned in 1819 that
President Monroe was planning to visit Kentucky, it expressed
a hope that he would take note of the languishing condition
of Lexington's factories and make an effort to encourage
domestic manufactures.[29]

If the South was not unanimous in its opposition to the
Baldwin bill, neither was the North a unit in its favor. In New
England, where manufactures were not yet supreme, the mercantile and shipping interests were happy to unite with the
bulk of the Southern planters against the forces of protection.
As William Lowndes of South Carolina pointed out in a letter
to Timothy Pickering, in the hope of enlisting that arch-Fed-
eralist in the antitariff campaign, it was natural that there
should be a "unity of view" on such an issue between the
carrying and exporting states.[30] Lewis Tappan, a Boston Federalist who later became an antislavery crusader, called the
Baldwin tariff a "mad project."[31] The Federalist Salem *Gazette*
applauded the agriculturists of Virginia for their memorial to
Congress against a tariff increase.[32] The Federalist Portland
Gazette believed that Baldwin's measure would injure the

[27] Charleston *Southern Patriot, And Commercial Advertiser,* May 13, 1820.

[28] Washington *Gazette,* October 1, 1819. The hemp growers of Kentucky
were also protectionists. See James F. Hopkins, *A History of the Hemp Industry in Kentucky* (Lexington, 1951), 88, 128.

[29] Lexington *Gazette,* July 2, 1819.

[30] William Lowndes to Timothy Pickering, April 19, May 22, 1820; John
Lowell to Pickering, October 25, 1820, Pickering Papers.

[31] Lewis Tappan to Benjamin Tappan, June 7, 1820, Tappan Papers.

[32] Salem *Gazette,* January 14, 1820.

mercantile part of the community and that the merchants might well exclaim in the language of Shylock: "You take my life, when you take the means whereby I live; you take my house when you take the prop, which doth support my house."[33] The *Gazette's* Democratic rival, the Portland *Eastern Argus,* was of the same opinion.[34] The Boston *Daily Advertiser,* a Federalist journal, placed at the head of its editorial columns an anonymous letter from Washington which asserted that a suitable title for the Baldwin bill would be, "an act to prevent all trade beyond the Cape of Good Hope, to inhibit ship-building, to destroy the distilleries of spirits from molasses, and discourage the growth of the navy."[35] The Baldwin bill was also condemned by certain Federalists in the Middle states. Rufus King, though he voted for it, privately admitted that he was not sorry to see it postponed until the next session.[36]

In spite of the attitude of the shipping interests, the tariff of 1820 was not only supported by an overwhelming majority of the Northern congressional delegation but became entwined with the Missouri question. Henry Baldwin, chief sponsor of the tariff bill, voted consistently with the South in the Missouri contest. He deemed it wise to make concessions on the slavery issue in order to reconcile Southerners to the economic legislation that the North desired.[37] There were other protectionists who sympathized with the South or supported the compromises of 1820 and 1821, among them William Henry Harrison, Representative Charles Kinsey of New Jersey, and John Binns, publisher of the Philadelphia *Democratic Press.*

In general, however, the protectionists were intensely anti-Southern and believed that a long-range protective policy would not be possible until the expansion of slavery and Southern political influence were definitely checked. At Steubenville,

---

33 Portland *Gazette,* April 18, 1820.

34 Portland *Eastern Argus,* May 9, 1820.

35 Boston *Daily Advertiser,* April 19, 1820.

36 King, *Rufus King,* VI, 336, 338. See also antiprotectionist editorial in Robert Walsh's paper, the Philadelphia *National Gazette and Literary Register,* October 14, 1820.

37 Van Tyne, *Letters of Daniel Webster,* 83.

Ohio, a meeting was held for the double purpose of petitioning Congress to increase the tariff and to prohibit slavery in Missouri.[38] In this case the advocates of a high tariff and the Missouri restriction were identical. The Clintonian press, which was ardently protectionist, constantly harped upon the connection between the Missouri question and the tariff. This was especially true of William Duane's Philadelphia *Aurora*. Although the Clintonians were mostly to be found in New York, the *Aurora* could best be characterized as Clintonian rather than Democratic, since it supported Clinton for President in 1820 against Monroe, the regular Democratic nominee. In February, 1820, the *Aurora* declared that the attitude of Virginians toward Missouri and the tariff presented "a shocking evidence of . . . degeneracy—the same men . . . who are about, as they tell us, to *risk every thing to extend slavery,* are as malignantly vociferous in their hostility to the free *industry of the country.*"[39] An anonymous writer in the *Aurora* denounced the Virginia agricultural societies which were opposing higher tariff rates and imputed their "insensibility and hardness of heart" to their association with slavery. Later the same writer expressed concern over Southern threats to dissolve the Union. But, he observed, disunion would be dictated by necessity if the slave system was to be extended and the South continued to deny protection to Northern industry.[40] Another writer in the *Aurora* asserted that the prayers of the North for tariff protection and other favors were no more heeded than the whistling of the wind in the forest and that Northerners were treated as if they "were only another order of slaves, fit only to hew wood and draw water, like the Israelites for Egyptian taskmasters." Addressing himself to the North, the writer continued: "you merit this insult and this ingratitude; for you gave them a power to *legislate for you;* to exercise a *legislative power* under the name of a *representation of slaves.*"[41] During the gubernatorial election of 1820 in Pennsylvania, a mass meeting

[38] Steubenville *Western Herald,* December 18, 1819.
[39] Philadelphia *Aurora,* February 26, 1820.
[40] *Ibid.,* February 12, March 18, 1820.   [41] *Ibid.,* May 5, 1820.

at Carlisle prepared a list of grievances against Governor William Findlay. One of these was "his cold indifference and inactivity upon the great question recently agitated in Congress, concerning the introduction of Slavery into the new state of Missouri, to the prejudice of the non-slave holding states and of their just influence in the scale of the Union, operating against the encouragement of domestic manufactures & riveting the chains of slavery forever upon thousands of unborn generations."[42] A writer in the *Columbian,* the Clintonian organ of New York City, predicted that the Baldwin bill would be defeated by Southerners and Northern "dough faces." "Our representation in Congress," he wrote, "is but a farce—our men with *'dough faces'* as John Randolph calls them, can be *obtained* to answer any *purpose* which the gentlemen of the south desire, whether it be to extend slavery into Missouri—to support foreign work shops instead of our own, or to aid foreign speculators by our auctions and our custom-house credits."[43]

The House of Representatives passed the Baldwin tariff bill on April 29, 1820, by a vote of 91 to 78.[44] The rejoicing that followed in manufacturing circles was promptly cut short on May 4 when the Senate, by a vote of 22 to 21, postponed the consideration of the bill until the next session of Congress.[45] Under the circumstances, the vote on postponement was equivalent to a vote on the merits of the bill itself. The vote by states on the Baldwin tariff was:

STATE	House for	House against	Senate for	Senate against
New Hampshire		5	1	1
Vermont	1	4	1	1
Massachusetts	10	7		2
Rhode Island	2		2	

[42] Carlisle *Republican,* April 11, 1820.
[43] New York *Columbian,* May 6, 1820.
[44] *Annals of Congress,* 16 Cong., 1 Sess., 2155-56; *Journal of the House of Representatives,* 16 Cong., 1 Sess., 466-68. The *Annals* omit the name of one representative who voted for the bill—Joseph S. Lyman of New York.
[45] *Annals of Congress,* 16 Cong., 1 Sess., 672.

STATE	House for	House against	Senate for	Senate against
Connecticut	5	1	2	
New York	26		2	
New Jersey	6		2	
Pennsylvania	22	1	2	
Ohio	6		2	
Indiana	1		1	1
Illinois	1		1	1
Delaware	2		2	
Maryland	2	7		1
Virginia	1	18		2
North Carolina	1	12		2
South Carolina	1	7		2
Georgia		6		2
Kentucky	4	3	2	
Tennessee		5	1	1
Alabama				2
Mississippi		1		2
Louisiana		1		2
Total	91	78	21	22

An analysis of the vote on the Baldwin bill reveals some interesting facts. In the first place, the voting was along North-South lines. It is obvious that the South rather than New England was largely responsible for the bill's defeat. In order to tip the scales against a tariff increase, Southerners needed and received the aid of four New England senators, two of whom (Mellen and Otis of Massachusetts) happened to be Federalists. Thus, while Eastern Federalists were bitter against the "dough face" minority with whose assistance the South defeated the restrictionist clause of the Missouri bill, they themselves helped to make up the Northern minority which gave the slaveholding states a victory in the tariff controversy. Of all the slaveholding states, only Delaware and Kentucky cast a majority of their votes for the tariff. The only Virginian who voted for it was Thomas Newton, who was accused of supporting a measure which made Virginia tributary to Rhode Island and rendered the agricultural states colonial dependencies of the manufacturers.[46]

The defeat of the tariff of 1820 provoked an outburst of criticism aimed at the slaveholding states. Hezekiah Niles, editor of *Niles' Register*, was all for driving the government into a policy of direct taxation, letting "the slave states pay for their power of representation, if they refuse to the rest the means of prosperity."[47] The Pittsburgh *Statesman*, though it pursued a moderate course in the Missouri Controversy, asked after the defeat of the tariff: *"Do the slave-holding states wish to dissolve the Union, or make the manufacturing states their tributaries?"*[48] The Clintonian New York *Columbian* observed that the rejection of Baldwin's bill would cause "deep regret to the suffering manufacturers of the middle and northern states. Like another Missouri question, this has called forth local feeling, and some few 'dough faces' of the north have smiled upon a policy which goes to injure us in our interests and our honor."[49] An anonymous letter published in the *Columbian* declared that two essential maxims of the South were that *"Every new state must have its slaves"* and *"Every northern state shall be deprived of its manufactories."*[50] According to Duane's Philadelphia *Aurora*, the manufacturers had been optimistic when the tariff was approved by the House of Representatives but would not have been if they had understood *"that art* which is calculated to convert a *great republic* into a *small oligarchy,* or that morality which makes one man the *property* of another; the master often not half as worthy as the *property.*"[51] The *Aurora*'s favorite correspondent, "BRUTUS" (thought by some to be Duane himself), contended that the system of slave representation was destroying the North's

[46] Richmond *Enquirer,* quoted in New York *Columbian,* May 16, 1820.
[47] Hezekiah Niles to William Darlington, May 5, 1820, Darlington Papers, Library of Congress.
[48] Pittsburgh *Statesman,* May 10, 1820.
[49] New York *Columbian,* May 8, 1820.   [50] *Ibid.,* November 21, 1820.
[51] Philadelphia *Aurora,* May 9, 1820.

means of life and comfort.[52] The *Aurora* expressed a doubt that "this black despotism can be much longer endured." It agreed with "BRUTUS" that "the present system as to those who forge *hob nails, make hats,* or pursue any other *productive art or industry*—is only a change of British oppression for tyrants more unfeeling, because they compose part of the same nation—and could not exist independently of the free people they proscribe, and oppress, and impoverish."[53]

Northern bitterness over the defeat of the Baldwin bill is reflected in the toast given at a Fourth-of-July celebration at Harrisburg, Pennsylvania, in 1820: "National Industry—It is held in fetters by the iron grasp of slavery; may it soon burst the bands, and give food, health and happiness to a virtuous people."[54] A writer in the Lancaster, Pennsylvania, *Gazette,* in discussing the Missouri question and the tariff, complained of the political power which the South derived from the representation of three fifths of the slaves. To two millions of slaves, said the writer, were sacrificed the North's manufactures, its agriculture, and its independence. Thus the North was a mere appendage of the Southern states, and its interests were held in contempt.[55] The Steubenville, Ohio, *Western Herald* wondered how the people of Pittsburgh could support Congressman Baldwin for re-election, notwithstanding his sponsorship of protective legislation, since he voted on the Missouri question with the very Southern slaveholders whose policies had ruined the manufacturing establishments of Pittsburgh.[56] The Harrisburg *Chronicle* remarked that the slave states, always inimical to a protective tariff, had been guaranteed a preponderance in the United States Senate by the Missouri Compromise and thus could "render abortive future attempts to extricate us from dependence upon the workshops of Europe. Hence by this act the misery entailed upon the black population to the

[52] *Ibid.,* May 8, 1820.   [53] *Ibid.,* January 23, 1821.
[54] *Ibid.,* July 14, 1820.
[55] Lancaster *Gazette,* quoted in Philadelphia *Aurora,* December 30, 1820.
[56] Steubenville *Western Herald,* June 10, 1820.

THE MISSOURI CONTROVERSY

south, is accompanied by the impoverishment and distress of the white population of the other parts of the union."[57]

While the manufacturers and their friends were emptying the vials of their wrath upon the slaveholders, they did not overlook the assistance which the latter received from New England. Referring bitterly to the political alliance between Virginia and certain elements in New England against the tariff, a writer in the Philadelphia *Aurora* declared that "On this altar, reared by Jew and Gentile hand, to filthy lucre, the manufactures of the country are to be sacrificed."[58] In 1821 the Providence *Manufacturers' & Farmers' Journal,* an organ of the manufacturing interests of Rhode Island, urged the voters of Massachusetts to elect a Democratic governor. It charged that Governor John Brooks, the Federalist incumbent, was under the thumb of Boston importers of piece goods and that the Bostonians had formed a coalition with Virginians to postpone the tariff bill.[59]

In spite of criticism, Eastern merchants and shipowners remained steadfast in opposition to increased protection. In the latter part of 1820 antitariff meetings were held in Boston; Portsmouth; Belfast, Maine; and Philadelphia.[60] Webster was one of the speakers at Boston. Similar meetings were being held in South Carolina at the same time.[61] When the Chambers of Commerce of New York, Philadelphia, Boston, and Salem joined in the antitariff campaign, a writer in the New York *Columbian* accused them of being allied with foreign industry and the South. Addressing himself to the South, he said: "Erect your heads, ye Demagogues of the South! *Behold your friends!* ready to bolster you to the last, to aid you in every

[57] Harrisburg *Chronicle,* quoted in Philadelphia *Aurora,* May 29, 1820.
[58] Philadelphia *Aurora,* October 20, 1820.
[59] Boston *Commercial Gazette,* March 19, 1821.
[60] *Ibid.,* October 5, 1820; Portsmouth *Oracle,* October 14, 1820; New Haven *Columbian Register,* September 23, 1820; *Poulson's American Daily Advertiser* (Philadelphia), November 8, 1820.
[61] Charleston *Southern Patriot, And Commercial Advertiser,* September 14, 15, November 1, 6, 20, 1820.

project that shall keep down the rising fortunes of the north and the west, and perpetuate your political ascendency at Washington!"[62]

Oddly enough, although the manufacturers believed that the extension of slavery would injure the cause of protection, the leading antirestrictionist organ of Missouri, the St. Louis *Enquirer,* announced in July, 1820, that Missourians were in favor of an increase in tariff rates. The *Enquirer* had a long editorial praising Congressman Baldwin and listing four articles that the people of Missouri were "immensely" anxious to protect from foreign competition: lead, iron, salt, and hemp. Such commodities, said the *Enquirer,* could be produced in Missouri. In September the *Enquirer* asserted that Missouri wanted even more protection for these items than was provided by the Baldwin tariff.[63] When in 1824 a thoroughgoing protective tariff measure was finally enacted, it received the support of the entire Missouri congressional delegation.[64]

In the same session of Congress which saw the defeat of the Baldwin tariff, two other measures sponsored by the manufacturers were lost—a bill requiring the cash payment of import duties and another laying a heavy tax on foreign goods sold at auction. The House rejected the cash duty proposal by a vote of 91 to 55, a majority of the votes in favor of rejection being cast by Southerners.[65] The auction sales bill, after being passed in the House over Southern opposition, was later postponed until the next session of Congress because of developments in the Senate.[66] Advocates of the cash duty and auction bills correctly ascribed their defeat to the South.[67]

[62] New York *Columbian,* September 1, 1820. In the case of Pennsylvania, the commercial interests which opposed the Baldwin bill are said to have constituted less than 4 per cent of the state's population. Malcolm R. Eiselen, *The Rise of Pennsylvania Protectionism* (Philadelphia, 1932), 55.

[63] St. Louis *Enquirer,* July 1, September 30, 1820.

[64] *Annals of Congress,* 18 Cong., 1 Sess., 743-44, 2429-30; Stanwood, *American Tariff Controversies,* I, 239.

[65] *Annals of Congress,* 16 Cong., 1 Sess., 2171-72.

[66] *Ibid.,* 2184-85, 2201-2202.

[67] New York *Daily Advertiser,* May 20, 1820.

Southerners were also criticized for their opposition to legislation which would establish a uniform system of bankruptcy throughout the United States. Such a law had been enacted in 1800 but repealed in 1803.[68] Rufus King declared in 1818 that the South and West, in refusing to sanction a new bankruptcy bill, were withholding from the Eastern states a system of law that was necessary for commercial prosperity.[69] The Philadelphia *Aurora*, two years later, denounced the slaveholders as feudal lords who would not aid Northern merchants in obtaining protection by a bankrupt law.[70] That there was truth in the accusation is shown by the fate of a bankruptcy bill in the Senate in March, 1820. Northern senators voted 10 to 9 in its favor, but the slaveholding states killed it with an adverse vote of 14 to 5.[71]

Internal improvements, constructed at the expense of the national government, were another apple of sectional discord in 1819-1821. Ever since President Madison's veto of the Bonus Bill in 1817 many citizens of the Middle states had believed that the vetoes of Southern Presidents were denying them the roads and canals which they so ardently desired. The Philadelphia *Aurora's* correspondent, "BRUTUS," charged in 1820 that Monroe professed to regard federal internal improvements as unconstitutional, "lest improvement should augment population in the middle states, and by that means throw a weight of political influence into the scale, which would overweigh the slave states in representative power, in wealth, in strength, and in the force of popular principles; to retard the prosperity of the old states, and to augment the artificial and poisonous influence of slave representation."[72]

The fact that the national government had aided in the construction of the Cumberland Road project seemed to some Northerners to show favoritism, since the road ran through

---

[68] F. Regis Noel, *A History of the Bankruptcy Clause of the Constitution of the United States of America* (Gettysburg, n.d.), 124-33.

[69] King, *Rufus King*, VI, 119-20.

[70] Philadelphia *Aurora*, December 28, 1820.

[71] *Annals of Congress*, 16 Cong., 1 Sess., 561.

[72] Philadelphia *Aurora*, May 8, 1820.

Cumberland and Wheeling in the slave states of Maryland and Virginia. New Yorkers and New Englanders wished to know why similar assistance was not forthcoming for roads and canals in their states. The Federalist Portland *Gazette* referred to the Cumberland Road as an "internal improvement of a limited and sectional nature." It asked: "Why must the money of the North, be so lavishly expended in pulling down the mountains of the South? *Over a million and a half of dollars* laid out on one single road 130 miles long, while we cannot obtain $30,000, all we want, to make the notch of the *White Hills* passable. Is all internal improvement to be made at the South, and nothing done at the North?"[73] Additional embarrassing questions were asked by Evert K. Vanderveer in a letter published in the New York *Columbian*. "What," he wrote, "made Mr. Madison refuse the bonus of $90,000 for your [Erie] canal, when he signed a law for appropriating money for a Virginia road? Do you know that your northern people pay money out of your pockets to make Virginia turnpikes?— and that you will be compelled to do so while such men as Noah [pro-Southern Tammany editor] print for you—such men as Meigs [New York representative who voted against the Missouri restriction] act for you."[74]

The scruples of Presidents Madison and Monroe regarding the constitutionality of federal internal improvements were not shared of course by all the people of the slaveholding states. When Monroe visited Kentucky in 1819 he was distinctly given to understand that Kentuckians did not agree with him on this subject.[75] There were many more who did not agree with him in Maryland, South Carolina, Georgia, and the states of the Southwest.[76] Nevertheless, an analysis of the voting in the

[73] Portland *Gazette*, April 4, 1820.

[74] New York *Columbian*, April 14, 1820.

[75] Lexington *Gazette*, August 20, 1819.

[76] Phillips, *Georgia and State Rights*, 114; John W. Walker to Charles Tait, January 19, 1819, Tait Papers; Homer C. Hockett, *Western Influences on Political Parties to 1825* (Columbus, Ohio, 1917), 125. Of all the Southwestern states, Tennessee was probably least interested in the federal aid movement in 1820. Stanley J. Folmsbee, *Sectionalism and Internal Improvements in Tennessee 1796-1845* (Knoxville, 1939), 49.

Sixteenth Congress indicates that a majority of the Southern congressmen were opposed to federal internal improvements at the time of the Missouri Compromise. Thus it was not only the President but also a large bloc of Southern congressmen who were thwarting the desires of the Middle states. In April, 1820, Southern senators, with the aid of New England, almost succeeded in postponing indefinitely a bill authorizing the appointment of commissioners to survey routes for two canals in Delaware, Maryland, and New Jersey as well as a route for the continuation of the Cumberland Road from Wheeling to the Mississippi. Fourteen Southerners and five Northerners voted for postponement, while sixteen Northerners and five Southerners (counting Delaware and the Old Southwest as Southern) voted against it.[77] In May, 1820, the Senate voted on a measure authorizing the appointment of commissioners to lay out a route for a canal connecting the waters of Lake Erie with the Ohio (if a practicable route could be located). The measure was supported by seventeen Northerners and three Southerners and was opposed by eleven Southerners and two Northerners.[78] On May 3 Senator William Smith of South Carolina attempted to postpone for a year the consideration of the bill authorizing the appointment of commissioners to survey a route for the continuation of the Cumberland Road from Wheeling to the Mississippi, this bill having now been separated from the one pertaining to canals. Smith's postponement motion was defeated by a vote of 27 to 11,[79] the tally by states being:

SLAVE STATES	for	against	FREE STATES	for	against
Delaware		2	New Hampshire		1
Maryland		1	Vermont		2
Virginia	2		Massachusetts	1	
North Carolina	1	1	Rhode Island		2
South Carolina	2		Connecticut		2
Georgia		2	New York		2
Kentucky		1	New Jersey		2

[77] Annals of Congress, 16 Cong., 1 Sess., 625. [78] Ibid., 683.
[79] Ibid., 655.

SLAVE STATES			FREE STATES		
	for	*against*		*for*	*against*
Tennessee	2		Pennsylvania		2
Alabama	2		Ohio		2
Mississippi	1	1	Indiana		2
Louisiana			Illinois		2
Total	10	8	*Total*	1	19

The defeat of Smith's motion cleared the way for the passage of the Cumberland Road extension survey bill in the Senate. In the House of Representatives the bill was subsequently approved by a vote of 74 to 35.[80] The House vote was:

SLAVE STATES			FREE STATES		
	for	*against*		*for*	*against*
Delaware			New Hampshire	3	2
Maryland	5	1	Vermont	2	
Virginia	2	8	Massachusetts	6	3
North Carolina		6	Rhode Island	1	
South Carolina	3	1	Connecticut	2	3
Georgia	1	2	New York	13	5
Kentucky	3		New Jersey	5	
Tennessee		1	Pennsylvania	17	3
Alabama	1		Ohio	6	
Mississippi	1		Indiana	1	
Louisiana	1		Illinois	1	
Total	17	19	*Total*	57	16

This vote, despite the large number of congressmen who were absent when it was taken, leaves no doubt about which way the wind was blowing. President Monroe did not veto the bill, although two years later he did veto a measure for making repairs on the Cumberland Road.[81]

[80] *Ibid.*, 2244.

[81] Jeremiah S. Young, *A Political and Constitutional Study of the Cumberlandland Road* (Chicago, 1902), 66-70. While the Cumberland or National Road passed through Maryland and Virginia, it was too far north to be of much benefit to the South. For an account of Southern opposition to the use of federal funds for its construction, see Philip D. Jordan, *The National Road* (Indianapolis, 1948), 159-75.

Interestingly enough, while Missouri regarded the Northern congressmen as its persecutors, it actually had more in common with them, as far as internal improvements were concerned, than with the representatives of the slaveholding states. In June, 1819, the St. Louis *Enquirer* listed thirteen things which the people of Missouri needed federal aid in obtaining. The first was admission to statehood. Among the others were: the development of Missouri salt springs and lead mines, a national road to Washington, a post road to New Orleans, post routes throughout the territory, a post route from St. Louis to Louisville by way of Vincennes, a canal between Lake Michigan and the Illinois River, and a canal to unite the Mississippi River and Lake Superior.[82] This was one of the most sweeping demands for federal internal improvements that was made during the period from 1819 to 1821, and it amazed the seaboard states. The Savannah *Georgian* declared that "When we read this long list of wants we almost expected it to end with— 14th. A canal through the isthmus of Darien, and 15. Another through the isthmus of Suez!"[83] The Federalist Philadelphia *Union* concluded that there was just no satisfying the demands of Missouri.[84]

In conclusion it may be said that the conflicting economic interests of the free and slaveholding states were an important factor in the Missouri Controversy. Undoubtedly each side was less conciliatory and more determined to add Missouri to its sphere of influence because of the fear that a victory for its adversary might injure its own economy. Speaking for the North, former Governor William Plumer of New Hampshire expressed a fear that a slaveholding minority might rule a free majority by means of slave representation. He pointed out that the free states were interested in agriculture, commerce, and manufactures but that in the slave states agriculture alone constituted the principal business. It would therefore be

[82] St. Louis *Enquirer*, June 16, 1819.
[83] Savannah *Georgian*, quoted in Washington *Gazette*, August 24, 1819.
[84] Philadelphia *Union*, February 16, 1820.

natural, he argued, for the South, if vested with power, to neglect manufacturing and commerce.[85] The Steubenville, Ohio, *Western Herald* lamented the failure of Congress to increase the tariff, to pass the bill for requiring prompt payment of duties on imports, to lay a duty on sales at auction, and to enact a bankrupt law. "Thus," said the *Western Herald*, "has southern policy, as in the Missouri question again triumphed over the hopes and interests of the nation—thus are tens of thousands of our people doomed to beggary, to jails and to death."[86] In opposing the re-election of President Monroe in 1820, the Philadelphia *Aurora's* correspondent, "BRUTUS," accused him of being responsible for the defeat of the Missouri restriction and of being an enemy of internal improvements and domestic manufactures. In advocating the election of De Witt Clinton as President, "BRUTUS" asserted that Clinton would "encourage manufactures with a paternal care" and "prosecute internal improvements, with an impartial, but liberal hand."[87] Evert K. Vanderveer wrote from Washington in March, 1820, to a friend in New York that Virginians dominated the government because they were united among themselves. "Do you not perceive," he said, "that they are obtaining the advantage of you on every great national question. They have carried the *bank* question, because they are *united*—they have carried the *Missouri* question, because they were *united*—they have rejected the bill for encour[ag]ing *your manufactures,* because they were *united*—and they will reject the bankrupt bill— and have president after president from their *own state,* because they are united."[88]

The South was quite as fearful of economic oppression as the North. The Louisville *Public Advertiser* wondered whether the North might secure control of the government by means of the Missouri Controversy and then proceed to promote manufacturing, by prohibitory duties, at the expense of agri-

[85] William Plumer to William Plumer, Jr., February 28, 1820, Plumer Papers.
[86] Steubenville *Western Herald*, May 27, 1820.
[87] Philadelphia *Aurora*, October 26, November 1, 1820.
[88] New York *Columbian*, April 7, 1820.

culture and commerce.[89] Linn Banks, Speaker of the Virginia
House of Delegates, warned that the free states, after securing
control of the West, would have the power to tax Southern
agriculture in the interest of their manufactures.[90] An unnamed
member of the Virginia congressional delegation, writing to the
editor of the Petersburg *Intelligencer,* urged that the Unioin be
dissolved immediately unless a constitutional amendment could
be secured to protect the South against Northern aggression.
Otherwise, said the congressman, "Abolition societies and that
general spirit of wild fanatical zeal which pervades the North,
(directed by the chief jugglers who act unseen) will continually press this subject [slavery restriction] upon congress from
this time forward, whilst we shall continue (in despite of all
we may *say*) to be taxed by their manufacturers and by their
stockholders and their banks."[91] An elaborate economic interpretation of the Missouri Controversy from a Southern standpoint was advanced by John Taylor of Caroline, who believed
that he could discern the real cause of the dispute in the words
"ambition, avarice, exclusive privileges, bounties, pensions and
corporations." Taylor's thesis was that "The great pecuniary
favour granted by congress to certificate-holders, begat banking; banking begat bounties to manufacturing capitalists; bounties to manufacturing capitalists begat an oppressive pension
list; these partialities united to beget the Missouri project;
that project begat the idea of using slavery as an instrument
for effecting a balance of power; when it is put in operation,
it will beget new usurpations of internal powers over persons
and property, and these will beget a dissolution of the union."[92]

[89] Louisville *Public Advertiser,* February 14, 1821.

[90] Tyler, "Missouri Compromise. Letters to James Barbour," 21.

[91] Petersburg *Intelligencer,* quoted in Baltimore *Patriot & Mercantile Advertiser,* March 11, 1820.

[92] Taylor, *Construction Construed,* 293-94, 298. See also Henry H. Simms,
Life of John Taylor (Richmond, 1932), 166-70; Eugene T. Mudge, *The Social
Philosophy of John Taylor of Caroline* (New York, 1939), 208.

"I take it for granted that the present question is a mere preamble—a title-page to a great tragic volume."—JOHN QUINCY ADAMS[1]

CHAPTER XI

SIGNIFICANCE OF THE MISSOURI CONTROVERSY

*T*HE MISSOURI Controversy did not, as some had hoped and others had feared, result in an immediate realignment of political parties along North and South lines, nor did it lead to a resurgence of Federalism. In the elections of 1820-1821, factional fights within the Democratic party overshadowed contests between Democrats and Federalists in the key states of New York and Pennsylvania. In New Hampshire the Federalists made slight gains, but in Rhode Island they merely held their own, while in Connecticut and New Jersey the Democrats won by better than normal majorities.[2] When Delaware replaced its Federalist governor with a Democrat in 1821, Massachusetts had the distinction of being the only remaining Federalist state in the Union.[3]

For the most part, the Anti-Missourians did not attempt to prevent the re-election of Monroe in 1820. Congressman John Sloane of Ohio, a militant restrictionist, wrote privately that everyone with whom he discussed the subject regarded the President as weak and inefficient but that any opposition to his candidacy would be unavailing.[4] The Clintonian organ, the New York *Columbian,* while it grudgingly attributed Monroe's re-election to the apathy of the voters rather than their unanimity, significantly made no effort to secure his defeat.[5]

Rival slates of candidates for the electoral college were placed in the field in New York by the Bucktail and Clintonian factions, and the Canandaigua *Ontario Messenger* characterized the Bucktail slate as the "SLAVE TICKET" and that of their opponents as the "ANTI-SLAVE TICKET." The candidates on the "ANTI-SLAVE TICKET" were said to be favorable to Monroe, though they did not have a chance to demonstrate it, since the "SLAVE TICKET" defeated them in the legislature by a vote of 72 to 54.[6]

As the President of the so-called era of good feelings, Monroe had won the respect of many Federalists,[7] and it was only in Philadelphia that his re-election was seriously opposed. Here the erratic William Duane and his newspaper, the *Aurora*, sponsored an electoral ticket pledged to the support of De Witt Clinton. Charging Monroe with the responsibility for the passage of the Missouri Compromise, the *Aurora's* star correspondent, "BRUTUS," denounced him as the candidate of slavery.[8] Another writer in the *Aurora* called upon Pennsylvanians to enter a solemn protest "against being any longer submissive vassals to a slave aristocracy."[9] In the city of Philadelphia Clinton polled 793 votes as against 1,233 for Monroe. Penn Township, Northern Liberties, and Southwark cast a total of 1,197 votes for Monroe and 433 for Clinton.[10] Elsewhere in Pennsylvania the Clintonian vote was negligible.[11] When the

1 Adams, *Memoirs of J. Q. Adams*, IV, 502.

2 Concord (New Hampshire) *Patriot & State Gazette*, March 19, 1821; Providence *Patriot*, September 2, 1820; Hartford *American Mercury*, April 11, 1820; Trenton *True American*, October 21, 1820.

3 Hartford *Times, and Weekly Advertiser*, October 17, 1820.

4 John Sloane to Benjamin Tappan, May, 1820, Tappan Papers.

5 New York *Columbian*, November 22, 1820.

6 *Ibid.*, December 4, 1820; Canandaigua *Ontario Messenger*, November 14, 1820; New York *Commercial Advertiser*, November 27, 1820.

7 See Lewis Tappan to Benjamin Tappan, March 31, 1820, Tappan Papers; New York *Evening Post*, December 4, 1819.

8 Philadelphia *Aurora*, October 26, 1820.   9 *Ibid.*, October 27, 1820.

10 Philadelphia *Democratic Press*, November 4, 1820.

11 Harrisburg *Republican*, November 10, 1820; Philadelphia *Franklin Gazette*, November 8, 15, 1820.

electoral returns from all the states were canvassed, it was found that only one elector—former Governor Plumer of New Hampshire—had voted against Monroe.[12]

In general the hope of the Anti-Missourians was not that Monroe would be defeated in 1820 but that there would be no more Presidents from the slave states after the expiration of his second term. A writer in a Newark newspaper summed up the sentiments of a multitude of Northerners when he predicted that the Missouri question would eventuate "in the exclusion, after the present wearisome and threadbare presidential incumbent retires from office, of all slave presidents and slave cabinets from the councils of the nation."[13] If Monroe had retired in 1821 instead of 1825, Missouri slavery would probably have been the main issue in the presidential election of 1820. It was widely assumed that it would be the main issue in 1824, and with some of the voters, it was. According to Jabez D. Hammond, the historian of New York politics, many Northern Democrats voted for John Quincy Adams partly because they were tired of defending themselves against the accusation of supporting Southern men for the presidency.[14] Nevertheless, for every voter who was influenced by the Missouri Controversy in casting his ballot in 1824, there were many more who were not. The years between 1820 and 1824 had erased the controversy from the minds of most men and replaced it with issues like "King Caucus" which, at the moment, seemed more vital. In Ohio, where the Adams supporters attempted unsuccessfully to make a major issue out of slavery even in the final phase of the election of 1824, no less an Anti-Missourian than James Wilson, editor of the Steubenville *Western Herald,* finally gave his support to Henry Clay, a slaveholder. Wilson explained

[12] Plumer opposed Monroe because he believed that the latter had shown "a want of foresight & economy." William Plumer to William Plumer, Jr., January 8, 1821, Plumer Papers; Charles O. Paullin, "The Electoral Vote for John Quincy Adams in 1820," in *American Historical Review,* XXI (1916), 318-19; William Plumer, Jr., *Life of William Plumer* (Boston, 1857), 493-95.

[13] Newark *Centinel of Freedom,* September 26, 1820.

[14] Hammond, *History of Political Parties in New-York,* II, 127.

that he had hoped that the Missouri question would have a strong effect upon the election. As such had not been the case, he was now prompted to vote for Clay by closer and more important interests.[15]

So soon as the Missouri Controversy had subsided, the public was happy to forget it for a season, and its immediate effect upon political parties was not great. Its significance lay rather in what it clarified and foreshadowed. It was an epitome of the entire sectional controversy before 1860, containing all of the important elements of previous and future antagonisms. There was little about it that was original, since there was scarcely one strand in its whole texture whose origin cannot be traced back to an earlier day. Yet its clarifying effects were not only great but appalling, and it was these which startled thoughtful men in 1820.

In short, the Missouri Controversy was the first occasion on which all of the strands in the fabric of North-South sectionalism were brought together and paraded before the public in magnitudinous proportions. This was the first full-scale dress rehearsal (with nothing omitted) for the great sectional contest which was to dominate the last two decades of the ante bellum era. The westward expansion of slavery was an issue upon which a united North could be arrayed against a united South and one far more to be dreaded than the Hartford Convention, which only represented a segment of Northern opinion. It was not necessary for farsighted men like Jefferson and John Quincy Adams to live until 1860 to know what the future held in store. The events of the forties, fifties, and sixties were unmistakably foreshadowed in the clarification of sectional issues wrought by the Missouri Controversy. Here, clearly, was the "knell of the Union," the "title-page to a great tragic volume."

As has been shown in preceding pages, it would be difficult to name a single item in the twenty-year fracas before the Civil War that did not have its precedent or counterpart in the contest over Missouri. Abolitionism and fire-eating, gradualism

---

[15] Eugene H. Roseboom, "Ohio in the Presidential Election of 1824," in *Ohio Archaeological and Historical Quarterly*, XXVI (1917), 161-62, 193-94.

and immediatism, secession, the higher law, squatter sover-eignty, bleeding Kansas, the Kansas-Nebraska Act, the idea of redressing the balance of power by means of a sectional poli-tical party—all these were present in 1819-1821. The Feder-alist and Clintonian philanthropists of the Missouri Controversy were the spiritual forebears of the abolitionists of a later day. As in the case of Lewis Tappan and William Lloyd Garrison, many of the later abolitionists were ex-Federalists or of Feder-alist descent, and the abolitionist movement was always spear-headed by middle and upper class humanitarians and politicians rather than by proletarians and labor unions.[16] The motives of the Anti-Missourians, like those of the Republicans and aboli-tionists three decades afterward, were partly humanitarian, partly political, and partly economic. In the absence of exact measuring instruments for computing human emotions, it is im-possible to determine the relative weights of these factors.

Clearly foreshadowed by the events of 1819-1821 was the manner in which the question of slavery expansion would later, by entwining itself with international relations, lead to endless complications. The ratification of the Adams-Onís Treaty, by which the United States acquired Florida but re-linquished its claim to Texas, took place contemporaneously with Missouri's admission and was inevitably affected by the slavery debates. John Quincy Adams stated in his diary that the Missouri question prejudiced every section of the nation against the treaty, the North dreading the acquisition of addi-tional slave territory in the form of Florida and the South and West being unwilling to part with Texas, since they wanted all the land to the Rio Grande for more slave states.[17]

In the North there were indeed misgivings over the Spanish cession of Florida. Robert Walsh's Philadelphia *Gazette* re-marked that the desire of the free states to secure the Floridas

[16] If the abolitionists had based their appeal on the solidarity of labor, ir-respective of color, this "might have made the anti-slavery movement more of a mass agitation and less of one led by intellectuals and kind-hearted philan-thropists." Williston H. Lofton, "Abolition and Labor," in *Journal of Negro History*, XXXIII (1948), 261.

[17] Adams, *Memoirs of J. Q. Adams*, V, 53.

must suffer considerable abatement upon the reflection that there would be no restriction of slavery in those provinces.[18] The Richmond *Enquirer* reported early in 1821 that Northern members of Congress would attempt to annex Florida to Georgia and Alabama in order to avoid the erection of another slave commonwealth within the Union.[19] About a year later Congress was buzzing with the rumor—backed up by a memorial from the American Convention for Promoting the Abolition of Slavery which actually made a request to that effect— that slavery restriction would be agitated again when it came time to organize a government for Florida.[20]

Meanwhile, as Adams had correctly stated, some Southerners frowned upon the Adams-Onís Treaty because it abandoned the American claim to Texas. "The Western politicians," wrote Senator John Walker of Alabama, "look with more solicitude to Texas since the agitation of the odious Missouri question."[21] Immediately after the adoption of the compromise of 1820, the Richmond *Enquirer* asserted that now the South and West "owe it to themselves, to keep their eye firmly fixed on Texas. If we are cooped up on the north, we must have elbow room to the west."[22] In condemning the Adams-Onís Treaty because of its relinquishment of Texas, the Frankfort, Kentucky, *Argus of Western America* contended that "the West and South have . . . motives for the retention of that territory. It is necessary to maintain the balance between the north and the south, to preserve for the slave holding states their due portion of poli-

18 Philadelphia *National Gazette and Literary Register*, April 5, 1820.
19 Richmond *Enquirer*, February 3, 1821.
20 Henry R. Warfield to Henry Clay, December 18, 1821, Clay Papers; *Minutes of the Seventeenth Session of the American Convention for Promoting the Abolition of Slavery*, 46-48; Edward Needles, *An Historical Memoir of the Pennsylvania Society, for Promoting the Abolition of Slavery* (Philadelphia, 1848), 72. Former Governor Plumer of New Hampshire wrote, regarding the acquisition of Florida: "We have too much territory to covet more. We have too many slave States to seek for land over which slavery will be further extended." William Plumer to William Plumer, Jr., March 27, 1820, Plumer Papers.
21 John W. Walker to Charles Tait, January 28, 1821, Tait Papers.
22 Richmond *Enquirer*, March 7, 1820.

tical power and afford a vent to their surplus population."[23] John Randolph denounced the treaty on the ground that it sacrificed a vast amount of territory "south of thirty-six and a half of north latitude."[24] One of Missouri's senators, apparently David Barton, considered the treaty "a twin brother to the opposition to Missouri," since it surrendered enough of the Southern border country to form several slave states at some future day.[25]

On the other hand, there were Northerners like Rufus King who opposed the acquisition of Texas for fear that it would increase the political power of the South.[26] Adams could probably have secured part or all of Texas for the United States if he had insisted upon it in the negotiations with Onís, but President Monroe did not encourage him to do so.[27] Adams and Onís placed their signatures on the treaty in February, 1819, about one week after Tallmadge presented his famous amendment to the Missouri bill. A year later Monroe wrote Andrew Jackson that, "Having long known the repugnance, with which the Eastern portion of our Union, . . . have seen its aggrandizement to the West, and South, I have been decidedly of opinion, that we ought to be content with Florida, for the present, and until the public opinion, in that quarter, shall be reconciled to any further change." The Missouri dispute made

[23] Frankfort *Argus of Western America*, March 9, December 7, 1820.

[24] *Annals of Congress*, 17 Cong., 1 Sess., 1248.

[25] Hodder, "Missouri Compromises," 158. See also Benton, *Thirty Years' View*, I, 14-15; [Darlington], *Desultory Remarks on the Question of Extending Slavery*, 35. In spite of the fact that some Southerners wished to use Texas as a means of preserving the sectional equilibrium, the colonization of the province by American immigrants was a normal frontier movement and not a slaveholders' "conspiracy." On this point, see Eugene C. Barker, "Notes on the Colonization of Texas," in *Southwestern Historical Quarterly*, XXVII (1923), 117-19; Chauncey S. Boucher, "In Re That Aggressive Slavocracy," in *Mississippi Valley Historical Review*, VIII (1921), 21-24. While the main thesis of Barker and Boucher is correct, they underestimate the sectional motive that prompted many Southerners to advocate the annexation of Texas in 1819-1821.

[26] King, *Rufus King*, VI, 289-90; *Poulson's American Daily Advertiser* (Philadelphia), April 15, 1820.

[27] Samuel F. Bemis, *John Quincy Adams and the Foundations of American Foreign Policy* (New York, 1949), 339-40.

Monroe more willing to renounce Texas; for, as he pointed out to Jackson, the country was now confronted with internal difficulties which did not exist before.[28]

John Quincy Adams, though he had himself negotiated the treaty, stated privately in 1820 that he was unwilling to have either Texas or Florida annexed to the United States except with the understanding that they should be free of slavery. In a conversation with Senator Ninian Edwards in March, 1820, while the final approval of the treaty was still pending, Adams went so far as to declare that if he were a member of Congress he would offer resolutions to the effect that the treaty ought not now to be ratified without an article prohibiting slavery in the territory to be acquired. He added that he had been expecting one of the Northern congressmen to present such a resolution.[29] Adams' antislavery proposal was important, not because of any likelihod that it would be adopted, but because it foreshadowed and so closely resembled the Wilmot Proviso of the Mexican War period.

While the Missouri Controversy was thus clearly marking out the lines of the future Northern attack against slavery expansion, it was, at the same time, doing much to clarify the South's attitude toward the "peculiar institution." As has already been shown, the Southerners who opposed the Missouri restriction in 1819-1821 can be divided into three groups: (1) those who were sincerely antislavery but regarded immediate abolition or congressional restriction as unwise; (2) those who would have liked to defend slavery per se but did not yet dare to; and (3) those (mostly Georgians and South Carolinians) who openly defended slavery as a positive good. The second group was a large and important one and held the key to the South's future. It was to the people of this group that John Quincy Adams was referring when he wrote in his diary that "The discussion of this Missouri question has betrayed the secret of their souls. In the abstract they admit that

28 James Monroe to Andrew Jackson, May 23, 1820, Monroe Papers, Library of Congress.
29 Adams, *Memoirs of J. Q. Adams*, V, 54.

slavery is an evil. . . . But when probed to the quick upon it, they show at the bottom of their souls pride and vainglory in their condition of masterdom."[30] The editor of the Georgetown, D. C., *Metropolitan* was typical of those who made up the second group. The *Metropolitan* admitted (as it was fashionable for educated Southerners to do in 1820) that slavery was "a curse," and it wished "to God that some Moses would lead them [Negroes] out of the 'house of bondage to the promised land.'" So far so good. No abolitionist could have done any better! But then, as if frightened by its own rashness, the *Metropolitan* hastened to add: "That our slaves are ill treated, no man who has ever looked around him will assert. See them in their quarters—See them in the interior of Louisiana—see them in the town of Orleans, assembled on the levee, after their work is done, and a sad face among a groupe of negroes will be found as rare, as courteous language in the London Courier towards this country—the Violin and Bandjeau are ever in tune, and tripping it lightly to the air of their favorite song '*Massa, Misses, kill a duck,*' they are more heedless of the morrow than . . . ourselves."[31]

To swing the mass of Southern public opinion into the proslavery column it was necessary first of all to push the waverers —those who conceded that slavery was evil but did so reluctantly and in some cases hypocritically—into the arms of the ultras who were already defending it as a positive good. The dispute over Missouri certainly helped to accomplish this, thus bearing out the contention of a Kentucky newspaper that, instead of promoting the cause of emancipation, the attempted restriction would protract the existence of slavery.[32] John Randolph of Roanoke sensed such a tendency when he wrote: "These Yankees have almost reconciled me to negro slavery. They have produced a revulsion even on my mind, what then must the effect be on those who had no scruples on the subject."[33]

[30] *Ibid.*, 10-11.   [31] Georgetown *Metropolitan*, February 15, 1820.
[32] Lexington *Western Monitor*, March 20, 1821.
[33] Garland, *John Randolph*, II, 133.

The Missouri Controversy marked the end of the liberal phase of ante bellum Southern history, during which the thinking of Southern statesmen had been dominated by the philosophy of the Age of Enlightenment, even though that philosophy had not always been put into practice.[34] From 1820 to 1835 there was a transitional period, followed by the two and a half orthodox and proslavery decades that preceded the Civil War. Between 1820 and 1860 the definitive defense of slavery was formulated (mainly by rehashing old arguments) and was gradually accepted by most of the Southern people. Increased profits from cotton, Northern criticism of Southern institutions, and the fear of slave revolts are generally cited as the factors which produced Southern unanimity in defense of slavery. The Missouri Controversy provided the first large-scale Northern assault against the territorial expansion of slavery, accompanied by vigorous Northern condemnation of the Southern way of life. This was followed in 1822 by the abortive Vesey insurrection in the South Carolina low country.

Stimulated by the course of events, South Carolinians in the 1820's worked out a comprehensive defense of slavery. There was never a time when some Southerners did not attempt to justify Negro bondage, but the intensive defense of the institution was launched by Senator William Smith of South Carolina in his addresses on the Missouri question.[35] These were augmented, between 1822 and 1826, by the proslavery writings of such South Carolinians as Edwin C. Holland, Frederick Dalcho, Richard Furman, Whitemarsh B. Seabrook, Edward Brown, and Thomas Cooper.[36] Though the influence exerted by the Vesey

[34] For a discussion and evaluation of the liberal period of Southern history, see Eaton, *Freedom of Thought in the Old South*, 3-31; Virginius Dabney, *Liberalism in the South* (Chapel Hill, 1932), 1-23; Niels H. Sonne, *Liberal Kentucky 1780-1828* (New York, 1939), 1-45.

[35] *Annals of Congress*, 16 Cong., 1 Sess., 266-75; Avery Craven, *The Coming of the Civil War* (New York, 1942), 155; Jenkins, *Pro-Slavery Thought in the Old South*, 66, 71.

[36] For a summary of the proslavery argument of the 1820's, see Craven, *The Coming of the Civil War*, 155-59; Jenkins, *Pro-Slavery Thought in the Old South*, 71-77.

insurrection overshadowed everything else in the proslavery tracts of the 1820's, the effect of the Missouri Controversy was also in evidence. Edwin Holland's brochure of 1822 contained a number of references to the controversy and quoted Senator Smith's remarks on that occasion.[37] Whitemarsh Seabrook's pamphlet quoted the Missouri debates and asked significantly: "Did not the unreflecting zeal of the North and East, and the injudicious speeches on the Missouri question animate Vesey in his hellish efforts?"[38] The essays of Edward Brown and Thomas Cooper further reflected the influence of the Missouri debates.[39] Formerly an antislavery man, Cooper had published an article in defense of slavery, in connection with the Missouri restriction, in a Pennsylvania newspaper in 1819. While not yet willing to admit that he favored the abstract principle of human bondage, Cooper maintained in 1819 that the latter was defensible by the law of nature, the law of God, and the municipal statutes of most civilized nations. He also contended that slaves were property, that Negroes had no right to object to slavery, that Congress did not have the power to enact the proposed Missouri restriction, and that under present circumstances it was not expedient to do so.[40] By 1826 Cooper was ready to go all lengths to justify the "peculiar institution" of his adopted state, and by the close of the decade South Carolinians had left no stone unturned in preparing their defense arguments. After 1831, thanks to the Garrisonian blast and events in Virginia, the citizens of other Southern states would come to their assistance.

[37] [Edwin C. Holland], *A Refutation of the Calumnies Circulated Against The Southern & Western States, Respecting the Institution and Existence of Slavery Among Them* (Charleston, 1822).

[38] Whitemarsh B. Seabrook, *A Concise View of the Critical Situation, and Future Prospects of the Slave-Holding States, in Relation to Their Coloured Population* (Charleston, 1825), 14.

[39] Edward Brown, *Notes on the Origin and Necessity of Slavery* (Charleston, 1826), 40-42; Thomas Cooper, *Two Essays: 1. on the Foundation of Civil Government: 2. on the Constitution of the United States* (Columbia, S. C., 1826), 44-46.

[40] Philadelphia *Democratic Press*, December 22, 1819, January 6, 1820. Cooper wrote the article in the *Press* signed "T. C."

If the contest over Missouri foreshadowed the sectional tension of the forties and fifties, it also provided a formula by which this tension might be kept under control. The Missouri Compromise was probably the most satisfactory solution of a difficult problem that could have been devised at the time and under the circumstances. It set definite legal limits to the expansion of slavery while at the same time placing a reasonable amount of western territory at the disposal of the slaveholding portion of the population. One cannot but be impressed, moreover, by the inevitability of the compromise. The plains of Kansas and Nebraska could not have supported a plantation economy, and Congress, in prohibiting slavery in the territories north of 36° 30', was merely placing its stamp of approval upon the laws of nature.[41] On the other hand, only a civil war or the dissolution of the Union could have prevented the erection of a slave state in Missouri, and civil strife and disunion most Americans did not want. John Quincy Adams, when asked his opinion of the advisability of a compromise, replied that "the question could be settled no otherwise than by a compromise."[42] In truth it could not have been. Without an arrangement similar to the one actually made, the Union would have disintegrated before the 1820's were half over. As for solving the problem by force, as was done in 1861-1865, that was out of the question, since the free states did not have the strength and resources for such an undertaking in 1820. Neither did they possess the necessary internal unity. It was the party of Jefferson, not Lincoln, which ruled the nation. Northern Democrats, mistrustful of the antislavery motives of Federalists and Clintonians and naturally inclined to compromise with the South, could not possibly have worn in the 1820's the mantle that Lincoln assumed in the sixties.

Had the compromise line of 36° 30' been preserved inviolate in later decades and extended to the Pacific as the frontier expanded, it would almost certainly have held the nation to-

[41] Charles W. Ramsdell, "The Natural Limits of Slavery Expansion," in *Mississippi Valley Historical Review*, XVI (1929), 161-62.
[42] Adams, *Memoirs of J. Q. Adams*, IV, 530.

gether until such time as the South, yielding to the humanitarian spirit of the age and the inexorable decree of economic law, should abolish slavery of its own volition. The compromise remained in effect for thirty-four years. Though outflanked by the acquisition of Texas and the Mexican War, it continued until the day of its repeal to be a major factor in preserving the harmony of the Union. Its repeal in 1854 set in motion the chain of events which culminated in the Civil War and was easily the second greatest tragedy in American history, the greatest being the original introduction of slavery among a people who were, in other respects, democratically inclined.

BIBLIOGRAPHY

Manuscript Correspondence

James Barbour Papers, New York Public Library
Nicholas Biddle Papers, Library of Congress
Elias Boudinot Papers, Princeton University
Breckinridge Family Papers, Library of Congress
Henry Clay Papers, Library of Congress
De Witt Clinton Papers, Columbia University
Edward Coles Papers, Chicago Historical Society
John J. Crittenden Papers, Library of Congress
William Darlington Papers, Library of Congress
William Darlington Papers, New-York Historical Society
William Dillwyn, Samuel Emlen, and Susanna Emlen Papers,
 Ridgway Branch Library, Philadelphia
Ninian Edwards Papers, Chicago Historical Society
William Eustis Papers, Library of Congress
Gideon and Francis Granger Papers, Library of Congress
Bolling Hall Papers, Alabama Department of Archives and History
David Holmes Papers, Governor's Correspondence, Series E, No. 2,
 Mississippi Department of Archives and History
John Holmes Papers, Maine Historical Society
Joseph Hopkinson Papers, Historical Society of Pennsylvania
David Hosack Papers, New-York Historical Society
Rufus King Papers, New-York Historical Society
William King Papers, Maine Historical Society
William Lowndes Papers, Library of Congress
John B. C. Lucas Papers, Missouri Historical Society
James Monroe Papers, Library of Congress
James Monroe Papers, New York Public Library
Hugh Nelson Papers, Library of Congress
Timothy Pickering Papers, Massachusetts Historical Society
William Plumer Papers, Library of Congress
George Poindexter Papers, Governor's Correspondence, Series E,
 No. 4, Mississippi Department of Archives and History

John Randolph–James M. Garnett Correspondence, manuscript
    transcript, Library of Congress
Thomas and Caesar A. Rodney Papers, Library of Congress
John Sergeant Papers, Historical Society of Pennsylvania
Charles Tait Papers, Alabama Department of Archives and History
Tallmadge Family Papers, New-York Historical Society
Benjamin Tappan Pappers, Library of Congress
John W. Taylor Papers, New-York Historical Society
Jesse B. Thomas Papers, Illinois State Historical Library
William Tudor Papers, Massachusetts Historical Society
Martin Van Buren Papers, Library of Congress
Roberts Vaux Papers, Historical Society of Pennsylvania
John W. Walker Papers, Alabama Department of Archives and
    History

Other Manuscript Material

"Manumission Society New York City—Minutes July 15, 1817–Jan.
    11, 1842," New-York Historical Society
Memorials and petitions of state legislatures and public meetings
    regarding the Missouri Controversy, National Archives, Legisla-
    tive Division
Street, Joseph M., Notice of runaway Negro named London, Shaw-
    neetown, Illinois, August 15, 1820, Chicago Historical Society

Newspapers and Magazines

(Dates are for the period of the Missouri Controversy unless
otherwise specified)

ALABAMA:
Huntsville *Alabama Republican*
The Halcyon, And Tombeckbe Public Advertiser (St. Stephens)

CONNECTICUT:
Hartford *American Mercury*
Hartford *Connecticut Courant*
The Times, and Weekly Advertiser (Hartford)
New Haven *Columbian Register*
The Connecticut Journal (New Haven)
The Republican Advocate (New London)

DELAWARE:

Wilmington *American Watchman*
Wilmington *Delaware Gazette*

DISTRICT OF COLUMBIA:

The Metropolitan (Georgetown)
Georgetown *National Messenger*
City of Washington Gazette (later called *Washington Gazette*)
Washington *Daily National Intelligencer*
The National Register (Washington)

GEORGIA:

Augusta Chronicle & Georgia Gazette
Milledgeville *Georgia Journal*
Savannah Daily Republican

ILLINOIS:

Edwardsville Spectator
The Illinois Intelligencer (Kaskaskia)
The Illinois Gazette (Shawneetown)

INDIANA:

Brookville Enquirer
Vincennes *Indiana Centinel*
Vincennes *Western Sun & General Advertiser*

KENTUCKY:

Frankfort *Argus of Western America*
The Commentator (Frankfort)
Lexington *Kentucky Gazette*
Lexington *Western Monitor*
Louisville Public Advertiser

LOUISIANA:

New Orleans *Orleans Gazette and Commercial Advertiser* (Country
Edition)

MAINE:

The Eastern Argus (Portland)
The Portland Gazette

MARYLAND:

Baltimore *American & Commercial Daily Advertiser*
Baltimore Patriot & Mercantile Advertiser
Niles' Weekly Register (Baltimore)

MASSACHUSETTS:

Boston Commercial Gazette
Boston Daily Advertiser
Boston Intelligencer & Evening Gazette
Boston Patriot & Daily Mercantile Advertiser
Boston Yankee
Boston *Columbian Centinel*
Boston *New-England Palladium & Commercial Advertiser*
Pittsfield Sun
Salem *Essex Register*
The Salem Gazette
Stockbridge *Berkshire Star*
Worcester *National Aegis*
Thomas's Massachusetts Spy, or Worcester Gazette

MICHIGAN:

Detroit Gazette

MISSISSIPPI:

Natchez *Mississippi Republican*
The Mississippi State Gazette (Natchez)

MISSOURI:

Jackson *Missouri Herald*
The Missourian (St. Charles)
St. Louis *Missouri Gazette & Public Advertiser*
St. Louis Enquirer

NEW HAMPSHIRE:

Concord Observer
Concord *New-Hampshire Patriot & State Gazette*
Keene *Newhampshire Sentinel*
Portsmouth *New-Hampshire Gazette*
The Portsmouth Oracle

NEW JERSEY:

The Burlington Mirror (Mount Holly)
The Centinel of Freedom (Newark)

The Fredonian (New Brunswick)
The True American (Trenton)

NEW YORK:

The Albany Argus
The Albany Register
The New-York Statesman (Albany)
Canandaigua *Ontario Messenger*
Newburgh *Political Index*
The American (New York)
New York *Commercial Advertiser*
The National Advocate (New York)
The New-York Columbian
New-York Daily Advertiser
The New-York Evening Post
New-York Gazette & General Advertiser
Poughkeepsie *Dutchess Observer*

NORTH CAROLINA:

New Bern *Carolina Centinel*
Raleigh Register, and North-Carolina Gazette

OHIO:

Chillicothe *Scioto Gazette, and Fredonian Chronicle*
Cincinnati Inquisitor Advertiser
Liberty Hall and Cincinnati Gazette
Western Spy, and Cincinnati General Advertiser
The Crisis (Columbus), issue of December 14, 1864
Cleaveland Herald
Mount Pleasant *Genius of Universal Emancipation*
The Philanthropist (Mount Pleasant)
Western Herald & Steubenville Gazette

PENNSYLVANIA:

The Carlisle Republican
Harrisburg Chronicle
Harrisburg Republican
Philadelphia *Aurora*
The Democratic Press (Philadelphia)
Philadelphia *Franklin Gazette*
The Friend (Philadelphia), issues of August 23, 1828, and April 2,
   1836

The National Gazette and Literary Register (Philadelphia)
Poulson's American Daily Advertiser (Philadelphia)
The Union (Philadelphia)
The Pittsburgh Gazette
The Statesman (Pittsburgh)
West Chester *Village Record*

RHODE ISLAND:

Newport Mercury
Newport *Rhode-Island Republican*
Providence Gazette
Providence Patriot
Providence *Rhode-Island American, And General Advertiser*

SOUTH CAROLINA:

The Charleston Courier
Charleston *City Gazette And Commercial Daily Advertiser*
Charleston *Southern Patriot, And Commercial Advertiser*

TENNESSEE:

Clarksville Gazette
The Emancipator (Jonesboro); all quotations from *The Emancipator* in this monograph are taken from Elihu Embree, *The Emancipator (Complete)*, Reprint, Nashville, B. H. Murphy, 1932
Knoxville Register
The Clarion, and Tennessee Gazette (later called *The Nashville Clarion*)
The Nashville Whig

VERMONT:

Middlebury *National Standard*
Windsor *Vermont Republican & American Yeoman*

VIRGINIA:

The Independent Virginian (Clarksburg)
Clarksburg *Republican Compiler*
The Virginia Herald (Fredericksburg)
The Norfolk and Portsmouth Herald
Richmond Enquirer
Warrenton *Palladium of Liberty*

Pamphlets, Memorials, Circulars, and Contemporary Magazine Articles

Bell, Samuel, *Message From His Excellency the Governor, Communicating Sundry Resolutions of the Legislature of Virginia on the Missouri Question,* n.p., 1820

[Blunt, Joseph], *An Examination of the Expediency and Constitutionality of Prohibiting Slavery in the State of Missouri. By Marcus,* New York, C. Wiley & Co., 1819

[Carey, Mathew?], *Considerations on the Impropriety and Inexpediency of Renewing the Missouri Question. By a Pennsylvanian,* Philadelphia, M. Carey & Son, 1820

A Caveat; or Considerations Against the Admission of Missouri, With Slavery, Into the Union, New Haven, A. H. Maltby, 1820

Cummings, Asa, *A Discourse Delivered at Brunswick, (Maine,) April 6, 1820, the Day of the Annual Fast in Maine and Massachusetts,* Brunswick, Joseph Griffin, 1820

[Darlington, William], *Desultory Remarks on the Question of Extending Slavery into Missouri: As Enunciated During the First Session of the Sixteenth Congress, by the Representative from Chester County, State of Pennsylvania,* West Chester (Pa.), Lewis Marshall, 1856

[Everett, Edward?], "Mr. Walsh's Appeal," *The North American Review,* X (1820), 334-71

Hamilton, James, Jr., *An Account of the Late Intended Insurrection Among a Portion of the Blacks of This City. Published by the Authority of the Corporation of Charleston,* Charleston, A. E. Miller, 1822

Hill, Mark L., *Fellow Citizens of the State of Maine,* Washington, 1820

[Hillhouse, William], *The Crisis, No. 1. or Thoughts on Slavery, Occasioned by the Missouri Question,* New Haven, A. H. Maltby, 1820

[_____], *The Crisis, No. 2. or Thoughts on Slavery, Occasioned by the Missouri Question,* New Haven, A. H. Maltby, 1820

[_____], *Pocahontas; A Proclamation: With Plates* [New Haven, J. Clyme, 1820]

Holmes, John, *Mr. Holmes' Letter to the People of Maine,* Washington, 1820

————————; Kinsley, Martin; Hill, Mark L.; Parker, James; Cushman, Joshua; Whitman, Ezekiel, *Representation of the Members of the House of Representatives, from That Part of Massachusetts Hitherto Known as the District of Maine*, Washington, Gales & Seaton, 1820

King, Rufus, *Substance of Two Speeches, Delivered in the Senate of the United States, on the Subject of the Missouri Bill*, New York, Kirk and Mercein, 1819

————————, *The Substance of Two Speeches, Delivered in the Senate of the United States, on the Subject of the Missouri Bill* [Philadelphia, Clark & Raser, 1819]

Kinsley, Martin; Cushman, Joshua; Whitman, Ezekiel; Lincoln, Enoch, *An Address to the People of Maine*, Washington, Davis and Force, 1820

Learned, Joseph D., *A View of the Policy of Permitting Slaves in the States West of the Mississippi: Being a Letter to a Member of Congress*, Baltimore, Joseph Robinson, 1820

Letter to the Edinburgh Reviewers: by "An American." First Published in the National Intelligencer of November 16, 1819, n.p., n.d.

Madison, James, *Jonathan Bull and Mary Bull, An Inedited Manuscript*, Washington, J. C. M'Guire, 1856

Memorial of Sundry Inhabitants of the City of Baltimore. January 10, 1820 (House Documents, 16 Cong., 1 Sess., III, No. 40), Washington, Gales & Seaton, 1820

Memorial of the Citizens of Missouri Territory, St. Louis, S. Hall, n.d.

Memorial of the Legislature of Missouri, for a Division of the Territory, &c., Washington, E. De Krafft, 1818

A Memorial to the Congress of the United States, on the Subject of Restraining the Increase of Slavery in New States to be Admitted into the Union, Boston, Sewell Phelps, 1819

Miner, Charles, *The Olive Branch; or, the Evil and the Remedy*, Philadelphia, T. K. & P. G. Collins, 1856

Papers Relative to the Restriction of Slavery. Speeches of Mr. King, In the Senate, And of Messrs. Taylor & Talmadge, In the House of Representatives, of the United States, On the Bill For Authorising the People of the Territory of Missouri to Form a Constitution And State Government, And For the Admission of the Same

Into the Union. In the Session of 1818-19. With a Report of a Committee of the Abolition Society of Delaware, Philadelphia, Hall & Atkinson, 1819

Preamble and Resolutions on the Subject of the Missouri Question, Agreed to by the House of Delegates of Virginia, and the Amendment of the Senate, Proposed Thereto, Richmond, John Warrock, 1820

Raymond, Daniel, *The Missouri Question,* Baltimore, Schaeffer & Maund, 1819

Scott, John, Mr. *Scott's Speech on the Missouri Question, in the House of Representatives of the United States,* Washington, Davis and Force, 1820

[Shaw, Lemuel], "Slavery and the Missouri Question," *The North American Review,* X (1820), 137-68

Tallmadge, James, *Speech of the Honorable James Tallmadge, Jr. of Duchess County, New-York, in the House of Representatives of the United States, on Slavery. To which is Added, the Proceedings of the Manumission Society of the City of New-York, and the Correspondence of Their Committee with Messrs. Tallmadge and Taylor,* New York, E. Conrad, 1819

To the Honorable Senate, and the House of Representatives, of the Commonwealth of Massachusetts, in General Court Assembled, n.p. [1820]

[Walsh, Robert], *Free Remarks on the Spirit of the Federal Constitution, the Practice of the Federal Government, and the Obligations of the Union, Respecting the Exclusion of Slavery from the Territories and New States. By a Philadelphian,* Philadelphia, A. Finley, 1819

Wheaton, Josephus, *The Equality of Mankind and the Evils of Slavery, Illustrated: A Sermon, Delivered on the Day of the Annual Fast, April 6, 1820,* Boston, Samuel T. Armstrong, 1820

Wright, John, *A Refutation of the Sophisms, Gross Misrepresentations, and Erroneous Quotations Contained in 'An American's' 'Letter to the Edinburgh Reviewers,'* Washington, the Author, 1820

Documents

In addition to the *American State Papers, Annals of Congress, Congressional Globe,* House and Senate *Journals, Journals of the*

Continental Congress, and *Statutes at Large,* these were used:

Carter, Clarence E. (ed.), *The Territorial Papers of the United States,* 18 vols. to date, Washington, Government Printing Office, 1934–

Catterall, Helen T. (ed.), *Judicial Cases Concerning American Slavery and the Negro,* 5 vols., Washington, Carnegie Institution, 1926-1937

Clarke, L. H. (ed.), *A Report of the Debates and Proceedings of the Convention of the State of New-York; Held at the Capitol, in the City of Albany, on the 28th Day of August, 1821,* New York, J. Seymour, 1821

Constitution of the New-Jersey Society for the Suppression of Vice and Immorality, and for the Encouragement of Virtue and Good Morals, New Brunswick, W. Myer, 1818

Constitution of the State of Missouri, St. Louis, I. N. Henry, 1820

Donnan, Elizabeth (ed.), *Documents Illustrative of the History of the Slave Trade to America,* 4 vols., Washington, Carnegie Institution, 1930-1935

Harrison, James L. (ed.), *Biographical Directory of the American Congress 1774-1949,* Washington, Government Printing Office, 1950

Hurd, John C., *The Law of Freedom and Bondage in the United States,* 2 vols., Boston, Little, Brown, 1858-1862

Journal of the Missouri State Convention, St. Louis, I. N. Henry, 1820

Journal of the Thirtieth House of Representatives of the Commonwealth of Pennsylvania, Harrisburg, James Peacock, 1819-1820

Laws of the State of Missouri, Passed at the First Session of the Fourteenth General Assembly, Jefferson City, James Lusk, 1847

Miller, Hunter (ed.), *Treaties and Other International Acts of the United States of America,* 8 vols. to date, Washington, Government Printing Office, 1931–

Minutes of the Proceedings of a Special Meeting of the Fifteenth American Convention for Promoting the Abolition of Slavery, and Improving the Condition of the African Race, Assembled at Philadelphia, on the Tenth Day of December, 1818, and Continued by Adjournments until the Fifteenth of the Same Month, Inclusive, Philadelphia, Hall & Atkinson, 1818

Minutes of the Sixteenth American Convention for Promoting the Abolition of Slavery, and Improving the Condition of the African

Race. Held at Philadelphia, on the Fifth of October, and the Tenth of November, 1819, Philadelphia, William Fry, 1819

Minutes of the Seventeenth Session of the American Convention for Promoting the Abolition of Slavery, and Improving the Condition of the African Race. Convened at Philadelphia, On the third day of October, 1821, Philadelphia, Atkinson & Alexander, 1821

Norton, Margaret C. (ed.), Illinois Census Returns 1820, Springfield, Illinois State Historical Library, 1934

Pease, Theodore C. (ed.), Illinois Election Returns 1818-1848, Springfield, Illinois State Historical Library, 1923

Potter, David M., and Manning, Thomas G., Nationalism and Sectionalism in America 1775-1877, New York, Henry Holt, 1949

Richardson, James D. (ed.), A Compilation of the Messages and Papers of the Presidents 1789-1907, 11 vols., New York, Bureau of National Literature and Art, 1908

The Seventh Census of the United States: 1850, Washington, Robert Armstrong, 1853

Other Printed Source Material

Adams, Charles F. (ed.), Memoirs of John Quincy Adams, Comprising Portions of His Diary from 1795 to 1848, 12 vols., Philadelphia, Lippincott, 1874-1877

Barck, Dorothy C. (ed.), Letters from John Pintard to His Daughter Eliza Noel Pintard Davidson 1816-1833, 4 vols., New York, New-York Historical Society, 1940-1941

Bassett, John S. (ed.), Correspondence of Andrew Jackson, 7 vols., Washington, Carnegie Institution, 1926-1935

Benton, Thomas H., Thirty Years' View, 2 vols., New York, Appleton, 1854-1856

Bonney, Mrs. Catharina V. R., A Legacy of Historical Gleanings, 2 vols., Albany, J. Munsell, 1875

Boucher, Chauncey S., and Brooks, Robert P. (eds.), "Correspondence Addressed to John C. Calhoun 1837-1849," in Annual Report of the American Historical Association for the Year 1929, Washington, Government Printing Office, 1930, pp. 125-533

Brown, Everett S. (ed.), The Missouri Compromises and Presidential Politics 1820-1825 from the Letters of William Plumer, Junior, St. Louis, Missouri Historical Society, 1926

_____, "The Senate Debate on the Breckinridge Bill for the Government of Louisiana, 1804," The American Historical Review, XXII (1917), 340-64

Burnett, Edmund C. (ed.), *Letters of Members of the Continental Congress*, 8 vols., Washington, Carnegie Institution, 1921-1936

Cabell, Nathaniel F. (ed.), *Early History of the University of Virginia, as Contained in the Letters of Thomas Jefferson and Joseph C. Cabell*, Richmond, J. W. Randolph, 1856

Coleman, Mrs. Chapman (ed.), *The Life of John J. Crittenden*, 2 vols., Philadelphia, Lippincott, 1871

Colton, Calvin (ed.), *The Private Correspondence of Henry Clay*, New York, A. S. Barnes, 1855

Darby, John F., *Personal Recollections of Many Prominent People Whom I Have Known*, St. Louis, G. I. Jones, 1880

Dix, Morgan (ed.), *Memoirs of John Adams Dix*, 2 vols., New York, Harper, 1883

Faux, William, *Memorable Days in America: Being a Journal of a Tour to the United States*, London, W. Simpkin and R. Marshall, 1823

Fitzpatrick, John C. (ed.), *The Autobiography of Martin Van Buren*, in *Annual Report of the American Historical Association for the Year 1918*, II, Washington, Government Printing Office, 1920

Flint, Timothy, *Recollections of the Last Ten Years*, Boston, Cummings, Hilliard, 1826

Ford, Paul L. (ed.), *The Writings of Thomas Jefferson*, 10 vols., New York, Putnam's, 1892-1899

Ford, Worthington C. (ed.), *Writings of John Quincy Adams*, 7 vols., New York, Macmillan, 1913-1917

Goodrich, Samuel G., *Recollections of a Lifetime*, 2 vols., New York, Miller, Orton and Mulligan, 1856

Hamilton, Stanislaus M. (ed.), *The Writings of James Monroe*, 7 vols., New York, Putnam's, 1898-1903

Hammond, Jabez D., *The History of Political Parties in the State of New-York*, 2 vols., Albany, C. Van Benthuysen, 1842

Hillard, George S., *Memoir and Correspondence of Jeremiah Mason*, Cambridge, Riverside Press, 1873

Hunt, Gaillard (ed.), *Disunion Sentiment in Congress in 1794—a Confidential Memorandum Hitherto Unpublished Written by John Taylor of Caroline Senator from Virginia for James Madison*, Washington, W. H. Lowdermilk, 1905

Jameson, J. Franklin (ed.), *Correspondence of John C. Calhoun*, in *Annual Report of the American Historical Association for the Year 1899*, II, Washington, Government Printing Office, 1900

Johnston, Henry P. (ed.), *The Correspondence and Public Papers of John Jay*, 4 vols., New York, Putnam's, 1890-1893

King, Charles R. (ed.), *The Life and Correspondence of Rufus King*, 6 vols., New York, Putnam's, 1894-1900

"Letters of Spencer Roane, 1788-1822," *Bulletin of the New York Public Library*, X (1906), 167-80

Mansfield, Edward D., *Personal Memories Social, Political, and Literary with Sketches of Many Noted People 1803-1843*, Cincinnati, Robert Clarke, 1879

Morison, Samuel E., *The Life and Letters of Harrison Gray Otis Federalist 1765-1848*, 2 vols., Boston, Houghton Mifflin, 1913

"Original Letters," *William and Mary College Quarterly*, XXI (1912), 75-84

Owen, Thomas M. (ed.), "Letters from John C. Calhoun to Charles Tait," *The Gulf States Historical Magazine*, I (1902), 92-104

Raymond, Daniel, *Thoughts on Political Economy*, Baltimore, Fielding Lucas, Jun'r, 1820

Seaton, Josephine, *William Winston Seaton of the "National Intelligencer,"* Boston, James R. Osgood, 1871

Smith, Margaret B., *The First Forty Years of Washington Society* (ed. by Gaillard Hunt), New York, Scribner's, 1906

Sparks, W. H., *The Memories of Fifty Years*, Philadelphia, Claxton, Remsen and Haffelfinger, 1870

Story, William W. (ed.), *Life and Letters of Joseph Story*, 2 vols., Boston, Little and Brown, 1851

Taylor, John, *Construction Construed, and Constitutions Vindicated*, Richmond, Shepherd and Pollard, 1820

Tyler, Lyon G. (ed.), "Missouri Compromise. Letters to James Barbour, Senator of Virginia in the Congress of the United States," *William and Mary College Quarterly*, X (1901), 5-24

Van Tyne, Claude H. (ed.), *The Letters of Daniel Webster*, New York, McClure, Phillips, 1902

Walsh, Robert, Jr., *An Appeal from the Judgments of Great Britain Respecting the United States of America*, Philadelphia, Mitchell, Ames, and White, 1819

Warren, Charles, *Jacobin and Junto or Early American Politics as Viewed in the Diary of Dr. Nathaniel Ames 1758-1822*, Cambridge, Harvard University Press, 1931

Washburne, Elihu B. (ed.), *The Edwards Papers; Being a Portion of the Collection of the Letters, Papers, and Manuscripts of Ninian Edwards*, Chicago, Fergus Printing Co., 1884

Weed, Harriet A., and Barnes, Thurlow W., *Life of Thurlow Weed,* 2 vols., Boston, Houghton Mifflin, 1883-1884

Secondary Works

Adams, Alice D., *The Neglected Period of Anti-Slavery in America (1808-1831),* Boston, Ginn, 1908

Adams, James T., "Disfranchisement of Negroes in New England," *The American Historical Review,* XXX (1925), 543-47

——————, *New England in the Republic 1776-1850,* Boston, Little, Brown, 1926

Alexander, De Alva S., "John W. Taylor, New York's Speaker of the House of Representatives," *The Quarterly Journal of the New York State Historical Association,* I (1920), 14-37

——————, *A Political History of the State of New York,* 3 vols., New York, Henry Holt, 1906-1909

Alvord, Clarence W. (ed.), *Governor Edward Coles,* Springfield, Illinois State Historical Library, 1920

Ambler, Charles H., "Life of John Floyd," *The John P. Branch Historical Papers of Randolph-Macon College,* V (1918), 5-117

——————, *Thomas Ritchie,* Richmond, Bell Book and Stationery Co., 1913

Anderson, Hattie M., "Missouri, 1804-1828: Peopling a Frontier State," *The Missouri Historical Review,* XXXI (1937), 150-80

Aptheker, Herbert, *American Negro Slave Revolts,* New York, Columbia University Press, 1943

Ashe, Samuel A., *History of North Carolina,* 2 vols.: I, Greensboro, Charles L. Van Noppen, 1925; II, Raleigh, Edwards and Broughton, 1925

Babcock, Kendric C., *The Rise of American Nationality 1811-1819 (The American Nation: A History,* XIII), New York, Harper, 1906

Bancroft, Frederic, *Slave-Trading in the Old South,* Baltimore, J. H. Furst, 1931

Barker, Eugene C., "The Influence of Slavery in the Colonization of Texas," *The Mississippi Valley Historical Review,* XI (1924), 3-36

——————, "Notes on the Colonization of Texas," *The Southwestern Historical Quarterly,* XXVII (1923), 108-19

Barnes, Gilbert H., *The Antislavery Impulse 1830-1844,* New York, Appleton-Century, 1933

Barnhart, John D., "The Southern Influence in the Formation of Illinois," *Journal of the Illinois State Historical Society*, XXXII (1939), 358-78

—————, "The Southern Influence in the Formation of Indiana," *Indiana Magazine of History*, XXXIII (1937), 261-76

—————, "The Southern Influence in the Formation of Ohio," *The Journal of Southern History*, III (1937), 28-42

Barrett, Walter (pseud. for Joseph A. Scoville), *The Old Merchants of New York City*, 5 vols., New York, Worthington Co., 1889

Bean, W. G., "Anti-Jeffersonianism in the Ante-Bellum South," *The North Carolina Historical Review*, XII (1935), 103-24

Bemis, Samuel F., *John Quincy Adams and the Foundations of American Foreign Policy*, New York, Knopf, 1949

Beveridge, Albert J., *The Life of John Marshall*, 4 vols., Boston, Houghton Mifflin, 1916-1919

[Bledsoe, A. T.?], "The Missouri Compromise of 1820," *The Southern Review*, III (1868), 346-77

Bobbé, Dorothie, *De Witt Clinton*, New York, Minton, Balch, 1933

Bond, Beverley W., Jr., *The Civilization of the Old Northwest*, New York, Macmillan, 1934

Boucher, Chauncey S., "In Re That Aggressive Slavocracy," *The Mississippi Valley Historical Review*, VIII (1921), 13-79

Bridenbaugh, Carl (ed.), *The Partisan Leader*, by Nathaniel Beverley Tucker, New York, Knopf, 1933

Brigham, Clarence S., *History and Bibliography of American Newspapers 1690-1820*, 2 vols., Worcester, American Antiquarian Society, 1947

Brown, Everett S., *The Constitutional History of the Louisiana Purchase 1803-1812*, Berkeley, University of California Press, 1920

Brush, Edward H., *Rufus King and His Times*, New York, Nicholas L. Brown, 1926

Buley, R. Carlyle, *The Old Northwest Pioneer Period 1815-1840*, 2 vols., Indianapolis, Indiana Historical Society, 1950

Burnett, Edmund C., *The Continental Congress*, New York, Macmillan, 1941

Burns, Josephine E., "Daniel P. Cook," *Journal of the Illinois State Historical Society*, VI (1913), 425-44

Carpenter, Jesse T., *The South as a Conscious Minority 1789-1861*, New York, New York University Press, 1930

Carr, Lucien, "An Error in the Resolution of Congress admitting Missouri into the Union," *Proceedings of the Massachusetts Historical Society*, Second Series, XIII (1900), 448-54

Carroll, Joseph C., *Slave Insurrections in the United States 1800-1865*, Boston, Chapman and Grimes, 1938

Cleaves, Freeman, *Old Tippecanoe, William Henry Harrison and His Time*, New York, Scribner's, 1939

Cooley, Henry S., *A Study of Slavery in New Jersey* (*Johns Hopkins University Studies in Historical and Political Science*, XIV, Nos. 9-10), Baltimore, Johns Hopkins Press, 1896

Coulter, E. Merton, "The Great Savannah Fire of 1820," *The Georgia Historical Quarterly*, XXIII (1939), 1-27

Craven, Avery, *The Coming of the Civil War*, New York, Scribner's, 1942

Cresson, William P., *James Monroe*, Chapel Hill, University of North Carolina Press, 1946

Curti, Merle, *The Growth of American Thought*, New York, Harper, 1943

Dangerfield, George, *The Era of Good Feelings*, New York, Harcourt, Brace, 1952

Dixon, Mrs. Archibald, *The True History of the Missouri Compromise and its Repeal*, Cincinnati, Robert Clarke, 1899

Dodd, William E., "Chief Justice Marshall and Virginia, 1813-1821," *The American Historical Review*, XII (1907), 776-87

Dorsey, Dorothy B., "The Panic of 1819 in Missouri," *The Missouri Historical Review*, XXIX (1935), 79-91

Drake, Thomas E., *Quakers and Slavery in America*, New Haven, Yale University Press, 1950

Du Bois, William E. B., *The Suppression of the African Slave-Trade to the United States of America 1638-1870*, New York, Longmans, Green, 1896

Dumond, Dwight L., *Antislavery Origins of the Civil War in the United States*, Ann Arbor, University of Michigan Press, 1939

Dunn, J. P., Jr., *Indiana A Redemption from Slavery*, Boston, Houghton Mifflin, 1905

Eaton, Clement, *Freedom of Thought in the Old South*, Durham, Duke University Press, 1940

Edwards, Ninian W., *History of Illinois, from 1778 to 1833; and Life and Times of Ninian Edwards*, Springfield, Illinois State Journal Co., 1870

Ellis, James F., *The Influence of Environment on the Settlement of Missouri*, St. Louis, Webster Publishing Co., 1929

Fee, Walter R., *The Transition from Aristocracy to Democracy in New Jersey 1789-1829*, Somerville (N. J.), Somerset Press, 1933

Ferguson, Russell J., *Early Western Pennsylvania Politics*, Pittsburgh, University of Pittsburgh Press, 1938

Ford, Thomas, *A History of Illinois, from its Commencement as a State in 1814 to 1847*, Chicago, S. C. Griggs, 1854

Fowler, William C., *The Sectional Controversy; or, Passages in the Political History of the United States, Including the Causes of the War Between the Sections*, New York, Scribner, 1863

Fox, Dixon R., *The Decline of Aristocracy in the Politics of New York*, New York, Columbia University Press, 1919

————, "The Negro Vote in Old New York," *Political Science Quarterly*, XXXII (1917), 252-75

Fox, Early L., *The American Colonization Society 1817-1840 (Johns Hopkins University Studies in Historical and Political Science*, XXXVII, No. 3), Baltimore, Johns Hopkins Press, 1919

Franklin, John H., *From Slavery to Freedom, a History of American Negroes*, New York, Knopf, 1948

Fuess, Claude M., *Daniel Webster*, 2 vols., Boston, Little, Brown, 1930

Gabriel, Ralph H., *The Course of American Democratic Thought*, New York, Ronald Press, 1940

Garland, Hugh A., *The Life of John Randolph of Roanoke*, 2 vols., New York, Appleton, 1850

Goebel, Dorothy B., *William Henry Harrison A Political Biography*, Indianapolis, Historical Bureau of the Indiana Library and Historical Department, 1926

Goldberg, Isaac, *Major Noah: American-Jewish Pioneer*, Philadelphia, Jewish Publication Society of America, 1936

Greeley, Horace, and Cleveland, John F. (comps.), *A Political Text-Book for 1860*, New York, Tribune Association, 1860

Green, Duff, *Facts and Suggestions Relative to Finance and Currency, Addressed to the President of the Confederate States*, Augusta (Ga.), J. T. Paterson, 1864

Hale, Edward E., *James Russell Lowell and His Friends*, Boston, Houghton Mifflin, 1901

Harris, N. Dwight, *The History of Negro Servitude in Illinois*, Chicago, A. C. McClurg, 1904

Hatch, Louis C. (ed.), *Maine, a History,* 3 vols., New York, American Historical Society, 1919

Henry, Howell M., *The Police Control of the Slave in South Carolina,* Emory (Va.), 1914

Hibben, Paxton, *Henry Ward Beecher,* New York, George H. Doran, 1927

Hinsdale, Burke A., *The Old Northwest The Beginnings of Our Colonial System,* Boston, Silver, Burdett, 1899

Hockett, Homer C., *The Constitutional History of the United States,* 2 vols., New York, Macmillan, 1939

_____, "Rufus King and the Missouri Compromise," *Missouri Historical Review,* II (1908), 211-20

_____, *Western Influences on Political Parties to 1825 (The Ohio State University Bulletin,* XXII, No. 3), Columbus, Ohio State University, 1917

Hodder, Frank H., "Dough-faces," *The Nation,* C (1915), 245

_____, "Side Lights on the Missouri Compromises," in *Annual Report of the American Historical Association for the Year 1909,* Washington, Government Printing Office, 1911, pp. 151-61

Honeywell, Roy J., *The Educational Work of Thomas Jefferson,* Cambridge, Harvard University Press, 1931

Hoss, E. E., *Elihu Embree, Abolitionist (Publications of the Vanderbilt Southern History Society,* No. 2), Nashville, University Press Co., 1897

Houck, Louis, *A History of Missouri from the Earliest Explorations and Settlements until the Admission of the State into the Union,* 3 vols., Chicago, R. R. Donnelley, 1908

Jay, John, *Memorials of Peter A. Jay Compiled for his Descendants,* privately printed, 1929

Jenkins, William S., *Pro-Slavery Thought in the Old South,* Chapel Hill, University of North Carolina Press, 1935

Jensen, Merrill (ed.), *Regionalism in America,* Madison, University of Wisconsin Press, 1951

Jervey, Theodore D., *Robert Y. Hayne and His Times,* New York, Macmillan, 1909

Klein, Philip S., *Pennsylvania Politics 1817-1832,* Philadelphia, Historical Society of Pennsylvania, 1940

Lloyd, Arthur Y., *The Slavery Controversy 1831-1860,* Chapel Hill, University of North Carolina Press, 1939

Lochemes, Sister Mary F., *Robert Walsh: His Story,* New York, American Irish Historical Society, 1941

Locke, Mary S., *Anti-Slavery in America from the Introduction of African Slaves to the Prohibition of the Slave Trade (1619-1808)*, Boston, Ginn, 1901

Lofton, John M., Jr., "Denmark Vesey's Call to Arms," *The Journal of Negro History*, XXXIII (1948), 395-417

Lofton, Williston H., "Abolition and Labor," *The Journal of Negro History*, XXXIII (1948), 249-83

Lynch, William O., "The Influence of Population Movements on Missouri Before 1861," *The Missouri Historical Review*, XVI (1922), 506-16

Martin, Asa E., "Anti-Slavery Activities of the Methodist Episcopal Church in Tennessee," *Tennessee Historical Magazine*, II (1916), 98-109

—————, *The Anti-Slavery Movement in Kentucky Prior to 1850* (*Filson Club Publication*, No. 29), Louisville, Standard Printing Co., 1918

—————, "Pioneer Anti-Slavery Press," *The Mississippi Valley Historical Review*, II (1916), 509-28

McCormick, Richard P., *Experiment in Independence New Jersey in the Critical Period 1781-1789*, New Brunswick, Rutgers University Press, 1950

McLaughlin, Andrew C., *A Constitutional History of the United States*, New York, Appleton-Century, 1935

McMaster, John B., *A History of the People of the United States from the Revolution to the Civil War*, 8 vols., New York, Appleton, 1884-1913

Meigs, William M., *The Life of Thomas Hart Benton*, Philadelphia, Lippincott, 1904

Merkel, Benjamin G., "The Abolition Aspects of Missouri's Anti-slavery Controversy 1819-1865," *Missouri Historical Review*, XLIV (1950), 232-53

—————, *The Antislavery Controversy in Missouri 1819-1865* (abstract of doctoral dissertation), St. Louis, Washington University, 1942

Meyer, Leland W., *The Life and Times of Colonel Richard M. Johnson of Kentucky*, New York, Columbia University Press, 1932

"The Missouri Compromise," *The Collector: A Magazine for Autograph and Historical Collectors*, XIX (1906), 62

Moffat, Charles H., "Jefferson's Sectional Motives In Founding the University of Virginia," *West Virginia History*, XII (1950), 61-69

Morse, Jarvis M., *A Neglected Period of Connecticut's History 1818-1850*, New Haven, Yale University Press, 1933

Moses, John, *Illinois, Historical and Statistical Comprising the Essential Facts of its Planting and Growth as a Province, County, Territory, and State*, 2 vols., Chicago, Fergus Printing Co., 1889-1892

Myrdal, Gunnar, *An American Dilemma, The Negro Problem and Modern Democracy*, 2 vols., New York, Harper, 1944

Needles, Edward, *An Historical Memoir of the Pennsylvania Society, for Promoting the Abolition of Slavery; the Relief of Free Negroes Unlawfully Held in Bondage, and for Improving the Condition of the African Race*, Philadelphia, Merrihew and Thompson, 1848

Owsley, F. L., "Two Agrarian Philosophers: Jefferson and Du Pont de Nemours," *Hound & Horn*, VI (1932), 166-72

Parrington, Vernon L., *The Romantic Revolution in America 1800-1860 (Main Currents in American Thought, II)*, New York, Harcourt, Brace, 1927

Paullin, Charles O., *Atlas of the Historical Geography of the United States*, Washington, Carnegie Institution, 1932

Pease, Theodore C., *The Frontier State 1818-1848 (The Centennial History of Illinois, II)*, Springfield, Illinois Centennial Commission, 1918

Phillips, Ulrich B., *The Course of the South to Secession* (ed. by E. Merton Coulter), New York, Appleton-Century, 1939

_____, *Georgia and State Rights*, in *Annual Report of the American Historical Association for the Year 1901*, II, Washington, Government Printing Office, 1902, pp. 1-224

Platt, Edmund, *The Eagle's History of Poughkeepsie*, Poughkeepsie, Platt & Platt, 1905

Purcell, Richard J., *Connecticut in Transition 1775-1818*, Washington, American Historical Association, 1918

Quillin, Frank U., *The Color Line in Ohio, A History of Race Prejudice in a Typical Northern State*, Ann Arbor (Mich.), George Wahr, 1913

Quincy, Edmund, *Life of Josiah Quincy*, Boston, Ticknor and Fields, 1868

Ramsdell, Charles W., "The Natural Limits of Slavery Expansion," *The Mississippi Valley Historical Review*, XVI (1929), 151-71

Randall, Henry S., *The Life of Thomas Jefferson*, 3 vols., New York, Derby and Jackson, 1858

Ravenel, Mrs. St. Julien, *Life and Times of William Lowndes of South Carolina 1782-1822*, Boston, Houghton Mifflin, 1901

Roseboom, Eugene H., "Ohio in the Presidential Election of 1824," *Ohio Archaeological and Historical Quarterly*, XXVI (1917), 153-224

——————, and Weisenburger, Francis P., *A History of Ohio*, New York, Prentice-Hall, 1934

Rowland, Kate M., *The Life of Charles Carroll of Carrollton 1737-1832*, 2 vols., New York, Putnam's, 1898

Sargent, Epes, and Greeley, Horace, *The Life and Public Services of Henry Clay, Down to 1848*, Philadelphia, Porter & Coates, 1852

Savelle, Max, *Seeds of Liberty, The Genesis of the American Mind*, New York, Knopf, 1948

Scarborough, Ruth, *The Opposition to Slavery in Georgia Prior to 1860*, Nashville, George Peabody College, 1933

Schlesinger, Arthur M., Jr., *The Age of Jackson*, Boston, Little, Brown, 1945

Schmeckebier, L. F., "How Maine Became a State," *Collections and Proceedings of the Maine Historical Society*, Second Series, IX (1898), 146-72

Shoemaker, Floyd C., *Missouri's Struggle for Statehood 1804-1821*, Jefferson City, Hugh Stephens Printing Co., 1916

——————, "Traditions Concerning the Missouri Question," in *Annual Report of the American Historical Association for the Year 1921*, Washington, Government Printing Office, 1926, pp. 186-88

Simms, Henry H., *Life of John Taylor*, Richmond, William Byrd Press, 1932

Simpson, Albert F., "The Political Significance of Slave Representation, 1787-1821," Ph.D. dissertation, Vanderbilt University, 1940

——————, "The Political Significance of Slave Representation, 1787-1821," *The Journal of Southern History*, VII (1941), 315-42

Snyder, J. F., "Forgotten Statesmen of Illinois. Hon. Jesse Burgess Thomas," *Transactions of the Illinois State Historical Society for the Year 1904*, Springfield, Illinois State Historical Library, 1904, pp. 514-23

The South in the Building of the Nation, 13 vols., Richmond, Southern Historical Publication Society, 1909-1913

Stackpole, Everett S., *History of New Hampshire*, 4 vols., New York, American Historical Society, n.d.

Stanwood, Edward, *American Tariff Controversies in the Nineteenth Century*, 2 vols., Boston, Houghton Mifflin, 1903

_____, A History of the Presidency, Boston, Houghton Mifflin, 1898

_____, "The Separation of Maine from Massachusetts," Proceedings of the Massachusetts Historical Society, Third Series, I (1907), 125-64

Stevens, Walter B., Centennial History of Missouri (the Center State), 6 vols., St. Louis, S. J. Clarke, 1921

_____, "The Travail of Missouri for Statehood," The Missouri Historical Review, XV (1920), 3-35

Stimpson, George W., Nuggets of Knowledge, New York, George Sully, 1928

Stone, Frederick D., "The Ordinance of 1787," The Pennsylvania Magazine of History and Biography, XIII (1889), 309-40

Swisher, Carl B., Roger B. Taney, New York, Macmillan, 1935

Sydnor, Charles S., The Development of Southern Sectionalism 1819-1848 (A History of the South, V), Baton Rouge, Louisiana State University Press, 1948

Talmadge, Arthur W., The Talmadge, Tallmadge and Talmage Genealogy, New York, Grafton Press, 1909

Taussig, Frank W., The Tariff History of the United States, New York, Putnam's, 1931

Trent, William P., William Gilmore Simms, Boston, Houghton Mifflin, 1895

Trexler, Harrison A., Slavery in Missouri 1804-1865 (Johns Hopkins University Studies in Historical and Political Science, XXXII, No. 2), Baltimore, Johns Hopkins Press, 1914

Turner, Edward R., The Negro in Pennsylvania, Washington, American Historical Association, 1911

Turner, Frederick J., Rise of the New West 1819-1829 (The American Nation: A History, XIV), New York, Harper, 1906

_____, The Significance of Sections in American History, New York, Henry Holt, 1932

Tyler, Alice F., Freedom's Ferment, Phases of American Social History to 1860, Minneapolis, University of Minnesota Press, 1944

[Tyler, Lyon G.?], "The Missouri Compromise," Tyler's Quarterly Historical and Genealogical Magazine, XIII (1932), 149-75

[Tyson, John S.], Life of Elisha Tyson, the Philanthropist, Baltimore, B. Lundy, 1825

Van Deusen, Glyndon G., The Life of Henry Clay, Boston, Little, Brown, 1937

————, *Thurlow Weed, Wizard of the Lobby*, Boston, Little, Brown, 1947

Viles, Jonas, "Missouri in 1820," *The Missouri Historical Review*, XV (1920), 36-52

Wagstaff, Henry M., *State Rights and Political Parties in North Carolina—1776-1861* (*Johns Hopkins University Studies in Historical and Political Science*, XXIV, Nos. 7-8), Baltimore, Johns Hopkins Press, 1906

Weeks, Stephen B., "Anti-Slavery Sentiment in the South," *Publications of the Southern History Association*, II (1898), 87-130

————, "The History of Negro Suffrage in the South," *Political Science Quarterly*, IX (1894), 671-703

Weisenburger, Francis P., "The Middle Western Antecedents of Woodrow Wilson," *The Mississippi Valley Historical Review*, XXIII (1936), 375-90

Wesley, Charles H., "Negro Suffrage in the Period of Constitution-Making 1787-1865," *The Journal of Negro History*, XXXII (1947), 143-68

Wiltse, Charles M., *John C. Calhoun Nationalist, 1782-1828*, Indianapolis, Bobbs-Merrill, 1944

Woodburn, James A., "The Historical Significance of the Missouri Compromise," in *Annual Report of the American Historical Association for the Year 1893*, Washington, Government Printing Office, 1894, pp. 249-97

Woodfin, Maude H., "Nathaniel Beverley Tucker: His Writings and Political Theories; With a Sketch of His Life," *Richmond College Historical Papers*, II (1917), 9-42

Wright, Benjamin F., Jr., *American Interpretations of Natural Law*, Cambridge, Harvard University Press, 1931

INDEX

Abolitionists, 343
Adams, John Quincy, 11, 39-40, 96, 97, 124, 127, 196-97, 284, 339, 341, 343-46, 350
Adams-Onís Treaty, 343-46
Alabama, 172, 220, 246
Allen, Paul, 225
American Convention for Promoting the Abolition of Slavery, 34-35, 176, 344
"American System," 243
Ames, Fisher, 11-12
Ames, Nathaniel, 313
"Anti-Missourian Crusade," 67
Aristocracy, issue in Missouri Controversy, 310-14
"Aristocrats with liberal views," 251-56
Arkansas Territory, 59-64
Atrocity stories, 269-70, 284
Auction sales bill, 331
Austin, James T., 82

Bailhache, John, 205-206
Baily, Abraham, 130
Balance of power, 22-25, 75, 87, 114-15, 126-28, 143, 160-62, 241, 279, 298-300
Baldwin, Henry, 101, 105, 157, 211-12, 322, 324
Baldwin tariff bill, 322-30; analysis of vote on, 326-27
Baltimore, 224-26
Bank question, 310, 337, 338
Bankruptcy bill, 105-106, 332, 337
Banks, Linn, 338
Baptists, 263, 265
Barbados, 296
Barbour, James, 93, 113, 153, 236-37
Barbour, Philip, 46-47, 169
Barbour-Clay compromise, 152-53, 159
Barton, David, 146, 160, 262, 266, 345
Bateman, Ephraim, 157
Bates, Edward, 266
Bates, Elisha, 29

Beecher, Henry W., 193
"Benevolent empire," 76
Benton, Thomas H., 40, 98, 129, 136, 146, 159, 160, 250, 260, 262, 266, 309
Biddle, Nicholas, 163, 164, 287
Binney, Horace, 80
Binns, John, 188, 324
Blake, George, 82
Bleeding Kansas, 136
Bloodworth, Timothy, 6
Bloomfield, Joseph, 101, 157, 212-13
"Bluelight" Federalists, 14
Blunt, Joseph, 177, 289, 306
Boone, Daniel, 14
Booth, James, 221
Boston, 81-82, 216-17, 251-52
Boucher, Jonathan, 2
Boudinot, Elias, 65, 68-73, 76
Bourne, George, 28
Brackenridge, H. M., 116, 225
Bradford, Alden, 82
Breck, Samuel, 80
Breckinridge, Joseph C., 229
Breckinridge Bill, 30, 31, 315
Bridgham, Samuel W., 215-16
Bringhurst, Joseph, 222-23
Brookens, Ephraim, 307
Brooks, John, 198, 330
Brown, Edward, 348, 349
Brown, William, 152, 162, 312
"BRUTUS," 328-29, 332, 337, 340
Bryan, Daniel, 231
Buchanan, James, 80
Bucktails, 16, 169, 180, 340
"Bunk," origin of term, 92
Burke, Edmund, 313
Burlington County (New Jersey), 67-73; Burlington meeting, 67-70
Burrill, James, 61, 128
Butler, Pierce, 23, 320
Byrd, William, 2

Calhoun, John C., 20, 124, 246-47, 250

Cambreling, Churchill C., 168, 185
Canals, 20-21, 334, 336
Carey, Mathew, 134
Carlisle (Pennsylvania), 210-11, 325-26
Carroll, Charles, 251, 253
Case, Walter, 101, 213-14
Cash import duty bill, 331
Chandler, John, 143, 159
Charless, Joseph, 261-62, 265, 269
Charleston, 218, 219, 250, 295
Cheswell, Wentworth, 301
Cheves, Langdon, 159, 250-51
Cincinnati meeting, 80-81, 306
Clark, Robert, 157
Clarkson, Matthew, 78-79
Clay, Henry, 43-44, 45-46, 63, 87; sponsors compromises, 94-95, 102-103, 147-48, 152-53, 154-60, 164
Clinton, De Witt, 16-18, 20-21, 39-40, 106, 138, 180-83, 192, 229, 233, 253, 264, 340
Clintonians, 16-17, 83, 106, 135, 175, 177-78, 181-83, 184, 191, 194, 196, 197-98, 200, 203, 214, 310, 316, 325, 339-40, 350; Clintonian philanthropists, 129, 316, 343
Cobb, Thomas W., 39, 50, 59
Coles, Edward, 286, 287
Coles, John B., 78-79
Colonization Society, 26-27
Colston, Edward, 45, 50
"Compact" theory, 111-112
Congress, Capitol galleries, 91; unpopularity of Sixteenth Congress, 173-75
Congress of Vienna, 314
Connecticut, 192-94, 214-15
Constitutional Convention of 1787, 7-8
Constitutionality of slavery restriction, 42-43, 45, 46, 48, 60, 63-64, 105, 119-24
Cony, Daniel, 274
Cook, Daniel P., 85, 94, 283-84, 285
Cooper, Thomas, 257, 348, 349
Correspondence committees, Trenton-Burlington committee, 71-72, 80, 82; New York committee, 79, 80-81, 82
Cotton gin, 318
Coyle v. Oklahoma, 121
Crawford, William H., 124
Crittenden, John J., 119

Cumberland Road, 20, 332-33, 334-35
Cummings, Asa, 288
Cushman, Joshua, 161-62, 279, 280

Daggett, David, 166
De Wolf, James, 298
Dearborn, H. A. S., 178-79
Decatur, Stephen, 14
Declaration of Independence, 307, 308-309
Delaware, 221-24
Democracy, issue in Missouri Controversy, 310-14; Greek democracy, 314
Democrats, attitude toward Missouri question, 17-18, 21-22, 66-67, 69, 82, 106-107, 109, 113, 142, 150-51, 160-64, 177-97, 199-200, 207, 213, 214-16, 223, 280-81, 350
"Diffusion" argument, 46-47, 51, 292-93
Dillwyn, William, 134
Disunion, threats of, 3, 5, 9, 12, 49, 50, 56-57, 59, 92-94, 105, 151, 175, 242
"Dough faces," 103-106, 188, 201-203, 209-17, 326
Dowse, Edward, 107
Dred Scott case, 123, 166
Du Ponceau, Peter S., 80
Duane, William, 188, 325, 328-29, 340
Dwight, Theodore, 74-76, 78, 130, 131, 134, 136, 168, 175, 191, 193, 194, 198, 200, 203, 240, 306, 319

Eaton, John H., 144
Economic issues, 18-22, 44, 63, 318-38
Eddy, Samuel, 101, 157, 215-16
Eddy, Thomas, 79, 181
Edgefield burning, 296-97
Education, Southern, 254-57
Edwards, Henry W., 101, 104-105, 214-15
Edwards, Ninian, 53-54, 62, 85, 112, 159, 282, 285
Ely, Isaac M., 73, 75, 79
Embree, Elihu, 230, 249
Emlen, Samuel, 69-72, 134
Emmet, Thomas A., 181
England, attitude toward Missouri question, 314-15
Enlightenment, 251, 256
Era of good feelings, 340

Erie Canal, 20-21
Europe, attitude toward slavery, 314-15
Eustis, William, 140, 147, 167
Everett, Charles, 238

Federalists, 10-16, 66-83, 106-107, 160-64, 175, 177-80, 183-85, 188-203, 204, 215-16, 221-22, 223, 226, 251, 280-81, 316-17, 339, 340, 350; Federalist philanthropists, 73, 76-79, 142, 343
Findlay, William, 326
Fithian, Philip, 2
Florida, 23, 161, 343-44, 345, 346
Floyd, John, 153, 232
Foot, Samuel A., 101, 112, 214-15
Ford, William D., 157
Frontier influence, 259, 270
Fry, William, 131
Fuller, Timothy, 44-45, 124
Fullerton, David, 101, 210-11

Gaillard, John, 247
Gales and Seaton, 41, 227
Gallison, John, 82
Garnett, James M., 218, 321
Garrison, William L., 74, 343, 349
Georgetown (D.C.), 227-28
Georgia, 14, 27, 31, 245, 294, 300
Goldsborough, Robert H., 226
Gore, Christopher, 199, 217
Gradualism and immediatism, see Slavery
Granger, Gideon, 16-17
Grayson, William, 31
"Great American Desert," 115-18
Green, Duff, 283-84
Griffith, William, 70-71, 212-13
Gross, Ezra, 119-20
Grundy, Felix, 21
Guyon, James, 157

Hackley, Aaron, 157
Haines, Charles G., 181, 182
Hale, Salma, 49, 86, 140, 186-87
Hall, Willard, 52, 101, 145, 223-24
Hamilton, James, Jr., 246
Hardin, Benjamin, 151-52
Harper, Robert G., 226
Harrison, William H., 205, 324
Hartford Convention, 12, 74, 76, 162, 164, 189, 190, 191, 194, 195, 229

Hay, George, 235, 238
Hayne, Robert Y., 248
Hemphill, Joseph, 112, 122
Henry, Isaac, 269
Herculaneum (Missouri), 265
Herring, John S., 232
"Higher law," 307-308
Hill, Isaac, 186-87, 199
Hill, Mark L., 101, 105, 106, 157, 277-78, 279-80
Hillhouse, James, 31
Hillhouse, William, 177, 240
Hoffman, John, 225
Holland, Edwin C., 348-49
Holley, Horace, 257
Holmes, John, 100, 101, 106, 126, 143, 159, 171, 277, 278, 279-80
Hooper, James, 274
Hopkinson, Joseph, 69, 71-72, 106, 107, 142, 191
Horsey, Outerbridge, 223
Hosack, David, 301
Humanitarian movement of 1820's, 28-29, 74, 76-78
Hunter, William, 109, 159

Illinois, 14, 34, 54, 85, 281-87
Immigration, 270-71, 286
Indentured servants, 281, 282
Indiana, 14, 207-209; legislature, 139, 208
Ingersoll, Jared, 80
Internal improvements, 20-22, 332-36, 337
Irvine, Baptist, 133, 159
Irving, John T., 78-79

Jackson, Andrew, 231, 271, 295
Jay, John, 3-6, 72-73
Jay, Peter A., 77-79, 191, 306
Jay-Gardoqui treaty negotiations, 3-6
Jefferson, Thomas, 125, 203, 232, 243, 251, 253-56, 271-72, 292, 303
Johnson, Edward, 224
Johnson, Reverdy, 225
Johnson, Richard M., 312, 317
Jones, Francis, 93-94, 151

Kane, Elias K., 285, 287
Kansas-Nebraska Act, 134
Kell, Thomas, 225
Kelton, James, 130
Kemp, James, 225

Kendall, Amos, 116, 228
Kenrick, John, 28
Kentucky, 23, 228-30, 256-57, 312, 323, 333; legislature, 229
King, Rufus, 7, 24, 55-59, 73-74, 82, 96-97, 106, 107, 116-17, 127, 156, 324, 332, 345; motives in Missouri Controversy, 179-80, 183-84; South's opinion of, 233, 252, 253, 264, 295; higher law doctrine, 307-308
King, William, 197, 276, 277, 278
Kinsey, Charles, 100-101, 212, 213, 324
Kinsley, Martin, 279

Labor, Southern attitude toward, 43-44, 47, 311-13; labor unions, 343
Lacock, Abner, 32, 94, 127
Lancaster meeting, 80
Langdon, Richard C., 248
Lanman, James, 87, 193
Learned, Joseph D., 226, 304
"Legitimates" of Europe, 314
Lewis, Morgan, 177
Lexington (Kentucky), 323
Liberal Southerners, 251-56, 292, 317, 348
Lincoln, Abraham, 184, 350
Lincoln, Enoch, 279, 280
Lindsey, John, 313
Livermore, Arthur, 33, 45, 50, 153
Local self-government, see Popular sovereignty
Long, Stephen H., 115-16
Louisiana, 12, 30, 31, 42-43, 243-44
Louisiana Purchase, 12, 48
Lowell, James R., 202
Lowell, John, 198
Lowndes, William, 122, 139-40, 145, 323
Lowrie, Walter, 94, 107, 150-51, 159
Lucas, John B. C., 265, 266
Lundy, Benjamin, 263, 265

McLane, Louis, 63, 64, 122, 166, 223-24, 304
McLean, John, 85, 283, 287
McNair, Alexander, 262, 268
Macon, Nathaniel, 109, 125, 128, 144, 159, 219, 304
Maddox, John W., 209, 313
Madison, James, 16, 20, 124, 251, 252, 332, 333

Maine, 273-81; bill for admission of, 86-90, 100-103
Mallary, Rollin C., 148-49
Malthus, Thomas R., 293
Mansfield, Edward, 192
Marshall, John, 167, 234, 243
Maryland, 224-26
Mason, Jeremiah, 187-88
Mason, Jonathan, 101, 106, 198, 203, 216-17
Massachusetts, 195, 198-99, 216-17; militia claims, 81, 198
Meigs, Henry, 101, 105, 157, 213-14, 291
Mercer, Charles F., 101, 290
Middle states, buffer between North and South, 3, 6-7; disagree with South on economic issues, 18-22, 67
Mills, Elijah, 40
Mine a Burton, 117, 266
Minority groups, 77, 136-37, 167
Miscegenation, 289, 307
Missionaries, 314
Mississippi, 24, 30, 31, 248-49, 250, 322
Mississippi River navigation, dispute over, 3-6
Missouri, early history, 31-32; attitude toward Missouri Controversy, 258-73; "solemn public act," 272; admission to Union, 272-73; disagrees with South on economic issues, 331, 336
Missouri bill, introduced, 33, 35; attempt to amend, 35; debated, 41-59, 87-100; passed, 100-103
Missouri Compromise of 1820, 64, 86, 88-89; passage of, 100-107; analysis of vote on, 107-11; origin of, 112; attitude of congressmen toward, 113-15; Northern desire to abrogate, 130-34, 137-39, 148-49; attitude of press and public toward, 199-203, 204, 205-207, 208-209, 209-217, 230, 236-39, 244-48, 264-65, 277-78
Missouri Compromise of 1821, 155-64, 203, 245
Missouri constitution, 134-36; rejected by House, 145; provisions, 267-68, 273
Monroe, James, 5-6, 95, 123-24, 152-53, 169, 196, 234-38, 251-52, 323, 332, 333, 335, 339-41, 345-46

Montgomeryville (Indiana), 209

Moore, Samuel, 157, 158

Morril, David, 127, 150-51, 159, 166-67

Moultrie, William, 125

Mount Pleasant *Philanthropist*, 29

Natchez, 248-49, 322

Nationalism, Virginian, 241-43; American, 243, 246-48; Southern, 250

Natural law, 307-309

Negroes, as voters, 37, 165, 301, 316-17; interested in Missouri question, 91; free Negro and mulatto citizenship issue, 135, 142-43, 155, 165-67; status in free states, 301-303; amalgamation and equality, 304-307

Nelson, Hugh, 157

Neville, Morgan, 21-22

New England, sectionalism, 2, 10-15

New Hampshire, 186-88

New Jersey, 7, 67-73, 189-90, 212-13

New York, 16-17, 20-21, 190-92, 213-14; New York City meeting, 73, 78-79; legislature, 139, 178

New York *Daily Advertiser,* 74-75

New York Manumission Society, 27-28, 176

Newbold, William, 68-71

Newport (Rhode Island), 297-98

Newspapers, aid in passage of compromise of 1821, 162-63; Northern Democratic press denounces antislavery movement, 188-97; attitude of Northern press toward compromises of 1820 and 1821, 199-201, 203; attitude of press in Old Northwest, 205-207, 208-209; attitude of Southern press, 232-34, 236, 239, 243-45; Missouri press, 260-62

Newton, Thomas, 327-28

Niles, Hezekiah, 21, 225, 328

Noah, Mordecai M., 191-92

Nonslaveholders, views of, 230, 286; status in South, 47, 312-13

North, lack of unity, 6-7, 142-43, 177-85, 188-99, 250, 327, 350; attitude toward Missouri question, 107-109, 113, 170-217

North Carolina, 5, 6, 31, 114, 231

Ohio, 204-207; legislature, 205; "Ohio Controversy," 310

Old Northwest, 52-53, 61-62, 121-22, 203-209, 281-87

Ordinance of 1787, 31, 121-22, 281, 282

Otis, Harrison G., 85, 94, 113, 198, 240, 327

Palmer, Barnabas, 171

Pamphlets, 83, 176-77

Panic of 1819, 172-73, 220-21, 271, 320-21

Parker, James, 71

Parris, Albion K., 171

Parrott, John F., 87, 109, 159, 187

Patronage, 196-97

Pearce, Dutee J., 215

Peddlers, hostility toward, 13, 256-57

Peek, Harmanus, 101, 213

Pell, Ferris, 181, 182

Pennsylvania, 162-64, 188-89, 210-12

Pennsylvania Society for Promoting the Abolition of Slavery, 131, 202

Percy, Thomas G., 172, 246

Philadelphia meeting, 80

Pinckney, Charles, 6, 114-15, 122, 125-26, 166, 218, 304, 311

Pinckney, Henry L., 247

Pindall, James, 120, 121

Pinkney, William, 97-99, 120, 308

Pintard, John, 65, 181, 300

Pittsburgh, 204

Plumer, William, 187, 336-37, 341, 344

Plumer, William, Jr., 113, 149-50, 153-54, 161

Poindexter, George, 249

Popular sovereignty, 63-64, 123

Portsmouth (New Hampshire) meeting, 186-87

Preble, William P., 171, 179, 277

Presidential election of 1820, 152-53, 236-38, 339-41

Presidential election of 1824, 341-42

Providence (Rhode Island), 80, 215-16

Public meetings, 66-83, 219, 221, 224-25, 258, 260, 262-63, 265

Public opinion, indifference toward Missouri question, 65-66, 170-75, 186, 218, 219-21; indifference temporarily overcome, 83, 175-77, 219; attitude toward "dough faces," 209-17; in Missouri, 259-66

Quakers, 25, 26, 28, 67, 69, 70, 95, 99, 221, 222-23, 224, 225, 231, 287
Quincy, Josiah, 12, 82, 198
Quincy, Josiah, Jr., 2

Race relations, 301-307
Ralston, Robert, 80
Randolph, John, 93, 96, 102-104, 125, 152, 153, 156-57, 175, 240, 241, 251-52, 308, 321, 345, 347
Rankin, Christopher, 119
Rawle, William, 80
Raymond, Daniel, 177, 225, 226, 293
Reid, Robert, 93, 124
Republicans, see Democrats
Republicanism, issue in Missouri Controversy, 44-45, 310, 311, 313-14
Rhode Island, 194-95, 215-16, 297-98
Richmond, 234
Richmond Enquirer, 232-33, 236
Ritchie, Thomas, 232-34, 236, 239, 241, 250
Roane, Spencer, 237, 295
Roberts, Jonathan, 87-88, 107, 124, 127, 150-51, 159
Rodney, Caesar A., 221, 223-24
Rogers, Thomas J., 157, 158
Root, Erastus, 178, 316

Sage, Ebenezer, 305
San Domingo, 295
Savage, John, 20-21
Savannah fire, 294
Scott, John, 47-50, 93, 146, 309
Seabrook, Whitemarsh B., 348, 349
Seaton, Mrs. William W., 91
Sectionalism, prior to the Missouri Controversy, 1-32; effect of Controversy on, 250-51
Sergeant, John, 35, 96, 127, 139-40, 141-42, 150, 160-61, 210
Seward, William H., 307
Shaw, Henry, 101, 157, 216
Simkins, Eldred, 322-23
Slave representation, see Three-fifths ratio
Slavery, prior to Missouri Controversy, 25-32; issue in Missouri Controversy, 38-39, 45, 46-47, 50-51, 71, 79, 124-26, 265-67, 288-90, 299; slave trade, 43, 50-51, 290, 297-98; slave revolts, 45, 47, 50, 295, 348-49; emancipation proposals, 290-92;

slave codes, 296-97; gradualism and immediatism, 303-304; slave breeding, 319; proslavery argument of 1820's, 346-49
Sloane, John, 339
Smith, Bernard, 101, 105, 157, 212, 213
Smith, Humphrey, 269, 292
Smith, Jeremiah, 187
Smith, Samuel, 52, 226
Smith, William, 28, 109, 125, 159, 247-48, 295, 297, 312, 334-35, 348, 349
Solid South, 6, 250
South, sectionalism in, 2-6, 8-9; decline of sectionalism, 10; attitude toward Missouri question, 107-11, 113-15, 218-57
South Carolina, 246-48, 257, 296-97
Southard, Henry, 157, 158
Southard, Samuel L., 159
Speakership, contest for in 1820, 139-41
Spencer, Ambrose, 181-82
Spencer, John C., 118, 138-39, 181
Squatter sovereignty, see Popular sovereignty
St. Louis, 262, 263, 265, 266, 269-70
St. Louis Enquirer, 260-61
State rights, 46, 119-20, 243, 249-50, 309-10
Steubenville, 207, 324-25
Stevens, James, 101, 157, 193, 214-15
Stockbridge (Massachusetts), 216
Stokes, Montfort, 114
Stone, William L., 136-38, 203
Storer, Clement, 187
Storrs, Henry R., 101, 112, 157, 213-14
Story, Joseph, 80, 106, 191, 202
Street, Joseph M., 282, 285
Strother, George, 311
Stuart, Archibald, 239-40
Suffrage, 77, 78, 83, 136, 316-17
Supreme Court, 120-21, 122, 167, 243

Tait, Charles, 24, 127, 220, 246, 251
Tallmadge, James, Jr., 17, 33, 34, 35-40, 50-51, 176, 315, 317
Tallmadge, Matthias, 17
Tallmadge amendment to Missouri bill, 35, 47, 52-55, 59
Tammany Hall, 21, 69, 169

Taney, Roger B., 166, 226
Tappan, Lewis, 170, 217, 323, 343
Tariff question, 18-19, 21-22, 105, 211, 236, 320-31, 337-38
Taylor, John (of Caroline), 22, 56-57, 243, 338
Taylor, John W., 33, 39-40, 41-44, 49, 60, 63, 64, 86, 89; elected Speaker, 139-40; impartiality as Speaker, 141, 144-45, 147, 154; defeated in 1821, 169
Taylor, Waller, 54, 62, 87, 159, 208, 209
Tennessee, 230-31, 333
Tennessee Manumission Society, 230-31
Texas, 343, 344-46
Thomas, Jesse B., 53-54, 62, 85, 88-89, 90, 100, 112-13, 159, 282, 285, 287
Thomas proviso, see Missouri Compromise of 1820
Three-fifths ratio of slave representation, 7-8, 11-12, 51, 58, 126-28, 236, 298, 325
Tolerationists, 192, 193
Tompkins, Caleb, 101, 213-14
Tompkins, Daniel D., 91, 152-53, 181-82, 182-83
Treaty of 1803, 48
Trenton meeting, 70-71
Troup, Robert, 202
Tucker, Henry St. George, 237
Tucker, Nathaniel Beverley, 241-42, 260
Tudor, William, 82
Tyler, John, 92, 123, 124
Tyson, Elisha, 224-25

Udree, Daniel, 157
University of Virginia, 255
Upson, Jesse, 70

Van Buren, Martin, 170, 178, 185
Van Dyke, Nicholas, 223
Van Ness, William W., 181, 182
Van Rensselaer, Solomon, 140, 181-82
Vanderveer, Evert K., 21, 333, 337
Varick, Richard, 78

Vassalboro (Maine), 275
Vaux, Roberts, 80, 131, 142, 210, 287
Vermont, 22-23, 139, 195, 303
Vesey, Denmark, 295, 348-49
Virginia, 1-2, 25-26, 231-44, 245-46, 250, 254-55, 337
Virginia Dynasty, 16, 21, 243
Vose, R. C., 278

Walker, David, 100
Walker, Felix, 63, 92
Walker, Freeman, 93, 125, 311
Walker, John W., 115, 140
Walsh, Robert, Jr., 80, 83, 131-32, 140-41, 168-69, 177, 191, 203, 291, 307-308, 343-44
War Hawks, 23
War of 1812, 12-13, 14
Ware, Ashur, 277, 278
Warren, Hooper, 283, 284-85
Washington (D. C.), 226-27
Washington Intelligencer, 227
Webster, Daniel, 69, 82, 106, 107, 191, 330
West, separatist movement in, 5; North-South rivalry in, 10, 24-25, 30-31, 60, 113-15, 319-20
West Chester (Pennsylvania) meeting, 81
West Virginia, 231-32
Wheaton, Josephus, 310
"White slaves," 300-301
Whitman, Ezekiel, 62, 279, 280
Williamson, William D., 276
Wilmington (Delaware), 221-22
Wilmot Proviso, 346
Wilson, James, 133, 135, 207, 212, 341-42
Wilson, James J., 190, 212
Wirt, William, 124
Wolcott, Oliver, 192, 311
Woodbury, Levi, 187
World opinion, 314-15

Yancey, Charles, 234, 236, 237
Yankees, hostility toward, 13-15, 229-30, 258, 281-82, 347
Yeomen, 311, 312-13
Yorkers, 13, 14-15